WHAT WORKS?

Evidence-based policy and practice in public services

Edited by Huw T.O. Davies, Sandra M. Nutley
and Peter C. Smith

The POLICY PRESS

First published in Great Britain in July 2000 by

The Policy Press
34 Tyndall's Park Road
Bristol BS8 1PY
UK

Tel +44 (0)117 954 6800
Fax +44 (0)117 973 7308
e-mail tpp@bristol.ac.uk
http://www.policypress.org.uk

British Library Cataloguing in Publication Data

A catalogue record for this book is available from the British Library

ISBN 1 86134 191 1 paperback

ISBN 1 86134 192 X hardback

Cover design by Qube Design Associates, Bristol.

The right of Huw T.O. Davies, Sandra M. Nutley and Peter C. Smith to be identified as editors of this work has been asserted by them in accordance with Sections 77 and 78 of the 1988 Copyright, Designs and Patents Act.

The statements and opinions contained within this publication are solely those of the editor and contributors and not of The University of Bristol or The Policy Press. The University of Bristol and The Policy Press disclaim responsibility for any injury to persons or property resulting from any material published in this publication.

The Policy Press works to counter discrimination on grounds of gender, race, disability, age and sexuality.
Printed and bound in Great Britain by Hobbs the Printers Ltd, Southampton.

Contents

Part Two: Thematic analysis

Concluding remarks

Foreword

During the past few years there has been a surge of interest in the theory and practice of 'evidence-based policy', both in the academic community and among policy makers. In early 1999, two important national conferences on evidence-based policy were held: one under the auspices of the Association of Research Centres in the Social Sciences (ARCISS), and the other convened by the School of Public Policy at University College London in association with the Cochrane Centre at Oxford. These key events coincided with the finalisation of the ESRC's plans for a new national Resource Centre for Evidence-Based Policy which will draw together high-quality research evidence to support policy makers and practitioners in a variety of policy domains; at the same time, the journal *Public Money and Management* devoted a special issue to a series of case studies on evidence-based policy. The current volume stems from that seminal collection.

In searching for an explanation of why this surge of interest has occurred at the present time the editors rightly point to such factors as the expansion and availability of relevant social science knowledge, the decline in deference to government and the demand for greater public accountability. Correspondingly, the enthusiasm on the part of government for systematic and well-focused evidence reflects, as they perceive it, the rapidly changing and more complex character of the society with which they have to deal: a challenge which requires foresight, accurate knowledge and rigorous analysis. These high-level concerns about the need to improve the quality of policy making form a distinct stream within the *Modernising government* White Paper which was published in March 1999. They have led to the creation of new units within the Cabinet Office such as the Social Exclusion Unit (SEU) and the Performance and Innovation Unit (PIU), whose job it is to develop policy initiatives in a much more research based way through cross-departmental teams (including the involvement of experts from outside Government). The Centre for Management and Policy Studies (CMPS), which began its work in June 1999, has been given the special task of developing a new approach to policy making based on the latest techniques of knowledge management. CMPS, PIU and SEU are, therefore, important 'customers' for high-quality research evidence and exemplify the new interface between policy makers and knowledge producers which will begin to unfold over the next few years.

The chapters in the present volume add up to a fascinating state-of-the-art review of evidence-based policy making. The varied picture across such a wide range of policy areas is illuminating and provides many interesting contrasts and comparisons. Running through all these contributions, however, are some key questions which need to be confronted if this general vision is to be realised.

Firstly, the relationship between research evidence, on the one hand, and policy and practice, on the other, is not a simple or straightforward one. In much the same way that innovation is now seen by most social scientists as a non-linear process, so the production of scientific knowledge is closely interlinked with user perspectives. The varied sources of evidence which government draws on will, therefore, inevitably have been shaped to some degree by the different institutional interests, values and discourses of those who produced and commissioned them. Establishing the quality of research evidence is a key item on any future agenda.

A second key factor, which is related to the first, concerns the range of evidence to which policy makers need to gain access. For the purposes of designing policies or other forms of intervention, randomised controlled trials (RCTs) and large-scale surveys are typically strong on general quantitative relationships, but relatively weak on the more finely grained understanding of specific context and the meanings which individuals give to those contexts. Policy makers need evidence of both kinds, and would benefit from a research community in which there are strong bridges between qualitative and quantitative approaches.

Finally, there are some practical issues to do with how the research and policy-making communities can work with each other more effectively. The recent Cabinet Office study on *Professional policy making for the 21st century* (1999) establishes some useful guidelines of good practice, but it was not part of its remit to explore the mechanisms of engagement in detail. That is now being taken forward by the CMPS as it develops pilot 'knowledge pools' to support selected policy areas. With the development of the government's IT strategy to facilitate rapid access to data and documentation, these will be important vehicles for drawing in the best research evidence and stakeholder perspectives, including the views of those who will implement policy. This initiative in turn raises the difficult question of how to incentivise staff and to generate their commitment to new ways of working. Chapter Fifteen provides us with some very useful insights into this key issue, examined in both micro and macro terms. All this serves to remind us that policy making is, in the end, a process with distinctive institutional behaviours which have to be modified and managed if we are to move towards greater knowledge sharing and 'joined-up thinking'.

One of the main merits of this book is to raise some of the key methodological and management challenges in a realistic way yet, at the same time, to provide strong encouragement and a sense of direction. It has come at just the right time to help policy makers see the benefits of greater openness and academic researchers the value of closer engagement with practice. Donald Schon perhaps went too far in once describing the policy process as "a swampy lowland where solutions are confusing messes incapable of technical solutions". Like the contributors to this volume, I believe that there is firmer ground. We should mark it out and occupy it.

Professor Ron Amann
Director General
Centre for Management and Policy Studies
Cabinet Office

Editors' preface

The editors began this work after some chance observations on the apparent similarities between service areas in the problems faced in assessing 'what works?', and the seeming differences between areas on how such vital questions are tackled. Some years later we now know a lot more about both these similarities and differences. In the presentation and exploration of these we hope to enable the many and diverse parts of the public sector to achieve greater insight into their own areas through a reflection on the strategies used by others.

Along the way we have been helped by many generous people. In September 1998 we held a small cross-discipline seminar at the University of St Andrews. We thank all those participants who gave so freely of their time and ideas, enriching our understanding and providing added momentum to this project. This St Andrews seminar was financed in part by the Russell Trust in Fife, whose financial support we gratefully acknowledge. We also thank our many contributors to this text, for sharing their knowledge, and for their forbearance under the many demands we placed on them for more information or clearer explications. Early versions of some of these assembled papers appeared in a special edition of the journal *Public Money and Management* (1999, vol 19, issue 1). Hence we are very grateful to the editor of this journal, Francis Terry, for encouraging us to build on this early effort.

Over the period September 1998 to August 1999, one of us (Huw Davies) was a Harkness Fellow in Health Care Policy based at the Institute for Health Policy Studies at the University of California, San Francisco. Huw is very grateful for the financial support of the Commonwealth Fund, New York City, which allowed him the freedom to develop some of the ideas contained in this volume.

Finally, we acknowledge our deep debt to the many people with whom we have engaged in scholarly or frivolous debate about evidence-based everything over recent years. The evidence-based agenda is enormous, and every conversation reveals new pearls to be squirrelled away, which then re-emerge as part of larger arguments later on. We are only too aware that in attempting to draw threads from such diverse areas, and weave them into a coherent whole, we have borrowed liberally (and sometimes unknowingly) from many sources. Our indebtedness is tempered only by our passion for sharing – in pursuit of knowledge, understanding and creative new thinking. We express our greatest appreciation to the many individuals – named contributors or shadowy influences – whose insights have accreted so well into this volume.

Huw Davies, Sandra Nutley, Pete Smith
University of St Andrews, May 2000

List of acronyms

ADL	activities of daily living
AfC	Action for Cities
AVID	Advancement Via Individual Determination
CBA	cost-benefit analysis
CC	City Challenge
CCETSW	Central Council for Education and Training in Social Work
CCT	compulsory competitive tendering
CCTV	closed circuit television
CDP	Community Development Project
CES	Centre for Environmental Studies
CHI	Commission for Health Improvement
CORE	COntinuous REcording
CPRS	Central Policy Review Staff
CRD	Centre for Reviews and Dissemination
CURS	Centre for Urban and Regional Studies
DETR	Department of the Environment, Transport and the Regions
DfEE	Department for Education and Employment
DHSS	Department of Health and Social Security
DICE	Design Improvement Controlled Experiment
DoH	Department of Health
DoT	Department of Transport
DSS	Department of Social Security
DTI	Department of Trade and Industry
EA	Estate Action
EBM	evidence-based medicine
EBP	evidence-based practice
ED	enumeration district
EPOC	Effective Practice and Organisation of Care Group
ESRC	Economic and Social Research Council

EZ	Enterprise Zone
FACTS	Framework for Appropriate Care Throughout Sheffield
GCSE	General Certificate of Secondary Education
GP	general practitioner
GRiPP	Getting Research into Practice and Purchasing
HIP	Housing Investment Programme
HMI	Her Majesty's Inspectorate
HMIP	Her Majesty's Inspectorate of Probation
HTA	Health Technology Assessment
ISS	Information Systems Strategy
IT	information technology
JSA	Jobseeker's Allowance
LEA	local education authority
MLR	multiple linear regression
MRC	Medical Research Council
NEMIS	National Online Manpower Information Service
NERF	National Educational Research Forum
NHP	Nottingham Health Profile
NHS	National Health Service
NICE	National Institute for Clinical Excellence
NRR	National Research Register
NRTF	National Road Traffic Forecasts
NVQ	National Vocational Qualification
Ofsted	Office for Standards in Education
ORGS	Offender Group Reconviction Scale
PACE	Promoting Action on Clinical Effectiveness
PACTS	Parliamentary Advisory Committee on Transport Safety
PFI	Private Finance Initiative
PRG	Police Research Group
QALYS	Quality Adjusted Life Years
QCA	Qualifications and Curriculum Authority
R&D	Research and Development
RCEP	Royal Commission on Environmental Pollution
RCT	randomised controlled trial

RDS	Research Development and Statistics
RSG	Revenue Support Grant
SACTRA	Standing Advisory Committee on Trunk Road Assessment
SAUS	School for Advanced Urban Studies
SCORE	Scottish COntinuous REcording
SCPR	Social and Community Planning Research
SER	school effectiveness research
SES	socio-economic status
SRB	Single Regeneration Budget
TOPSS	Training Organisation for Personal Social Services
TRL	Transport Research Laboratory
TTA	Teacher Training Agency
TVEI	Technical and Vocational Education Initiative
UDC	Urban Development Corporation
UPA	Urban Poverty Area

List of contributors

Dr Huw T.O. Davies, Reader in Health Care Policy and Management, University of St Andrews

Dr Philip Davies, Director of Social Sciences, Department for Continuing Education, University of Oxford

Dr Joe Doherty, Senior Lecturer in Geography, University of St Andrews and Director, Joint Centre for Scottish Housing Research, Universities of St Andrews and Dundee

Professor Carol T. Fitz-Gibbon, Professor of Education, University of Durham

Tony Harrison, Head of School of Housing and Urban Studies, University of the West of England

Professor John P. Hutton, Professor of Economics and Econometrics, University of York

Dr Gloria Laycock, formerly Head of Policing and Reducing Crime Unit, Home Office, and currently International Visiting Fellow at the National Institute of Justice, Washington, DC

Professor Geraldine M. Macdonald, Professor of Social Work, Centre for Family Policy and Child Welfare, School for Policy Studies, University of Bristol

Dr Sandra Nutley, Senior Lecturer in Public Sector Management, University of St Andrews

Judy Sebba, Senior Adviser (Research), Standards and Effectiveness Unit, Department for Education and Employment

Professor Trevor Sheldon, Professor of Health Studies, Department of Health Studies, University of York

Professor Peter C. Smith, Professor of Economics, University of York

Professor Nick Tilley, Professor of Sociology, The Nottingham Trent University (currently on secondment to The Home Office)

Francis Terry, Secretary, National Institute of Economic and Social Research and Visiting Fellow, London School of Economics and Political Science

Professor Robert Walker, Professor of Social Policy, University of Nottingham

Jeff Webb, Principal Lecturer in Public Policy and Management, The Nottingham Trent University

ONE

Introducing evidence-based policy and practice in public services

Huw Davies, Sandra Nutley and Peter Smith

The rise of evidence

A striking change in government in the 20th century was the massive rise in the number of organisations seeking explicitly to advise or influence governments in their actions. Examples include pressure groups of one sort or another, university researchers, independent 'think–tanks', professional bodies and statutory organisations. One of the most important instruments used by such organisations is the assembly and presentation of 'evidence' of one sort or another. With a few startling exceptions (most notably Margaret Thatcher's doctrine of 'conviction politics', echoed in William Hague's 'common sense revolution'), governments have become increasingly receptive to certain types of evidence. This rise of *evidence-based policy* reached its apotheosis in 1997, when a Labour government was elected with the philosophy of 'what matters is what works' – on the face of it signalling a conscious retreat from political ideology. Subsequent government initiatives, which aim to take forward the *Modernising government* agenda, have confirmed the central role that evidence is expected to play in policy making for the 21st century (see Chapter Two).

There has also in recent years arisen an atmosphere of increasing public and political scepticism towards the actions of professionals charged with delivering public services. At the start of the 20th century there appears to have been a general assumption that doctors, police officers, teachers and other professionals were the experts, whose judgement was to be trusted, and who were therefore left relatively unchallenged to carry out their duties. By the end of the century this culture of public trust had been severely diluted, as an increasingly educated, informed and questioning public sought reassurance that its taxes were being well spent. In contrast to the preceding culture of largely judgement-based professional practice, there has arisen the important notion of *evidence-based practice* as a means of ensuring that what is being done is worthwhile and that it is being done in the best possible way.

This rise in the role of evidence in policy and practice is the result of a number of factors, which include: the growth of an increasingly well-educated and well-informed public; the explosion in the availability of data of all types, fuelled by developments in information technology (IT); the growth in size and capabilities of the research community; an increasing emphasis on productivity and international competitiveness, and an increasing emphasis on scrutiny and accountability in government. In the UK, one merely needs to observe the relatively recent emergence of organisations such as the Audit Commission, the National Audit Office, Parliamentary select committees and numerous watchdogs and regulators to get an idea of the way that evidence now drives policy and practice in a hitherto unimagined way.

The nature of evidence

In discussing this topic, we immediately enter a debate as to what constitutes 'evidence'. *Chambers Dictionary* gives a number of definitions, including:

- means of proving an unknown or disputed fact
- support for a belief
- an indication
- information in a law case
- testimony
- witness or witnesses collectively.

This range of possibilities hints at the difficulties that emerge when disputes arise as to what constitutes evidence. At one extreme, it might be argued that all evidence must conform to certain scientific rules of proof (the first definition). In other circumstances, any observation on an issue (whether informed or not) might be considered evidence (the last definition). However, perhaps the unifying theme in all the definitions is that the evidence (however construed) can be independently observed and verified, and that there is broad consensus as to its contents (if not its interpretation).

The presumption in this book is that evidence takes the form of 'research', broadly defined. That is, evidence comprises the results of "systematic investigation towards increasing the sum of knowledge" (*Chambers* again). Chapter Two explores this further and explains the current government's broader vision as to what counts as 'evidence'. Contributing authors describing progress on the evidence-based agenda in different sectors have rightly interpreted this definition widely to include almost any conscious assembly of facts. In doing so, it becomes clear that the accepted rules of evidence differ greatly between research cultures. Whereas our definition largely excludes evidence presented in forms such as expert judgement, anecdote, or theory unsupported by empirical evidence, each of these categories remains influential, and would include the medical consultant's tacit knowledge, education inspectors' reports from site visits, or social work practice influenced by sociological theories of human behaviour. Nonetheless, the majority of research evidence considered in this text is the output from more formal and systematic enquiries, generated by government departments, research institutes, universities, charitable foundations, consultancy organisations, and a variety of agencies and intermediaries such as the Audit Commission, or Office for Standards in Education (Ofsted).

While all sorts of systematic enquiry may have much to offer the rational development of public services, our primary interest is in evidence of what works, hence the title of this volume. We will to some extent assume that policy goals have been articulated and that client needs have been identified. The crucial question that remains is what interventions or strategies should be used to meet the goals and satisfy the client needs? This necessarily limits the catch when we trawl for accounts of evidence-based policy and practice. For example, most of our contributors say little about needs assessment, forecasting, scenario planning or a range of other analytic approaches that can inform the policy process. It is not that these approaches are not valuable, it is just that, in order to focus on issues of commonality across sectors, we have concentrated more on the debates surrounding evidence of effectiveness. This emphasis on effectiveness means that there is relatively little examination of the related questions of efficiency and cost-effectiveness. In part, this reflects the infancy of cost-effectiveness and cost-benefit analyses in the public sector, and the relative paucity of activity in this area.

Users of evidence

By examining public sector policy and practice we presume that there are two broad users of evidence: policy makers and practitioners. There are many others who may use various elements of the evidence collected for these parties – most notably individual citizens, seeking to become more informed about issues that concern them, or organised groups with vested interests. The importance of such constituencies should not be underestimated, especially when their activities succeed in radically altering the basic premises of key debates (such as the impact of environmental groups on redefining transport issues or the influence of lobby groups such as Age Concern, Child Poverty Action Group, or Shelter on healthcare, social care and welfare debates). However, this book is primarily concerned with an examination of the official policy process and the day-to-day delivery of services.

Our purpose is:
- to document some of the history of evidence that has formed policy and practice in important public services;
- to explain the current role of evidence in those services, assessing the strengths and weaknesses of evidence generation and use;
- to present the key generic issues relating to the commissioning, assembly, analysis, presentation and use of evidence.

What works in different parts of the public sector?

The book is organised first by exploring the role of evidence in different models of the policy process, and then by focusing on the role of evidence in specific public policy areas (healthcare, education, criminal justice, social care, welfare, housing, transport and urban renewal). The second half of the book then picks up some of the recurrent themes to explore cross-sectoral issues of evidence generation (especially the methodological concerns surrounding the assessment of 'what works'), before moving on to consider evidence implementation.

In assessing what works, questions of methodology arise throughout. In each of the sector-specific chapters the authors describe the legitimacy issues that arise in the creation of evidence. They explore, for example, the balance and debates between quantitative and qualitative approaches to assessing what works; the use of cross-sectional surveys or longitudinal studies; and, most especially, the disputes over the appropriateness of true experiments (randomisation) in generating robust evidence. These debates are laid out without requiring detailed technical knowledge; nonetheless those with limited methodological expertise may well benefit from reviewing the arguments in Chapters Twelve to Fourteen in parallel or even prior to examining the sector-specific accounts. To assist the process of finding specific methodological explanations, Table 1.1 depicts the key approaches and the location of some of the key discussions.

In Chapter Two, Nutley and Webb set out the generic role of evidence as it relates to policy in the UK. They focus on the policy process, and emphasise the many influences that come together to make policy, of which evidence is only one element. A range of models of the policy process are put forward, such as rationality, 'satisficing', incrementalism and mixed scanning. Evidence is likely to play a different role depending on which of these models holds – and subsequent chapters suggest that there may be considerable variations in the type of models that hold sway in different service areas in the UK public sector. This chapter also discusses the various roles that evidence might play in the policy making process, of which informing on 'what works' may be only one.

The following eight chapters describe the emergence and nature of evidence in some of the most important services in the UK public sector. Authors describe the *generation* of evidence in their given sector, the *dissemination* structures by which such evidence is communicated, and the efforts made to *incorporate* such evidence into policy and practice. They account for the changing relationship between evidence on the one hand, and policy and practice on the other, including those areas that remain contested or otherwise controversial. What emerge are rich accounts of the many and diverse activities in each sector, and insight into the ebb and flow of evidence as guidance to policy and practice. The precise treatment of the material varies between chapters, depending on the nature of the service being discussed, and the historic role played by evidence in the sector under consideration.

Evidence is well to the fore in healthcare (Davies and Nutley, Chapter Three), with an emerging consensus as to what constitutes evidence and a willingness to consider evidence as an essential component of decision making. Nonetheless, many obstacles remain in bridging the gap between what is known about effective care and the care that patients actually receive. Many of the larger policy questions – such as the formation of fundholding general practices, and their subsequent abandonment – are not so well supported as the more detailed service issues such as choice of first-line therapy.

Table 1.1: Methodological approaches to assessing what works

Primary research

Primary research involves organised systematic empirical enquiry. The terminology used for different research designs is not always consistent but the table below provides an outline guide.

Qualitative methods	Pluralistic approaches	Quantitative methods				
		Cross-sectional designs	Longitudinal designs			
			Observational only	Quasi-experimental	Theory-driven evaluation	True experiments (randomisation)
eg focus groups, indepth interviews, ethnographic approaches, and discourse analysis (see Chapter Fourteen)	eg multi-method strategies, indepth case studies with quantitative and qualitative data gathering. Qualitative work carried out as preparation for large-scale quantitative work. Qualitative work carried to explore and explain quantitative findings (see Chapter Fourteen and Chapter Seven)	eg surveys of users' and providers' experiences of services (see eg Chapter Six)	eg cohort studies (prospective follow-up studies), case-control studies (retrospective designs), statistical modelling techniques (econometrics) (see Chapter Thirteen)	eg before-and-after studies with limited control over extent and timing of interventions (see Chapters Twelve and Thirteen)	eg pluralistic approaches underpinned by comprehensive theory, perhaps involving quasi and true experimentation (see Chapter Twelve)	eg random allocation to experimental or control groups (see Chapter Twelve and Chapter Three)

Table 1.1: continued

Secondary research

The accumulation of research findings into a robust body of knowledge has become a preoccupation of methodologists and policy makers over recent decades. Central to this interest has been the development of the techniques of **secondary research** – research that takes as its objects of study *primary* research studies. Key strategies developed have been **systematic reviews** (where all studies relevant to a given evaluation issue are uncovered, assessed for methodological quality, and synthesised), and **meta-analysis** (which allows for a quantitative estimate of overall effect size aggregated across a given group of primary studies).

Research hierarchies

A preoccupation with avoiding bias and increasing the precision of estimates of effect size has led to the idea of 'methodological hierarchies' for quantitative methods, ie the notion that some study designs are more able than others to provide robust evidence of effectiveness (eg see Chapter Three). These hierarchies usually prefer high quality secondary research to single studies, true randomised experiments to quasi-experiments, and experiments to pure observation. Such hierarchies are not without their critics (eg see Chapters Twelve and Fourteen).

Education should, on the face of it, offer similar opportunities for evidence to influence teaching as evidence has influenced healthcare. The educational career of children has been referred to as '15,000 hours of compulsory treatment'. However, as Fitz-Gibbon shows in Chapter Four, the relationship between research and education policy and practice has been fraught with disputes, often methodological or even philosophical in nature. While research findings from diverse sources are brought to bear on education debates, robust evidence from rigorous experimental trials has largely been lacking.

Within the criminal justice system there is renewed interest in the role that evidence can play in shaping crime reduction policies and practices. In Chapter Five, Nutley and Davies chart the shift from the conclusion in the 1970s that 'nothing works' to the active search for 'what works' in the 1990s. Criminal justice research is characterised by its methodological plurality and, particularly in the UK, a belief in the need for a theory-driven approach to evaluation (in order to understand not only what works but also why it works). One of the issues highlighted by this chapter is the potential danger of adopting tentative research results as firm effective practice principles. An evidence-based approach requires the implementation of current evidence to be carefully balanced and integrated with ongoing evaluations of effectiveness.

The approach to decision making exemplified by evidence-based healthcare has also been urged upon social services. In Chapter Six, Macdonald outlines the sometimes acrimonious debates that have arisen as a result. There is no consensus about the nature of evidence in social care, and only a minority voice in favour of the need for experimentation (particularly randomised controlled trials). Nevertheless, there have been several notable regional initiatives to develop evidence-based social care, and parts of the voluntary sector are pioneering in this area.

Welfare policy has a long and distinguished history of being informed by research evidence. As Walker shows in Chapter Seven, some of the most influential studies were landmarks in social policy research – from Charles Booth and Seebohm Rowntree, through to Brian Abel-Smith and Peter Townsend. Walker shows that research on welfare has had to be both eclectic and inventive in order to provide policy-relevant findings. Even so, frustration arises from the almost complete inability to mount experimental studies in this field, as well as from the speed with which carefully designed research can be overtaken by political imperatives.

There is also a long history of association between housing research and housing policy in the UK, described by Doherty in Chapter Eight. However, as we enter the 21st century there is a paradox whereby, at a time of unprecedented research output, research evidence rarely impacts directly on housing policy formulation and implementation. Three possible explanations are explored: the operational focus of housing research, which is of limited help in setting policy agendas; the growing complexity of housing policy, which has moved beyond the mere provision of shelter to be implicated in a range of social and economic problems; and the dominant role of political ideology in setting the housing policy agenda. Each of these means that, despite the wealth of research on housing issues, evidence-based housing policy seems some way off.

The danger of an over-reliance on a single government-controlled source of research evidence is well illustrated in the overview by Terry in Chapter Nine of the use of research in transport policy making. Up to the mid-1990s the effect of this was that transport research focused mainly on operational issues and was geared to simply fulfilling established and unquestioned policy objectives. In road policy there was a 'predict and provide' approach, the efficacy of which was eventually only challenged by researchers outside of government. The result has been a paradigm shift in transport policy and the opening up of transport research to a wider variety of providers.

Of all the areas discussed, perhaps urban policy faces some of the most formidable problems in identifying what works. Nonetheless, as Harrison shows in Chapter Ten, the rhetoric of evidence figures large in the justification of many of the schemes aimed at improving the urban environment. Evaluation of the success (or otherwise) of many such schemes has been attempted. Naturally enough, methodological problems are legion – in particular, identifying suitable outcomes, identifying unwanted effects or displacements, and making causal attributions between any outcomes obtained and the activities undertaken. The response has been a growing body of case material, which provides rich individual accounts but few robust generalisations.

Learning across the sectors

The book concludes with a series of chapters that seek to integrate some of the ideas across the diverse sectors and to address issues of generic interest. Many of these chapters are concerned with the generation of evidence, both in organisational terms and methodologically, whereas the final contribution explores the all-important question of implementing evidence-based practice.

In Chapter Eleven, Davies, Laycock, Nutley, Sebba and Sheldon examine the attempts to shape the research supply to meet the demand for research evidence. They look at the research and development (R&D) process in three big government areas: the National Health Service (NHS), the Home Office, and the Department for Education and Employment (DfEE). Similar problems have emerged in each of these three areas: a lack of connection between research activity and pressing policy issues; and a failure of research to impact on day-to-day professional activities. The more proactive stance taken by each of these departments to redress these deficiencies is a sign of the growing importance of research to the government policy machine.

Interventions are delivered with the hope of achieving some outcome. Whether such interventions 'work' in terms of achieving the desired outcomes (and avoiding any deleterious side effects) is paramount. In the view of many, experimentation, in the form of the randomised controlled trial (RCT), has become the 'gold standard' in producing evidence of such effects. Within many parts of healthcare experimentation has become obligatory, and there are evangelical advocates for its adoption in other sectors (some represented in the earlier chapters of the book). However, Chapter Twelve (Davies, Nutley and Tilley) notes growing unease with experimentation in certain quarters for a number of reasons, fundamentally because it rarely offers useful insights into *why* a particular

9

intervention performs better than another. When the interest is in what works *in what context*, such information may be crucial, so the authors explore the use of theory-driven evaluation as one possible way forward.

For all the interest in experimentation, the majority of quantitative evidence used to form policy and practice takes the form of observational rather than experimental data. The volume of observational data now available is overwhelming, as the electronic capture of routine information becomes commonplace. Yet the use of such data gives rise to profound dangers of misinterpretation. In Chapter Thirteen, Hutton and Smith explore the dangers associated with the analysis of non-experimental data, and describe the increasingly powerful tools used to handle such problems that are emerging from the discipline of econometrics.

Quantitative evidence about 'what works' can tend to dominate debates about evidence-based policy and practice. In this respect, the chapter by Davies (Chapter Fourteen) is a welcome exploration of the contribution to evidence that can be made from qualitative research. Although qualitative methodologies are dismissed in some quarters as non-scientific, Davies demonstrates the rich potential offered by such methods to contribute to policy and practice. In particular, qualitative methods can help to formulate and focus the key evaluation questions, shed light on the underlying theories supporting intervention design, and highlight the outcomes to be examined. In doing so, qualitative methods address issues such as *why* one intervention may be better than another, and they can contribute to an understanding of the context within which policies must be framed and implemented.

For all the growth in a robust evidence base over recent decades, it has repeatedly been shown that such evidence often fails to have the impact that it might. Studies in healthcare show that it can take a decade or more before research evidence on the effectiveness of interventions percolates through the system to become part of established practice. The abandonment of ineffective treatments in the light of damning evidence can be equally slow. Other parts of the public sector, such as education, social care and criminal justice services are only beginning to grapple with what it means to be 'evidence-based'. Whereas the first substantive chapter of this book examines the policy process and the role of evidence (Chapter Two by Nutley and Webb), the concluding contribution (Chapter Fifteen by Nutley and Davies) focuses more on service delivery and professional practice. It uses a diverse set of ideas from the social sciences – such as the diffusion of innovations and theories of individual and organisational learning – to explore how evidence might impact on services in a more timely and organised manner. Finally, in Chapter Sixteen, the editors draw together a summary and set of conclusions from the wide-ranging contributions.

Concluding remarks

Some might argue that the overt basis of this book relies too heavily on rationality. Policy making, they might say, is a much more chaotic and political process than that implied by an explicitly 'evidence-based' approach. Yet the aims of many of those promoting the role of evidence are rather more modest than the term 'evidence-based' might imply. Many would argue that evidence-*influenced*, or even evidence-*aware* is the best that we can hope for. Some models of the policy process (such as the enlightenment model – see Chapter Two) make explicit recognition of this in that evidence is seen not as something on which decisions hinge, but more as pressure for a reframing of policy problems and potential solutions.

The turn of the century has seen evidence embedded in the political and policy rhetoric of the day, and infused in the newly transformed professional ethic of many service professionals. Bringing such diverse accounts from across the public sector together under a coherent framework will, we hope, offer new insights and scope for cross-sectoral learning. Our aim is an enhancement of understanding by exposure to parallel debates, and a reinvigoration of innovative thinking stimulated through cross-sectoral and interdisciplinary discourse.

TWO

Evidence and the policy process

Sandra Nutley and Jeff Webb

At the dawn of 2000, science and research evidence feature prominently in government pronouncements on food safety and agricultural policy in the UK. In the furore surrounding the French ban on British beef (part of the ongoing BSE saga) Nick Brown (the Minister for Agriculture at this time) frequently refers to the way in which the decisions of his ministry need to be guided by 'the science'. Thus the Chief Medical Officer was charged with reviewing the evidence for lifting the ban on purchasing beef on the bone. We are also told that research trials of genetically modified crops need to go ahead in order to provide the evidence on which to base longer-term policy decisions in this area. The White Paper on *Modernising government* (Cm 4310, 1999) makes it clear that policy decisions should be based on sound evidence. This includes evidence from the social sciences:

> Social science should be at the heart of policy making. We need a revolution in relations between government and the social research community – we need social scientists to help to determine what works and why, and what types of policy initiatives are likely to be most effective. (Blunkett, 2000)

The prominence of such calls for evidence might lead to speculation that we are living in the era of the 'scientifically guided society' (Lindblom, 1990). However, such a view would be misleading. The chapters in the first half of this book provide many alternative examples of policy initiatives that seem to either fly in the face of the best available research evidence on effectiveness or, at the very best, are based on flimsy evidence. For example, in education the evidence in support of the introduction of the literacy hour or the homework policy is disputed (see Chapter Four). Similarly, in healthcare the evidence to support the case for the introduction of the Patient's Charter and NHS Direct seems to be lacking. Even when policy decisions relate to areas that are highly technical and scientific, there is little evidence that technical arguments (based on science and research evidence) necessarily have much of a direct impact on the decisions made (Nelkin, 1992). Unsurprisingly, then, society appears to be guided more by politics than by science, and politics is more about the art of the possible or generally acceptable than what is rational or might work best (Stoker, 1999).

However, the chapters in the first half of the book also demonstrate that there is an ongoing interaction between evidence and public policy, although the nature of this relationship varies greatly with the policy area. It is in the light of this diversity in the use of research evidence that this chapter aims to provide an overview of the possible relationship(s) between evidence and public policy. In doing so, it provides a number of frameworks within which to situate the experiences of evidence-based policy and practice outlined in each of the policy areas covered in Part One of the book.

Given the complexity and ambiguity of the policy-making process, an early exploration of some of the terms used in this chapter is warranted. Some of the many definitions found in the policy studies literature are highlighted Box 2.1. The phrase *public policy* refers to those public issues defined as problems and the courses of action (or inaction) that arise to address these problems. This book is concerned with a subset of these courses of action by focusing on 'what works' in improving the effectiveness of public services.

Box 2.1: Definitions

- Public policy is concerned with "the public and its problems" (Dewey, 1927).

- The study of public policy considers "what governments do, why they do it, and what difference it makes" (Dye, 1976, p 1).

- The policy process refers to "all aspects of what is involved in providing policy direction for the work of the public sector. These include the ideas which inform policy conception, the talk and work which goes into providing the formulation of policy directions, and all the talk, work and collaboration which goes into translating these directions into practice" (Yeatman, 1998, p 9).

- Policymaking is defined as "the process by which governments translate their political vision into programmes and actions to deliver 'outcomes' – desired changes in the real world" (Cabinet Office – Strategic Policy Making Team, 1999, para 2.4)

The distinction between policy and practice, implied by the title of this book, is not a rigid one. Practitioners do not merely implement policy decisions that have been decided elsewhere. Policy is influenced from the bottom up (Lipsky, 1976, 1979) as well as practice being influenced from the top down. There are many different types of policy decisions (Carley, 1980) – from specific issues (decision making about day-to-day activities) to strategic issues (large-scale decisions between broad policy choices). Many decisions lie somewhere in between.

The phrase *policy making* does not usually relate to a clearly defined event or to an explicit set of decisions. Policy tends to emerge and accrete rather than being the outcome of conscious deliberation (Weiss, 1980). Policy making is a complex process without a definite beginning or end – "somehow a complex set of forces together produces effects called 'policies'" (Lindblom, 1980, p 5). The parties to this complex process, the so-called *policy makers*, are not confined to government ministers, senior civil servants and co-opted policy advisors. Politicians and officials at local government level and other activists (such as professional associations, pressure groups, journalists and other commentators) also influence the form that policies take. Practitioners (professional or otherwise), who operationalise policies, have their own distinctive role in shaping policies as they are experienced by clients or service users.

The introduction to this book comments on the diversity of what counts as evidence of policy and service effectiveness. This is a theme that will be returned to time and again throughout the book. Within policy studies, the phrase *policy analysis* is sometimes used to refer to the way in which evidence is generated and integrated into the policy making process. This represents analysis *for* the policy process, which needs to be distinguished from analysis *of* the policy process:

- *Analysis for the policy process* encompasses the use of analytical techniques and research to inform the various stages of the policy process.
- *Analysis of the policy process* considers how policy problems are defined, agendas set, policy formulated, decisions made and policy is subsequently implemented and evaluated. (Parsons, 1995, p xvi)

In this book, evidence arising from policy evaluation is considered to be one aspect of analysis *for* the policy process. No hard and fast distinctions are made between the prospective nature of policy analysis (analysis before the formation of policy) and the retrospective character of evaluation (analysis of the implementation of policy [Chelimsky, 1985]). Both are capable of informing subsequent policy formation.

This chapter is primarily concerned with analysis *of* the policy process in order to understand how evidence (arising from analysis *for* the policy process) could and should feed into policy making and implementation. In addressing these concerns the first section of the chapter provides a brief chronological overview of the relationship between research and public policy in the UK. This is followed by a section that considers the ways in which this relationship has been modelled. A third section summarises the conclusions of empirical studies that have explored the use of research evidence in practice. The fourth section highlights the importance of context in understanding the relationship between evidence and policy. It outlines one way of mapping this context by identifying and describing policy networks. The penultimate section discusses the implications of evidence-based policy making for democracy. The concluding section speculates about some possible futures for the relationship between evidence and policy.

A short history of the relationship between research and public policy in the UK

It can be argued that the origins of analysis for policy (and the role of research and knowledge within this) are as old as 'the state' itself (Parsons, 1995). However, the specific character of the relationship between social research and social policy in Britain was shaped during the expansion of both activities in the 19th and early 20th centuries (Abrams, 1968; Bulmer, 1982; Finch, 1986). The origins of social research in England are often associated with the Royal Commission on the Poor Law (1832-34). This was the first 'dramatically obvious' instance of the use of social research in policy making (Bulmer 1982, p 2). The character of the research–policy relationship established by this Commission set the framework for the subsequent development of that relationship. Finch (1986, p 18) summarises the main aspects of this framework as:

- a belief in the importance of collecting accurate facts about the social world as a basis for formulating government policies;
- quantification and accurate statistics seen as essential to the definition of such facts;
- adherence to a simple model of the relationship between social research and social reform; a model which posits a direct and unproblematic relationship between knowledge and reform.

Subsequent work by Booth, Rowntree and the Webbs remained within this broad framework of the research–policy relationship. The activities of the Fabian Society (founded in 1883) moved the agenda forward by establishing that research was of use in both formulating social policies and administering them (Abrams, 1968; Finch, 1986). The idea that research could and should be of direct use to government in determining and achieving its social policy objectives has been referred to as establishing a social engineering role for research (Janowitz, 1972; Bulmer, 1986; Finch, 1986).

The social survey research of the 19th century continued and developed during the 20th century. Survey techniques developed in their sophistication (Bulmer, 1982) and there was also consideration of how the capacity to provide such research should be expanded. There were several government reports during the 20th century about ways to ensure sufficient research capacity. The Haldane Report in 1917 reviewed the government's provision for research and argued that it should be substantially expanded. One of the principles expounded in this Report related to the need for a separate government research department (rather than research units within each government department) to ensure that research is given its own voice and that results are not subordinated to administrative interests. Subsequent government reports – Clapham Report (HMSO, 1946), Heyworth Report (HMSO, 1965) and two reports by Lord Rothschild (Rothschild, 1971; HMSO, 1982) – revisited such issues.

Following Lord Rothschild's recommendations in 1971, there was tighter control on research commissioned by the government (each individual project was expected to have a clearly identified customer who commissions a contractor to carry out the work on specified items). In Chapter Nine, Francis Terry states that one effect of this reform seems to have been a reduction in the scope for government-sponsored research and development to range very far outside the framework of current policies.

To be fair, Lord Rothschild recognised the dangers of this in his 1982 report on what was then the Social Science Research Council. In this he acknowledges that, although ministers cannot be expected to fund research that is likely to be highly critical of their departments, governments do more generally have a duty to sponsor social science research which challenges prevailing orthodoxies. Such concerns led Sir Douglas Wass, in one of his Reith lectures, to argue that it is essential for democracy that governments should not be the only (or even the primary) source of information and analysis on policy-related topics (Wass, 1983). More recently the government has reiterated the analytical dangers of insularity and has proposed that inhouse policy analysis, particularly long-term quantitative models, should be published and be subjected to external audit and peer review (Cabinet Office – Performance and Innovation Unit, 2000).

While the government's capacity to provide research information grew in the middle years of the 20th century, academic institutions also began to expand to provide a base for such research. With the development of the social sciences after the Second World War the production of organised knowledge about social problems became more institutionalised (Parsons, 1995). However, such was the demand for social knowledge that by the 1970s the range of organisations conducting such research had grown rapidly in the UK, as in all industrialised countries (Crawford and Perry, 1976).

The 1960s are considered to be the high point of a social engineering role for research. This was followed by increasing disillusionment about such an approach, coupled with a breakdown of the social democratic consensus in British politics more generally:

> The collapse of the social democratic consensus and a recognition on the political left that previous attempts at social engineering through education (and elsewhere) had largely been ineffective called into question the whole enterprise of creating social knowledge for direct use by governments. (Finch 1986, p 35)

It was in this climate of disillusionment with social engineering, during the 1970s and 1980s, that an expansion took place in the number, type and variety of 'think-tanks' (Weiss, 1992; Parsons, 1995). These think-tanks and related research bodies aim to influence the policy agenda through the publication of research and policy advocacy (see Box 2.2 for examples). The growth in their number signifies an increasing plurality of 'knowledge-providers', but they still represent the idea of a centralised policy process where inputs are fed into the centre (Parsons, 1995). Since the 1980s the sources of knowledge and advice, and the mechanisms by which they operate, have become more diverse, as indicated by the concepts of policy 'networks', and 'communities', described further later in this chapter.

Despite the earlier tradition of social engineering and the subsequent proliferation of research 'providers', there have long existed mechanisms for keeping research evidence at arm's length from government. For example, the practice in the UK of appointing special commissions of inquiry to collate and evaluate evidence for particular policy decisions. The use of research councils to allocate funding for a wide range of policy issues has also encouraged an arm's length relationship between government departments and researchers in many policy areas. This distancing or even this dismissal of research was particularly apparent with the ideologically driven government of the 1980s.

Box 2.2: Examples of think-tanks in Britain	
1883	• The Fabian Society (one of the oldest think-tanks) whose aim was to promote socialism through gradual change
1920s and 1930s	• Chatham House – an institute for international affairs
	• Political and Economic Planning (merged with the Centre for Studies in Social Planning in 1976 to form the Policy Studies Institute) – occupies the middle ground on the political spectrum
1955	• Institute for Economic Affairs – right wing and framed much of the policy agenda adopted by the Thatcher government
1976	• Adam Smith Institute – right wing and at the forefront of the campaign for privatisation
1988	• Institute for Public Policy Research – left of centre, developed by the Labour Party
1993	• DEMOS, an organisation that draws support for its activities from across the political spectrum; tries to focus on long-term issues

Much has been written about the way in which the gap left by the crumbling of the social democratic consensus was filled by a 'new right ideology' with the election of the Thatcher government in 1979 (for example, Flynn, 1993). Policy making throughout the 1980s and in part in the early 1990s was driven by this ideology. However, the concurrent development of a management agenda in the public sector led to a greater focus on programme evaluation, an explosion in performance indicator systems and increased powers for audit and inspection regimes (Pollitt, 1990; Hood, 1991). These in turn provided systematic information on the effects of policy and practice interventions that was sometimes fed into the policy-making process. For example, when the Audit Commission took over audit responsibilities for NHS trusts (in the early 1990s), it conducted value-for-money studies on the cost–effectiveness of day-case surgery. The findings of these studies subsequently contributed to the development of a policy agenda that promoted the benefits of day-case surgery.

The recent political history of the UK might signal the re-emergence of a more evidence-informed policy process in the social engineering mould. The election of a Labour government in the UK in May 1997, with slogans such as 'what counts is what works', has reignited interest in the role of research evidence in the policy process. During 1998 and 1999 there were several initiatives launched by government departments and allied bodies to improve both the evidence-base on intervention effectiveness and its use in policy formation and service delivery practice. Many of these initiatives are linked to the Comprehensive Spending Review, conducted by the Labour government during 1998, which demonstrated the many gaps in existing knowledge about 'what works'. Some of the undertakings affecting different policy areas are described in the chapters in the first half of this book. This chapter provides a brief overview of recent government pronouncements on 'professional policy making' as part of the *Modernising government* agenda.

The *Modernising government* White Paper (Cm 4310, 1999) promises changes to policy making to ensure that policies are strategic, outcome focused, joined-up (if necessary), inclusive, flexible, innovative and robust. One of the changes identified as important was making sure that in future policies were evidence-based. Two subsequent publications have sought to identify how such a goal could be achieved. *Adding it up* (Cabinet Office, 2000) calls for a fundamental change in culture to place good analysis at the heart of policy making. *Professional policy making* (Cabinet Office, 1999) examines what modernised policy making should look like (see Box 2.3) and how it might be achieved.

A broad definition of evidence is found within these recent government documents (Box 2.4), but a central role for research evidence is nonetheless advocated. There is recognition that at present little of the research commissioned by government departments or other academic research appears to be used by policy makers. As part of a series of initiatives to address this, the new Economic and Social Research Council (ESRC, 1999) Centre for Evidence-based Policy is seen as important in improving the accessibility of research evidence. However, just making research more accessible is unlikely to be enough to ensure evidence-based policy making. Hence further initiatives are proposed to improve departments' capacity to make best use of evidence (cf Chapter Eleven). A central role is envisaged for the Centre for Management and Policy Studies in the Cabinet Office, which has been given the task of promoting practical strategies for knowledge-based policy making, including the effective sharing of information and training officials in how to interpret, use and apply evidence.

It is not entirely clear why there appears to be an opportunity for research evidence to have substantial impact on public policy and practice at the present time. Media comment has included the view that the 'what works' orthodoxy offers a credible means of keeping public spending in check:

> Both Tony Blair and Gordon Brown seem to agree that the option of reaching for the Treasury contingency reserves when in political difficulty is not open to ministers, nor even to the prime minister.... Having decided not to throw money at problems, Blair seems determined to throw information instead. As a tactic it might even work.' (Travis, 1999)

However, promises to increase NHS funding to bring it in line with the European average demonstrates that the Labour government is not adverse to dipping into Treasury reserves and relaxing public expenditure targets, especially as the spectre of the next general election begins to loom large. Another explanation for the renewed interest in evidence focuses on the complexity of the problems facing government:

> ...the political world has become a place where ideological certainties have been undermined, the world's problems seem more complex and solutions more uncertain. In this context evidence could be a bigger player than in the previous era of conviction-driven, ideological politics. (Stoker, 1999, p 1)

Box 2.3: A descriptive model of 'professional policy making'

The model aims to describe what an ideal policy-making process would look like. It is intended for use by government departments in benchmarking their current policy making against the standards outlined in the *Modernising government* White Paper (Cm 4310, 1999). Its genesis is traced back to the Business Excellence Model (British Quality Foundation, undated) and is a deliberate attempt to move away from the traditional policy-making cycle model (cf Figure 2.1) because this does not reflect the realities of policy making.

The model comprises:

- nine features of a policy making process which should produce fully effective policies
- three themes (vision, effectiveness and continuous improvement) that a fully effective policy making process will need to encompass
- nine core competencies that relate to each theme
- definitions of the core competencies with an indication of the evidence that might be relevant to showing that the competencies are being met.

The nine core competencies are said to encapsulate all the key elements of the policy-making process. For this reason they are reproduced below to summarise the model.

- *Forward looking* – takes a long-term view, based on statistical trends and informed predictions, of the likely impact of policy.
- *Outward looking* – takes account of factors in the national, European and international situation and communicates policy effectively.
- *Innovative and creative* – questions established ways of dealing with things and encourages new ideas; open to comments and suggestions of others.
- *Using evidence* – uses best available evidence from a wide range of sources and involves key stakeholders at an early stage.
- *Inclusive* – takes account of the impact on the needs of all those directly or indirectly affected by the policy.
- *Joined-up* – looks beyond institutional boundaries to the government's strategic objectives; establishes the ethical and legal base for policy.
- *Evaluates* – builds systematic evaluation of early outcomes into the policy process.
- *Reviews* – keeps established policy under review to ensure it continues to deal with the problems it was designed to tackle, taking account of associated effects elsewhere.
- *Learns lessons* – learns from experience of what works and what doesn't.

Source: Abstracted from Cabinet Office (1999)

Box 2.4: What counts as evidence for policy making?

The raw ingredient of evidence is information. Good quality policy making depends on high quality information, derived from a variety of sources – expert knowledge; existing domestic and international research; existing statistics; stakeholder consultation; evaluation of previous policies; new research, if appropriate; or secondary sources, including the Internet. Evidence can also include analysis of the outcome of consultation, costings of policy options and the results of economic or statistical modelling.

There is a tendency to think of evidence as something that is only generated by major pieces of research. In any policy area there is a great deal of critical evidence held in the minds of both front-line staff in departments, agencies and local authorities and those to whom the policy is directed.

Source: Abstracted from Cabinet Office (1999, paras 7.1 and 7.22)

The rhetoric of the Labour government stresses the need for collaboration (to identify what matters) as well as evidence (to discover what works). This has presented enormous challenges for policy makers, practitioners and researchers. Central government ministers have offered to work with local agencies to develop and test out new models of service delivery (Martin and Sanderson, 1999). As part of this initiative they have launched a series of pilot projects, policy review groups and public consultations in areas such as crime prevention, employment, education and social welfare. Managing this piloting and review process, and making sense of the information it provides, is a complex process, made more difficult by the demands of a fast-moving policy process (see Box 2.5 for one example; others are provided in Chapter Seven). Researchers are having to combine their traditional role of providing impact analysis with a new role as facilitators and process consultants.

Concerns have been raised about the possible effect of the evidence-based policy agenda on 'objective' research. For example, Janet Lewis, Research Director at the Joseph Rowntree Foundation, has commented that "evidence led may mean what we want for our own political purposes" (Walker, 2000). There are still clear indications that unpalatable evidence is not welcomed:

> ... no-one with the slightest commonsense could take seriously suggestions by Durham University researchers that homework is bad for you. (Blunkett, in Major, 2000)

23

Box 2.5: Best Value pilot programme

On taking up office in 1997 the Labour government in the UK pledged to abolish compulsory competitive tendering (CCT) in local government. Instead, they laid out their plans to give local authorities new legal obligations: a 'duty to consult' and a 'duty of Best Value'. Before imposing these duties on all local councils the Local Government Minister selected 40 local authorities and two police forces to pilot a variety of ways of complying with them. The pilot period was set as April 1998 to April 2000.

The Department of the Environment, Transport and the Regions (DETR) appointed researchers to evaluate the Best Value pilot programme. Their brief is to:

- produce a summative evaluation of the impacts of the pilot programme;
- monitor processes in the pilots to develop an understanding not only of what works but also why it works;
- assist in managing the piloting process to maximise the chances of capturing and disseminating learning from the pilots.

Despite the fact that the pilots had only just begun, in 1998 the DETR issued a series of key policy documents outlining the ways in which central government expects the Best Value framework to operate. Piloting is not therefore designed to test whether the Best Value framework should replace CCT – ministers are already committed to this course of action. The piloting process is more about exemplifying rather than experimenting. The main aim seems to be to create a cadre of 'trail blazing' authorities that will provide instances of 'good practice' that can be adopted by other councils. As well as assisting in the identification of good practice, the evalution of impacts is also intended to provide evidence to reassure the Treasury and the Prime Minister's office that abandoning CCT will not lead to a large increase in local taxes or a marked deterioration in local services.

Evaluators must struggle to combine the requirement for rigorous measurement of long-term impacts with the short-term demand for rapid feedback to inform a fast-moving policy process. The former 'rational-objectivist' approach is very different from the 'argumentative-subjectivist' approach that is likely to be more effective in promoting policy learning.

The reflexive and collaborative approach to policy making, which the Best Value pilot programme is intended to exemplify, places new demands on local and central government as well as on evaluators. The demand is for a move away from a model of central direction, coupled with local compliance, to a situation where local and central government work in partnership to develop new models of local service delivery.

Source: Abstracted from Martin and Sanderson (1999)

This brief chronology of the relationship between research and policy in the UK has already mentioned one way to model this relationship – social engineering. The next section discusses further possible models of the interaction between research and policy.

Modelling the relationship between research and policy

Ideas, knowledge and research evidence have played and will continue to play a role in the policy process (Stoker, 1999). There is a considerable literature devoted to understanding the possible relationships and roles (see Parsons, 1995). This section aims to outline a few key models of the policy-making process and, in doing so, considers how each model envisages research evidence feeding into the process.

Keynes is often cited as the main proponent of the importance of ideas and knowledge in policy making. He argued that policy makers should make rational decisions based on knowledge and 'reasoned experiment' (Keynes, 1971, vol xxi, p 289). As a consequence, the model of policy making he envisaged was one in which ideas rather than interests shaped decisions. This echoes Bacon's 17th-century vision of the New Atlantis, which is a place where policy is informed by knowledge, truth, reason and facts.

The call for policy choices to be made in the light of research evidence on what works fits well with a rational decision-making model of the policy process. Five main stages can be identified in rational models, with research evidence mainly feeding in during stages 2 and 3:

1. A problem which requires action is identified. The goals, values and objectives related to the problem are set out.

2. All important possible ways of solving the problem or achieving the goals or objectives are listed. These are alternative strategies, courses of action or policies.

3. The important consequences which would follow from each alternative strategy are predicted and the probability of those consequences occurring is estimated.

4. The consequences of each strategy are then compared to the goals and objectives identified under (2).

5. Finally, a policy or strategy is selected in which consequences most closely match goals and objectives, or the problem is most nearly solved. (Bulmer, 1986, p 5)

Building on the rational model, the policy process is often characterised as a cycle of activities, where the final stage of one move through the cycle becomes the starting point for the next (see Figure 2.1). The role of evaluation in the post-decision phase provides an important source of evidence for subsequent rounds of policy analysis.

Figure 2.1: The policy cycle

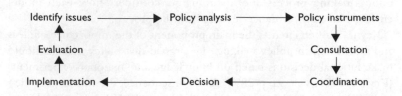

Source: Adapted from Bridgman and Davis (1998)

There have been many criticisms of the idealism of the rational model. From within the rationalist tradition Simon (1957) has been influential in setting out the limits of rationality. For Simon, organisational decision making is characterised by satisficing rather than maximising behaviour. This 'bounded rationality' does not involve the examination of all the alternative courses of action. Nevertheless, he argues that the task is to design the organisational environment so that "the individual will approach as close as practicable to rationality (judged in terms of the organisation's goals) in his [sic] decisions" (1957, p 241). He considers that some arrangements are better than others for achieving a more rational decision-making process. These include:

- the creation of specialist groups and organisations that can deal with routine and repetitive decisions;
- the introduction of market mechanisms to provide a way to restrict the amount of information needed to operate and reach tolerable if not optimal arrangements;
- the use of adversarial proceedings as a means of increasing the consideration of relevant information and arguments;
- greater use of technical tools to improve decision analysis;

- improving the pool of knowledge about the effectiveness of policy alternatives as a precursor to a more rational decision-making process.

Many of the criticisms of the rational model focus on its inadequate representation of the policy-making process in practice. Critics, such as Lindblom, also argue that it is flawed as a normative model. For Lindblom, policy making neither can nor ought to follow the stages of the rational model. Instead, he offers an alternative description of the policy-making process – disjointed incrementalism (Braybrooke and Lindblom, 1963) – and his normative model for good policy making advocates 'the science of muddling through' (Lindblom, 1959).

Incrementalism, as a model, was born out of dissatisfaction with the rational view of decision making. As a result of an analysis of decisions in public sector organisations, proponents (Dahl and Lindblom, 1953; Lindblom, 1959; Braybrooke and Lindblom, 1963) argued that decisions are not made as a movement towards predetermined goals, based on a thorough analysis of the situation. Instead, the process is more piecemeal. Problems are tackled a bit at a time in the process of muddling through.

Whereas the rational model implies that research evidence is fed in at a particular stage (or stages) in the policy-making process, incrementalism envisages a much more diffuse role for research. Within the incrementalist model research evidence can feed into the process at many different points in time and can be targeted separately to the many different parties to the policy-making process. Under such a model:

> ... analysis operates as an indispensable element, but less as the rational arbiter between alternative courses of action. It becomes a way of exerting control by means of which groups and individuals involved in the policy-making process use knowledge to influence others in the process of political interaction. (Bulmer, 1986, p 12)

Lindblom's early work on incrementalism was within the pluralist tradition. Multiple interests were said to impact on the policy-making process. The resulting policy emerges via a process of mutual adjustment to achieve consensus. Such a view of policy making was criticised as being politically naïve (Dror, 1964, 1989; Etzioni, 1967). The argument was that policy change does not always proceed by reaching consensus between the parties involved; instead, the more powerful tend to dominate. By the end of the 1970s, Lindblom had revised his ideas on pluralism. In his later work he recognised that not all interests and participants in incrementalist politics are equal – some have considerably more power than others.

Following the exposition of the rational and incremental models (and in particular the work of Simon and Lindblom) there was much interest in identifying some form of middle or mixed approach (see Dror, 1964; Etzioni, 1967). For example, Etzioni's 'mixed scanning approach' was founded on a distinction between fundamental and more routine (incremental) decisions. Fundamental decisions should, he argued, adopt a rationalist approach, whereas more routine decisions can be made in a more incremental fashion.

There are clear differences between rational and incremental models of the policy-making process. However, there are also some common concerns underpinning these two models and the various mixed approaches derived from them:

> ... what Simon, Lindblom, Dror and Etzioni all have in common is their belief in the improvement of decision-making through changing the relationship of the political process to knowledge and information.
> (Parsons, 1995, p 299)

Some other models of policy formation and decision making do not share this underlying belief. For example, garbage can theories of decision making (Cohen et al, 1972; March and Olsen, 1976) alert us to the possibility that the identification of policy solutions does not necessarily arise from problem identification and analysis. Instead, pre-existing solutions can result in a search for problems to which they can become attached. The garbage can is a metaphor for the choice situation in which various components of the decision-making process are mixed and become attached to one another. The components include: problems or issues, solutions, participants, and choice opportunities (situations when participants are expected to match a solution with a problem and thereby make a decision). A choice situation is thus viewed as "a garbage can into which various problems and solutions are dumped by participants" (Cohen et al, 1972, p 2).

The garbage can model considers the way in which social and economic structure determines who will participate in choice situations and it also discusses the way in which cultural values operate to limit the number of choice outcomes. The role of culture and language is accorded even greater weight in more recent post-modern analyses of the policy process. For example, the argumentative approach (Fischer and Forester, 1993) is the study of how language shapes the way in which we make sense of the world. It is concerned with understanding how policy discourses emerge and how these frame the way in which problems and agendas are constructed. Power arises from establishing the discourse within which problems are framed. An example of the complex relationship between policy discourses, ideology and power is provided in Chapter Eight. Doherty discusses the way in which ideologies act as purposeful 'filters' through which evidence is passed before it impacts on housing policy.

How research evidence is used in practice

Having outlined some of the key models of the policy-making process and their implications for the use of research evidence, we now turn our attention to the way in which research is utilised and what this implies for models of the policy process. We still know relatively little about the dynamics of the policy process and how research evidence impacts on this process (although case studies such as those provided by James, 1997; Marinetto, 1999; Laycock, 2001: forthcoming are of some help).

Much of the pioneering work in this area has been undertaken by Carol Weiss and her colleagues in the USA. Weiss (1979) outlines the ways in which research might be utilised (see Box 2.6) — although in practice she finds more evidence for the last four than for the first two. The problem-solving model relates to the rational model of decision making outlined earlier. The interactive model fits with an incremental view of the policy process. The political and tactical models of research utilisation imply a far more political view of the policy process than those outlined so far in this chapter. Such a framework may be pluralist/ élitist in approach (for example, Dahl, 1961; Bachrach and Baratz, 1970; Lukes, 1974) or neo-Marxist (for example, Milliband, 1982). The first five models outlined in Box 2.6 relate to direct, although diverse, uses of research findings. The direct use of research in problem solving is often contrasted with its indirect use in developing conceptual thinking, as per the final enlightenment model.

Box 2.6: The many meanings of research utilisation

- *Knowledge-driven model* – derives from the natural sciences. The fact that knowledge exists sets up pressures for its development and use.

- *Problem-solving model* – involves the direct application of the results of a specific study to a pending decision.

- *Interactive model* – researchers are just one set of participants among many. The use of research is only one part of a complicated process that also uses experience, political insight, pressure, social technologies and judgement.

- *Political model* – research as political ammunition; using research to support a predetermined position.

- *Tactical model* – research as a delaying tactic in order to avoid responsibility for unpopular policy outcomes.

- *Enlightenment model* – the indirect influence of research rather than the direct impact of particular findings in the policy process. Thus the concepts and theoretical perspectives that social science research engenders pervade the policy making process.

Source: Weiss (1979)

The debate about the role for policy-related research is often framed (following Janowitz, 1972) in terms of engineering versus enlightenment. While support for the enlightenment model of research use has grown, there have been criticisms. For example, Blume (1979) thinks the enlightenment model is too pessimistic about what can be achieved in the shorter term. Others argue that although the social engineering model may be discredited, this relates to Utopian versions of social engineering rather than a more incrementalist ('piecemeal') version (Finch, 1986). The term enlightenment may, in itself, be misleading. Discussion of research utilisation usually assumes that the use of research necessarily improves policy making and that an increase in its use is always desirable (Finch, 1986). Yet when research diffuses to the policy sphere through indirect and unguided channels, it dispenses invalid as well as valid generalisations that can result in 'endarkenment' (Weiss, 1980).

The direct use of research findings appears to be limited, both in Britain and elsewhere (Finch, 1986; Weiss, 1998; and Chapters Four to Ten of this book). Researchers have sought to explain this lack of use. For example, there are said to be a number of limitations on the use of analytical work in the decision-making process (Heinemann et al, 1990, pp 62-4). These include the information overload that exists in the policy process and analysts' lack of a power base and their weak position vis-à-vis political and bureaucratic interests. It appears to take an extra-ordinary set of circumstances for research to influence policy decisions directly (Weiss, 1979). However, there are conditions that are more likely to suit the instrumental use of research:

- if the implications of the findings are relatively non-controversial, neither provoking rifts nor running into conflicting interests;
- if the changes that are implied are within a programme's existing repertoire and are relatively small-scale;
- if the environment of a programme is relatively stable, without big changes in leadership;
- when a programme is in crisis and nobody knows what to do (Weiss, 1998, pp 23-4).

These observations all relate to a generic policy context. Unsurprisingly, the extent and nature of the impact of research findings is greatly influenced by the settings within which evidence emerges and policies are shaped. This is the subject of the next section. Chapter Fifteen considers the more operational question of how to get research to impact on practice.

Policy networks and communities

Models of research utilisation need to be considered in context. The enlightenment model arises from USA research and should not be unquestioningly accepted as appropriate in explaining research utilisation in the UK:

> The character of social research and its effects on the public agenda and social policy depend upon the structure of the political economy in which it is financed and used; hence, US social scientists have less influence on policy than their counterparts in several other rich democracies where there are tighter relations between knowledge and power. (Wilensky, 1997, p 1242)

The apparent lack of influence of social scientists in the USA may seem surprising given the USA's strong reputation for policy analysis and evaluation. There seems to be an inverse relationship operating here. The USA has a reputation for careful evaluation research but in the fragmented and decentralised political economy of that country this is often single-issue research, focusing on short-run effects and used for political ammunition rather than policy planning. In contrast, the more 'corporatist' European systems (such as those found in Sweden, Norway and Austria) foster dialogue between researchers, bureaucrats and politicians. The result is (according to Wilensky) that even though the evaluation research industry may be less well developed in these European countries, research findings are more often used for policy planning and implementation.

> Compared to other countries, we [the USA] are loaded with experts and academicians, but their voices are typically cast to the winds. (Wilensky, 1997, p 1249)

A useful framework for analysing the context for policy making and research utilisation is provided by the concepts of policy networks and policy communities. The concept of a policy network focuses on the pattern of formal and informal relationships that shape policy agendas and decision making. For example, it is suggested that the policy-making networks in Britain are characterised by a fragmented collection of sub-systems: a "series of vertical compartments or segments, each segment inhabited by a different set of organisational groups" (Richardson and Jordan, 1979, p 174). A close working relationship between the government, the research community and industry, identified as 'iron triangles' (Jordan, 1981), applies in the UK to a few areas, such as defence.

The types of network can be distinguished according to their degree of integration (Rhodes, 1988). At the one end of a continuum are policy communities, which have stable and restricted memberships. At the other end are issue networks that represent a much looser set of interests and are less stable and non-exclusive. Networks are found to vary considerably across policy sectors and between states. One possible explanation for this variability is that:

- policy communities are more likely to develop where the state is dependent on groups for implementation;
- policy communities are more likely to develop where interest groups have important resources they can exchange;
- issue networks will develop in areas of lesser importance to government, of high political controversy, or in new issue areas where interests have not yet been institutionalised (Smith, 1993, p 10).

The diverse nature of policy networks/communities across policy areas (such as health, education and criminal justice) shapes the way in which policy is made and implemented. The form of the network also affects the ways in which research evidence is sought and considered by members of the network. This can vary over time. For example, analysis of the development of food policy in the wake of the salmonella-in-eggs scare in the late 1980s suggests that the scare resulted in a shift away from the previous consensual food policy community towards a more pluralistic, less consensual, issue network (Smith, 1991).

One of the important means by which research evidence becomes known and is discussed within policy networks/communities is through the process of advocacy. Around many major issues in contention, there have evolved a group of people who have long-term interests and knowledge in shaping policy (Weiss, 1987, p 280). These interest groups are important purveyors of data and analysis:"It is not done in the interests of knowledge, but as a side effect of advocacy" (Weiss, 1987, p 278).

The concepts of policy networks and communities highlight the potential for more open participation in the policy process. This is explored further in the next section by considering the relationship between evidence, policy and democracy.

Evidence, policy and democracy

> The rise of power based on knowledge in the form of experts or technocrats has been a key feature of the analysis of policy-making in the post war era. (Parsons, 1995, p 153)

The rise of policy analysis (analysis *for* policy) and the resulting impact of a new technocracy on decision making has led to fears that this poses a threat to liberal democratic policy making (Sartori, 1962; Bell, 1976; for a review see Fischer, 1991). However, fears that experts would come to dominate the decision-making process, and hence threaten democracy, have not materialised (Jenkins-Smith, 1990).

The textbook approach to policy analysis has been described as promoting the idea of a 'scientifically guided society', which can be contrasted with an alternative model of the 'self-guiding society' (Lindblom, 1990). In the latter model, social science and research evidence provide enlightenment rather than prescribe a particular form of social engineering. Purveyors of research evidence are only one among a variety of voices in the policy-making process. Research evidence has a limited framing and organising role; it facilitates decisions but does not determine them (Stoker, 1999, p 3). There are a number of reasons why this may be more appropriate than an over-reliance on technical/rational problem solving:

• all knowledge is inconclusive;
• social science is an aid, not an alternative, to ordinary inquiry;
• some problems are intractable to social science;
• learning needs to take place among ordinary citizens;
• democracy and participation are vital for good problem solving;
• the self-guiding society must leave room for problem solving, rather than deliberately designing organisations and assigning problems to solvers;
• the self-guiding society has limited faith in reason and is not motivated by general laws or holistic theories. (Abstracted from Parsons, 1995, p 439)

The need for experts to be 'on tap but not on top' is a theme also addressed in the vision of an active society (Etzioni, 1968, 1993). In such a society, social science can serve an engineering function, and so improve society, but this requires knowledge and power to be distributed widely among members of the community. An active society involves the public in analysis: intellectuals, experts and politicians should interact with the public in a form of 'collective reality testing' (Etzioni, 1968, pp 155-70). Thus the active society uses knowledge and social science to become a self-critical society – active in its use of knowledge (Etzioni, 1968, p 190). The paradox is that while policy analysis clearly contributes to public knowledge and understanding, it can also inhibit change:

> ... its tendency to inhibit change on larger issues may reduce the ease with which popular expression can work its way through the policy process to a new policy. (Jenkins-Smith, 1990, p 218)

Concluding remarks

The idea of evidence-based policy and practice fits most naturally with rational models of the policy-making process. However, rational models have been subjected to sustained criticism throughout the latter half of the 20th century. A major debate exists in the policy studies literature about the scope and limitations of reason, analysis and intelligence in policy making (Stoker, 1999). It appears that the most that can be expected is some form of bounded rationality. But even then we need to consider the political question of 'rational for whom?'

A pluralist view of the nature of interests and power in society opens up the possibility of an alternative incremental model of the policy process; one where research evidence enters the arena through the process of advocacy. Research evidence is thus a political weapon but 'when research is available to all participants in the policy process, research as political ammunition can be a worthy model of utilisation" (Weiss, 1979). A problem arises when certain groups in society do not have access to research evidence and, even if they did, their ability to use this evidence is restricted due to their exclusion from the networks that shape policy decisions.

Recent developments in the provision of evidence over the Internet may encourage more open debates which are not confined to those operating in traditional expert domains. Similarly, the establishment of intermediary bodies (such as the National Institute for Clinical Excellence) to digest existing evidence may facilitate the opening up of evidence-based policy debates.

Developing the sort of active or self-guiding societies envisaged by Etzioni and Lindblom may offer possibilities for the future. This is unlikely to be an easy task. It is hard enough to encourage research to impact on policy in single-issue domains. Many major issues are multisectoral, such as social exclusion, and the problems of research utilisation here are more difficult still. Given the differing nature of policy networks and communities across policy areas, certain sectors may offer more fertile environments than others within which to nurture such a vision.

Questions about how to achieve a more evidence-based policy process are not just practical or technical in nature – ethical and normative issues underlie the debate (Stoker, 1999). The role for academics is not just in providing evidence about 'what works':

> The search for vision and values – especially to any government committed to radical reform – means that there remains scope for social scientists to offer themselves as not just technocrats but also as "gurus".
> (Stoker, 1999, p 3)

One scenario for the future is that initiatives that encourage consultation through policy action teams, will widen the membership of policy communities. The involvement of wider interests in these teams is likely to set a different agenda and lead to a more practice-based view of policy options. The use of research evidence under such a scenario is likely to be diffuse and researchers will be required to answer questions not only on what works, but also on how and why it works.

Another, more pessimistic, scenario is that social scientists and other researchers will continue to bemoan the fact that politicians and other policy makers continue to pay insufficient attention to their research findings. In this scenario, evidence-based policy is likely to continue to be the exception rather than the rule; a situation sustained by the many 'enemies' of a more evidence-based approach (see Box 2.7).

Box 2.7: Seven enemies of evidence-based policy

- *Bureaucratic logic* – the logic that says things are right because they have always been done this way

- *The bottom line* – the logic of the business environment and the throughput measurement that goes with this

- *Consensus* – this involves extensive consultation to find out what matters, followed by an inclusive task force drawn from all interested parties to determine the limits of a solution that will satisfy everyone, which is defined as that which will work

- *Politics* – the art of the possible rather than what is rational or what might work best

- *Civil service culture* – in particular a strong distrust of information generated outside the system

- *Cynicism* – an attitude of mind that allows us to go along with the 'company view' or 'conventional wisdom' even though we know it to be false

- *Time* – no wonder there is so little room for evidence-based policy: there is scarcely room even to think

---

Source: Abstracted from Leicester (1999)

This review demonstrates the shortcomings of simplistic notions of evidence–action–review cycles. It emphasises a more complex conceptualisation of the interactions between stakeholders in policy networks. Teasing out 'what works, when?' in influencing the policy process will be as important as generating evidence for policy in the first place.

References

Abrams, P. (1968) *The origins of British sociology 1834-1914*, Chicago, IL: University of Chicago Press.

Bachrach, P.S. and Baratz, M. S. (1970) *Power and poverty, theory and practice*, New York, NY: Oxford University Press.

Bell, D. (1976) *The coming of post-industrial society: A venture into social forecasting*, Harmondsworth: Penguin Books.

Blume, S. (1979) 'Policy studies and social policy in Britain', *Journal of Social Policy*, vol 8, no 3, pp 311-34.

Blunkett, D. (2000) 'Blunkett rejects anti-intellectualism and welcomes sound ideas', *DfEE News,* http://www.dfee.gov.uk/newslist.htm, 2 February.

Braybrooke, D. and Lindblom, C. (1963) *A strategy of decision*, New York, NY: Free Press.

Bridgman, P. and Davis, G. (1998) *Australian policy handbook*, St Leonards, Australia: Allen and Unwin.

British Quality Foundation (undated) *Towards business excellence*, London: British Quality Foundation.

Bulmer, M. (1982) *The uses of social research*, London: Allen and Unwin.

Bulmer, M. (1986) *Social science and policy*, London: Allen and Unwin.

Cabinet Office – Strategic Policy Making Team (1999) *Professional policy making for the twenty first century*, London: Cabinet Office.

Cabinet Office – Performance and Innovation Unit (2000) *Adding it up: Improving analysis and modelling in central government*, London: Cabinet Office.

Carley, M. (1980) *Rational techniques in policy analysis*, London: Policy Studies Institute/Heinemann.

Chelimsky, E. (1985) 'Old patterns and new directions in program evaluation', in E. Chelmisky (ed) *Program evaluation: Patterns and directions*, Washington, DC: The American Society for Public Administration.

Cohen, M., March, J. and Olsen, J. (1972) 'A garbage can model of organizational choice', *Administrative Science Quarterly*, vol 17, pp 1-25.

Crawford, E. and Perry, N. (eds) (1976) *Demands for social knowledge: The role of research organisations*, London: Sage Publications.

Dahl, R. (1961) *Who governs? Democracy and power in an American city*, New Haven, CT: Yale University Press.

Dahl, R. A. and Lindblom, C. E. (1953) *Politics, economies and welfare*, New York, NY: Harper and Brothers.

Dewey, J. (1927) *The public and its problems*, New York, NY: Holt.

Dror, Y. (1964) 'Muddling through – "science" or "inertia"', *Public Administration Review*, no 24, pp 153-7.

Dror, Y. (1989) *Public policymaking reexamined* (2nd edn), New Brunswick, NJ: Transaction Publishers.

Dye, T. R. (1976) *What governments do, why they do it, what difference it makes*, Tuscaloosa, AL: University of Alabama Press.

ESRC (Economic and Social Research Council) (1999) *Evidence-based policy and practice: Research resources in the social sciences*, Call for submissions, Swindon: ESRC.

Etzioni, A. (1967) 'Mixed scanning: a "third" approach to decision-making', *Public Administration Review*, no 27, pp 385-92.

Etzioni, A. (1968) *The active society: A theory of societal and political processes*, New York, NY: Free Press.

Etzioni, A. (1993) *The spirit of community: Rights, responsibilities and the communitarian agenda*, New York, NY: Crown Publishers.

Finch, J. (1986) *Research and policy: The use of qualitative methods in social and educational research*, London: Falmer Press.

Fischer, F. (1991) 'American think tanks: policy elites and the politicisation of expertise', *Governance*, vol 4, no 3, pp 332-53.

Fischer, F. and Forester, J. (eds) (1993) *The argumentative turn in policy analysis and planning*, London: Duke University Press/UCL Press.

Flynn, N. (1993) *Public sector management*, Hemel Hempstead: Harvester Wheatsheaf.

Haldane Committee (1917) *Machinery of government*, Cm 9230, London: HMSO.

Heinemann, R.A., Bluhm, W.T., Peterson, S.A. and Kearney, E.N. (1990) *The world of the policy analyst: Rationality, values and politics*, Chatham, NJ: Chatham House.

HMSO (1946) *Report of the Committee on the Provision of Social and Economic Research*, Cmd 6868 (Clapham Report), London: HMSO.

HMSO (1965) *Report of the Committee on Social Studies*, Cmnd 2660 (Heyworth Report), London: HMSO.

HMSO (1982) *An enquiry into the Social Science Research Council*, Cmnd 8554 (Rothschild Report), London: HMSO.

Hood, C. (1991) 'A public management for all seasons?', *Public Administration*, no 69, pp 3-19.

James, S. (1997) *British government: A reader in policy making*, London: Routledge.

Janowitz, M. (1972) *Sociological models and social policy*, Morristown, NJ: General Learning Systems.

Jenkins-Smith, H. (1990) *Democratic politics and policy analysis*, Pacific Grove, CA: Brooks/Cole.

Jordan, A.G. (1981) 'Iron triangles, woolly corporatism or elastic nets: images of the policy process', *Journal of public policy*, no 1, pp 95-123.

Keynes, J.M. (1971) *The collected writings of John Maynard Keynes, Vols 1-30*, London: Macmillan.

Laycock, G. (2001: forthcoming) 'Hypothesis-based research: the repeat victimisation story', *Criminal Policy Journal*, Forthcoming.

Leicester, G. (1999) 'The seven enemies of evidence-based policy', *Publlic Money and Management*, vol 19, no 1, pp 5-7.

Lindblom, C. (1959) 'The science of muddling through', *Public Administration Review*, no 19, pp 79-88.

Lindblom, C. (1980) *The policy-making process*, Englewood Cliffs, NJ: Prentice Hall.

Lindblom, C.E. (1990) *Inquiry and change: The troubled attempt to understand and shape society*, New Haven, CT: Yale University Press.

Lipsky, M. (1976) 'Towards a theory of street-level bureaucracy', in W.D. Hawley (ed) *Theoretical perspectives on urban policy*, Englewood Cliffs, NJ: Prentice-Hall.

Lipsky, M. (1979) *Street level bureaucracy*, New York, NY: Russell Sage Foundation.

Lukes, S. (1974) *Power: A radical view*, London: Macmillan.

Major, L.E. (2000) 'Simply impossible', *The Guardian*, 1 February, 1H.

March, J. and Olsen, J. (1976) *Ambiguity and choice in organisations*, Bergen: Universiteforlaget.

Marinetto, M. (1999) *Studies of the policy process*, Englewood Cliffs, NJ: Prentice Hall.

Martin, S. and Sanderson, I. (1999) 'Evaluating public policy experiments: measuring outcomes, monitoring process or managing pilots?', *Evaluation*, vol 5, no 3, pp 245-58.

Milliband, R. (1982) *Capitalist democracy in Britain*, Oxford: Oxford University Press.

Nelkin, D. (ed) (1992) *Controversy: Politics of tehnical decisions* (3rd edn), London: Sage Publications.

Parsons, W. (1995) *Public policy*, Cheltenham: Edward Elgar.

Pollitt, C. (1990) *Managerialism and the public services*, Oxford: Blackwell.

Rhodes, R.A.W. (1988) *Beyond Westminster and Whitehall: The sub-central governments of Britain*, London: Unwin Hyman.

Richardson, J.J. and Jordan, A.G. (1979) *Governing under pressure: The policy process in a post-Parliamentary democracy* (2nd edn), Oxford: Martin Robertson.

Rothschild, Lord (1971) *A framework for government research and development*, Cmnd 4814, London: HMSO.

Sartori, G. (1962) *Democratic theory*, Detroit, MI: Wayne State University Press.

Simon, H.A. (1957) *Models of man: Social and rational*, New York, NY: John Wiley.

Smith, M.J. (1993) *Pressure power and policy: State autonomy and policy networks in Britain and the United States*, Hemel Hempstead: Harvester Wheatsheaf.

Smith, R. (1991) 'Where is the wisdom..? [editorial]', *BMJ*, vol 303, pp 798-9.

Stoker, G. (1999) Notes on Keynote address, ARCISS Conference, 27 January, London.

Travis, A. (1999) 'Super think-tanker', *The Guardian*, 6 September.

Cm 4310 (1999) *Modernising government White Paper*, London: The Stationery Office.

Walker, D. (2000) 'You find the evidence, we'll pick the policy', *The Guardian*, 15 February, p 3H.

Wass, D. (1983) 'Participation, the sole bond – Reith Lecture VI', *The Listener*, 15 December, pp 15-17.

Weiss, C.H. (1979) 'The many meanings of research utilisation', *Public Administration Review*, vol 39, no 5, pp 426-31.

Weiss, C.H. (1980) 'Knowledge creep and decision accretion', *Knowledge: Creation, Diffusion, Utilization*, vol 1, no 3, pp 381-404.

Weiss, C.H. (1987) 'The circuitry of enlightenment', *Knowledge: Creation, Diffusion, Utilisation*, vol 8, no 2, pp 274-81.

Weiss, C.H. (1992) *Organisations for policy analysis: Helping government think*, Newbury Park, CA: Sage Publications.

Weiss, C.H. (1998) 'Have we learned anything new about the use of evaluation?', *American Journal of Evaluation*, vol 19, no 1, pp 21-33.

Wilensky, H.L. (1997) 'Social science and the public agenda: reflections on the relation of knowledge to policy in the United States and abroad', *Journal of Health Politics, Policy and Law*, vol 22, no 5, pp 1241-65.

Yeatman, A. (ed) (1998) *Activism and the policy process*, Sydney, Australia: Allen and Unwin.

THREE

Healthcare: evidence to the fore

Huw Davies and Sandra Nutley

Introduction

Physicians and other health workers have always claimed special knowledge about what works – from this springs their legitimacy. Those outside the health professions have harboured more cynical thoughts. Benjamin Franklin said that "God heals, and the doctor takes the fees" (Tripp, 1973), and George Bernard Shaw castigated the medical profession for being "no more scientific than their tailors" (Shaw, 1911). However, until recent years healthcare has been characterised not by uncertainty about efficacy but by an often unwarranted surety of therapeutic success. For many doctors it is a case of "not so much that they don't know, but that they know so much that ain't so" (source unknown). More recently, the presence of uncertainty has been made explicit and healthcare workers (and many doctors in particular) have striven to become more 'evidence-based'.

Healthcare may be delivered by individual practitioners but they do so largely within the context of various national organisational structures. In the United Kingdom, the National Health Service has three main goals:
- to promote good health
- to diagnose and treat illness
- to provide healthcare for those in continuing needs (The Scottish Office, 1991).

Tellingly, these goals are qualified with the caveat 'within the resources available' (The Scottish Office, 1991). Thus, evidence on effectiveness is not simply the domain of healthcare practitioners. Managers and policy makers also need evidence to allow them to allocate resources, assess progress in meeting organisational objectives and manage performance.

This review of evidence in healthcare first describes the nature of evidence and the commonly accepted methodologies for deciding what works, before explicating some of the themes aimed at ensuring that the evidence impacts on healthcare policy, health service management and, most especially, clinical practice. It focuses primarily on evidence relating to effectiveness, and is largely confined to exploring how evidence is used in health service delivery. This is not to suggest that healthcare is the only (or even the prime) route to health, and recent work to develop evidence for public health shows that the themes in this chapter are beginning to be addressed outside of clinical services (Gowman and Coote, 2000).

Nature of evidence

Confidence in therapeutic effect has traditionally arisen from personal experience. Case reports and case series are "the age-old cornerstone of medical progress" (Anonymous, 1990). However, since the 1940s there has been growing recognition of the inadequacies of these approaches in discerning what works, and a new and dominant paradigm has emerged.

Need for greater rigour

Personal experience can mislead. Few therapeutic interventions are always successful: even the best sometimes fail to bring the expected relief. What is more, even quite hopeless therapies will sometimes appear to show benefits in individual cases. There are two main ways in which we can be misled: believing that useless or even harmful therapies are efficacious; or rejecting as ineffectual therapies that in reality offer benefits. Many factors conspire to make it difficult to distinguish between the helpful, the hopeless and the harmful (see Box 3.1).

Box 3.1: Need for rigorous methodology when assessing effectiveness

- *Ineffective treatments abound:* Even the most cursory study of the history of medicine shows a scenery littered with discredited therapies, from blood letting to thalidomide, radical mastectomy and cement-less hip prosthetics. New therapeutic approaches rise, shine and then fall away. We should be clear about one thing: for even the most outlandish and alarming therapies their proponents were (and are) largely convinced of their therapeutic value.

- *Limitations of clinical theory:* Therapeutic advances are often made on the basis of reasoning from an understanding of pathophysiology. Unfortunately, therapies based on inadequate models of complex biological processes are themselves sometimes inadequate. For example, throughout the 20th century attempts have been made to control chronic pain by cutting, burning, freezing and poisoning nerve fibres (neuroablation). Although this approach appeared reasonable by the then understanding of the nervous system as 'body wiring', the inescapable conclusion is that it frequently exacerbates the problem (Macrae et al, 1992).

- *Spontaneous improvements:* Most disease is self-limiting and many patients recover spontaneously. Even chronic diseases such as multiple sclerosis and rheumatoid arthritis fluctuate and sometimes temporarily abate. Distinguishing between natural improvements and physician-induced benefit is thus problematic.

- *Placebo effect:* Numerous studies attest to the power of the placebo at inducing real and measurable changes in patients' conditions. In the 1950s, sham surgery was shown to improve angina patients, not only in patient-reported outcomes but also in objective tests such as exercise tolerance (Cobb et al, 1959). Such effects may be therapist-induced but they are non-specific to the therapy.

- *Chance variability:* Biological variation greatly clouds judgements as to therapeutic effect. Inter- and intra-subject variability may lead to either Type I errors (erroneously accepting a therapy as efficacious) or Type II errors (falsely rejecting an intervention as useless).

- *Importance of small effects:* Dramatic improvements in patient outcomes are as rare as they are easy to spot. Far more commonly, healthcare has advanced through a number of improvements which are individually small but collectively worthwhile. Small improvements are easily submerged in a background of wide random variation. Some of the deleterious effects from therapies may be very rare but devastatingly serious (such as thrombosis from oral contraceptives). Finding these is as important as discovering the therapeutic effects.

Source: Adapted and extended from Crombie and Davies (1996)

The fundamental problem is one of comparisons. To assess effectiveness, the outcomes (however measured) of those receiving the new intervention have to be compared with the outcomes from some other group that has been treated in the standard way. Doing this should separate out the benefits of treatment from natural spontaneous improvements. The difficulty lies in choosing the comparison group. Unless the two groups are identical *in every respect other than the nature of the intervention received* then attributions of causality between intervention and outcome are unwarranted (Sheldon, 1994; Davies and Crombie, 1997; see also Chapters Twelve and Thirteen). Experience has shown that whenever comparison groups are chosen, whether historical or concurrent, the comparisons tend to exaggerate the value of a new treatment (Pocock, 1983; Colditz et al, 1989; Miller et al, 1989), although this may have more to do with the often poor methodological quality of non-randomised designs (Ottenbacher, 1992; Kunz and Oxman, 1998; Reeves et al, 1998).

New paradigm

Gradual recognition of the need for fair and rigorous comparisons has led to the ascendancy and eventual hegemony of *experimental* rather than observational designs in assessing effectiveness (see Chapter Twelve for more detailed exploration of this issue). It is now widely accepted that to achieve fair comparative groups patients should be *randomly assigned* to either the existing therapy or the intervention under test. This removal of *choice* from group allocation will on average lead to balanced groups (for both known and unknown prognostic factors), and is the basis of statistical testing that seeks to estimate whether any benefits seen are greater than would be expected by chance alone.

Other methodological enhancements have been developed so that there is now a standard 'package' of design features that figures in rigorous studies (see Box 3.2). Wherever possible, patients and healthcare workers should be 'blind to treatment allocation'. That is, no one should know (until the end of the analysis) whether patients are receiving the standard therapy or the innovative treatment. Blinding is intended to overcome the placebo effect and to reduce biased assessment of outcomes. It also contributes to keeping the comparison fair after allocation: ensuring that no one knows which patients are in the new group means that these patients cannot be treated any differently from usual.

Further care is taken during analysis to ensure that bias is minimised. First, patient groups are compared at the start of the study to look for any differences. Randomisation will on average lead to balanced groups but does not guarantee this, especially when numbers in the study are small (that is, dozens rather than hundreds). Second, great care is taken to ensure that all patients are followed up and that the main comparison made is between the groups as initially allocated. Even if subsequently patients move between groups (for example, patients stopping the new therapy and reverting to the old) an analysis based on the *initial intention to treat* precludes bias because of differential swapping between treatment groups. Finally, an assessment is made, using standard statistical procedures, as to the chances of either Type I or Type II errors (see Box 3.1 under Chance variability).

Box 3.2: Methodological features in the rigorous paradigm
• Random allocation to new therapy or existing best practice
• Single blinding: patients are unaware of their group allocation
• Double blinding: all healthcare staff are unaware of patients' group allocation
• Comparison of patients at the baseline to ensure balanced groups
• Full patient follow-up
• Objective and unbiased outcome assessment
• Analysis based on initial group allocation (an intention-to-treat analysis)
• The likelihood of the findings arising by chance alone is assessed
• The power of the study to detect a worthwhile effect is assessed

This approach to assessing the effectiveness of interventions is now widely accepted as the gold standard. This acceptance comes not just from the considerations outlined in Box 3.1 but from repeated demonstrations that studies lacking rigour are quite capable of misleading (Sacks et al, 1982; Green and Byar, 1984; Schulz et al, 1995; Kunz and Oxman, 1998; Moher et al, 1998). Despite widespread acceptance of this, some concerns remain as to the applicability of the method in several areas, notably, surgery and other therapies where there are important differences between practitioners in skills, approach and rapidity of learning (Pollock, 1989; Dundee and McMillan, 1992). Disputes also continue over technical details (for example, whether a frequentist or a Bayesian approach is most appropriate during analysis [Lilford et al, 1995]). Nonetheless, these are more arguments about implementation of the method than serious philosophical disagreements with the approach. While ethical debates do still occur, the ethical basis as to the use of patients in experimentation has largely been accepted, subject to the safeguards of informed consent (Passamani, 1991; Wager et al, 1995).

Even in areas where intervention studies cannot be designed according to the key principles, the gold standard laid out in Box 3.2 gives a high point against which less than ideal studies can be assessed. The question then becomes not 'is the study flawed?', but more 'how flawed is the study and do any biases weaken or vitiate the conclusions?' The key role of the double-blind randomised control trial has been formalised in 'hierarchies of evidence' summarised in Box 3.3 (Hadorn et al, 1996).

Box 3.3: Hierarchies of evidence

I-1   Systematic review and meta-analysis of two or more double-blind randomised control trials

I-2   One or more large double-blind randomised control trials

II-1   One or more well-conducted cohort studies

II-2   One or more well-conducted case-control studies

II-3   A dramatic uncontrolled experiment

III   Expert committee sitting in review; peer leader opinion

IV   Personal experience

Role of theories

The ascendancy of randomised control trials represents the triumph of pragmatism and empiricism. Theories abound in medicine (and more widely about the delivery of care). But precisely because these theories have misled so often (see Box 3.1 under Limitations of clinical theory) the top of the heap in terms of evidence is the *pragmatic* randomised control trial (Schwartz and Lellouch, 1967). Such trials do not try to explain *why* beneficial outcomes are achieved; they merely try to demonstrate that they *are* achieved.

The pragmatism embodied in the dominant methodology means that randomised intervention trials have been used to assess whole packages of care (for example, in assessing the role of health insurance on the demand for medical care [Manning et al, 1987]) or in evaluating the impact of a multidisciplinary management of chronic pain [Flor et al, 1992]). When this is done, often few attempts are made to 'unbundle' the package in pursuit of understanding of the mechanism(s) of action. It is not that such understanding is deemed unimportant – better understanding can lead to improved design of future interventions. It is just now widely accepted that even apparently clear understandings have to be tested in real-world settings; and, more importantly, even when understanding is imperfect, 'best-guess' interventions (or packages of interventions) can still be tested empirically.

Examining appropriate outcomes

The establishment of an appropriate methodology for assessing what works has not silenced debate. Much of this debate is centred around the distinction between 'does it work?' and 'does it matter?' The rise in methodological rigour has been accompanied by a shift towards patient-centred health outcomes rather than clinical or process measures of effectiveness (Davies and Crombie, 1995; Davies and Marshall, 1999). This ties in with the suspicion of theory outlined above: we may believe that interventions, approaches or technologies offer benefits to patient care but we still need to test these beliefs in pragmatic trials whose main effect measures are mortality, morbidity, quality of life and patient satisfaction.

For example, testing the effectiveness of new imaging equipment is not a matter of assessing whether good pictures are obtained but of demonstrating that these better images contribute to better patient care and hence improve patient outcomes. As another example, the fundamental issue in evaluating cancer screening (cervical cytology; mammography; prostate specific antigen) is not whether new cancer cases can be detected but whether mortality is reduced in consequence (Gøtzsche and Olsen, 2000). Identifying the important and relevant outcomes is a major concern in evaluating the effectiveness of any healthcare intervention.

Beyond effectiveness: introducing cost

For all that the healthcare community has successfully grappled with assessing 'what works?' (effectiveness), it is far less clear about assessing 'is it worth it?' (efficiency or cost-effectiveness). Whereas randomised control trials are (relatively) uncontroversial, bringing costs into the equation is viewed as highly problematic (some clinicians even regard it as unethical; their views are discussed and dismissed in an article by Williams [1992]). While many *do* accept the necessity of considering costs there is considerable doubt and uncertainty as to how to do so fairly and with rigour. Despite the rise of health economics and pharmacoeconomics as recognised disciplines, much work remains to build a solid theoretical and methodological platform.

For many individual practitioners lack of evidence on cost–effectiveness is of little immediate concern. Their foremost obligation is to the care of the patient in front of them, so questions of effectiveness take precedence over cost issues. However, for managers and policy makers who must work within the confines of limited budgets, cost–effectiveness is key. Lack of consensus on an accepted paradigm and the limited applicability of many existing methodological tools greatly hampers attempts at rationality in these areas.

Finally, it is not enough to identify that any intervention *can be* effective. Effectiveness may be quite context-dependent, and costs will vary between different settings. Therefore assessing the value of evidence, and making decisions on implementation, requires thorough consideration of local circumstances.

Evidence-based management

The enthusiasm for evidence in healthcare has percolated beyond the examination of clinical interventions. In particular, calls are now being heard for evidence-based management (Hewison, 1997) and evidence-based policy (Ham et al, 1995). Macro-organisational change such as hospital mergers (Garside, 1999) and quality improvement strategies such as Continuous Quality Improvement (Shortell et al, 1998) or Continuing Medical Education (Davis et al, 1992) are coming under closer scrutiny than hitherto. Such expansion of the doctrine has led some to observe that healthcare is interested in "evidence-based everything" (Fowler, 1997).

Gathering the evidence

Although methodological advance continued apace since the first randomised study on streptomycin (the first effective drug treatment for tuberculosis) in 1948 (Hill, 1990), a systematic approach to gathering evidence on the whole of healthcare was much slower to develop. Recognition of this deficiency grew during the 1980s and was given voice in an influential report from the House of Lords Select Committee on Science and Technology (1988). This identified that too little good quality research was being carried out which was relevant to practitioners, managers and policy makers (see Box 3.4).

In the UK, the arrival of the first NHS R&D strategy in 1991 (Peckham,

1991), headed up by Professor (now Sir) Michael Peckham, represented a major shift in approach to research (see also Chapter Eleven). For the first time the NHS now sought to identify its research needs (through a major consultation exercise with all stakeholders), articulate these research needs in the form of focused tractable research questions, and then direct significant research funding into these areas. The stated aim was to secure and direct 1.5% of total NHS spend into 'health services research' (see Box 3.5).

A major part of the NHS R&D strategy is aimed not just at generating new research but also at capitalising on the vast base of existing studies. To this end a number of initiatives (such as the Cochrane Collaboration, and the NHS Centre for Reviews and Dissemination [Sheldon and Chalmers, 1994]) aim systematically to review existing research on important clinical or operational questions, collate these findings, and then present them in a way that is accessible and relevant to decision makers. This whole new area (called research synthesis or secondary research — research that uses other research studies as its unit of analysis) has seen an explosion of activity in the 1990s. Rapidly developing its own rigorous methodological approaches (Oxman et al, 1994; Chalmers and Altman, 1995), research synthesis aims to provide unbiased summaries of existing knowledge.

Box 3.4: Deficiencies in healthcare research identified prior to the 1991 NHS R&D strategy

- Too little research being carried out in the important clinical areas
- Much existing research was ad hoc, piecemeal, poorly done, of limited power and sometimes repetitive
- Research agenda was driven by researchers — not practitioners, managers or policy makers
- Existing research funders were more reactive than proactive
- There was a lack of connect between researchers, their research findings, and decision makers; little systematic dissemination — let alone diffusion

---

> ### Box 3.5: Health services research
>
> Health services research is defined by the Medical Research Council as "the investigation of the health needs of the community and the effectiveness and efficiency of the provision of services to meet those needs" (MRC, 1993). Health services research differs from biomedical research, which is concerned with understanding normal and abnormal functioning of biological processes. For further definitions and discussion of health services research see Crombie and Davies, 1996, chapter 1 and Black et al, 1998.

Using the evidence

The problem

Securing evidence on effectiveness is only part of the story; what is also important is whether it is used to support the delivery of services. A notorious and oft-quoted *British Medical Journal* editorial in 1991 called 'Where is the wisdom?' claimed that "only 15-20% of medical interventions are supported by solid scientific evidence" (Smith, 1991). In a nice irony, this claim itself was not evidence-based, and subsequent studies attempted to refute the figures. Various empirical projects showed that perhaps 50-80% of *major* therapeutic decisions (taken in centres with an interest in evidence-based medicine) are largely evidence-based (Ellis et al, 1995; Gill et al, 1996; Summers and Kehoe, 1996). However, the main thrust of the editorial's argument remains well-supported by the extensive international evidence of medical practice variations (McPherson, 1994), widespread quality failings (Chassin and Galvin, 1998; Schuster et al, 1998) and medical errors (Kohn et al, 1999). While many *major* decisions may be evidence-based (for example, main diagnosis and first-line management of a health problem), there remains little research guidance on the finer-grained decisions made as part of everyday care (for example, the dosage, duration and exact formulation of drugs; the appropriateness of different dressings; the effectiveness of many nursing activities). Much of the healthcare delivered to patients is established through tradition rather than evidence-based.

In addition, numerous studies have found that therapies that have been proven useless and even harmful linger in practice long after the evidence for this is clear (Davies et al, 1993). Several seminal studies have demonstrated that, *even when the evidence supporting an intervention is almost incontrovertible,* there is often a lag of up to 10 years before that intervention becomes established standard practice (Antman et al, 1992; Lau et al,

1992; Ketley and Woods, 1993). As far as R&D is concerned, research may produce the evidence, but development is frequently lacking.

Too many of the wrong things are done to patients (interventions of dubious benefit, with high costs and high risks); too few of the right things are carried out (interventions of proven therapeutic benefit); and for many common practices we just do not know whether the benefits outweigh the discomfort, side-effects and potential harm.

Source of the problem

The reasons for this failure of healthcare to connect with the research evidence have been best studied in doctors. Doctors taught in the traditional way of accumulating knowledge find that knowledge diminishing and becoming dated as time passes (Ramsey et al, 1991). At the same time, there has been a vast increase in understanding and evidence of effectiveness and thus the gap widens between knowledge and practice. Traditional continuing medical education has been shown to be largely ineffectual (Davis et al, 1992, 1995).

In recognition of the lack of connection between evidence and practice two main responses can be discerned: the guidelines movement (Forrest et al, 1996; Huttin, 1997) and the new evangelism of evidence-based medicine (Rosenberg and Donald, 1995; Sackett et al, 1997). Although fundamentally different (the first is unavoidably top-down, while the latter is – at least in conception – bottom-up) these two interact and share common tools. It is not the case that individuals are either in one camp or the other: many healthcare professionals are in both camps and more still are in neither.

Guidelines movement

The guidelines movement is based around systematic attempts to bring the evidence to those who should be using it. This approach has been enthusiastically adopted by the Royal Colleges, government-sponsored bodies and many professional special interest groups. In essence, prescriptions for practice are prepared which outline correct management of specific disease groups or clinical problems. These should (but do not always) encapsulate a full and critical assessment of the research evidence (Sudlow and Thomson, 1997). Guidelines abound for a wide range of clinical areas but evidence on their implementation shows that on their own they are often unsuccessful in changing clinical practice (Grimshaw and Russell, 1993). At least part of this failure can be ascribed to the top-down and passive approach of guidelines, and their emphasis on knowledge content rather than on the process of using that knowledge. Nonetheless, the guidelines industry grows apace while research continues as to how to make the best use of its output.

As part of the incoming Labour government's healthcare reforms of the late 1990s, a new institute has been set up to help formalise and accelerate the guidelines movement. The new National Institute for Clinical Excellence (NICE, see http://www.nice.org.uk/) is a government-sponsored organisation that will collate and disseminate evidence on effectiveness and cost-effectiveness. The guidance from NICE will provide further top-down practice prescriptions for clinicians in the NHS.

Evidence-based medicine

All the preceding discussions have been about the evidence base and its application in healthcare. However, the term 'evidence-based medicine' (EBM) currently has a very specific meaning in healthcare (Rosenberg and Donald, 1995). It applies to a particular approach to personal professional practice, initially by doctors but now taken up by other professional groups such as nurses and the professions allied to medicine (such as physiotherapists, occupational therapists, chiropodists, speech and language therapists, dieticians and nutritionists, radiographers and clinical psychologists).

The EBM approach eschews the notion that professionals are simply repositories of facts deployed at relevant moments in the care of individuals. Instead, the evidence-based professionals are equipped with problem-solving skills which allow them to determine the best course of action for any given patient. The approach taken is outlined in Box 3.6 and involves defining a specific clinical problem from clinical practice (often but not exclusively about therapy), searching for and then appraising any evidence relevant to that question, and then applying that evidence in delivering care.

Box 3.6: Evidence-based medicine approach

- Identify a problem from clinical practice. This is often about choosing the most appropriate therapy, but may also be about the choice of a diagnostic test, an assessment of disease causation and prognosis, or an assessment of harm.

- Search a range of sources of published evidence looking for studies that relate to the specific clinical question.

- Appraise that evidence using standard criteria for methodological rigour and a detailed understanding of the potential of methodological flaws to mislead.

- Identify best practice by synthesising an understanding of biological processes and pathophysiology with evidence of effectiveness and with the patient's preferences. Acknowledge explicitly the presence of uncertainty.

- Assess the impact of any decisions and adapt practice accordingly.

An evidence-based practitioner gains knowledge along the way that may be redeployed at other opportune moments. Sometimes the whole process is short-circuited by concentrating on evidence sources that are known to offer high quality information (for example, from the Cochrane Collaboration, or from true evidence-based guidelines). Evidence-based medicine may utilise many of the other strands of activity aimed at bringing evidence to practitioners. Nonetheless, it is the questioning and dynamic nature of EBM that sets it apart as a philosophical approach to practice.

Evidence-based medicine has achieved an astonishingly rapid rise to prominence. Yet the approach is not without its critics, and a recent special issue of the *Journal of Evaluation in Clinical Practice* was devoted to their arguments (Various, 1997). Three main strands of dissent can be discerned. The first objects to the narrow definition of 'evidence' prominent in EBM – the emphasis on effectiveness demonstrated in double-blind randomised control trials and, what seems to some, a comparative neglect of qualitative methods. The concern is that the importance of holistic treatment tailored to individual patients is being neglected in favour of common approaches drawn from inappropriately aggregated data (Charlton, 1995; Hart, 1997). The second criticism centres around the emphasis on effectiveness in EBM and the comparative neglect of cost-effectiveness (Maynard, 1997). Finally, throughout the censure of EBM can be found laments to the lost art of practising medicine and the diminution of cherished clinical freedom.

Despite these concerted criticisms, EBM remains an impressive international movement with a radically different approach to incorporating evidence into practice which appears to have caught the imagination of many healthcare professionals.

Changing organisational structures and processes, and the role of evidence

Practitioners do not practice in a vacuum. Rapid and radical change in the organisational structure of healthcare in the United Kingdom has also contributed to changing attitudes to evidence. The 1989 government White Paper *Working for patients* (Secretary of State for Health, 1989) introduced the purchaser–provider split in the NHS. This reform separated out responsibilities for strategic and organisational matters, and introduced a quasi-market. Health authorities (health boards in Scotland) and GP fundholders now had responsibility for purchasing services from semi-independent healthcare providers ('trusts'). This sharpened the focus on who within the organisation was responsible for clinical effectiveness. Purchasers now had to identify local health needs and purchase services likely to meet those needs; providers needed to offer services with assurances that these services would address the identified health problems. Both parts of the NHS had greater incentives and a clearer responsibility to utilise research evidence on service effectiveness.

Following on from the White Paper, *Medical audit:Working Paper 6* (DoH, 1989) made medical audit part of the professional obligation of all doctors. This was later extended to other staff groups, under the umbrella term 'clinical audit'. Clinical audit is a systematic approach to setting local clinical standards and improving care to ensure that those standards are met (Crombie et al, 1993; Hopkins, 1996). The standards that are central to effective audit are most sustainable when they are evidence-based. The advent of widespread clinical audit provides another opportunity for healthcare professionals to grapple with and ultimately apply evidence on what works.

The NHS reforms arising from the election of a Labour government in 1997 (DoH, 1997) maintained the separation of planning and provision in UK healthcare, but emphasised cooperation rather than competition. Following on from this, healthcare performance is now monitored through a *National Performance Assessment Framework* (NHS Executive, 1998) which is intended to make extensive use of evidence. Key parts of this revitalised approach are the National Institute for Clinical Excellence (NICE) which provides evidence-based guidance, and the Commission for Health Improvement (CHI) which is essentially an NHS inspectorate.

The NHS reforms of the late 1990s also sought to strengthen managerial influence over quality of care issues (including evidence-based practice) with the introduction of clinical governance. Clinical governance means that healthcare managers, for the first time, have a statutory duty for quality of care to equal the pre-existing duty of financial responsibility (Black, 1998; Scally and Donaldson, 1998; Davies and Mannion, 1999). It remains to be seen whether the array of activities introduced under the rubric of clinical governance will succeed in bringing evidence more to the fore in healthcare practice but that, at least in part, is their intent.

The shift to evidence-based practice is supported by many of the national organisational changes and top-down initiatives, but ultimately applying evidence in treatment decisions remains a matter of individual responsibility.

International dimension

Healthcare organisation differs greatly between countries – although there has been some convergence during the last decade as policy makers have grappled with common problems (Wall, 1996). For all these differences, interest in evidence in healthcare is an international phenomenon. The evidence base on effectiveness is added to on a global basis and shaped through international joint working and initiatives such as the Cochrane Collaboration. Although lip-service is paid to recognising cultural differences across different settings, the transferability of much evidence is assumed (Davies and Marshall, 2000). Initiatives aimed at encouraging the uptake of evidence may be nationally or locally organised, but the ideas that drive them come from a research literature that pays little heed to national boundaries. The research community in healthcare is truly global, and the drive to evidence-based policy and practice is pandemic. The United States in particular has been very active in stimulating a debate over the lamentable quality of much of healthcare and is searching for creative solutions to improve matters (Chassin and Galvin, 1998; The President's Advisory Commission on Consumer Protection and Quality in the Health Care Industry, 1998; Kohn et al, 1999).

Concluding remarks

The scale, organisation and rigour of research on the effectiveness of healthcare is at an unprecedented level. Yet still a hunger for better knowledge exists at all levels in health systems of whatever ideological persuasion. We can expect accelerating activity in attempts to meet these evidence needs, at least in part because as knowledge solidifies it often serves to sharpen our view on the complexity of the situation and the extent of our ignorance.

There may be much for other client-focused public sector services to learn from the great strides taken in healthcare towards an evidence-based culture over the past two decades. Closer examination of the strengths and weaknesses of research in healthcare may assist researchers and policy makers in other areas to see more clearly what can be achieved and how to progress without unnecessarily covering old ground.

Strengths of research in healthcare

- A research culture with wide acceptance of the need for evidence and good agreement on the nature of acceptable evidence.
- An obsession with methodological rigour based on randomised intervention studies with meticulous attention to bias (perhaps also a weakness since randomisation has its limitations and 'rigour' is often confused with 'quantitative' – see Chapters Twelve and Fourteen).
- Ethical objections to human experimentation largely overcome through utilitarian considerations balanced against strong personal safeguards (informed consent).
- Practical difficulties overcome through force of will, ingenuity and resources.
- A distaste for poor quality research, with some commentators going so far as to suggest that poorly designed and conducted research 'is unethical' (Altman, 1994).
- Thorough exploitation of the existing research base through systematic reviews and meta-analyses.
- Use of a mixed top-down/bottom-up strategy to identify (and find answers to) key questions on effectiveness.
- Concerted and systematic attempts to tackle dissemination and implementation of research findings (albeit with limited success and little evaluation to date [*Effective Health Care Bulletin*, 1999]).

Despite these achievements, research in healthcare has by no means solved all the problems, and many methodological, ethical and philosophical debates continue. Identifying some of the key problem areas may identify avoidable pitfalls for other parts of the public sector or point up unresolved issues where experience from other service areas may provide valuable insight for healthcare.

Weaknesses of research in healthcare

- An obsession with discovering aggregate effects leading to a narrow focus on a positivistic paradigm (randomised control trials) to the relative exclusion of other methodological approaches (especially qualitative methods) (Greenhalgh, 1996).
- Much published research is in fact methodologically dubious (of poor internal validity) and of limited applicability (poor external validity) (Altman, 1994). Few healthcare professionals are adept at sorting good studies from bad, or even interpreting broad findings (Fahey et al, 1995).
- Even published guidelines may lack necessary rigour (perhaps being based on unsystematic reviews of the literature) and few are buttressed by clear links to published research (Sudlow and Thomson, 1997).
- Because of the emphasis on methodological rigour (especially in drug development), there are some concerns that this might militate against effective innovation (Horrobin, 1990).
- Much of the best quality research takes place in specialist treatment centres under idealised conditions. Thus there may be doubt as to how the findings translate into routine practice in different settings. The extent of applicability of research findings is open to debate, especially when extrapolating from hospital-based services to primary care.
- Most patient contacts in the health service are with practitioners in primary care and yet most research on effectiveness takes place in secondary care. This imbalance is shifting, but only slowly.
- Different methodological standards are applied to different classes of intervention in different settings. For example, bringing a new drug to market requires stringent trials to be submitted to a regulations agency; developing a new surgical procedure does not, although some (weak observational) evidence is usually proffered.
- The most rigorous methodology is seen in 'intervention on individual' type studies (a treatment model). Evaluation of organisational restructuring or models of service delivery is methodologically more uncertain, less rigorously executed or frequently omitted (for example,

where is the evidence for the creation of NHS trusts, the move to GP fundholding and its subsequent abandonment, the publication of league tables of performance, or the shift to community care?). Policy changes still tend to be more ideology-driven than evidence-based despite calls for change (Ham et al, 1995).

• Many methodological problems remain to be solved: for example, dealing with practitioner effects and learning curves; coping with bias where blinding is not possible (such as with surgical treatments); identifying and measuring important patient outcomes (reliably, validly, sensitively).

• The evidence-based approach in healthcare focuses largely on effectiveness and not cost-effectiveness. Integrating values (patients' and society's) into evidence-based decision making is largely implicit and idiosyncratic.

• Changing professional practice has not been easy. Interventions aimed at diffusion have often been haphazard and poorly informed by evidence (*Effective Health Care Bulletin*, 1999); good evidence is largely lacking in this area, despite a recent funding programme financed through the NHS Health Technology Assessment (HTA) scheme (see http://www.hta.nhsweb.nhs.uk/).

Evidence on effectiveness is more to the fore in healthcare than in any other public sector service (although evidence remains just one of many influences on decision makers). While other sectors may have much to learn from this progress there may well be areas where healthcare is blind to the progress made outside its own field. Perhaps there are ready lessons to be learned from education, social services or criminal justice which may eradicate some of the weaknesses outlined above. Sharing experience across the diverse settings may prompt important insights and advances that are of mutual benefit.

References

Altman, D. (1994) 'The scandal of poor medical research', *BMJ*, vol 308, pp 283-4.

Anonymous (1990) 'Should we case-control?' [editorial], *Lancet*, vol 335, pp 1127-8.

Antman, E.M., Lau, J., Kupelnick, B. and Chalmers, T.C. (1992) 'A comparison of results of meta-analyses of randomized control trials and recommendations of clinical experts', *JAMA*, vol 268, pp 240-8.

Black, N. (1998) 'Clinical governance: fine words or action?', *BMJ*, vol 326, pp 297-8.

Black, N., Brazier, J., Fitzpatrick, R. and Reeves, B. (eds) (1998) *Health services research methods: A guide to best practice*, London: BMJ Publishing.

Chalmers, I. and Altman, D.G. (eds) (1995) *Systematic reviews*, London: BMJ Publishing Group.

Charlton, B.G. (1995) 'Mega-trials: methodological issues and clinical implications', *Journal of the Royal College of Physicians of London*, vol 29, pp 96-100.

Chassin, M.R. and Galvin, R.W. (1998) 'The urgent need to improve health care quality. Institute of Medicine National Roundtable on Health Care Quality', *JAMA*, vol 280, no 11, pp 1000-5.

Cobb, L.A., Thomas, G.I., Dillard, D.H., Merendino, K.A. and Bruce, R.A. (1959) 'An evaluation of internal-mammary-artery ligation by a double-blind technic', *New England Journal of Medicine*, vol 260, pp 1115-18.

Colditz, G.A., Miller, J.N. and Mosteller, F. (1989) 'How study design affects outcomes in comparisons of therapy. I: Medical', *Statistics in Medicine*, vol 8, no 4, pp 441-54.

Crombie, I.K. and Davies, H.T.O. (1996) *Research in health care: Design conduct and interpretation of health services research*, Chichester: John Wiley & Sons.

Crombie, I.K., Davies, H.T.O., Abraham, S.C.S. and Florey, C.d.V. (1993) *The audit handbook: Improving health care through clinical audit*, Chichester: John Wiley & Sons.

Davies, H.T.O. and Crombie, I.K. (1995) 'Assessing the quality of care: measuring well supported processes may be more enlightening than monitoring outcomes', *BMJ*, vol 311, p 766.

Davies, H.T.O. and Crombie, I.K. (1997) 'Interpreting health outcomes', *Journal of Evaluation in Clinical Practice*, vol 3, pp 187-99.

Davies, H.T.O. and Mannion, R. (1999) 'The rise of oversight and the decline of mutuality', *Public Money and Management*, vol 19, no 2, pp 55-9.

Davies, H.T.O. and Marshall, M.N. (1999) 'Public disclosure of performance data. Does the public get what the public wants?', *Lancet*, vol 353, pp 1639-40.

Davies, H.T.O. and Marshall, M.N. (2000) 'UK and US health-care systems: divided by more than a common language', *The Lancet*, vol 355, p 336.

Davies, H.T.O., Crombie, I.K. and Macrae, W.A. (1993) 'Polarised views on treating neurogenic pain', *Pain*, vol 54, pp 341-6.

Davis, D.A., Thomson, M.A., Oxman, A.D. and Haynes, R.B. (1992) 'Evidence for the effectiveness of CME. A review of 50 randomized controlled trials', *JAMA*, vol 268, no 9, pp 1111-17.

Davis, D.A., Thomson, M.A., Oxman, A.D. and Haynes, R.B. (1995) 'Changing physician performance. A systematic review of the effect of continuing medical education strategies', *JAMA*, vol 274, pp 700-5.

DoH (Department of Health) (1989) *Medical audit:Working Paper 6*, London, HMSO.

DoH (1997) *The new NHS: Modern, dependable*, London: DoH.

Dundee, J. and McMillan, C. (1992) 'Some problems encountered in the scientific evaluation of acupuncture antiemesis', *Acupuncture in Medicine*, vol 10, no 1, pp 2-8.

Effective Health Care Bulletin (1999) vol 5, no 1, London: Royal Society of Medicine Press.

Ellis, J., Mulligan, I., Rowe, J. and Sackett, D.L. (1995) 'Inpatient general medicine is evidence based', *Lancet*, vol 346, pp 407-10.

Fahey, T., Griffiths, S. and Peters, T.J. (1995) 'Evidence based purchasing: understanding results of clinical trials and systematic review', *BMJ*, vol 311, pp 1056-60.

Flor, H., Fydrich, T. and Turk, D.C. (1992) 'Efficacy of multidisciplinary pain treatment centers: a meta-analytic review', *Pain*, vol 49, pp 221-30.

Forrest, D., Hoskins, A. and Hussey, R. (1996) 'Clinical guidelines and their implementation', *Postgraduate Medical Journal*, vol 72, pp 19-22.

Fowler, P.B. (1997) 'Evidence-based everything', *Journal of Evaluation in Clinical Practice*, vol 3, no 3, pp 239-43.

Garside, P. (1999) 'Evidence based mergers?', *BMJ*, vol 318, pp 345-6.

Gill, P., Dowell, A.C., Neal, R.D., Smith, N., Heywood, P. and Wilson, A.E. (1996) 'Evidence-based general practice: a retrospective study of interventions in one training practice', *BMJ*, vol 312, pp 819-21.

Gøtzsche, P.C. and Olsen, O. (2000) 'Is screening for breast cancer with mammography justifiable?', *Lancet*, vol 355, pp 129-34.

Gowman, N. and Coote, A. (2000) 'Evidence and public health. Towards a common framework', www.kingsfund.org.uk/publichealth (accessed 24 March 2000).

Green, S. and Byar, D.P. (1984) 'Using observational data from registries to compare treatments: the fallacy of omnimetrics (with discussion)', *Statistics in Medicine*, vol 3, pp 361-73.

Greenhalgh, T. (1996) '"Is my practice evidence-based?" should be answered in qualitative, as well as quantitative terms', *BMJ*, vol 313, pp 957-8.

Grimshaw, J.M. and Russell, I.T. (1993) 'Effect of clinical guidelines on medical practice: a systematic review of rigorous evaluations', *Lancet*, vol 342, pp 1317-22.

Hadorn, D.C., Baker, D., Hodges, J.S. and Hicks, N. (1996) 'Rating the quality of evidence for clinical practice guidelines', *Journal of Clinical Epidemiology*, vol 49, pp 749-54.

Ham, C., Hunter, D.J. and Robinson, R. (1995) 'Evidence based policy making. Research must inform health policy as well as medical care', *BMJ*, vol 310, pp 71-2.

Hart, J.T. (1997) 'What evidence do we need for evidence-based medicine?', *Journal of Epidemiology and Community Health*, vol 51, pp 623-9.

Hewison, A. (1997) 'Evidence-based medicine: what about evidence-based management?', *Journal of Nursing Management*, vol 5, pp 195-8.

Hill, A B (1990) 'Suspended judgement. Memories of the British streptomycin trial in tuberculosis', *Controlled Clinical Trials*, vol 11, pp 77-9.

Hopkins, A. (1996) 'Clinical audit: time for a reappraisal?', *Journal of the Royal College of Physicians of London*, vol 30, no 5, pp 415-25.

Horrobin, D. F. (1990) 'The philosophical basis of peer review and the suppression of innovation', *JAMA*, vol 263, pp 1438-41.

House of Lords Select Committee on Science and Technology (1988) *Priorities in medical research, Volume I – Report*, London: HMSO.

Huttin, C. (1997) 'The use of clinical guidelines to improve medical practice: main issues in the United States', *International Journal of Quality in Health Care*, vol 9, pp 207-14.

Ketley, D. and Woods, K.L. (1993) 'Impact of clinical trials on clinical practice: example of thrombolysis for acute myocardial infarction', *Lancet*, vol 342, pp 891-4.

Kohn, L., Corrigan, J. and Donaldson, M. (1999) *To err is human: Building a safer health system*, Washington, DC: Institute of Medicine, National Academy of Sciences.

Kunz, R. and Oxman, A.D. (1998) 'The unpredictability paradox: review of empirical comparisons of randomised and non-randomised clinical trials', *BMJ (Clinical Research Ed)*, vol 317, no 7167, pp 1185-90.

Lau, J., Antman, E.M., Jimenez-Silva, J., Kupelnick, B., Mosteller, F. and Chalmers, T.C. (1992) 'Cumulative meta-analysis of therapeutic trials for myocardial infarction', *New England Journal of Medicine*, vol 327, pp 248-54.

Lilford, R.J., Thornton, J.G. and Braunholtz, D. (1995) 'Clinical trials and rare diseases: a way out of a conundrum', *BMJ*, vol 311, pp 1621-5.

McPherson, K. (1994) 'How should health policy be modified by the evidence of medical practice variations?', in M. Marinker, *Controversies in health care policies: Challenges to practice*, London: BMJ Publishing Group, pp 55-74.

Macrae, W.A., Davies, H.T.O. and Crombie, I.K. (1992) 'Pain: paradigms and treatments' [editorial], *Pain*, vol 49, pp 289-91.

Manning, W.G., Newhouse, J.P., Duan, N., Keeler, E.B., Leibowitz, A. and Marquis, M.S. (1987) 'Health insurance and the demand for medical care: evidence from a randomized experiment', *American Economic Review*, vol 77, no 3, pp 251-77.

Maynard, A. (1997) 'Evidence-based medicine: an incomplete method for informing treatment choices', *Lancet*, vol 349, pp 126-8.

Miller, J.N., Colditz, G.A. and Mosteller, F. (1989) 'How study design affects outcomes in comparisons of therapy. II: Surgical', *Statistics in Medicine*, vol 8, no 4, pp 455–66.

Moher, D., Pham, B., Jones, A., Cook, D.J., Jadad, A.R., Moher, M., Tugwell, P. and Klassen, T.P. (1998) 'Does quality of reports of randomised trials affect estimates of intervention efficacy reported in meta-analyses?', *Lancet*, vol 352, no 9128, pp 609–13.

MRC (Medical Research Council) (1993) *The Medical Research Council scientific strategy*, London: MRC.

NHS Executive (1998) *The new NHS modern and dependable: A National Framework for Assessing Performance*, Leeds: NHS Executive.

Ottenbacher, K. (1992) 'Impact of random assignment on study outcome: an empirical examination', *Controlled Clinical Trials*, vol 13, no 1, pp 50–61.

Oxman, A.D., Cook, D.C. and Guyatt, G.H. (1994) 'Users' guides to the medical literature: VI. How to use an overview', *JAMA*, vol 272, pp 1367–71.

Passamani, E. (1991) 'Clinical trials – are they ethical?', *New England Journal of Medicine*, vol 324, no 22, pp 1589–92.

Peckham, M. (1991) 'Research and development for the National Health Service', *Lancet*, vol 338, pp 367–71.

Pocock, S.J. (1983) *Clinical trials: A practical approach*, Chichester: John Wiley & Sons.

Pollock, A.V. (1989) 'The rise and fall of the random trial in surgery', *Theoretical Surgery*, vol 4, pp 163–70.

President's Advisory Commission on Consumer Protection and Quality in the Health Care Industry (1998) *Quality first: Better health care for all Americans*, Washington, DC: US Government Printing Office.

Ramsey, P.G., Carline, J.D., Inui, T.S., Larson, E.B., Logerfo, J.P., Norcini, J.J. and Wenrich, M.D. (1991) 'Changes over time in the knowledge base of practicing internists', *JAMA*, vol 266, pp 1103–7.

Reeves, B.C., Maclehose, R.R., Harvey, I.M., Sheldon, T.A., Russell, I.T. and Black, A.M.S. (1998) 'Comparisons of effect sizes derived from randomised and non-randomised studies', in N. Black, J. Brazier, R. Fitzpatrick and B. Reeves, *Health services research methods: A guide to best practice*, London: BMJ Publishing, pp 73-85.

Rosenberg, W. and Donald, A. (1995) 'Evidence based medicine: an approach to clinical problem-solving', *BMJ*, vol 310, pp 1122-6.

Sackett, D.L., Richardson, W.S., Rosenberg, W. and Haynes, R.B. (1997) *Evidence based medicine: How to practice and teach EBM*, London: Churchill Livingston.

Sacks, H., Chalmers, T.C. and Smith, Jr, H. (1982) 'Randomized versus historical controls for clinical trials', *American Journal of Medicine*, vol 72, pp 233-40.

Scally, G. and Donaldson, L.J. (1998) 'Clinical governance and the drive for quality improvement in the new NHS in England', *BMJ*, vol 317, pp 61-5.

Schulz, K.F., Chalmers, I., Hayes, R.J. and Altman, D.G. (1995) 'Empirical evidence of bias: dimensions of methodological quality associated with estimates of treatment effects in controlled trials', *JAMA*, vol 273, pp 408-12.

Schuster, M.A., McGlynn, E.A. and Brook, R.H. (1998) 'How good is the quality of health care in the United States?', *Milbank Quarterly*, vol 76, pp 517-63.

Schwartz, D. and Lellouch, J. (1967) 'Explanatory and pragmatic attitudes in therapeutical trials', *Journal of Chronic Diseases*, vol 20, pp 637-48.

Scottish Office, The (1991) *Framework for action*, Edinburgh, The Scottish Office.

Secretary of State for Health (1989) *Working for patients*, London: DoH.

Shaw, G.B. (1911) *The doctor's dilemma*, Constable.

Sheldon, T.A. (1994) 'Please bypass the PORT – observational studies of effectiveness run a poor second to randomised controlled trials', *BMJ*, vol 309, pp 142-3.

Sheldon, T.A. and Chalmers, I. (1994) 'The UK Cochrane Centre and the NHS Centre for Reviews and Dissemination: respective roles within the Information Systems Strategy of the NHS R&D Programme; Coordination and principles underlying collaboration', *Health Economics*, vol 3, pp 201-3.

Shortell, S.M., Bennett, C.L. and Byck, G.R. (1998) 'Assessing the impact of continuous quality improvement on clinical practice: what it will take to accelerate progress', *Milbank Quarterly*, vol 76, no 4, pp 510, 593-624.

Smith, R. (1991) 'Where is the wisdom...?' [editorial], *BMJ*, vol 303, pp 798-9.

Sudlow, M. and Thomson, R. (1997) 'Clinical guidelines: quantity without quality', *Quality in Health Care*, vol 6, pp 60-1.

Summers, A. and Kehoe, R.F. (1996) 'Is psychiatric treatment evidence-based?', *Lancet*, vol 347, pp 409-10.

Tripp, R.T. (1973) *The international thesaurus of quotations*, London: George Allen & Unwin.

Various (1997) 'The limits of evidence-based medicine', *Journal of Evaluation in Clinical Practice*, vol 3, no 2, pp 83-172.

Wager, E., Tooley, P.J.H., Emanuel, M.B. and Wood, S.F. (1995) 'Get patients' consent to enter clinical trials', *BMJ*, vol 311, pp 734-7.

Wall, A. (1996) *Health care systems in liberal democracies*, London: Routledge.

Williams, A. (1992) 'Cost-effectiveness analysis: is it ethical?', *Journal of Medical Ethics*, vol 18, pp 7-11.

FOUR

Education: realising the potential

Carol Fitz-Gibbon

Introduction

Nobel Prize-winning economist, psychologist and computer scientist
H.A. Simon, in his classic text *The sciences of the artificial*, classified education
as a 'design' discipline:

> Everyone designs who devises courses of action aimed at changing
> existing situations into preferred ones.... The natural sciences are
> concerned with how things are.... Design, on the other hand, is
> concerned with how things ought to be, with devising artifacts to attain
> goals. (Simon, 1988, p 129)

This chapter takes the concept of education as a design discipline, and
considers its goals and the ways in which various forms of evidence are
used to formulate policies and practices with respect to these goals. In
doing so it explores the ongoing debate in education about the quality of
research, its relevance and its ability to influence policy and practice.
Some of these themes about supply-side defects in research and the demand
for research are picked up again in Chapter Eleven, which explicates the
UK government strategy with respect to research in education. However,
here the aim is to explain the current common sources of evidence in
education, their methodological features and their influence. Examples
are provided of the ways in which policy makers have responded to three
major types of evidence: survey data including more recently 'performance
indicators'; evaluation data arising from policy initiatives; and the findings
from experiments. This trichotomy follows the distinction drawn by a
president of the Royal Statistical Society, Sir David Cox. He suggested
three types of data: that which arises from passive observation (such as

surveys); that which is observed when there has been an intervention but one not fully under the control of the researcher (evaluations); and data arising from active intervention (true experiments).

Education: a guide to the territory

Having identified education as one of the design disciplines, Figure 4.1 provides a map of the goals and the contexts within which these goals are sought. This set of categories both reflects past research concerns in education, and informs the modern development of indicator systems. Bloom's 1956 *Taxonomy of educational objectives* suggested three types of goals for education: the widely recognised *cognitive* goals of learning; the important but more difficult to assess *affective* goals such as child happiness, aspirations, and satisfaction with school; the ever-challenging *behavioural* goals such as influencing students to attend school (and behave well while there), to adopt healthy eating habits, and to acquire important skills.

Figure 4.1: Typology of indicators for education

			Domains to be monitored
Goals		A*	*Affective* eg attitudes, aspirations, feelings
		B*	*Behavioural* eg skills, actions
		C*	*Cognitive* eg achievements, beliefs
Contextual factors		D	*Demographic descriptors* eg sex, ethnicity, socio-economic status
		E	*Expenditure* policies eg resources, time and money
		F	*Flow* policies eg who is taught what for how long – curriculum balance, retention, allocations, selection, admissions, recruitment

*cf Bloom (1956)

All the goals in Figure 4.1 could relate to pupils, parents, teachers, schools, LEAs or countries ie there is a third dimension to the diagram, that of the *unit of analysis*.

Cognitive goals

Cognitive changes, in the form of learning outcomes, are currently seen as the major responsibility of schools. Children are sent to school to learn and current political pressure is focused on 'driving up standards' of achievement. Politicians in England have set themselves targets for raising examination results, these have been passed to local education authorities

(LEAs) who in turn pass them on to the units whose work is seen as the key to delivering these targets: the schools.

The guardian of the all-important cognitive standards – the Qualifications and Curriculum Authority (QCA) – is now an agent of the government. School examination boards (originally developed by universities) have been forced to amalgamate from seven down to three and now operate only with the permission of the QCA. Thus cognitive outcomes are to some extent under the control of politicians through the Department for Education and Employment (DfEE). Public examinations can be withdrawn and the whole system is subject to politically-motivated revisions. The public cannot readily evaluate the education system nor even be sure how good or bad has been their own education. There is the possibility that, when it comes to cognitive goals, policy makers may be more interested in public perceptions than reliable evidence as to 'what works'.

Attitudinal goals

However, studies of parents frequently find that they are equally interested in affective and behavioural outcomes, as well as cognitive attainment. For example, they are concerned that their children are happy in school, develop good attitudes and do not cause trouble. Schools might also be expected to have some impact here.

Behavioural goals

Problems such as disaffection, disruption, missing lessons, truanting, drug-taking and delinquency, all cause considerable angst and sometimes considerable effects on the individual, other pupils and, indeed, teachers. The fact that these problems seem intractable, and vary independently of methods of addressing them, suggests that many of the interventions tried have been ineffective (compare with the 'nothing works' debate in criminal justice, see Chapter Five). In a few well-controlled trials of possible school interventions the results have even been unfavourable: those helped had worse outcomes than those in the randomly equivalent groups not provided with help (McCord, 1978, 1981). Although many of these behavioural outcomes are witnessed and influenced outside as well as inside school, since 15,000 hours of children's time is spent in schools the possibility of affecting these types of behaviour in a positive way must be an important consideration in education policies.

Contextual variables

In addition to the three major goal areas, Figure 4.1 identifies a range of other factors that are often presumed to affect outcomes, such as demographic characteristics (including gender, ethnicity, socio-economic status [SES], and family circumstances), service expenditure, and flow policies.

Grouping children by demographic variables, while easy, is not necessarily helpful. For example, in England in the 1990s there have been many graphs produced showing a strong negative relationship between two variables *measured at the school level*: the percentage of pupils eligible for free school meals and the average achievement outcomes of the schools on external examinations. However, relationships between variables seen when aggregate units are used (schools) may disappear when individual data is analysed (pupils). This is an example of what has become known as 'the ecological fallacy', that is, the detection of an association at the aggregate level that does not exist at the individual level.

In this case, the relationship appears strong only because schools are to a considerable extent segregated by social class, of which one index is the eligibility for free school meals. It is only because of this segregation that there appears to be a strong relationship between social class and achievement at the level of the school. *At the pupil level* the correlation between these variables is generally about 0.3, showing that the association of social class with achievement is able to 'explain' only about 9% of the variation in cognitive outcomes. Even this 9% 'explained' variation disappears once a prior achievement measure is included (Gray et al, 1986; Goldstein and Blatchford, 1998). This situation might have been different in the early years of the century before there was compulsory education to the age of 16, but it appears to be the case today that the determining influence of social class is not what it was. By focusing attention on numerous analyses of these demographic variables, education researchers are failing to address the issue of what can be done, the 'alterable variables' as Bloom called them (1979), or 'what works' in modern parlance.

Nature and use of evidence

Having mapped out the territory the three above-mentioned sources of evidence used to inform 'what works' in education will be discussed: observational data from surveys; evidence from specific evaluation projects;

and the findings from true experimental research. However, before this the role of another type of observational data will be considered, that arising from qualitative research (see also Chapter Fourteen).

Role of qualitative studies

Although ranked low in the currently circulated hierarchy of evidence, case studies and qualitative descriptions undoubtedly carry persuasive power. Careful studies of existing situations, such as Coffield's work on cycles of deprivation (Coffield et al, 1980, 1986) and Hargreaves et al's detailed studies of secondary schools (Hargreaves et al, 1975), were influential in drawing attention to important educational factors and in formulating, albeit informally, hypotheses regarding the causes of student attainment (or lack thereof). Such studies can be seen as setting agenda, raising issues and providing 'thick' descriptions comparable to ethnological studies (Geertz, 1973; Herriott and Firestone, 1983).

There is also an important strand of education research that goes beyond description and involves practitioners in action. Known as 'action research' (see, for example, Hustler et al, 1987; Scott and Driver, 1998), it has been promoted largely with a view to enhancing practitioner knowledge rather than influencing policy on a national scale. Views of professional action and tacit knowledge (such as *The reflective practitioner* by Schon, 1983) also fall in the last category of the hierarchy of evidence (case studies and personal experience). Their influence is widespread but the impact of the ideas they contain remains a matter for empirical investigation.

Informing policy with quantitative observational data

Survey data has fuelled a considerable number of inconclusive debates. This is not surprising given the inevitability of numerous confounds in such observational data ('correlation is not causation'). For example, in the UK, the publication of examination results in the School Performance Tables shows that better outcomes on examinations are not associated with those LEAs that have larger expenditures on education. This raises the issue of the impact of expenditure but it cannot provide answers since like is not compared with like. In the US, a debate has long raged regarding the interpretation of such survey data, particularly with respect to the impact of expenditures relating to 'class size' (Hanushek, 1989; Greenwald et al, 1996; Hedges et al, 1994). Since about 80% of the cost of running a school is attributable to staff salaries, the issue of the number of pupils taught by each member of staff is critical to the overall education budget. Reductions in class size would require considerable expenditures, and this has been a hotly debated topic for several years. Survey data has produced contested conclusions and has largely left the issue unresolved.

It was a policy question about the relationship between school expenditure and cognitive test outcomes that led to a major study in this area (Coleman et al, 1966). This landmark study established a particular genre of education research, now known as school effectiveness research (SER). In 1966, Coleman and colleagues published a survey which had been commissioned by national policy makers concerned with learning the extent to which underfunding of schools in poverty areas led to the low achievement that was seen in standardised test scores from such areas. On the basis of a survey of 600,000 pupils and their secondary schools, Coleman et al concluded that schooling in fact had little influence: family background largely determined outcomes, and schools with many students from more deprived backgrounds were not actually less well funded than other schools.

This seminal study led to many years' work and many volumes of controversy among researchers. The suggestion that there was evidence that schools had little impact on achievement was a threat to the hope that education was the way out of poverty for individuals and a way towards productivity for countries. However, there were many grounds on which the study, and particularly its interpretation, could be criticised. These will be considered shortly, but it must be noted that arguments over the interpretation of data generally leave policy makers uncomfortable with the use of research evidence. In this case the findings were particularly unwelcome, both to policy makers and to researchers. What is the point in working to obtain increased education funding if it is not going to yield results?

The first major challenge to Coleman et al's conclusion that schools had little impact was that the tests used measured *general aptitude* rather than *actual achievement*. Although Cooley and Lohnes (1976) argued that aptitudes were precisely what schools should affect, this is not generally accepted – schools might be expected to have more impact on teaching-related achievement rather than aptitudes (Carver, 1975). Three characteristics of the types of tests used in the Coleman study have increasingly come under attack: the tests were not related to any specific curriculum known to teachers; they required largely multiple choice ticks rather than authentic writing exercises or working out problems; they were probably seen as unimportant by pupils and teachers, merely an interruption to provide somebody with research data. These problems have now, many years later, been recognised and summarised in the demand for tests that are: *curriculum embedded* (testing what has been taught); *authentic* (requiring more than multiple choice ticks and employing tasks that are relevant to education and the workplace); *high-stakes* (that have consequences and are taken seriously by students and teachers).

The second major criticism of this ground-breaking report was that the choice of putting home background into the regression equation first ensured that home background appeared to 'explain' the major proportion of the variance. If prior achievement had been entered first, the conclusions drawn would have been different. Inevitably, as data accumulates and research proceeds, the questions that are asked become more refined. However, to policy makers this must seem like slow progress through contested concepts. They usually do not want to know whether the order in which the variables are entered into a regression equation is going to affect the conclusion or not. They would like clearer answers to policy questions.

Since it was in the UK that data on curriculum-embedded, authentic, high-stakes tests (ie, 'exams') was already available, it is not surprising that major challenges to the conclusions of the Coleman Report came from work using examination results (Madaus et al, 1979; Kellaghan and Madaus, 1979). An influential book followed (Rutter et al, 1979), based on a three-year study of 12 secondary schools that received pupils from a variety of primary schools in the London area. *Fifteen thousand hours: The effects of schools on pupils* was a major challenge to the 'schools make no difference' conclusion of the Coleman Report. The study also broadened the outcome measures from cognitive achievement to measures of delinquency and school attendance (in other words, behavioural outcomes).

School effectiveness research (as this body of work became known) turned education research away from a concern with theories from the underpinning disciplines – psychology and sociology – and towards large surveys that sought to locate 'effective' schools and to deduce 'what works' from the correlates or characteristics of such schools. The large datasets collected in school surveys, and the nature of the organisation of the data in hierarchies (students, teachers, departments, schools, LEAs, countries), stimulated the development of statistical models for such data ('hierarchical linear models' or 'multi-level modelling') and the development of several new computer programs for analysis (see, for example, Goldstein, 1987, 1995). This highly quantitative approach has produced many estimates of parameters in regression equations, but has also attracted criticism – both from qualitative researchers (Elliott, 1996) and from researchers concerned with establishing a more robust evidence base (Fitz-Gibbon et al, 1989; Coe and Fitz-Gibbon, 1998). On the positive side, SER has directed research firmly into the realms of the schools and their work, and has therefore caught the attention of policy makers. Unfortunately, work in this area has too often led to overstated claims to have established what makes schools effective. Thus Reynolds, a leading organiser of the first School Effectiveness Conference in 1988, stated:

> ... the knowledge base now exists to insist that all schools and practitioners possess it, reliably and without fault. From the academic world, we 'know' that some practices actually work. Yet this knowledge is not spread reliably within the educational system. (Reynolds, 1992, p 127)

This statement is open to considerable doubt and such claims militate against the development of sound evidence-based approaches to policy and practice.

Perhaps the most important outcome from SER has been the development of indicator systems with the data being fed back into schools for internal use. This was driven by universities and schools acting together to develop systems for 'value-added' analyses. These systems use a measure of the progress made by each student compared to the average progress of similar students in other schools (Donoghue et al, 1996; Fitz-Gibbon, 1996).

Perhaps frustrated with school effectiveness research and the debates that surround it, policy makers seem currently to depend largely on only three sources of routine observational information in making judgements about the functioning of the education system: examination results, inspection reports and international comparisons. These are discussed below.

Evidence from examination results

Public examinations have been part of the education system in the UK for decades but changes in recent years have significantly increased the pressure on schools to show good examination results. A major pressure has arisen from the publication of results on a school-by-school basis. Officially called the School Performance Tables, they are popularly referred to as league tables. Schools feel they are judged by their position in the rank-ordered league tables, and that parents will choose to send their children to schools high in the league table in preference to those lower in the league table. Since funds now follow pupils and represent a major income source for schools, a declining enrolment is a threat to the very existence of a school.

It is now widely recognised that a school's intake has a substantial impact on the examination results that it can achieve. Consequently, there is a need for fairer comparisons which take account of diverse intakes. Various attempts have been made to do this. For several years schools have been compared because they have the same percentage of pupils receiving free school meals. However, the intake profile of two schools that have, say, 20% of their pupils on free school meals, may actually be very different – and their examination results will depend heavily on the number of pupils enrolled from the higher end of the ability spectrum. This is another manifestation of the ecological problems referred to earlier. So-called 'bench-marking', whether based on free school meals or postcodes or other variables is essentially far less accurate and far less fair than data based on the progress made by individual pupils. Hence the year 2000 will see the introduction of unique pupil numbers as a first step towards creating individual progress measures ('value-added measures') for each pupil in each subject.

Undoubtedly, examination systems do provide pressure for change, especially when used to set policy targets. The UK government has set targets for ever-increasing percentages reaching what was previously an average score in national examinations. Whether the rise in grades seen over recent years is because standards have fallen or attainment has risen is debatable. Nonetheless these changes have necessitated the addition of an A* grade as an extra rung above the A grade at GCSEs (General Certificate of Secondary Education), the age 16 exams.

Target-setting is widely regarded by politicians as an effective method of raising achievement. However, the impact of target-setting, if any, may be due largely to the fact that it introduces measurement and feedback systems into schools. There has been no rigorous research to address whether it is actually effective, so answers are currently a matter of opinion. What is clear is that schools that are set unreasonable targets will suffer and therefore the equity of the target-setting process is critical.

Evidence from inspection reports

Another source of 'evidence' used by policy makers is that provided by inspection reports, although in reality this information is far from being research-based. From the middle of the 1800s until the creation of the Office for Standards in Education (Ofsted) in 1996, inspection activities were undertaken by highly selected and carefully trained individuals called Her Majesty's Inspectors (HMIs) (Hogg, 1990). HMIs saw their role as reporting to ministers and to the DfEE on general trends in schooling. Many schools were not inspected on a national basis but were left in charge of the LEA. Under Ofsted there is competitive tendering from private or public sector inspection teams.

At a cost of about £120 million per year the new Ofsted inspections have touched every school. The judgements made by inspectors are often (somewhat loosely) referred to as evidence. However, whether this evidence is reliable or valid requires careful evaluation of: the adequacy of the sample drawn (usually four days of observations during a *pre-announced* visit); the inter-inspector agreement levels; the validity of the judgements even should they agree. An evaluation of inter-inspector agreement (actually conducted by Ofsted) suggested that there were considerable difficulties around the borderline judgement of what might constitute a 'failing' lesson (Matthews et al, 1998). A further major independent study of Ofsted (Kogan, 1999) indicated an average cost to each secondary school of about £26,000 incurred by one inspection visit, and revealed widespread dissatisfaction with the result. Add to this the expenditures incurred by Ofsted itself, along with the commonly held view that little new is learned from the inspection, and the value for money of this source of evidence is clearly in doubt (Fitz-Gibbon, 1998).

Evidence from international comparisons

There have been a number of international comparative studies of achievement, particularly in mathematics and science (Keys, 1999; Comber and Keeves, 1973; Beaton et al, 1996). These must perforce rely on tests that may or may not match the curriculum of a particular country, but the samples are drawn to be nationally representative and the tests are carefully administered and objectively scored. Reference is quite often made to the variety of results that emerge from these international comparisons along the lines of 'we need to do better' or 'we are falling behind our international competitors'. Remarkably this seems to be a conclusion reached by politicians in many countries and seems most often to represent selective reporting. Are negative comments given more coverage, or are they actually chosen by politicians with an eye on voter approval ratings?

Informing policy with evaluation data

The interplay between policy and research and the 'Great Society' initiatives in the US led to a new discipline: evaluation (McLaughlin, 1975). Evaluation was social science demanding to be heard in the policy arena. Yet when innovations were trialed and the evaluation results became available, these were sometimes frustrating experiences for policy makers.

One of the most extensive funding initiatives to be evaluated in education in the UK was the Technical and Vocational Education Initiative (TVEI) which was introduced in 1983. This was the first to demand project bids from LEAs and ushered in an era of government-led innovation in education. Policy makers were at that time very confident that they knew what was wrong with schools: the lack of both vocational relevance and an enterprise ethos promoting self-reliance and initiative. Many believed that the TVEI programmes could set this right.

Funds to support the initiative were substantial and were given to the Department for Trade and Industry (DTI). LEAs had to bid for individual TVEI projects, which eventually involved about 4% of teenage pupils. In successful LEAs, entire rooms were furnished with computers (still in short supply in schools in the 1980s); pupils were individually counselled and advised; pupils were sent on two or three weeks of work experience; and pupils and teachers spent time on team-building, and on developing initiative, enterprise skills and links with industry and business. Staff and pupils also took part in 'outward bound' types of activities in the country as part of residential programmes.

Very properly, policy makers set aside funds for both national and local evaluation (Hopkins, 1990). The finding after two years, using what would now be called a value-added analysis, was that pupils on whom the substantial funds had been expended had actually made *less* progress than similar pupils in ordinary classes (Fitz-Gibbon et al, 1989) – very disappointing results for policy makers. Researchers might issue the necessary caveats that these were self-selected pupils (ie pupils selected in various ways by different schools – sometimes volunteers, sometimes chosen by teachers), so that they were not necessarily equivalent to those who did not join the TVEI projects (leaving the interpretation in doubt).

Nevertheless the lack of strong evidence in favour of the policy was undoubtedly highly unwelcome. However, the immediate paradoxical response was to extend the pilot to many more schools but with much lower rates of funding.

The important point for current concerns regarding evidence-based policies is that the only way to have assessed securely the impact of TVEI, both in the short term and the long term, would have been to have *equivalent* groups of pupils who did and did not participate in the initiative (Fitz-Gibbon, 1990). Ethically this would surely have been possible since there were funds for only 4% of pupils – and the methods for selecting this small proportion were not specified other than that a full range of ability levels should be involved. It was left to schools to recruit students by whatever procedures they liked. Any observed differences could then have been due to self-selection or the selection procedures adopted by the schools. There was no way in which such data could be interpreted with strong conclusions. Thus, haphazard intervention was considered acceptable when more systematic study using randomly allocated control groups could have yielded interpretable results and made long-term follow-up studies worthwhile.

Another missed opportunity for rigorous evaluation, possibly involving randomisation, was the Assisted Places Scheme, in which bright students were funded to attend independent rather than state schools. The impact of this intervention on subsequent achievements and careers is clearly important to assess but, without an equivalent group not so aided, any follow-up studies must be seen as inconclusive.

Interventions such as the TVEI, the Assisted Places Scheme, or any scheme involving selection-for-special-programmes (whether for the 'gifted and talented' or for 'special needs' students) are amenable to some experimental study. Developing randomised allocation only for borderline students (where there is genuine uncertainty as to whether the individuals will benefit) could accommodate some ethical objections. Creating a 'borderline control group' each year (Fitz-Gibbon and Morris, 1987, pp 156-60) could yield data showing if there were benefits at the borderline. If not, the size of the intake could be reduced. If there were benefits this would be strong evidence and permit cost-benefit analyses to be undertaken to inform the allocation of additional funds. In the absence of attempts to find out if special programmes do harm or confer benefits, policy is driven more by argument and pressure groups than by evidence.

Deriving evidence from experiments

Dissatisfaction with the credibility of evidence from observational or weak evaluations leads us to examine methodologies capable of providing more robust findings. In education research, the potential contribution of experiments to sound policy making has long been recognised. It was noted in 1913, for example, by John Dewey, who wrote:

> Where is there a school system having a sum of money with which to investigate and perfect a scheme *experimentally*, before putting it into general operation? ... is not the failure to provide funds so that *experts* may work out projects *in advance* a penny wise and pound foolish performance? (John Dewey, 1913, cited by Grissmer, 1999a, p 231; emphases added)

Some experimental studies have been conducted in the UK (for example, on the initial teaching alphabet) but only recently has there been a commitment of public funds to more randomised controlled trials in education (influenced by the Cochrane Collaboration in medicine and healthcare, see also Chapter Eleven). However, it is the US that has led the way with what is described as the first large-scale trial of an education *policy*, a randomised controlled trial of that old bone of contention: the influence of class size on achievement (the Tennessee Experiment).

The Tennessee Experiment in class size had three intervention groups: large classes with one teacher, large classes with a teacher aide, and small classes (13-17 pupils). Although there were occasional diversions from these stipulations, on the whole, thousands of pupils were randomly assigned to one of these three conditions. Pupils were taught in this way for four years and substantial numbers of students were included. The findings included a small positive effect of being taught in a small class, with effect sizes of about 0.15 to 0.2 (this being the difference in attainment between large and small class sizes, expressed as a fraction of the standard deviation in the larger classes). This increase was maintained even after pupils continued into larger classes in later years of schooling. A definitive finding was that the addition of a teacher aide in large classes had almost no impact on achievement.

There was no self-selection and no volunteering – none of the type of threats to internal validity that fatally flaw surveys. Editing a special issue of *Educational Evaluation and Policy Analysis*, David Grissmer (1999b) of the Rand Corporation stated:

> ... the results of the Tennessee Study are increasingly being interpreted by many as 'definitive' evidence that supplants the scores of studies using non-experimental data. (p 93)

The findings have apparently convinced many policy makers. More than a dozen US states are now implementing class size reductions, citing evidence from the Tennessee Experiment. Grissmer (1999b) noted that:

> Experimental evidence is more understandable, more credible, and more easily explained to policy makers than is the more complex and often contradictory evidence from non-experimental studies. So the Tennessee Experiment has had significant influence among policy makers. (p 93)

The Tennessee Experiment was not the only initiative using experimental methods in education research. Notable contributions regarding threats to validity, ethical issues and policy needs have been made over many years by researchers such as Donald T. Campbell and Robert Boruch (for example, Campbell and Stanley, 1966; Campbell and Boruch, 1975; Boruch, 1997). A recent and extremely important methodological advance was the development of meta-analysis by Gene Glass and others (for example, Glass et al, 1981; Hedges and Olkin, 1985; Hedges, 1987). This approach provides quantitative research synthesis using appropriate statistical aggregation – emphasising magnitude of effect rather than statistical significance. There have now been several meta-analyses of results derived from education experiments in the US, drawing much strength from the large numbers of PhDs conducted there. Topics have included, for example, cross-age tutoring (Cohen et al, 1982), computer-assisted instruction (Kulik and Kulik, 1991), combinations of these (Hartley, 1977), and interventions for gifted children (Kulik and Kulik, 1992; Kulik et al, 1990).

The Tennessee class-size experiment represents a randomised controlled trial of a major *policy* variable. The implementation of such policy can be simple: pass legislation to reduce class sizes, and provide the funds – the policy will in all likelihood be implemented. Progress on this front can certainly be easily monitored.

However, if we consider not *policy* variables but interventions relating to classroom *practice*, the implementation of any evaluated innovation often becomes much more problematic. The knowledge base is often confused, findings are more contingent, and monitoring of implementation is difficult. Simon's concept of design reflects the experience and reality of delivering education. His notion of designing to achieve goals involved what he called the generate-test cycle: "… think of the design process as involving first, the generation of alternatives and, then, the testing of these alternatives against a whole array of requirements and constraints". Most teachers would recognise the "array of requirements and constraints" and many feel the need to test out practices for themselves (even when these have been evaluated elsewhere).

With about one in three schools in England now receiving annual performance indicators from comprehensive monitoring systems, there is emerging a framework in which experiments can be conducted by practitioners. Evidence from such experimentation can then inform local practice. For indicator systems to be used in this way – as part of professional development and as a contribution to evidence-based practice – is preferable to their being used purely as managerial tools (Smith, 1990; Fitz-Gibbon, 1997).

Concluding remarks

Education is a universal, compulsory treatment. In the UK, you become liable to this treatment on reaching the age of five or, increasingly, at even younger ages. Both the Conservative government of the 1980s and early 1990s, and the Labour government of the late 1990s, have been highly critical of schools, and 'driving up standards' is a recurrent theme. In particular, the Labour government's mantra of *education, education, education* seems to be a code for *examinations, examinations, examinations*. Yet even for these highly measurable cognitive outcomes, there is little secure knowledge of policies that work.

The opportunities presented by near universal treatment are for plentiful multi-site field trials, with no shortage of participants. Alas, the opportunities have not as yet been taken. Education remains largely a product of plausible belief and convenient practice, admixed, particularly in recent years, with the need to adhere to policies that are mandated politically.

The absence of robust uncontested evidence leaves space for political intrusion into professional practice. The Secretary of State for Education, David Blunkett, even went so far (in 1999) as to specify the number of minutes per evening to be spent on homework for children in schools, primary and secondary – despite weak, mixed or conflicting evidence as to the efficacy of such prescriptions. The trials that were available in the literature had not shown benefits for primary school pupils. In contrast, the evidence at secondary level, from both surveys and from controlled experiments, suggests that assigning homework to secondary age pupils *is* effective. Politicians and policy makers seemed to believe that the negative findings for primary schools "flew in the face of common sense" (David Blunkett, as reported in *Daily Mail*, 19 July 1999). To assert that the superficially plausible is a sufficient guide to policies is somewhat removed from evidence-based policy making. A more reasonable position would be to call for further research and larger samples with better controls.

Is education important enough to need standards of evidence as strict as the clinical trial? Should demands be made that policies should have been tested by randomised controlled trials before they are mandated? Usually the failures of education research are not thought to be as life-threatening or expensive as failures in medicine. But are they? Since education is universal any effects are widespread. Even small costs and inefficiencies and failures add up to substantial damage. Schweinhart and Weikart (1993, 1997) recently reported a follow-up across 23 years of a randomised trial of different forms of nursery education. Those who had been taught by 'direct instruction' (sometimes called didactic teaching) rather than by more self-initiated learning regimes, had more convictions and were more likely to agree that they felt that 'people were out to get them'. This type of work on long-term outcomes needs much replication, and it takes decades. Ultimately, however, it is the long-term consequences of education that matter most to individuals and to society. If the 15,000 hours of education that society demands from pupils could be used for even small improvements, the beneficial effects could be substantial for criminology, health, and social stability. There is an urgent need to relate outcomes in all these areas back to the time when the state is intervening in the lives of children: back to the education provided.

In concluding, here is a summary of what are perceived to be the major strengths and weaknesses of research in education on 'what works'.

Strengths of research in education

- A wide acceptance of the need to adopt methodologies appropriate to the issues under investigation, including both qualitative and quantitative methods.
- Strong links with practitioners, particularly in action research and indicator systems.

- Early recognition of the need for randomised designs, and major contributions from education researchers to methodological development, for example:
  - nomenclature for designs (Campbell and Stanley, 1966)
  - randomised controlled trials and long-term follow-up in early childhood education (Lazar et al, 1977; Schweinhart and Weikart, 1993, 1997)
  - 'reforms as experiments' advocated (Campbell, 1969)
  - distinctions between statistical and substantive significance (Carver, 1978)
  - fallacy of 'vote counting' (Hedges and Olkin, 1985)
  - the introduction of 'effect sizes' which provide a measure of substantive (as compared to statistical) significance (Glass et al, 1981)
  - statistical advances in meta-analysis (Hedges and Olkin, 1985).
- Many feasible outcome measures: for example, a framework of *external* tests and examinations that permits progress in learning to be monitored.
- Successful 'bottom-up' strategies for locating effectiveness. For example, practitioners (teachers) in the UK who not only accept fair accountability measures (performance indicators) but who adopted these for the purposes of internal school management many years before the government commissioned studies for a national 'value-added' system.
- A strong tradition of experimentation in educational psychology and in some evaluation traditions.
- Psychometric testing, when taught in teacher training, provides an introduction of the concepts of standards of sampling, reliability and validity.

Weaknesses of research in education

- Paradigm wars are still fought by some, with the epithet 'positivism' attached to any quantitative work.
- There is both serious over-interpretation (as in the claims made on the basis of correlational observational data from surveys for cause-and-effect relationships that explain 'school effectiveness') and less serious labelling errors (as in the politically driven labelling of residuals from regression equations as 'value-added').
- Both practitioners and researchers acquiesce, perhaps of necessity, in policies promoted by sources of power that often lack both the experience of the practitioner and the knowledge of the academic

researcher and that fail to provide any evidence for the effectiveness of their policies.

• A lack of understanding of the role of randomisation is still widespread among education researchers.

• There is a lack of teaching of research methods in initial teacher training (although this may change with the adoption by the Teacher Training Agency of the concept of a 'research-based profession' [see Hargreaves, 1997]).

• When choosing strategies for school improvement there is a lack of attention to research findings.

• Particularly in the UK there is a dearth of primary research studies that are evidence-based/experimental. Consequently, there are scarcely any meta-analyses based on UK studies, leaving unexamined the extent to which effective practices generalise across contexts.

References

Beaton, A.E., Martin, M.O., Mullis, I.V.S., Gonzalez, E.J., Smith, T.A. and Kelly, D.L. (1996) *Science achievement in the Middle School Years: IEA's Third International Mathematics and Science Study (TIMSS)*, Chestnut Hill, MA: Boston College.

Bloom, B.E. (1956) *Taxonomy of educational objectives*, Ann Arbor, MI: Longmans.

Bloom, B.S. (1979) *Alterable variables: The new direction in educational research*, Edinburgh: Scottish Council for Research.

Boruch, R. (1997) *Randomised experimentation for planning and evaluation: A practical guide*, London: Sage Publications.

Campbell, D.T. (1969) 'Reforms as experiments', *American Psychologist*, vol 24, pp 409-29.

Campbell, D.T. and Boruch, R.F. (1975) 'Making the case for randomized assignment to treatments by considering the alternatives: six ways in which quasi-experimental evaluation in compensatory education tend to underestimate effects', in C.A. Bennett and A.A. Lumsdaine, *Evaluation and experiment*, New York, NY: Academic Press, pp 195-296.

Campbell, D.T. and Stanley, J.C. (1966) *Experimental and quasi-experimental designs for research*, Chicago, IL: Rand McNally.

Carver, R.P. (1975) 'The Coleman Report: using inappropriately designed achievement tests', *American Educational Research Journal*, vol 12, no 1, pp 77-86.

Carver, R.P. (1978) 'The case against statistical significance testing', *Harvard Educational Review*, vol 48, no 3, pp 378-98.

Coe, R. and Fitz-Gibbon, C.T. (1998) 'School effectiveness research: criticisms and recommendations', *Oxford Review of Education*, vol 24, no 4, pp 421-38.

Coffield, F., Borrill, C. and Marshall, S. (1986) *Growing up on the margins*, Milton Keynes: Open University Press.

Coffield, F., Robinson, P. and Sarsby, J. (1980) *A cycle of deprivation? A case study of four families*, London: Heinemann Education.

Cohen, P.A., Kulik, J.A. and Kulik, C.L. (1982) 'Educational outcomes of tutoring: a meta-analysis of findings', *American Educational Research Journal*, vol 19, no 2, pp 237-48.

Coleman, J.S., Campbell, E.Q., Hobson, C.J., McPartland, J., Mood, A.M., Weinfeld, F.D. and York, R.L (1966) *Equality of educational opportunity*, Washington, DC: US Government Printing Office.

Comber, L.C. and Keeves, J. (1973) *Science education in nineteen countries: An empirical study*, International Studies in Evaluation, New York, NY: J. Wiley & Sons.

Cooley, W.W. and Lohnes, P.R. (1976) *Evaluation research in education*, New York, NY: John Wiley & Sons

Donoghue, M., Thomas, S., Goldstein, H. and Knight, T. (1996) *DfEE study of value added for 16-18 year olds in England*, London: DfEE.

Elliott, J. (1996) 'School effectiveness research and its critics: alternative visions of schooling', *Cambridge Journal of Education*, vol 26, pp 199-224.

Fitz Gibbon, C.T. (1990) 'Learning from unwelcome data: lessons from the TVEI examination results', in D. Hopkins (ed) *TVEI at the change of life*, Clevedon: Multilingual Matters.

Fitz–Gibbon, C.T. (1996) *Monitoring education: Indicators, quality and effectiveness*, London: Cassell.

Fitz–Gibbon, C.T. (1997) *The value added national project: Final report*, London: School Curriculum and Assessment Authority.

Fitz–Gibbon, C. (1998) 'Ofsted: time to go?', *Managing Schools Today*, vol 7, no 6, pp 22-5.

Fitz–Gibbon, C.T. and Morris, L.L. (1987) *How to design a program evaluation*, London and Beverly Hills, CA: Sage Publications.

Fitz–Gibbon, C.T., Hazelwood, R.D., Tymms, P.B. and McCabe, J.J.C. (1989) 'Performance indicators and the TVEI pilot', *Evaluation and Research in Education*, vol 2, no 3, pp 49-60.

Geertz, C. (1973) 'Thick description: toward an interpretive theory of culture', in C. Geertz (ed) *The interpretation of cultures*, New York, NY: Basic Books.

Glass, G.V., McGaw, B. and Smith, M.L. (1981) *Meta-analysis in social research*, Beverly Hills, CA: Sage Publications.

Goldstein, H. (1987) *Multi-level models in educational and social research*, London: Griffin.

Goldstein, H. (1995) *Multilevel statistical models* (2nd edn), London: Edward Arnold.

Goldstein, H. and Blatchford, P. (1998) 'Class size and educational achievement: a review of methodology with particular reference to study design', *British Educational Research Journal*, vol 24, no 3, pp 255-68.

Gray, J., Jesson, D. and Jones, B. (1986) 'The search for a fairer way of comparing schools' examination results', *Research Papers in Education*, vol 1, no 2, pp 91-122.

Greenwald, R., Hedges, L.V. and Laine, R.D. (1996) 'The effect of school resources on school achievement', *Review of Educational Research*, vol 66, no 3, pp 361-96.

Grissmer, D. (1999a) 'Conclusion – class size effects: assessing the evidence, its policy implications, and future research agenda', *Educational Evaluation and Policy Analysis*, vol 21, no 2, pp 231-48.

Grissmer, D. (1999b) 'Introduction', *Educational Evaluation and Policy Analysis*, vol 21, no 2, pp 93-5.

Hanushek, E.A. (1989) 'The impact of differential expenditures on school performance', *Educational Researcher*, vol 18, no 4, pp 45-65.

Hargreaves, D.H. (1997) 'In defence of research for evidence-based teaching: a rejoinder to Martyn Hammersley', *British Educational Research Journal*, vol 23, no 4, pp 405-19.

Hargreaves, D.H., Hester, S.K. and Mellor, F.J. (1975) *Deviance in classrooms*, London: Routledge and Kegan Paul.

Hartley, S.S. (1977) 'A meta-analysis of effects of individually paced instruction in mathematics', PhD, University of Colorado.

Hedges, L. (1987) 'How hard is hard science, how soft is soft science? The empirical cumulativeness of research', *American Psychologist*, vol 42, pp 443-55.

Hedges, L.V. and Olkin, I. (1985) *Statistical methods for meta-analysis*, New York, NY: Academic Press.

Hedges, L.V., Laine, R.D. and Greenwald, R. (1994) 'Does money matter? A meta analysis of studies of the effects of differential school inputs on student outcomes', *Educational Researcher*, vol 23, no 3, pp 5-14.

Herriott, R.E. and Firestone, W.A. (1983) 'Multisite qualitative policy research: optimizing description and generalizability', *Educational Researcher*, vol 12, no 2, pp 14-19.

Hogg, G.W. (1990) 'Great performance indicators of the past', in C.T. Fitz-Gibbon (ed) *Performance indicators*, Clevedon: Multilingual Matters.

Hopkins, D. (1990) *TVEI at the change of life*, Clevedon: Multiligual Matters.

Hustler, D., Cassidy, T. and Cuff, T. (1987) *Action research in classrooms and schools*, Hemel Hempstead: Allen & Unwin.

Kellaghan, T. and Madaus, G.F. (1979) 'Within school variance in achievement: schooleffect or error?', *Studies in Educational Evaluation*, vol 5, pp 101-7.

Keys, W. (1999) 'What can mathematics educators in england learn from TIMSS?', *Educational Research and Evaluation*, vol 5, no 2, pp 195-213.

Kogan, M. (1999) *The Ofsted system of school inspection: An independent evaluation*, A report of a study by The Centre for the Evaluation of Public Policy and Practice and Helix Consulting Group, CEPPP Brunel University.

Kulik, C.-L.C. and Kulik, J.A. (1991) 'Effectiveness of computer-based instruction: an updated analysis', *Computers in Human Behaviour*, vol 7, pp 75-94.

Kulik, C.-L.C., Kulik, J.A. and Bangert-Drowns, R.L. (1990) 'Effectiveness of mastery learning programs: a meta-analysis', *Review of Educational Research*, vol 60, no 2, pp 265-99.

Kulik, J.A. and Kulik, C.-L.C. (1992) 'Meta-analytic findings on grouping programs', *Gifted Child Quarterly*, vol 36, no 2, pp 73-7.

Lazar, J., Hubbell, V.R., Murray, H., Rosche, M. (1977) *The persistence of preschool effects: A long term follow up of fourteen infants and preschool experiments*, Washington, DC: US Government Printing Office.

Madaus, G.F., Kellaghan, T., Rakow, E.A. and King, D. (1979) 'The sensitivity of measures of school effectiveness', *Harvard Educational Review*, vol 49, no 2, pp 207-30.

Matthews, P., Holmes, J.R., Vickers, P. and Caporael, A.M. (1998) 'Aspects of the reliability and validity of school inspection judgements of teaching quality', *Educational Research and Evaluation*, vol 4, no 2, pp 167-88.

McCord, J. (1978) 'A thirty-year follow-up of treatment effects', *American Psychologist*, vol 33, pp 284-9.

McCord, J. (1981) 'Considerations of some effects of a counseling program', in S.E. Martin, L.B. Sechrest and R. Redner, *New directions in the rehabilitation of criminal offenders*, Washington, DC: National Academy Press, pp 393-405.

McLaughlin, M.W. (1975) *Evaluation and reform: The Elementary and Secondary Education Act of 1965, Title I*, Cambridge, MA: Ballinger Publishing Company.

Reynolds, D. (1992) 'The high reliability school', in H. Horne (ed) *The school management handbook*, London: Kogan Page, pp 126-32.

Rutter, M., Maughan, B., Mortimore, P. and Ousten, J. (1979) *Fifteen thousand hours: The effects of schools on pupils*, London: Open Books.

Schon, D.A. (1983) *The reflective practitioner: How professionals think in action*, New York, NY: Basic Books.

Schweinhart, L.J. and Weikart, D.P. (1993) *A summary of significant benefits: The High/Scope Perry Pre-School Study through age 27*, London: Hodder and Stoughton.

Schweinhart, L.J. and Weikart, D.P. (1997) 'The High/Scope Pre-School Curriculum Comparison Study through age 23: Executive summary', *OMEP Updates* (Update 87), pp 1-2.

Scott, P. and Driver, R. (1998) 'Learning about science teaching: perspectives from an action research project', in B.J. Fraser and K.G. Tobin, *International handbook of science education*, Dordrecht: Kluwer, pp 67-80.

Simon, H.A. (1988) *The sciences of the artificial* (2nd edn), Cambridge, MA: The MIT Press.

Smith, P. (1990) 'The use of performance indicators in the public sector', *Journal of the Royal Statistical Society A*, vol 153, Part 1, pp 53-72.

FIVE

Criminal justice: using evidence to reduce crime

Sandra Nutley and Huw Davies

Introduction

Long-term rising crime rates and the public's reaction to this – both fear and anger – have meant that law and order are high on the political agenda in many countries. The majority of the British public appears to support an approach which is *tough on crime* (Tarling and Dowds, 1997) and, in Tony Blair's memorable phrase, *tough on the causes of crime*. This chapter is largely concerned with measures for dealing with offenders. However, punitive measures have done little to arrest the increase in crime and it is difficult to demonstrate that punishment achieves the effect of deterring offenders from reoffending (McGuire, 1995, p 4).

Crime is not a simple problem and reducing it is not a simple task. The criminal justice system consists of a variety of interests and agencies that need to work together in addressing this task. These include police forces, courts, prisons, and the probation service. The system as a whole seeks to prevent crime where possible, convict those who are guilty of crime, and provide appropriate forms of punishment and/or rehabilitation for known offenders. In addressing these aims policy makers and practitioners have available a large body of, sometimes conflicting, research evidence relating to the causes of criminal behaviour and the effectiveness of various prescriptions for dealing with it.

A recent review of the available research on what is effective in reducing offending (Home Office, 1998) considers the evidence on:
- promoting a less criminal society
- preventing crime in the community
- effective criminal justice interventions with offenders.

This chapter focuses on the last of these areas – criminal justice interventions with convicted offenders, particularly those provided by the probation service (some consideration of evidence-based policing is included as part of Chapter Eleven). This choice is not intended to imply that treatment is more important than prevention. We would not dissent from the view of those (such as Farrington, 1989; Gottfredson and Hirschi, 1990) who argue that emphasis should be on the early prevention of crime rather than on the treatment or rehabilitation of known offenders. However, treatment will always be an important issue as "there is no such thing as a crime-free society" (Home Office, 1997, p 1).

While many people commit crime, for most their criminal career is short (Tarling, 1993). The most appropriate response for such offenders may be minimal intervention (McGuire and Priestley, 1995). On the other hand, the few offenders who have extensive criminal careers account for a disproportionate amount of crime. It is these offenders with whom the criminal justice system is most concerned. The question that policy makers need to address is whether *any* form of response to convicted offenders can have an impact on reoffending rates. If so:

• which measures for which offenders?
• how to ensure the right measures are used in practice?
• how to generate an expanding body of valid knowledge on which to base policy and practice?

In seeking to review progress in answering these questions, this chapter proceeds by first considering the changing ethos with regards to the treatment of offenders. This is followed by an overview of the methodology employed to discern what works. The means for disseminating existing evidence and getting it used is then considered before finally discussing the strengths and weaknesses of current approaches to evidence-based policy and practice in the criminal justice system.

Services for convicted offenders: changing ethos

The aims of prisons and the probation service are multiple and can include:
• punishment of offenders
• restriction of liberty and incapacitation
• protection of the public
• reduction of reoffending (recidivism)
• rehabilitation of offenders into communities
• offender reparation to the community.

These aims are far from discrete and the emphasis given to each of them has varied over time. For example, probation service practice in Britain has moved through a series of phases that include: the idealism and reformism of the early missionaries (1870s to 1930s) that focused on the 'saving of souls' (McWilliams, 1983); a medical model (1930s to 1970s) that emphasised scientific diagnosis and treatment of offenders; a welfare model (1970s to 1980s) that focused on rehabilitation into the community; and a justice model (late 1980s onwards) that emphasised reparation, restriction of liberty and the confrontation of offending behaviour.

In contrast to many other professionals (such as doctors, lawyers and architects), staff working in the criminal justice system have been much more cautious about claiming special knowledge about what works. During the 1970s a number of researchers (Martinson, 1974; Lipton et al, 1975; Brody, 1976) argued that research evidence suggested that rehabilitative interventions did not make a significant difference to the level of subsequent reoffending. The conclusion drawn was that *nothing works*. This conclusion suited a variety of political views and this, together with the role played by the media (Palmer, 1978), led to the hegemony of nothing works thinking during the 1970s and 1980s.

Partly as a result of the conclusion that nothing works (and longitudinal/ criminal career research that suggests that, in any case, many young offenders will grow out of offending by the time they are aged 25 or so), the role of probation services shifted from welfare and rehabilitation to punishment and public protection during the 1980s. The resulting justice model of probation emphasised that the primary task of probation officers was restricting liberty, confronting offending behaviour and ensuring that offenders make some form of reparation to the community.

Ironically, government policy on probation practice shifted from rehabilitation to 'punishment in the community' (Home Office, 1988) just at the time when the conclusion that nothing works was fading in the UK. During the late 1970s and 1980s, this pessimism was increasingly questioned, first in Canada and then in the USA and Britain (for example Gendreau and Ross, 1980; Blackburn, 1980; McGuire and Priestley, 1985). Martinson (1979) even withdrew and revised his own initial conclusions. However, by this stage the "nothing works view had become deeply embedded in the thinking of most levels of the criminal justice system" (McGuire and Priestley, 1995, p 7). A breakthrough in this thinking was only achieved with the application of meta-analysis techniques to existing criminal justice research (Garrett, 1985; Losel and Koferl, 1989; Izzo and Ross, 1990; Andrews et al, 1990; Lipsey, 1992). Overall, these meta-analyses concluded that there are some things that work in reducing the likelihood of reoffending, and a tentative list of effectiveness criteria began to emerge. The key message was that structured supervision programmes that are focused could achieve significant reduction in offending behaviour (see Box 5.1).

Box 5.1: Key principles for achieving effectiveness
• Target high risk offenders
• Focus on offence behaviour or criminogenic behaviour and attitudes
• A community-based approach
• An emphasis on cognitive and behavioural methods
• A structured approach with clear objectives
• A directive approach and style
• Ensuring that completed work fulfils declared aims and methods

Source: Adapted from McGuire and Priestley (1995)

By the 1990s, the more upbeat *what works* label had largely replaced the negative *nothing works* slogan. This reinvigorated the search for evidence and renewed interest in using evidence in setting policy and defining effective practice. This culminated in the review of existing evidence as part of the Comprehensive Spending Review (Home Office, 1998) and the subsequent Crime Reduction Programme (Home Office, 1999a).

Britain is not alone in demonstrating renewed confidence that it is possible to determine what works. In 1996, a Federal law required the US Attorney General to provide Congress with an independent review of the effectiveness of state and local crime prevention programmes. The result was the University of Maryland review of what works (Sherman et al, 1997).

The next section considers the diverse range of methodologies used in deciding what works, before discussing the themes associated with getting evidence into criminal justice practice.

Nature of evidence

Range of approaches to discerning what works

Criminal justice research utilises a wide variety of research methods, including:
• qualitative field research such as ethnography and participant observation;
• survey research such as the British Crime Survey;
• longitudinal/criminal career research based on cohort studies;
• experimental research that underlies many evaluation studies (see below);
• meta-analysis used to collate findings from individual small-scale studies.

The most appropriate research method is (or should be) determined by the research question that is posed. When that question asks about the relative effectiveness of various ways of dealing with convicted offenders two main methods might be used: a retrospective observational study of the efficacy of existing interventions, or a prospective evaluation of a proposed intervention using an experimental design. If carefully constructed, the latter method is likely to produce the most objective, valid and relevant results (Tarling, 1993; Taylor, 1994). Criminal justice research of this nature falls into three categories: weak quasi-experiments, strong quasi-experiments, and true experiments (Taylor, 1994).

In weak quasi-experiments there is an experimental group and there may or may not be a control group. If a control group is present little is done to make it comparable (see, for example, Pearson and Harper, 1990). Strong quasi-experiments always include both an experimental group and a control group or control period. Steps are taken to make the control group comparable with the experimental group (see, for example, Ross, 1982; Rosenbaum, 1988; Jones, 1990), but there is no way of knowing if this has been achieved. True experiments always include experimental and control groups and cases are randomly assigned to each of these (see, for example, Petersilia, 1989). This may not guarantee equivalence of the two groups, but it places statistical limits on their likely similarity. As a result, this approach should be less susceptible to bias and erroneous conclusions (see Chapter Twelve for an extended discussion of these issues).

Role of theories

Pragmatism and empiricism are increasingly questioned in evaluations of criminal justice interventions. The question is not simply "what works for offenders as a whole?", but "which methods work for which type of offenders and under what conditions or in what types of settings?" (Palmer, 1975, p 150). There is much interest in trying to understand the assumed causal linkages within the black box of the treatment package. Only in this way, it is argued, will we "understand what the program actually does to change behaviours and why not every situation is conducive to that particular process" (Pawson and Tilley, 1997, p 11). The HM Inspectorate of Probation's (HMIP) report on the What Works Project (HMIP, 1998) reinforces this concern with the three Ws of *what* works for *whom* in *what* circumstances? HMIP's scrutiny of probation programmes as part of this project noted an apparent lack of clarity about the theoretical basis of the programme designs in use. Such designs, it is argued, should have a clear (theoretical) model of the way in which offender behaviour changes.

Need for greater rigour

There is no agreed gold standard for the evaluation of criminal justice interventions, although new guidance documents have been produced as part of the Crime Reduction Programme (Colledge et al, 1999). Evaluation studies that adopt a weak methodology convince few and may produce misleading results. Those evaluating the effectiveness of interventions with offenders generally accept the need for control groups or yardsticks against which to measure effectiveness, but true experimental designs are often considered to be unachievable:

> Aim to have a control or comparison groups so that robust analyses can be made of the additional effect of the programme compared with what would happen to the offenders anyway. The strongest design for an evaluation is random allocation of subjects and this should be considered and chosen if possible although it is often not achievable in criminal justice settings. If a control or comparison group is not possible, then a second best will be to compare with national trends and on the basis of these to model actual and predicted outcomes. (Colledge et al, 1999, p 12)

An increasingly popular yardstick is to compare reconviction rates following an intervention with estimates of the expected rate of reconviction without that intervention (Knott, 1995; Wilkinson, 1994). Various reconviction predictors have been developed for this and other purposes (Taylor, 1994; Wilkinson, 1994) and in 1996 the Home Office supplied an Offender Group Reconviction Scale (OGRS) to all probation service areas as an assessment and research tool.

The main problem with quasi-experimental designs is that they do not provide the rigour to enable substantive causal inferences to be made (see Chapters Twelve and Thirteen). Garrett (1985) demonstrated the need for greater rigour in evaluation in her meta-analysis of the effects of residential treatments on adjudicated delinquents. She found that effect size was lower in those studies that had adopted more rigorous control procedures. It seems that in this example weak designs inflated positive treatment effects, although this finding has not been replicated in all settings (see Chapter Twelve).

Tarling (1993) argues that despite the disagreement on some aspects of research design, there is consensus on the need for greater experimentation. However, this seems an optimistic conclusion; the case for true experimental designs (randomised controlled trials) in criminal justice evaluation research is certainly not generally accepted (for example, Farrington, 1983 versus Dennis, 1990). It is common for true experimentation to be perceived as impractical and unethical. The impracticalities include getting researchers involved before the intervention starts and getting the various agencies involved to agree to random allocation to experimental and control groups. Experimentation is seen as unethical for two reasons. Firstly, if the intervention is believed to be effective, there is the question of whether it should be withheld from the control group. Secondly, if the treatment is believed to be doubtful, there is the issue of whether researchers have the right to test it out on an experimental group, with possible attendant risks to the public. This led McIvor (1995) to conclude:

> For both practical and ethical reasons, the experimental paradigm cannot, however, be readily applied to the probation setting and other methods of evaluation are therefore usually required. (p 212)

Others are a little more optimistic. Dennis and Boruch (1989) suggest that a series of hurdle conditions should be satisfied before pursuing a true experiment in criminal justice research (Box 5.2).

> **Box 5.2: Conditions which Dennis and Boruch suggest should be present before pursuing a true experiment**
>
> • There must be broad agreement that current practices need improvement
> • Neither past research nor sound wisdom provides surety that the proposed programme will achieve the intended goal
> • Simpler, alternative research designs are inadequate for one reason or another
> • The results will prove relevant to social policy makers
> • Both researchers and treatment providers who will distribute the programme, must be satisfied that implementation meets ethical standards

Source: Dennis and Boruch (1989)

Given the importance attached to the role of theories (see above) true experimental designs are sometimes also perceived to be inappropriate. Pawson and Tilley (1997, p 8) argue that "the experimental paradigm constitutes a heroic failure". The methodology, they argue, promises much but tends to result in findings that are typically "non-cumulative, low impact, prone-to-equivocation". When a package of treatments is given to a broad range of subjects it is not surprising that for some it works and for others it fails. An evaluation needs to demonstrate which element of the package works for which subjects (and, possibly, hypothesise why it works). Pawson and Tilley argue that this is not readily achieved by ever more sophisticated statistical analyses within an experimental paradigm. They call for a realistic approach to evaluation which is theory and not method driven (for further discussion of the realist approach see Chapter Twelve). Such evaluations need to understand the subject's reasoning because "it is not programmes which work, as such, but people co-operating and choosing to make them work" (Pawson and Tilley, 1997, p 36).

Nonetheless, randomised controlled experimental designs have been used to assess criminal justice interventions. In Britain, back in the 1970s, the IMPACT study used an experimental design with randomised allocation to experimental groups and control groups (Smith, 1977). More recently, a randomised controlled experiment was implemented to evaluate 11 intensive supervision programmes in the US (Petersilia, 1989). In the latter, difficulties in implementing a total random assignment of offenders to experimental and control groups were encountered. Field personnel (particularly judges) put pressure on researchers to change random assignments. As a result deviations from random assignment (overrides) were allowed. A systematic search for criminal justice randomised experiments conducted during 1950-93 (and available in English), uncovered more than 300 experiments (Petrosino, 1998). An analysis of 150 of these found that together they have been used at every stage of the criminal justice process, from arrest to release, although nearly half relate to interventions with offenders by the probation or prison services (Petrosino, 1998).

Relevant outcomes

Good measures of the effectiveness of interventions with offenders should be valid, relevant, objective, multidimensional and lead to unbiased assessment. In practice, there are many outstanding problems relating to the identification and measurement of appropriate effectiveness criteria. These problems are particularly prominent when seeking to compare the results of similar interventions across different jurisdictions. For example, the definition of what is considered to be a successful outcome varies between studies and can include completion of a supervision order, the number of breaches during a supervision order, and the number of reoffences following completion of a supervision order. The measurement of the subsequent level of reoffending may use self-report information as well as official reconviction data. Both of these are problematic. For example:
- reconviction rates may not be an accurate measure of offending given that only 3% of offences result in conviction (Barclay, 1991);
- using a simple dichotomous measure of conviction (yes/no) treats as equally serious offences as different as murder and shoplifting (Wilkinson, 1994).

Maltz (1984) has listed nine different definitions of recidivism which have been used in the USA and all of these have more than one qualifying condition. The definition of the appropriate follow-up period is also important in assessing the effectiveness of an intervention, and in many studies this is six months or less. Despite the widely recognised limitations of reconviction rates (Lloyd et al, 1995), they are still seen as the key measure of intervention effectiveness. The main source of data on reconvictions in the UK is the Home Office Offender Index, which is updated quarterly, six months in arrears.

The problems associated with defining and measuring the final outcome of reduced recidivism have led several researchers to suggest that process compliance and intermediate outcomes (such as attitude change) should also be identified and measured (Roberts, 1995). This advice has been adopted by HM Inspectorate of Probation. In the report of the What Works Project (HMIP, 1998, p 7) the following criteria are suggested for assessing effectiveness in the supervision of offenders:

- reduced reoffending – usually measured by reconviction;
- programme completion;
- achieving rehabilitative purpose, including changes in attitude, behaviour and social circumstances;
- fulfilling public accountability – effective risk management, value-for-money, anti-discriminatory practice.

Combining studies

Meta-analysis appears to have been generally accepted as an appropriate technique for synthesising the results of criminal justice evaluations, although there are sceptics (for example, Mair, 1994). Meta-analysis creates a 'common metric' so that studies using different outcomes can be compared. A key issue is that meta-analysis is only as good as the studies on which it draws. Mair provides a telling critique of the studies included in Lipsey's meta-analysis (Box 5.3).

Box 5.3: Detailed look at Lipsey's meta-analysis

- Half of the studies in the review only have follow-up periods for the primary delinquency measure (which is not always recidivism) of less than six months
- Half of the studies were coded as having low treatment integrity, and 75% were either low or moderate on this rating
- 20% of the studies covered institutionalised juveniles, and 50% were non-juvenile justice interventions
- Almost two thirds of the programmes were less than two years old, which raises questions about the impact of initial enthusiasm
- Only one quarter of the programmes were administered by criminal justice personnel, and 20% by lay persons

Source: Mair (1994, p 7)

Cost-effectiveness

Much of the existing research on what works with convicted offenders does not consider the issue of costs. The review of research evidence for the Comprehensive Spending Review (Home Office, 1998) was specifically concerned with issues such as:

- what evidence is available on the likely costs of implementation?
- what is the likely timescale for the costs and benefits?

In relation to interventions with offenders, the review concluded that the limited information available on costs and outcomes meant that it was not possible to compare the cost-effectiveness of various rehabilitation programmes delivered in custody and in the community. Given that much of the basic information on the costs of intervention is difficult to obtain, it is not surprising that little is known about the wider costs and benefits of criminal justice interventions. The Crime Reduction Programme (Home Office, 1999a) aims to address the issue of cost-effectiveness by ensuring that evidence is gathered on the costs and benefits of all the interventions funded by the programme. A guidance document has been produced to enable this to happen (Dhiri and Brand, 1999).

There is a need for an ongoing debate about what constitutes rigour in the evaluation of criminal justice interventions, why rigour is important and how it can be achieved. This section, on the nature of evidence, began by stating that there is no agreed gold standard for the evaluation of criminal justice interventions. Various guidance documents are sharpening the debate about the appropriateness of different methodologies. In probation, HM Inspectorate of Probation guidance (HMIP, 1998) provides a baseline from which to work. This suggests that good practice within evaluation studies should include:

- clarity about time periods and study groups;
- appropriate reconviction measures, using reconviction predictors, comparison or control groups and considering offence type and seriousness;
- appropriate use of attitudinal measures;
- following up and analysing outcomes for all members of a study group, but analysing results for completers separately.

Using the evidence

Sharing the evidence

There have been systematic reviews of research evidence (for example, McGuire, 1995) and a number of influential meta-analyses (referred to above). The Home Office in Britain has sought, to some extent, to disseminate the results of research findings (see Chapter Eleven). They examined the options for establishing a national information/resource service on crime prevention and reduction (Home Office, 1997). This is now likely to form part of the ESRC Centre for Evidence-based Policy and associated nodes (see Chapter Two). Such a service is intended as a means of gathering and exchanging reliable information about what works in what circumstances. It is important for such information to be disseminated beyond those responsible for implementing interventions in the prison and probation services. In particular, those who make decisions about the sentences given to convicted offenders, the courts, seem to be the least informed about the results of effectiveness research.

In relation to the probation service, during 1995 there were several conferences on the theme of what works organised by the Home Office (some with the Association of Chief Officers of Probation and the Central Probation Council). A Probation Circular (No: 77/1995) was also issued in that year drawing attention to critical success factors for probation supervision programmes. In January 1996 HM Chief Inspector of Probation established the What Works Project. The project aims to provide probation areas with guidance on best practice regarding the supervision of offenders. The report of this project (HMIP, 1998) argues that there are key messages about effective supervision programmes to come through from the already large, but still limited and sometimes conflicting, evidence base (for example, Box 5.1 above).

It is acknowledged that the existing evidence on what works with offenders is partial (focusing in particular on interventions with juvenile offenders) and is dominated by US and Canadian studies (Losel, 1995; Mair, 1994). There are many factors involved in the design and implementation of offender interventions and many of these have not been studied in depth. There is a need for a strategy that identifies priority areas for research, articulates these in the form of focused research questions, and directs research funding to these areas. To some extent this is being addressed by the Crime Reduction Programme and the role of the What Works Project within this programme.

Before an evidence-based approach can be adopted by criminal justice agencies a number of key problems with the availability of evidence need to be overcome. These include the: patchy coverage of research on interventions with adult offenders; extent to which the impact of programmes may vary according to different legislative and agency settings; limited synthesis and dissemination of research results. In addition to improving the quality, coverage and availability of evidence, there is also a need to address the extent to which it is used.

There are a number of barriers to implementing evidence-based policy and practice in the criminal justice system. These fall into four categories: politics/ideology; the lack of a research-orientated practitioner culture; the individualism of practitioners; scepticism among policy makers and practitioners. These problem areas are discussed below, followed by a consideration of the strategies employed so far to tackle them.

Problems

Policy making at Home Office level in the UK has not always been guided by evidence on what works. Michael Howard's statement to the Conservative Party conference in 1993 that 'prison works' was based on flimsy evidence at best. Andrews (1995) argues that criminal justice practice should be based on rational empiricism. In contrast, much criminal justice policy has had more of a political and ideological flavour. The Conservative Party has long portrayed itself as the party of law and order. However, from the late 1980s onwards Labour has also sought to portray itself as equally tough on crime. The hardening of government policies on law and order during the 1990s can be seen partly as the result of both parties trying to out tough each other in the law and order debate. Pawson and Tilley (1997, p 12) argue that research functions not as a valid, tested body of propositions, but as ammunition for political debate and intraorganisational arguments.

The lack of a research culture in criminal justice agencies is another problem. Criminal justice agencies in general, and probation services in particular, have not devoted much attention to studying the effectiveness of different interventions. The House of Commons Select Committee on Home Affairs (1998) concluded that:

> The absence of rigorous assessment of the effectiveness of community
> sentences is astonishing ... when viewed in the context of the overall
> expenditure on the criminal justice system, and the further costs of

crime both to the victims and to society, the figures spent nationally on research are risibly minuscule. (p 2)

Where research has been conducted it has had limited impact on probation policies and practices (McIvor, 1995). The probation service has lacked a clear vision of how effectiveness should be judged and this has fostered a disregard for the need to obtain evidence of supervision effectiveness (Burnett, 1996). Another possible reason for the lack of a research culture is that the training of probation officers has not equipped them to act as evidenced-based practitioners (Roberts, 1995). There are exceptions to this picture. For example, in the UK, Greater Manchester and Mid-Glamorgan probation areas have had active research programmes. However, a survey of evaluation practice (HMIP, 1998) found that although many probation areas claimed to evaluate intervention effectiveness, when this evaluation activity was studied in more detail, only 11 studies were identified as having some value as examples of good evaluation practice.

The roots of the probation service in the right of individual courts to appoint their own probation officers has meant a long history of largely autonomous probation officers working to a particular petty sessional division or court. This has led to an individualised approach to service delivery:

> Today, work done by individual practitioners with individual offenders has often developed into a presumed permission to practise some personally selected forms of social work. (Roberts, 1995, p 229)

This presents problems in implementing evidence-based practice:
- tentative research results suggest that while one-to-one supervision may continue to have an important role, structured programmes of intervention, centred on group work, are the way forward;
- the integrity of the interventions, which is important in achieving the desired outcomes, can be threatened by an individualist approach – this is not just a British problem; reflecting on their experiences in Canada, Gendreau and Ross (1987) comment: "We are absolutely amateurish at implementing and maintaining our successful experimentally demonstrative programmes within the delivery systems provided routinely" (p 395).

The problems encountered in implementing interventions means that when there are negative outcome results it can be difficult to distinguish implementation weaknesses from programme theory failure. Implementation problems not only arise from the individual autonomy of practitioners but also from the individualism of different parts of the criminal justice system. The implementation of effective policies and practices requires improvements in the ability of the diverse departments, agencies and organisations which constitute the criminal justice system to work together (to become better at horizontal and vertical 'joining up').

Finally, there is an ongoing scepticism about evidence that purports to show what works. This is not surprising given over a decade of being told that nothing works. Much of the evaluation of effectiveness has been undertaken by psychologists and their conclusions promote a psychological approach to offender treatment (mainly in the form of cognitive and behavioural therapy). This has led to some scepticism and resistance from those who have previously adopted a sociological framework for their work with offenders.

There are, then, problems in ensuring that criminal justice policy and practice is informed by the results of evaluation research. These problems need not be insurmountable. The next section considers the strategies currently being employed – starting first with the general context of the Crime Reduction Programme, before focusing on the What Works Project in the probation service.

Strategies

In 1999 the Labour government launched the Crime Reduction Programme, which is described as "the biggest single investment in an evidence-based approach to crime reduction which has ever taken place in any country" (Home Office 1999a, p 3). Some £250m has been committed to this initiative over the three years 1999-2002. The programme covers five broad themes:
- working with families, children and schools to prevent young people becoming the offenders of the future;
- tackling crime in communities, particularly high volume crime such as domestic burglary;
- developing products and systems that are more resistant to crime;
- providing more effective sentencing practices;
- working with offenders to ensure that they do not reoffend.

The programme is intended to contribute to crime reduction by ensuring that resources are allocated where they will achieve the greatest impact. This is to be determined by investing in crime reduction initiatives that show early promise (based on existing evidence) and subsequently evaluating whether the promise is delivered in practice. Those initiatives that are successful are intended to form the basis of future mainstream programmes; those that are not should be dropped. However, initiatives to tackle crime problems do not fall neatly within the domain of the Home Office and the Crime Reduction Programme forms part of the government's 'joined-up approach' to tackling public policy problems.

A number of pre-existing initiatives, aimed at promoting evidence-based policy and practice (such as the work of the Police Research Group, discussed in Chapter Eleven), have been incorporated into the Crime Reduction Programme. One of these initiatives is the probation services' What Works Project. There are two prongs to the 'what works' agenda for the probation service:

- the hypothesised principles of effective practice (see Box 5.1) are recommended for use in the design of probation programmes (and the national implementation plan sets probation service areas the goal of ensuring that every offender is supervised in accordance with the 'what works' principles by the year 2003);
- probation service areas are being encouraged to conduct ongoing evaluations of the effectiveness of their interventions with offenders.

There are clear dangers with both strands of this strategy. First, if the tentative nature of much of the existing evidence (Mair, 1994) is overemphasised this could result in a familiar boom and bust cycle of activity:

> Administrators and policy-makers ... may rush first into wholesale buy-in, as the promises of impact on recidivism are made, but then into wholesale sell-out, as the generalised reductions in recidivism seem not to be realised. (Porporino and Robinson, 1995, p 186)

Second, if inhouse evaluation is overemphasised this could lead to the continuing proliferation of poorly conceived, inconclusive, small-scale studies which add little to the existing body of evidence.

There is an evangelical feel to the present what works movement (Pitts, 1992, calls it a crusade), and there is a danger that the notion of evidence-based practice will be interpreted as implementing a set of treatment principles rather than an ongoing quest to be evidence-based practitioners.

Given that the individualism of practitioners has been identified as one of the barriers to implementing an effective practice agenda, there have been calls for probation areas to adopt health-style protocols as a means of ensuring quality and effective practice (Thomas, 1996). At present there are no such protocols at a national level (Home Office National Standards in Britain say little about the interaction between the offender and probation officers). However, local protocols are being developed to reflect the what works principles. These aim to ensure effective practice and intervention integrity.

The What Works initiative (HMIP, 1998; Home Office 1999b) signals a move towards increased standardisation across probation areas which may help to overcome the fragmentation of the service. There has been a tendency for each area to develop its own internal programmes for working with offenders. At the core of the What Works initiative is the development of a 'national curriculum' of evidence-based offender programmes. Some 35 promising offender programmes have been selected as 'pathfinders'. These will be evaluated on a national basis. Successful pathfinder programmes will be put forward for accreditation by a new Joint Prison and Probation Accreditation Panel. Programmes that are shown to deliver positive results will receive formal accreditation. They will then form part of a developing menu of effective programmes for the probation and prison services. The plan is that once sufficient programmes are available the prison and probation services will be required to run only accredited programmes (for further details see Furniss and Nutley, 2000).

The two prong strategy of the What Works agenda for the probation service needs to be carefully balanced and extended if it is to succeed in developing evidence-based policy and practices. The danger is that it will sell programmatic solutions when: "what seems to work universally is strategic thinking and a systematic, data-driven approach to defining the problem, determining a possible solution on the basis of some principles of human behaviour, proper implementation, and monitoring or evaluation thereafter' (from Laycock, Chapter Eleven in this book). Many barriers to the appropriate use of evidence remain.

Concluding remarks

The renewed interest in evidence on what works in the delivery of criminal justice services has resulted in a real opportunity for policy and practice to be evidence-based. However, the lack of methodological rigour in many of the evaluation studies and the adoption of tentative results as firm effective practice principles, may cause the bubble of enthusiasm to burst before evidence-based practice is placed on a firm footing. An examination of the strengths and weaknesses of what has happened in the criminal justice arena may assist researchers and policy makers to avoid this fate. Those in other public services may also learn from the experience of gathering and using criminal justice evidence.

Strengths of evaluation research in criminal justice

- There is an established research culture in criminology which uses a plurality of approaches (including qualitative and quantitative techniques) to investigate offending behaviour and the nature of criminal careers.
- There is an interest in theory and a desire to understand the causal linkages within the 'black box' of the treatment package.
- There is a renewed belief that criminal justice interventions can make a difference and that it is possible to discover what works best, with whom and in what contexts.
- There is a commitment on the part of some staff to evaluate the effectiveness of their practice.
- There has been some exploration of existing research results through systematic reviews and meta-analyses.
- The Home Office and practitioner bodies (such as the Association of Chief Officers of Probation) have encouraged discussion of what works and have provided advice on how to introduce evidence-based policy and practice.
- The Home Office has committed a substantial level of resources to developing an evidence-based approach to crime reduction. This should help fill the gaps in existing knowledge identified as one of the existing weaknesses below.

Weaknesses of evaluation research in criminal justice

- There are diverse views as to the best methodological approach for discovering what works in what circumstances.
- There is a lack of methodological rigour in many existing evaluations of interventions leading to a poor basis for inferring causality.

- There is a lack of acceptance of the true experiment as an appropriate, practical and ethical means of evaluating many criminal justice interventions.
- Existing research is not comprehensive in its coverage (focusing mainly on juvenile offenders) and may be of limited generalisability (given that most research has been conducted in the USA and Canada).
- The managers of criminal justice services have not always provided good role models. They continue to make decisions about structure and organisational processes that are not clearly evidence-based.
- There continue to be many problems in identifying and measuring (validly and reliably) appropriate outcomes for judging the effectiveness of criminal justice interventions.
- In the past there has been little attempt to integrate the issue of cost with that of effective practice – this is to be addressed by the Crime Reduction Programme.

These are exciting times for those interested in the implementation of evidence-based criminal justice policy and practice. The climate for considering the issues discussed in this chapter is favourable. Time will tell whether initiatives such as the Crime Reduction Programme will achieve the move towards policies and practices that are firmly rooted in evidence of what works. However, given the prominence of law and order on the political agenda, it may be hard to move away from the ideological battle that has resulted in extraordinary swings in penal policy during the past two decades.

References

Andrews, D. (1995) 'The psychology of criminal conduct and effective treatment', in J. McGuire (ed) *What works: Reducing reoffending*, Chichester: Wiley, pp 35-62.

Andrews, D., Zinger, I., Hoge, R., Bonta, J., Gendreau, P. and Cullen, F. (1990) 'Does correctional treatment work? A clinically relevant and psychologically informed meta-analysis', *Criminology*, vol 28, no 3, pp 369-404.

Barclay, G.C. (ed) (1991) *A digest of information on the criminal justice system*, London: Home Office Research and Statistics Department.

Blackburn, R. (1980) 'Still not working? A look at some recent outcomes in offender rehabilitation', Scottish Branch of British Psychological Society Conference on Deviance, University of Stirling, February.

Brody, S. (1976) *The effectiveness of sentencing*, Home Office Research Study No 35, London: HMSO.

Burnett, R. (1996) *Fitting supervision to offenders: Assessment and allocation decisions in the Probation Service*, Home Office Research Study 153, London: Home Office.

Colledge, M., Collier, P. and Brand, S. (1999) *Crime Reduction Programme and constructive regimes in prisons – Programmes for offenders: Guidance for evaluators*, Research, Development and Statistics Directorate, London: Home Office.

Dennis, M. (1990) 'Assessing the validity of randomized field experiments: an example from drug abuse treatment research', *Evaluation Review*, vol 14, no 4, pp 347-73, August.

Dennis, M.L. and Boruch, R.F. (1989) 'Randomized experiments for planning and testing projects in developing countries: threshold conditions', *Evaluation Review*, vol 13, pp 292-309.

Dhiri, S. and Brand, S. (1999) *Crime reduction programme – Analysis of cost and benefits: Guidance for evaluators*, Research, Development and Statistics Directorate, London: Home Office.

Farrington, D.P. (1989) *The origins of crime: The Cambridge Study in Delinquent Development*, Research Bulletin No 27, London: Home Office Research and Planning Unit, pp 29-32.

Farrington, D.P. (1983) 'Randomized experiments on crime and justice', in M. Tonry and N. Morris (eds) *Crime and justice: An annual review of research*, vol 4, Chicago, IL: University of Chicago Press, pp 257-308.

Furniss, J. and Nutley, S. (2000: forthcoming) 'Implementing what works with offenders – the Effective Practice Initiative', *Public Money and Management*, vol 20, no 4.

Garrett, C. (1985) 'Effects of residential treatment on adjudicated delinquents', *Journal of Research in Crime and Delinquency*, vol 22, pp 287-308.

Gendreau, P. and Ross, R.R. (1980) 'Effective correctional treatment: bibliotherapy for cynics', in R.R. Ross and P. Gendreau (eds) *Effective correctional treatment*, Toronto, Canada: Butterworths.

Gendreau, P. and Ross, R.R. (1987) 'Revivication of rehabilitation: evidence from the 1980s', *Justice Quarterly*, vol 4, pp 349-407.

Gottfredson, M. and Hirschi, T. (1990) *A general theory of crime*, Standford, CA: Stanford University Press.

HMIP (HM Inspectorate of Probation) (1998) *Strategies for effective offender supervision*, Report of the HMIP 'What Works' Project, London: Home Office.

Home Office (1988) *Punishment, custody and the community*, Green Paper, London: Home Office.

Home Office (1997) *Getting to grips with crime: A new framework for local action*, A consultation document, London: Home Office.

Home Office (1998) *Reducing offending: An assessment of research evidence on ways of dealing with offending behaviour*, Home Office Research Study 187, London: Home Office Research and Statistics Directorate.

Home Office (1999a) *Reducing crime and tackling its causes: A briefing note on the Crime Reduction Programme*, London: Home Office.

Home Office (1999b) *What works – Reducing offending: Evidence-based practice*, London: Home Office.

Izzo, R.L. and Ross, R.R. (1990) 'Meta-analysis of rehabilitation programmes for juvenile delinquents', *Criminal Justice and Behavior*, vol 17, pp 134-42.

Jones, P.R. (1990) 'Community corrections in Kansas: extending community-based corrections or widening the net?', *Journal of Research in Crime and Delinquency*, vol 27, pp 79-101.

Knott, C. (1995) 'The STOP programme: reasoning and rehabilitation in a British setting', in J. McGuire (ed) *What works: Reducing reoffending*, Chicester: Wiley, pp 115-26.

Lipsey, M. (1992) 'Juvenile delinquency treatment: a meta-analytic inquiry into the variability of effects', in T.D. Cook (ed) *Meta-analysis for explanation: A casebook*, New York, NY: Russell Sage Foundation.

Lipton, D., Martinson, R. and Wilks, J. (1975) *The effectiveness of correctional treatment: A survey of treatment evaluation studies*, New York, NY: Praeger.

Lloyd, C., Mair, G. and Hough, M. (1995) *Explaining reconviction rates: A critical analysis*, Home Office Research Study 136, London: Home Office.

Losel, F. (1995) 'The efficacy of correctional treatment: a review and synthesis of meta-evaluations', in J. McGuire (ed) *What works: Reducing reoffending*, Chicester: Wiley, pp 79-114.

Losel, F. and Koferl, P. (1989) 'Evaluation research on correctional treatment in West Germany: a meta-analysis', in H. Wegener, F. Losel and J. Haisch (eds) *Criminal behavior and the justice system: Psychological perspectives*, New York, NY: Springer-Verlag.

McGuire, J. (ed) (1995) *What works: Reducing reoffending*, Chicester: Wiley.

McGuire, J. and Priestley, P. (1985) *Offending behaviour: Skills and stratagems for going straight*, London: Batsford.

McGuire, J. and Priestley, P. (1995) 'Reviewing "What works": past, present and future', in J. McGuire (ed) *What works: Reducing reoffending*, Chicester: Wiley, pp 3-34.

McIvor, G. (1995) 'Practitioner evaluation in probation', in J. McGuire (ed) *What works: Reducing reoffending*, Chicester: Wiley, pp 209-20.

McWilliams, W. (1983) 'The mission to the English Police Courts 1876-1936', *Howard Journal*, vol 22, pp 129-47.

Mair, G. (1994) 'Standing at the crossroads: what works in community penalties', National Conference for Probation Committee Members, Scarborough, 7-9 October.

Maltz, M. (1984) *Recidivism*, London: Academic Press.

Martinson, R. (1974) 'What works? Questions and answers about prison reform', *Public Interest*, vol 35, pp 22-54.

Martinson, R. (1979) 'New findings, new views: a note of caution regarding sentencing reform', *Hofstra Law Review*, vol 7, pp 243-58.

Palmer, T. (1975) 'Martinson revisited', *Journal of Research in Crime and Delinquency*, July, pp 133-52.

Palmer, T. (1978) *Correctional intervention and research: Current issues and future prospects*, Lexington, MA: DC Heath and Co.

Pawson, R. and Tilley, N. (1997) *Realistic evaluation*, London: Sage Publications.

Pearson, F.S. and Harper, A.G. (1990) 'Contingent intermediate sentences: New Jersey's intensive supervision program', *Crime and Delinquency*, vol 36, pp 75-86.

Petersilia, J. (1989) 'Implementing randomized experiments: lessons from BJA's intensive supervision project', *Evaluation Review*, vol 13, no 5, pp 435-58, October.

Petrosino, A.J. (1998) 'A survey of 150 randomised experiments in crime reduction: some preliminary findings', *The Justice Research and Statistics Association Forum*, vol 16, no 1, pp 1 and 7.

Pitts, J. (1992) 'The end of an era', *The Howard Journal*, vol 31, no 2, pp 133-49, May.

Porporino, F. and Robinson, D. (1995) 'An evaluation of the reasoning and rehabilitation program with Canadian federal offenders', in R.R. Ross and R.D. Ross (eds) *Thinking straight: The reasoning and rehabilitation program for delinquency prevention and offender rehabilitation*, Ottawa: Air Training Publications.

Roberts, C. (1995) 'Effective practice and service delivery', in J. McGuire (ed) *What works: Reducing reoffending*, Chicester: Wiley, pp 221-36.

Rosenbaum, D. (1988) 'A critical eye on neighborhood watch: does it reduce crime and fear?', in T. Hope and M. Shaw (eds) *Communities and crime reduction*, London: HMSO, pp 126-45.

Ross, H.L. (1982) *Deterring the drunk driver*, Lexington, MA: Lexington.

Select Committee on Home Affairs (1998) *Alternatives to prison: Third Report – List of conclusions and recommendations*, London, House of Commons.

Sherman, L.W., Gottfredson, D.C., MacKenzie, D.L., Eck, J., Reuter, P. and Bushway, S.D. (1997) *Preventing crime: What works, what doesn't, what's promising*, Office of Justice Programs Research Report, Washington, DC: US Department of Justice.

Smith, D. (1977) *Impact – The major findings*, Home Office Research Bulletin, No 4, London: Home Office.

Tarling, R. (1993) *Analysing offending. Data, models and interpretations*, London: HMSO.

Tarling, R. and Dowds, L. (1997) 'Crime and punishment', in R. Jowell, J. Curtice, A. Park, L. Brook and K. Thomson, C. Bryson (eds) *British social attitudes: The 14th Report*, Aldershot: Ashgate Publishing, pp 197-214.

Taylor, R.B. (1994) *Research methods in criminal justice*, New York, NY: McGraw-Hill.

Thomas, M. (1996) 'What works: quality management and professional protocols', *Vista*, pp 54-61, May.

Wilkinson, J. (1994) 'Using a reconviction predictor to make sense of reconviction rates in the probation service', *British Journal of Social Work*, vol 24, pp 461-75.

SIX

Social care: rhetoric and reality

Geraldine Macdonald

Introduction

The term 'social care' was originally used to distinguish a range of practical services and functions of social services departments from the professional activity of social work (see Webb and Wistow, 1987). For reasons outlined below, social care has now been recast to cover the entire spectrum of welfare provision within the personal social services *including* social work. This breadth of activity makes it difficult to summarise, but the problems do not rest here. Particularly as it relates to social work, social care is a rather dubious name for the range of activities and responsibilities which cluster beneath this umbrella term. This is because while 'caring' is a central theme, the care of some (such as vulnerable children) inevitably involves the control or policing of others (such as parents). In pursuing long-term 'caring' goals, social care can entail activities that restrict people's liberties, such as interventions in the lives of those with serious mental illness (to protect them or others) and interventions aimed at preventing recidivism (youth justice). In decision-making terms, many of these functions rest with social workers.

The range of groups that fall within the scope of social care is wide, covering children and young people, older people, physically disabled people, the learning disabled, the mentally ill, and the homeless. Viewing social care through a 'problems' lens, rather than a 'client group' lens, reveals a similarly broad range of problems that it encounters and/or seeks to address: abuse and neglect, substance misuse, mental illness, alcoholism, chronic physical illness and disability, inadequate parenting, delinquency, to name but a few. The services provided span residential and daycare, group work, domiciliary services, counselling and other forms of intervention aimed at changing or improving behaviour, relationships or individual well-being. The focus of social care is also difficult to summarise succinctly. Generally speaking it is concerned with individually manifested problems with a social dimension amenable to social intervention. However, history and bureaucratic happenstance isolate some areas – such as education, transport, housing and many aspects of healthcare – that might, were we to start afresh, properly be seen as social care.

In the UK there is a large statutory sector (local government social services departments) which operates on the basis of statutory responsibilities and duties, coupled with a wide range of permissory powers. The latter are usually exercised in accordance with available resources, such as preventive and supportive services, and provide one source of the diversity of user experience across local authorities. The local authority (or 'public') sector increasingly operates within a 'mixed economy of welfare', commissioning large tranches of services from the private and voluntary sectors (such as daycare, residential care, domiciliary or homecare services), but retaining a key role in the assessment of an individual's need. The voluntary sector has always played a major role in certain areas of service provision, but the purposeful change of balance between the three sectors that has taken place within the last decade marks a significant departure from the provision of personal social services in the 1970s and 1980s (Brenton, 1985; Cooper, 1988, 1989). In principle, it marks part of an attempt to develop a more needs-led service and one which is more finely attuned to the wishes of those it seeks to serve. More ideologically, it reflects a belief in the market as a means of best securing consumer choice and high quality provision.

Within social care, political ideology plays a major role in shaping policy and practice. The volatility inherent in the way that social problems are conceived, and therefore how they are responded to, also impacts on the shape and nature of social care provision. Sheltering beneath these ideological umbrellas are more considered views of the need to rethink structures developed as a means of solving social problems and delivering services, some of which have themselves become problematic, some of which we simply can no longer afford. The move towards a mixed economy of welfare provision is in part the result of one such 'rethink'.

The boundary issues and problems of coordination between organisational sectors and professional groups comprise a major focus for improving effectiveness and efficiency, with an increasing emphasis on interdisciplinary and multidisciplinary (or professional) communication and collaboration. The term 'social care' is often deployed to capture not only the range of activities that fall within its scope, but also the diversity of the workforce which provides services. Social work is only one of a number of services provided, and social workers only one of a number of groups involved in social care. Numerically they represent a small percentage of the workforce. However, they are important as gatekeepers to resources, and are pivotal decision makers across a range of social care and social work tasks. As a group they are perhaps more particularly concerned with issues of skilled professional practice (rather than direct provision of practical services), and as a result are a central focus of the evidence-based practice debate within social care. Even among social workers there is debate and conflict.

For professional social workers, most of whom are employed by local authorities, there is a well-documented tension between the requirements of professional accountability and those of employing organisations (Bamford, 1990; Etzioni, 1969). The trend – as in other sectors – has been to curtail professional freedom. There is certainly a need to ensure that staff comply with important legislative and procedural requirements, but this does not require the suspension of professional accountability. The imminent establishment of a General Social Care Council and the transfer of responsibilities for social work training from the Central Council for Education and Training in Social Work (CCETSW) to the new Training Organisation for Personal Social Services (TOPSS) will need to address this tension.

Finally (though by no means exhaustively), as part of a wider concern with raising standards in the public sector and a need to keep costs to a minimum, the skills and knowledge required for particular tasks have come under increasing scrutiny. Questions are being asked about the range of tasks that require social work rather than other forms of service or case management. In 1999 the government reviewed the content, level and delivery of social work training as one part of a more major endeavour to map the occupational standards and qualifications required of people on the training continuum, at pre-qualifying (National Vocational Qualifications[NVQs]), qualifying and post-qualifying awards. So, yet more change to professional training is under way. An important consideration in this area is whether the developments that have taken place in the organisation and delivery of social care (particularly community care) now require us to consider whether we need a new type of hybrid animal within the social care sector, one who can encompass the range of knowledge and skills necessary for care management in particular.

It is in this context of change and threat to professional identity that the implementation of evidence-based approaches to policy and practice has to be considered. The concept of evidence-based practice is potentially as much a political tool as a professional concern, and as in other areas much will depend on how it is defined, how it is used, and what it is seen to deliver. In social care, as elsewhere, this is currently a major challenge, as yet unsettled. For the reasons indicated above, this chapter takes social work as a case study to explore the issues, dilemmas and challenges inherent in developing evidence-based social care.

The chapter proceeds by first discussing the nature of the evidence base for social care. This is followed by a consideration of the extent to which there is an evidence-based practice agenda in social care. The pioneering role of the voluntary sector in both extending the evidence base and getting it used in practice is then outlined, before considering more broadly the issues that need to be addressed in developing evidence-based practice in social care. The chapter concludes with a summary of the strengths and weaknesses of outcome research in social care.

Nature of evidence

In social care, those who share the core assumptions about evidence that underpin evidence-based healthcare comprise a minority voice. The majority of academics and researchers in the social care field are at best sceptical, and at worst antipathetic towards the transferability of the particular approaches to evaluation that are the hallmark of evidence-based practice in health (see, for example, Everitt and Hardiker, 1996; Everitt et al, 1992). In particular, they are concerned about the emphasis on randomised controlled trials as the gold standard of research, heading a hierarchy of research methods at the bottom of which lie the research designs most frequently deployed in social care: client opinion studies and pre-test-post-test or post-test only designs. This is not to say that studies with these designs do not have a role to play in the development of policy and practice in social care. In particular, client-opinion studies make an important contribution to ensuring that the views of clients, users and carers influence the shape, content and process of practice, and also the research agenda itself (see Macdonald, 1997a; Oliver, 1997). Rather, if the task is to evaluate the effects of interventions on measures other than, or in addition to, user views, then these studies are not sufficient (see Macdonald 1997a, 1997b).

More importantly, those who argue that no distinction should be made between the relative merits of different research designs, or who oppose the use of experimental methods in social care, change the nature of 'evidence-based practice' by endeavouring to redefine the term 'evidence-based'. Such ambivalence – and oft-times antipathy – is prevalent in key areas of research and training within social care (see below). In the field, there is more enthusiasm, but here practitioners are struggling in an environment which does not support the close relationship between practice and research (of any kind); and practitioners are not equipped by qualifying and post-qualifying training to exercise the discrimination required to identify, critically appraise, and use research, or syntheses of research. This is one reason why one of the strategies employed by the Centre for Evidence-Based Social Services at Exeter University has been to train professional and managerial staff in critical appraisal skills. Where this has been done (and it has been done quite extensively over 14 local authorities) it has been very well received and appears to have enabled people to develop basic knowledge and skills (CASP, 1999).

Social services departments undertake a great deal of 'inhouse' research, including outcome or effectiveness research. Most of this work is at the weaker end of what – in *outcome* research –would be seen as a hierarchy of research methods in health, that is, non-experimental methods and surveys of users' views, although of its kind it is often of good quality (see Kent Social Services Department's *Research Bulletin)*. Such methods fit most easily with the working realities of many departments and have an important part to play in routine monitoring and evaluation. However, as indicated above, they are not sufficient, in and of themselves, to constitute a secure basis for decision making with regard to policy or individual practice. That requires studies that score well on internal validity. Put more simply, studies are needed that can maximise our confidence that any pattern of results (good or bad, intended or unintended) can be attributed to the intervention we are trying to evaluate. This means ruling out as many alternate explanations as possible to account for a pattern of results (see Macdonald and Roberts, 1995 or Macdonald with Winkley, 2000). All things being equal (that is to say, if everything is done well and goes according to plan – see Chapter Twelve) the studies best able to do this are randomised controlled trials (RCTs). Randomisation of people to one of two or more groups means that if there is anything else 'going on' which we are unaware of, it is likely to be going on in both the group receiving the intervention and the group not receiving it. We can therefore ignore it as a possible account of any findings. However, RCTs are typically challenging to mount, and costly, which are some of the reasons why we would expect these to be the subject of externally-funded studies, conducted by independent researchers with minimal (preferably no) investment in a particular outcome.

The Department of Health (DoH) has its own division responsible for social care research, as well as inspection and regulation. It is one of a handful of major funders within the UK and, on the surface of it, a key player in the promotion of evidence-based practice in this field. For example, one of its projects referred to earlier concerned the identification and evaluation of meaningful outcomes in social care, and the feasibility of preparing and disseminating reviews of research. It pump-primed the establishment of the Centre for Evidence-Based Social Services and the phrase 'evidence-based approach' has begun to appear in its more recent policy documents (such as DoH, *Framework for the assessment of children in need and their families*, 2000). However, little of its research is, or has been, outcome research per se, by which is meant the evaluation of the effects of particular interventions (compared with others, or – more problematic – with not intervening at all).

Perhaps as a result of its political brief, the DoH has invested most resource into the monitoring of legislative and procedural change, for example, in monitoring the effects of the implementation of the Children Act 1989. Again, these monitoring studies are essential, but are not sufficient for developing accountable and effective services within social services. Other, vital areas of practice remain largely under-researched. For example, the decisions made by individual practitioners about the best way to respond to a child who has been sexually abused is of major importance to that child's future development and well-being. Such decisions (when resources permit any service to be offered) remain largely a matter of professional judgement: judgement that is rarely challenged on the basis of evidence of effectiveness (Macdonald, 1998).

Few studies funded in social care by the DoH – or by any other UK funder – deploy research designs of the kind that would be recognised in health as adequately rigorous to justify the wholesale adoption of particular policies and practices. Instead, there is a preponderance of descriptive or exploratory studies, and evaluations using non-experimental designs. For example, in a review of the effectiveness of social work covering the period 1979-90 (Macdonald and Sheldon, 1992) the authors were only able to identify 95 studies in Anglophone peer-reviewed journals (across the breadth of work undertaken by social workers – all client groups, all social problems), of which only 23 were experimental, 87% of which were American. This was the period in which the Children Act 1989 was drafted, received Royal Assent and was about to be implemented, yet only 13 of the studies concerned the effects of work with abused and neglected children, of which only two were experimental, with a further three quasi-experimental (matched group comparisons). Most were conducted in the USA. Generally speaking, in the last 15 years the number of trials of social work and social care per se has fallen; those conducted are generally smaller, and less methodologically secure than in earlier years (for details see Macdonald and Sheldon, 1992; Macdonald, 1998).

It might be assumed that this is all historical happenstance and not a conscious rejection of the need for experimentation. After all, research in social care is expensive and a range of technical, political and ethical challenges present themselves to the would-be user of RCTs. Examples of these challenges include:

- randomised trials generally increase the cost of research; the numbers needed to provide sufficient statistical power mean that studies can take a long time;
- it is difficult to guarantee the stability of the research context in social services departments, with consequent threat to the internal validity of trials;
- the introduction of national or intradepartmental 'across the board' changes in policy and practice make it difficult to espouse other than non-experimental designs, which are fraught with the very threats to internal validity that experimental designs seek to control (for example the weaker the research design, and poorer the methodological quality, the greater the effect sizes observed or recorded – see Schultz et al, 1995);
- these problems are exacerbated in social care in a way that they are not in health, by the fact that policy and practice are often dictated by political and ideological decisions; this is not only a question of resources, but the ways in which social problems are perceived, and responses selected (for example, perceptions of the causes and optimal responses to crime) – politicians perceive themselves more competent to judge 'social' than 'medical' issues;
- a strong, anti-scientific lobby within the social services research community minimises the likelihood of social care researchers entering the marketplace with a pro-trial disposition;
- the minimal appetite of researchers for experimental methodology is reinforced by the apparent lack of sustenance on offer from funders;
- few researchers in social care have ever been involved in this type of research (Tilda Goldberg and Jane Gibbons are rare exceptions in our

field – see Goldberg, 1970 and Gibbons et al, 1978) and some funders report the lack of researchers with the necessary skills.

So is the limited application of randomised experiments in social care just a reflection of the difficulties of mounting such experiments, rather than a rejection of their appropriateness? There is some evidence that the dearth of rigorous evaluations of social care interventions funded by the DoH reflects at best a lack of understanding of the issue of internal validity, and at worst an antipathy towards the deployment of scientific methodology within social care. The major obstacle to the adoption of an evidence-based approach to social work appears to be a view that such an approach amounts to narrow-minded empiricism (see Harrison and Humphries, 1997, 1998). Antagonists are endeavouring to redefine the concept of evidence-based practice in ways that leave the methodological *status quo* untouched, by rejecting the term 'evidence-based' and offering alternatives such as 'knowledge-based' (Fisher, 1998) and 'research-minded' (CCETSW, 1995). Such attempts imply that the nature of evidence is purely a matter of individual preference, rather than an important technical and ethical issue. This places the least powerful groups in society at risk of a double standard of operating by those more securely placed. The point is eloquently summed up by Pinker:

> If the characteristic patterns of risk and dependency confronting social workers were to spread to the majority of the population, the general public would very soon demand services of the highest quality from professional social workers of the highest calibre, and the idea of applying egalitarian principles to standards of knowledge and skill would be laughed out of court. (Pinker, 1980, pp 257-8)

Such methodological clashes invariably generate most heat over the role of qualitative methodologies. Although health has a long history of qualitative research (Light and Pillemar, 1985), this has typically been conducted in parallel with outcome research, rather than as an integral part of the latter (see Alderson et al, 1996) – Chapter Fourteen considers such complementarity in more detail. While the history of social work effectiveness research has much to teach healthcare about the importance of attending simultaneously to process and outcome within the context of experimental methods, social care has much to gain by increasing (and in some cases introducing) the use of experimental designs in its evaluative endeavours. While those in healthcare are grappling with the challenges of undertaking research where randomisation of participants is either technically or ethically inappropriate, and of synthesising the results of such studies, few in social care even acknowledge that both are problems that need resolving. Similarly, while those in healthcare are exploring ways to address long-standing problems in healthcare research, such as attention to outcomes of relevance to patients, social care researchers and funders still use outmoded and stereotypical notions of the 'medical model' as one plank in their rebuttal of the methodological assumptions underpinning evidence-based healthcare (see Macdonald, 1997a, 1997b).

In short, if evidence-based practice is to deliver in social care what it appears to be delivering in healthcare, it will need a more informed and strategic approach from senior policy makers, civil servants, government funders, as well as the research community, than it has enjoyed to date. While the language of 'evidence-based practice' is permeating policy documents, such as *Modernising social services* and a *Framework for the assessment of children in need and their families* (DoH, 1998, 2000), if you prod at the rhetoric you do not find much of substance or encouragement. Whatever is intended, it is not a replication of the meaning of the term as it is used in healthcare.

Using the evidence

Evidence-based practice

In recent years, the approach to decision making exemplified by evidence-based healthcare (see Chapter Three) has been urged upon the personal social services. In 1995 the President of the Royal Statistical Society commented favourably on the work of the Cochrane Collaboration in preparing and disseminating systematic reviews of the effects of healthcare interventions and proposed that its methods should be extended to other areas of public activity such as education and the penal system (Smith, 1996). The DoH's review of the position of personal social services research identified the need for the collation of existing research and recommended the:

- establishment of a recognised, national clearing-house for research available to practitioners and service users;
- preparation and publication of research and development reviews which would be accessible in style, have an easily recognisable format, and carry credibility and authority (Davies et al, 1994).

In 1996, the then Secretary for State for Health Steven Dorrell said in an interview to *The Guardian*:

> The commitment to evidence-based medicine increasingly pervades modern medical practice. This kind of commitment should be extended to the social services world. (Dorrell, 1996)

The late 1990s also saw a resurgence of interest in what would previously have been called the therapeutic aspects of social care, possibly as a reaction to the very managerial approaches that had swept social services during the 1980s, and also in response to the rediscovery by policy makers of the importance of supportive and preventive work – never lost, it should be noted, to practitioners (see, for example, Levin and Webb, 1997).

Moves towards a closer integration of research and practice also received unprecedented support from local authority directors of social services, some of whom placed both their weight and a portion of their budgets into new developments to achieve this, notably the establishment of Research in Practice (an initiative to disseminate childcare research to childcare practitioners, and to enable them to use it) and the funding of the Centre for Evidence-based Social Services at the University of Exeter.

The latter arose from the recommendations of the DoH's own review (Davies et al, 1994). It began as a joint initiative between the DoH and a group of local authorities in the South West to:
- establish a centre to promote the dissemination of research findings relevant to the work of the social services generally;
- identify gaps in existing knowledge;
- commission research to fill these;
- develop empirically-based training in social services departments and courses in higher education.

This project is now in its third year, and directors of the participating local authorities have pledged to fund it for a further period. This is no mean testimony to the influence of the Centre which, over a relatively short period of time, has placed not only the issue of evidence-based approaches to policy and practice very firmly on the agenda of practice agencies, but has gone some way to setting up mechanisms for helping managers and practitioners move towards that goal.

To date, no organisation or system has been established whereby practitioners, managers and policy makers in social services can access or commission systematic reviews. The Centre for Evidence-based Social

Services has commissioned some reviews, which have had considerable influence (see Simons and Watson, 1999), but they are not quite the same animal as those currently available within health. This is in part because the Centre has not established an explicit policy on, or guidelines for, systematic reviews of the effects of interventions (this might stimulate activity within the field), but also because it has neither the staff nor the funding to do so. Other initiatives have made contributions, such as the DoH's Outcomes in Social Care Initiative, in which one project was designed to explore the feasibility of systematically reviewing evidence of effectiveness within services to adults. This project immediately encountered a core problem in developing evidence-based practice, namely, what shall count as evidence? Its approach was essentially 'anything' – but this is unlikely to deliver the types of improvements in practice and service delivery that the concept of evidence-based practice is designed to deliver.

Voluntary sector: pioneers again?

Barnardo's has played a major role in placing the issue of evidence-based policy and practice in social care firmly on the public agenda. The UK's largest childcare charity, it delivers direct services to 40,000 children and families in all four UK countries. Its contribution, with the Social Science Research Unit (Institute of Education, University of London), raised the profile of this issue in influential places – something Barnardo's has an admirable track record in doing. Subsequently, Barnardo's has sought to tackle the issues within its own services for children and families. It is unique as an organisation providing direct social welfare services in having an explicit commitment to evidence-based practice. This policy is operationalised in a series of publications aimed at providing staff with readily accessible and up-to-date overviews of evidence on effective interventions in a range of areas relevant to children's lives (see Box 6.1). Further, it sponsored an ESRC studentship to examine in detail what the obstacles are to evidence-based practice. This complements the work of its own research and development department which provides a strong intellectual commitment to this area, evidenced in its research activity, its commissioned publications, its policy briefing documents and its training initiatives.

Box 6.1: Barnado's publications on 'what works'

What works in the early years? (Macdonald and Roberts, 1995)

What works in family placement? (Thoburn and Sellick, 1997)

What works in leaving care? (Stein, 1996)

What works in inclusive education? (Sebba and Sachdev, 1998)

What works in services for families with a disabled child? (Beresford et al, 1998)

What works in maintaining stability in care? (Jackson and Thomas, 1999)

What works in parenting education? (Lloyd, 1999)

What works in family support? (Buchanan, 1999)

In press are:

What works for parents with a learning disability? (McGraw, 1999)

What works in child protection? (Macdonald with Winkley, 1999)

In preparation are:

What works in community development? (Craig, 1999)

What works in community based alternatives for young offenders? (Utting and Vennard, 1999)

What works in reducing inequalities in child health? (Roberts, 1999)

In 1999-2000, Barnardo's funded a series of workshops for practitioners specifically around the use of evidence in practice. These are being carried out collaboratively with practice staff and Barnardo's national training and development coordinator. Barnardo's is acutely aware of the gap between research and practice, and the challenge of reorientating a large organisation in an evidence-based direction. It is experimenting with how best to achieve this, and analysing the difficulties is a key step. Its work has recently been acknowledged by a key funder of social care research, the Joseph Rowntree Foundation, which has commissioned Barnardo's to produce a report on the use of good evidence in practice, and the means to achieve this. This will certainly contribute to the debate, and may well help further the development of evidence-based practice. As in so many other areas, the voluntary sector is somewhat ahead of so-called 'mainstream' services. However, to guarantee the permeation of this philosophy as a basis for decision making across social

---

work and across the social care sector, a number of other areas need attention.

Developing evidence-based practice in social care

The development of evidence-based practice needs to begin some way 'upstream' of the evaluation of interventions. The troubles we encounter in training and in practice arise not only because of difference of opinion about legitimate approaches to evaluation. The problem is more fundamental, and an evidence-based approach in social work requires practitioners to take a more rigorous approach when choosing between ways of understanding. The two issues are linked. Effectiveness in tackling social problems is, in part, a function of the ability accurately to locate factors that contribute to social problems and that are amenable to influence. Here is an example from medicine. It is suggested that if doctors 50 years ago had been given erythropoietin, one of biotechnology's successful drugs and an excellent treatment for many anaemias, they would have discarded it, since they did not have the right classification of anaemias to be able to pick out the patients who would respond (*Economist*, 1995). The problems that fall within the remit of social work and social care are every bit as complex and challenging. Such difficulties in social work's knowledge base are exacerbated when empirically-tested theories are deemed to have no especial claim on our attention. It is little use funding research, however well-designed, if the problems being targeted are conceptualised in ways that themselves enjoy no empirical support, or which do not lend themselves to empirical verification. In distributing scarce resources, it would not be unreasonable to require researchers to demonstrate the validity of their problem formulations and the logical relationship these conceptualisations hopefully enjoy with the intervention proposed. This is particularly important when would-be helpers, having settled on a hammer during training, perceive everything to be amenable to a brief, task-centred 'tap'. Such an approach to theory would also enable a dramatic streamlining of social work curricula.

This worryingly democratic approach to the relationship between theory, research and practice in the social services is a long-standing problem (see Sheldon, 1978). It is the inevitable consequence of an epistemological position that refuses to recognise any qualitative difference in the status of data generated by research studies of different methodologies. The extent to which evidence-based practice will improve the effectiveness of services within social care will depend on the extent to which funders, researchers, educators and practitioners, can move away from the methodologically *laissez-faire* position currently dominating CCETSW and still present in the social care division of the DoH.

Assuming that an epistemological consensus, of the kind that generally exists in healthcare (see Chapter Three), was achieved, the development of evidence-based practice in social care would depend on the following:

- the generation of good quality data concerning effectiveness (see Campbell and Stanley, 1973; Cook and Campbell, 1979);
- a workforce able critically to appraise evidence and contribute to the process of systematic reviews of research findings (see Gambrill, 1997);
- the dissemination of data and/or research syntheses in a readily accessible form to professionals, managers, policy makers and to service users – this is a methodological, as well as technical challenge (Chalmers and Altman, 1995; Macdonald, 1998);
- a work and policy environment that facilitates, rather than impedes, the development of practices that reflect 'best evidence' (Macdonald, 1990; see also Chapter Fifteen).

So far, this chapter has focused on the dearth of good quality research into the effectiveness of the personal social services, and the lack of leadership (or even support) from some key research funders and from within academia. The next section considers what is required to facilitate evidence-based practice in social care/work, and some of the obstacles that need to be negotiated, beginning with a consideration of what is required in relation to primary research.

Generating the evidence-base – primary research

Evidence-based practice requires an increased investment in experimental and quasi-experimental research, wherever these are ethically and technically feasible. This requires not only a financial investment, but investment in the strategies designed to address the undoubted technical challenges that social care settings present to scientific evaluation (see Chapter Twelve). It is less the complexity of the subject matter (which randomised controlled trials are well placed to manage), but rather its fluidity. Social services departments, for example, rarely stand still long enough to achieve the stable environment required to conduct an experiment from which we can draw conclusions with confidence. Problems change, sometimes daily; today's difficulties oust previous priorities. But we should remember Kuhn's aside about the messiness of social science:

> A paradigm can ... insulate the [scientific] community from those socially important problems that ... cannot be stated in terms of the conceptual and instrumental tools the paradigm supplies.... One of the reasons why normal science seems to progress so rapidly is that its practitioners concentrate on problems that only their own lack of ingenuity should keep them from solving. (Kuhn, 1970, p 37)

Evaluating the effectiveness of personal social services provides researchers and statisticians with a rich set of technical and analytical problems to address, which will need to be tackled if the principles of evidence-based practice are to be extended to these areas. These challenges are currently used as a means to dismiss the relevance of certain research designs, rather than to stimulate debate about how such problems might be overcome. Large sums of money are currently invested in evaluations that are technically not capable of providing the answers to questions about 'what works?' The appropriateness of asking service users and staff to participate in such studies raises important ethical issues of a kind rarely discussed in social care. At least some of these monies could be redistributed in the direction of more scientifically sound projects.

Generating the evidence-base – systematic reviews

Broadly speaking, systematic reviews entail a series of techniques for minimising bias and error, primarily through the use of *protocols* which state, prior to the review being undertaken, what the criteria are that will guide the review – search strategies, exclusion and inclusion criteria, standards of methodological adequacy, the precise definition of the intervention in question, unbiased estimation of aggregate effect and so on. Given the wealth of studies in some areas, of different research designs, with varying definitions and approaches, and often with contradictory findings, a rigorous approach to research synthesis is a necessary prerequisite to an effective dissemination strategy. An infrastructure now exists within health to develop, maintain and disseminate such reviews (see Chapter Three). Such an infrastructure does not exist, as yet, in social care. That said, in February 2000 the Inaugral Meeting of the Campbell Collaboration took place in Philadelphia, USA. The Campbell Collaboration is a sibling organisation to the Cochrane Collaboration. This organisation aims to prepare, maintain and make accesible high quality reviews relevant to the fields of social, educational and criminological interventions. This organisation will have to face the same challenges about 'what shall count as evidence' but close links with the Cochrane Collaboration (such as pooling their resources and sharing Methods Working Groups) should keep the issues raised in this chapter firmly on the agenda. Meanwhile a database of RCTs has been developed, partly as a result of research sponsored by the Northern Ireland Office. The Review Group that was also established as a result of that work (the Cochrane Developmental, Psychosocial and Learning Problems Group) is producing a range of relevant reviews, available on the Cochrane Library (see Box 6.2). It is possible that this will be one of a number of groups that will span both the Cochrane and Campbell Collaborations, given the essentially multidisciplinary nature of the problems it covers and the interventions designed to address them.

Box 6.2: Output from the Cochrance Developmental, Psychosocial and Learning Problems Group

Reviews

'Home-based social support for socially disadvantaged mothers' (Review: Hodnett and Roberts, 1997)

'Day care for pre-school children' (Zoritch et al, 1997)

Protocols

'Family and parenting interventions for conduct disorder and delinquency in children aged 10-17' (Woolfenden and Williams, 2000)

'Cognitive-behavioural interventions for sexually abused children' (Macdonald et al, 2000)

Skills

Good quality reviews require reviewers with both content expertise and methodological expertise, who can articulate sensible research questions. For practitioners to make sense of published reviews requires that they too have new expertise in critical appraisal. In the longer term the role of systematic reviews and the skills required to conduct and use them, should be addressed in qualifying and post-qualifying training. In the short term other solutions are needed. At present the only training on offer to social care staff is that provided in healthcare settings such as the Systematic Review Training Centre at the Institute of Child Health. It is usually costly, and can be intimidating for those with no training in research methods. Ironically, the Centre for Evidence-based Social Services has no brief to prepare reviews and no brief directly to train staff in these skills. This is perhaps not surprising given their small numbers, but it represents a lost opportunity and must surely undermine its long-term goals. Insofar as the skills required critically to appraise the quality of research studies overlap with those needed to undertake reviews, the commissioning of critical appraisal skills training by the Centre may begin to stimulate work in this area, as might the involvement of social care staff in Cochrane Collaboration Review Groups. Time will tell whether or not these developments make a difference in the intended direction, but in any event their impact will be limited by the availability of accessible and reliable summaries of research. If and when the Campbell Collaboration gets off the ground, this is an area it will need to address, as will professional training bodies.

Dissemination

Social care has long been a 'doing' rather than a 'reflective' occupation. Pressure of work, both in volume and in riskiness, inhibits the development of conditions that are conducive to evidence-based practice, such as time (and permission) to read, time to share and debate practice issues with colleagues, study leave and so on. Unlike healthcare, where libraries and journals are often part and parcel of the work environment, social care staff can live and work 90 miles away from a bookshop, and further still from a university library. Dissemination is a key challenge, particularly when electronic support is also often absent.

At the present time we still lack "a recognised, national clearing–house for research, available to practitioners and service users" and an infrastructure for "the preparation and publication of research and development reviews which would be accessible in style, have an easily recognisable format, and carry credibility and authority" (see Davies et al, 1994). The success of the Campbell Collaboration in preparing, maintaining and disseminating reviews relevant to social interventions will depend, in part, on its ability to secure adequate financial backing. The Cochrane Collaboration has enjoyed substantial support from the NHS and although it undoubtedly provides good value for money, the financial support has made a tremendous difference to its productivity.

The DoH in the UK will need to decide whether and how to support the general enterprise of research synthesis and dissemination, particularly in a field where computers and similar resources are still inaccessible to most managers and practitioners, and where offices (unlike many hospitals) are not situated near to (or linked with) libraries or other resources where access to electronic databases is easily available.

Organisational context

If evidence-based practice is to flourish then changes need to take place in the culture and practices of organisations. In recent years the greatest impetus for change within social services has come from grass-roots practitioners and directors of social services, for example, the consortium of local authorities backing the Centre for Evidence-based Social Services, and a resurgence of interest in the content of practice (as opposed to its organisation). The latter is admittedly an impressionistic view, based on requests for seminars and training that address practice issues in general, and issues of effective practice in particular. But an evidence-based approach to practice requires that hard choices be made, not only by managers and practitioners who find that their preferred ways of working are not those supported by the best evidence available, but by politicians and the public. Defensive practice (one consequence of recent changes in legislation and 'political climate') does not necessarily sit easily with evidence-based practice, which might justify taking more risks than some would care to choose (see Macdonald and Macdonald, 2000: forthcoming). It is one thing to fund a centre, but it is another to be willing to develop internal policies and strategies that nail your organisational commitment firmly to the mast, and enable the realisation of such an approach in day-to-day practice.

Concluding remarks

For the reasons given above, evidence-based practice in social care is at an early and turbulent stage of development. At the grass-roots there is a resurgence of interest in the content of practice, and this appears to be carrying alongside it an appetite for evidence about the relative effectiveness of different approaches to social problems. Despite a series of initiatives intended to promote evidence-based practice, most are fundamentally compromised by the unwillingness of funders, particularly at government level, to address important epistemological issues. This ambivalence, or possible antipathy, is mirrored in other important arenas such as training and the research community. Together with a lack of investment in rigorous primary research this threatens the future of this approach to social care, with the ultimate costs being borne by service users and carers, and possibly by professionals who are unable adequately to demonstrate their 'value-added'.

Strengths of outcome research in social work and social care

- An informative history of well-conducted research using experimental methods. Social work was the first among the helping professions to subject its good intentions to rigorous scrutiny (see Mullen and Dumpsen, 1972; Fischer, 1973).
- A rich portfolio of approaches to evaluation, and a particularly strong history of client-opinion research. If appropriately valued this range of methodologies could form the basis of a step-wise approach to evaluation and the development of evidence-based theory and practice.
- An appropriate and well-developed concern with ethical issues associated with research in general and the scientific paradigm in particular. Health has much to learn from this, and from the ways that these problems have been tackled within social care research.
- A growing commitment and enthusiasm to evaluate practice and policy, especially among those at the coal face.
- Strategic and influential backing from organisations well placed to influence policy and practice such as Barnardo's, the Joseph Rowntree Foundation, the Social Science Research Unit, and pockets of support within government departments responsible for policy, regulation, inspection and research.
- Support from colleagues and organisations in health such as the Cochrane Collaboration, and the York Centre for Reviews and Dissemination. As well as having an interest in social care, there are also areas of overlapping interest such as primary healthcare.
- The development of a potential sister organisation to the Cochrane Collaboration, the Campbell Collaboration.

Weaknesses of outcome research in social work and social care

- A lack of consensus about what shall count as evidence.
- Antipathy towards scientific methodology which affects not only how interventions are evaluated but undermines the development of sound theories and exploration of the nature of social problems.
- Poor methodological quality of research, even *within* research designs.
- A lack of political and fiscal support for improving the evidence base of social care, both with regard to primary research and research synthesis.
- Ambivalence of many within the DoH about the relevance and transferability of scientific methodology to social care.
- Lack of skills among practitioners in methodological appraisal.
- The absence of dissemination structures.
- Organisational structures and cultures that do not facilitate evidence-based practice.

References

Alderson, P., Brill, S., Chalmers, I., Fuller, R., Hinkley-Smith, P., Macdonald, G.M., Newman, T., Oakley, A., Roberts, H. and Ward, H. (1996) *What works? Effective social interventions in child welfare*, Barkingside: SSRU/Barnardo's.

Bamford, T. (1990) *The future of social work*, Basingstoke: Macmillan.

Beresford, B., Sloper, P., Baldwin, S. and Newman, T. (1998) *What works in services for families with a disabled child?*, Barkingside: Barnardo's.

Brenton, M. (1985) *The voluntary sector in British social services*, London: Longman.

Buchanan, A. (1999) *What works in family support?*, Barkingside: Barnardo's/Wiltshire Social Services.

Campbell, D.T. and Stanley, J.C. (1973) *Experimental and quasi-experimental designs for research*, Chicago, IL: Rand McNally College Publishing Company.

CASP (1999) *Critical Appraisal Skills Project Report*, available from the Centre for Evidence-based Social Services, University of Exeter.

CCETSW (1995) *Assuring quality in the Diploma in Social Work – 1 Rules and Requirements for the DipSW*, London: CCETSW

Chalmers, I. and Altman, D.G. (eds) (1995) *Systematic reviews*, London: BMJ Publishing Group.

Cook, T.D. and Cambell, D.T. (1979) *Quasi-experimention: Design and analysis issues for field settings*, Chicago, IL: Rand McNally College Publishing Company.

Cooper, J. (1988) 'The mosaic of personal social services: public voluntary and private', *British Journal of Social Work*, vol 18, pp 237-50.

Cooper, J. (1989) 'The end is where we start from' [T.S. Eliot], *British Journal of Social Work*, vol 19, no 3, pp 177-88.

Craig, G. (1999) *What works in community development?*, mimeo, Barkingside: Barnardo's.

Davies, C., Morgan, J., Packman, J., Smith, G. and Smith, J. (1994) *A wider strategy for research and development relating to personal social services*, London: HMSO.

DoH (Department of Health) (1998) *Modernising social services*, London: DoH.

DoH (2000) *Framework for the assessment of children in need and their families*, London: DoH, DfEE, Home Office.

Dorrell, S. (1996) *The Guardian*, 19 June.

Economist (1995) 'Biotechnology and genetics: survey', 25 February, p 15.

Etzioni, A. (1969) *The semi-professions and their organisations*, New York, NY: Free Press.

Everitt, A. and Hardiker, P. (1996) *Evaluation for good practice*, Basingstoke: Macmillan.

Everitt, A., Hardiker, P., Littlewood, J. and Mullender, A. (1992) *Applied research for better practice*, Basingstoke: Macmillan.

Fischer, J. (1973) 'Is casework effective?', *Social Work*, vol 17, pp 1-5.

Fisher, M. (1998) 'Research, knowledge and practice in community care', *Issues in Social Work Education*, vol 17, no 2, pp 1-14.

Gambrill, E.D. (1997) *Social work practice: A critical thinker's guide*, New York, NY: Oxford University Press.

Gibbons, J.S., Butler, J., Urwin, P. and Gibbons, J.L. (1978) 'Evaluation of a social work service for self-poisoning patients', *British Journal of Psychiatry*, vol 133, pp 111-18.

Goldberg, E.M. (1970) *Helping the aged*, London: Allen and Unwin.

Harrison, C. and Humphries, C. (1997) *Keeping research in mind: Standards of research-mindedness in CCETSW's Award Programmes: Developing a framework of indicators – Report of a survey*, London: CCETSW.

Harrison, C. and Humphries, C. (1998) *Keeping research in mind: Final report and recommendations for future developments in social work education and training*, London: CCETSW.

Hodnett, E.D. and Roberts, I. (1997) 'Home-based social support for socially disadvantaged mothers' (Cochrane Review), *The Cochrane Library*, Issue 2, Oxford: Update Software.

Jackson, S. and Thomas, N. (1999) *What works in maintaining stability in care?*, Barkingside: Barnardo's.

Kuhn, T.S. (1970) *The structure of scientific revolutions* (2nd edn), Chicago, IL: University of Chicago Press (original published in 1962).

Levin, E. and Webb, S. (1997) *Social work and community care: Changing roles and tasks*, London: NISW.

Light, R.J. and Pillemar, D.B. (1985) *Summing up: The science of reviewing research*, Cambridge, MA: Harvard University Press.

Lloyd, E. (ed) (1999) *What works in parenting education?*, Barkingside: Barnardo's.

Macdonald, GM. (1997a) 'Social work research: the state we're in', *Journal of Interprofessional Care*, vol 11, no 1, pp 57-65.

Macdonald, G.M. (1997b) 'Social work: beyond control?', in A. Maynard and I. Chalmers (eds) *Non-random reflections on health services research. On the 25th anniversary of Archie Cochrane's* Effectiveness and Efficiency, Plymouth: BMJ Publishing Group.

MacDonald, G.M. (1990) 'Allocating blame in social work', *British Journal of Social Work*, vol 20, no 6, pp 525-46.

Macdonald, G.M. (1998) 'Developing evidence-based practice in child protection', *Child Psychology and Psychiatry*, vol 3, no 1, pp 1-23.

Macdonald, G.M. and Roberts, H. (1995) *What works in the early years? Effective interventions in health, education and welfare*, Barkingside: Barnardo's.

Macdonald, G.M. and Sheldon, B. (1992) 'Contemporary studies of the effectiveness of social work,' *British Journal of Social Work*, vol 22, no 6, pp 615-43.

Macdonald, G.M. and Sheldon, B. (1998) 'Changing one's mind: the final frontier?', *Issues in Social Work Education*, vol 18, p 1.

Macdonald, G.M. with Winkley, A. (2000) *What works in child protection?*, Barkingside: Barnardo's.

Macdonald, G.M., Ramchandani, P., Higgins, J. and Jones, D.P.H. (2000) 'Cognitive-behavioural interventions for sexually abused children' (Cochrane Protocol), *The Cochrane Library*, Issue 1, Oxford: Update Software.

Macdonald, K.I. and Macdonald, G.M. (2000: forthcoming) 'Perceptions of risk', in P. Parsloe (ed) *Risk assessment in social care and social work*, Aberdeen: Research Highlights.

McGraw, S. (1999) *What works for parents with a learning disability?*, Barkingside: Barnardo's.

Mullen, E.J. and Dumpson, J.R. (1972) *Evaluation of social intervention*, San Francisco, CA: Jossey Bass.

Oliver, S. (1997) 'Exploring lay perspectives on questions of effectiveness', in A. Maynard and I. Chalmers (eds) *Non-random reflections on health services research. On the 25th Anniversary of Archie Cochrane's* Effectiveness and Efficiency, Plymouth: BMJ Publishing Group.

Pinker, R. (1980) 'An alternative view: a note by Professor R.A. Pinker', in *Social workers: Their role and tasks*, London: Bedford Square Press/ NISW.

Roberts, H. (1999) *What works in reducing inequalities in child health?*, Barkingside: Barnardo's.

Schultz, K.F., Chalmers, I., Hayes, R.J. and Altman, D.G. (1995) 'Empirical evidence of bias: dimensions of methodological quality associated with estimates of treatment effects in controlled trials', *JAMA*, vol 273, pp 408-12.

Sebba, J. and Sachdev, D. (1998) *What works in inclusive education?*, Barkingside: Barnardo's.

Sheldon, B. (1978) 'Theory and practice in social work: a re-examination of a tenuous relationship', *British Journal of Social Work*, vol 8, no 1, pp 1–22.

Simons, K. and Watson, D. (1999) *New directions? Day services for people with learning disabilities in the 1990s. A review of the research*, Exeter: Centre for Evidence-based Social Services, University of Exeter.

Smith, A.F.M. (1996) 'Mad cows and ecstasy: chance and choice in an evidence-based society', *Journal of the Royal Statistical Society*, vol 159, no 3, pp 367–83.

Stein, M. (1996) *What works in leaving care?*, Barkingside: Barnardo's.

Thoburn, M. and Sellick, C. (1997) *What works in family placement?*, Barkingside: Barnardo's.

Utting, D. and Vennard, J. (1999) *What works in community based alternatives for young offenders?*, Barkingside: Barnardo's.

Webb, A. and Wistow, G. (1985) *The personal social services*, London: Longman.

Woolfenden, S. and Williams, K. (2000) 'Family and parenting interventions for conduct disorder and delinquency in children aged 10-17' (Cochrane Protocol), *The Cochrane Library*, Issue 1, Oxford: Update Software.

Zoritch, B., Roberts, I. and Oakley, A. (1997) 'Day care for pre-school children' (Cochrane Review), *The Cochrane Library*, Issue 2, Oxford: Update Software.

SEVEN

Welfare policy: tendering for evidence

Robert Walker

Introduction

Welfare policy in Britain – defined to include both contribution-based social security and means-tested social assistance – was born in its current form at the turn of the 20th century as the twin of systematic social enquiry. Research evidence has continued to shape policy ever since although it has seldom been the dominant influence, outweighed by ideology, political ambition and expediency (Bulmer, 1987).

The chapter begins with a brief account of the origins of evidence-based welfare policy before focusing on the role and limitations of welfare research at the turn of the 21st century. The primary focus is on the research that is most closely integrated into the policy process, namely that which is undertaken and commissioned by the Department of Social Security (DSS), since it best reveals the various purposes to which research is put. It is important, however, not to deny the importance of other types of research especially in helping to define new policy problems and agendas (Thomas, 1987). Pressure groups, exemplified by the Child Poverty Action Group, commission much secondary and some primary research that tends to focus on the failures of current policy. The Joseph Rowntree Foundation is also a key player, funding the strategic, blue-sky research that government seldom commissions, and other major research charities also play a role. Think-tanks are comparatively new entrants to the policy arena but are increasingly influential, typically spinning new ideas from pre-existing research evidence and offering variable doses of rhetoric and ideology. Quite often the same researchers and research organisations appear in different guises conducting research for government and research trusts, and writing for pressure groups and think-tanks.

Notwithstanding the range of other research stakeholders, this chapter focuses on the bilateral relationship between the DSS and its research contractors. The process of commissioning research within the DSS is briefly discussed and the types of evidence generated are described. Examples of specific research projects are provided to illustrate the range of research and its growing sophistication before discussing innovations demanded by new approaches to policy making. While evidence-based policy may be more developed in welfare than in some other areas of public policy, the chapter nevertheless concludes with a downbeat assessment of the significance of research evidence.

A history of evidence in welfare reform

It is impossible in the space available to detail fully the developing, symbiotic relationship between research and policy spanning over a century. Instead, a selective account is offered that is built around the contributions of three very influential researchers: Seebohm Rowntree, Peter Townsend and Richard Berthoud.

'A study of town life'

In 1892 Charles Booth published *Life and labour of the people of London* (Booth, 1892) which introduced the concept of a poverty line – a level of income below which people were counted as poor – and for the first time provided serious empirical estimates of the number of poor people in London (Marshall, 1981). The book attracted the interest of Seebohm Rowntree, heir to the Rowntree chocolate firm based in York, who remained unconvinced that poverty on the scale found in London could exist in a town such as York. Trained as a research chemist – but acting as a socially concerned businessman – Rowntree (1901) set out to employ his scientific training not only to establish the level of poverty in York but also to determine the reasons for it (Veit-Wilson, 1987).

Rowntree's investigators visited 11,560 households in York in 1899 – those of almost all the wage-earners in the town excluding those employing servants. Keen to distinguish between households with incomes too low to achieve a non-poor life-style (primary poverty) from those living in visible poverty for other reasons (secondary poverty), Rowntree devised a threshold level of income below which people could not maintain physical fitness. He concluded that 28% of the domestic population of York was poor and that 10% experienced primary poverty. The risk of poverty was highest among people without work, the aged and families with children. These findings – together with analysis by William Beveridge (1909) that showed that unemployment was beyond the control of any individual – were stimuli to the introduction of retirement pensions in 1908 and unemployment benefits in 1911 (Bruce, 1968).

Rowntree (1941) undertook a second study of social conditions in York in 1935. In this he used a new measure of poverty based on surveys of the budgets of working-class families, augmented by a 'minimal but conventional' diet, rent for 'decent' housing and a limited range of conventional social expenditures. Rowntree's work informed the Beveridge Committee's setting of the new National Assistance benefit levels, although the scales proposed were noticeably lower than the threshold used by Rowntree. There is some debate about whether this was due to muddle or mendacity (Veit-Wilson, 1992).

Rowntree lived to conduct another survey in York in 1950 (which for the first time used sampling techniques). It showed that the proportion of the working-class population with poverty-level income had fallen from 31% in 1936 to 2.7% in 1950 and that the new welfare measures were the biggest single cause. This study fed the belief that the postwar welfare state had succeeded in eradicating poverty, a view that was to prevail for half a generation.

'The poor and the poorest'

Complacency over the success of the welfare state was shattered in 1965 with the publication of Brian Abel-Smith and Peter Townsend's monograph *The poor and the poorest* (Bull, 1971). Based on an analysis of the 1960 Family Expenditure Survey, an official nationally representative probability sample, they concluded that two million people (3.8% of the population) had incomes below the National Assistance, means-tested, safety net (Abel-Smith and Townsend, 1965). In total, 7.7 million people (14.2%) had incomes below 140% of this level.

Townsend (1957) had earlier demonstrated that one third of a sample of pensioners in Bethnal Green had incomes below the National Assistance minimum and that between one fifth and one quarter were not receiving the National Assistance to which they were entitled. This stimulated an official enquiry by the Ministry of Pensions (MoP) which also revealed considerable poverty and non-take-up of benefits, seemingly because many pensioners viewed National Assistance as charity (MoP, 1966). What *The poor and the poorest* showed was that children accounted for a larger proportion of the poor than did pensioners (something that New Labour has recently rediscovered [Walker, 1999]). The creation of the Child Poverty Action Group, a research-based pressure group, followed and led indirectly to the introduction of Child Benefit in 1979 (Deacon and Bradshaw, 1983).

The Labour government's reaction in 1966 was to replace National Assistance with Supplementary Benefit. This blurred the distinction between insurance and the assistance benefits. It also included a more generous 'long-term' rate for all pensioners receiving a means-tested pension and for other claimants (excluding the unemployed) who had been on benefit for more than two years.

Reform of Supplementary Benefit

Supplementary Benefit was extensively reformed in 1980. By then, a Social Research Branch had been established in the Department of Health and Social Security (DHSS) that both undertook and commissioned research for the department. It commissioned Richard Berthoud (Policy Studies Institute) to evaluate the reform in what was one of the first large-scale evaluations of a social security benefit in Britain (Berthoud, 1984). The study is notable for its significant impact on policy, contributing to a comprehensive review of British social assistance and insurance provision in 1985 (Cmnd 9518, 1985a) that preceded the introduction of a number of new schemes in 1988 (including Income Support, Family Credit and the Social Fund).

A key component of the 1980 reform was to replace a discretionary system for meeting the exceptional needs of social assistance claimants with one based on regulation, and it was on this objective that the Policy Studies Institute focused. However, the evaluative components of the research were given rather less weight than the descriptive ones. The main report lists four project objectives: the first two were concerned with how 'normal families' managed 'their normal budgets on so low a level of weekly income' and the extent and nature of any exceptional expenses. The third objective was to assess 'how the [policy] arrangements for meeting special expenses worked out in practice', while the fourth included, almost as an afterthought, the question 'Has the 1980 formula produced the best system for meeting the needs of claimants?' (Berthoud, 1984).

The research comprised a home interview survey of a national probability sample of 1,772 claimants, interviews with a sample of 170 staff from the areas in which the claimant survey was drawn, analysis of claimants' social security records relating to claims for exceptional needs, and direct observation and discussion with staff in local benefits offices (Figure 7.1). An additional sub-study entailed local authority welfare rights officers visiting a proportion of the claimant sample to assess eligibility for payments to meet exceptional needs.

Figure 7.1: Evaluation of the 1980 changes to Supplementary Benefit

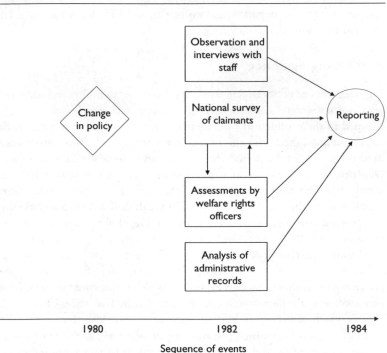

The study uncovered considerable financial hardship especially among couples with children. It revealed high levels of ignorance about the structure of the scheme and concluded that complexity made the scheme difficult for staff to understand. It also identified the pressures created by a labyrinthine paper-based system, problems in distinguishing exceptional need against a back-cloth of general hardships, and a de facto reliance on discretion because of the complexity of regulation leading to wide variation in the treatment accorded to claimants. This catalogue of 'failings' was sufficient to build a case for reform, but the absence of comparative data meant that the study provided only limited insight into whether the 1980 reforms improved or exacerbated the initial levels of financial hardship.

These three case studies illustrate that, even before the modern policy era, welfare policy in Britain was forged in the context of research evidence. Research techniques developed and improved with the advance of social science. The routine collection of statistics was increasingly accompanied by systematic analysis, and research moved into the heart of government, first serving ad hoc departmental enquiries and later forming a regular element in day-to-day policy making.

Purchasing evidence

The Department of Social Security (DSS) currently employs economists, operational researchers, statisticians and social researchers who are variously engaged in the production of evidence for policy. Much of their work remains unpublished with the result that it is impossible for an outsider to assess its impact on policy. Since the early 1980s virtually all of the Department's external research programme has been proactive and has mostly been let through competitive tender. Following a precedent established by the old Department of Health and Social Security, the Department now core funds two research centres (Policy Studies Institute, University of Westminster and Centre for Research in Social Policy, Loughborough University).

The visible tip of the Department's research effort is evident in the research programme published each year, which is informed by an annual consultation with the research community, and by two series of research reports which have been published since 1990 and 1993. Since virtually all externally commissioned research is published, the sustained growth in the number of reports published can be taken to index the increased importance of research, at least as measured in volume terms (Figure 7.2).

The balance in the objectives of the research programme, as reflected in the published reports, shifted over the 1990s in response to changes in policy preoccupations (Figure 7.3). There is of course a lag in these figures due to the time-lapse between commissioning and publishing research. Policy analysis studies, the objective of which variously involved some combination of the definition, specification and measurement of aspects of the policy environment, accounted for around half of the reports published in the 1990s. Customer satisfaction studies were most prevalent in the mid-1990s following the development of executive agencies and the inclusion of customer satisfaction as a performance criterion a little earlier. The policy focus on implementation, which was a feature of this period when efficiency savings were being sought as a method of holding back the escalating cost of welfare, is also evidenced by the growth of research concerned with operational efficiency.

Figure 7.2: Number of research reports published by the DSS (1990-99)

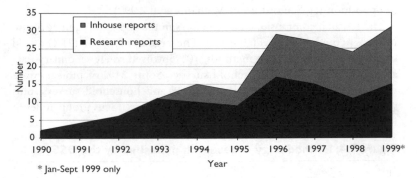
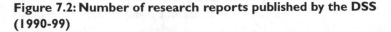

* Jan-Sept 1999 only

Figure 7.3: Objectives of research published by the DSS (1990-99)

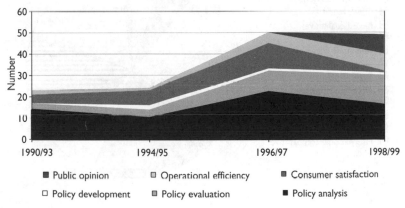
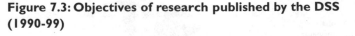

An increase in evaluation studies is the most marked feature of the late 1990s and, in part, reflects the commitment of the 1997 Labour government to piloting ahead of full policy implementation (see below). In fact, prior to 1996 it was not possible to undertake an impact evaluation or pilot a social security scheme prior to implementation since the law prohibited any geographical variation in the levels of benefits. However, the upturn in evaluation studies occurred some years before the 1997 election on account of HM Treasury's insistence that new policies should all be subject to post-implementation evaluation. This, in turn, was a response to the advance of the so-called new public management which placed increasing emphasis on financial control and monitoring (Carter and Greer, 1993; Stewart, 1996; Walker, 1997). The public opinion studies published in 1998 and 1999 reflect Labour ministers' initial desire to continue using polling and focus groups to develop policy as had happened in opposition (eg Stafford, 1998; Williams et al, 1999).

The research commissioned by the DSS in the 1990s was quite eclectic in terms of methodology (Figure 7.4). The largest proportion (21%) mixed quantitative and qualitative methods, 10% involved solely secondary data analysis and 10% solely household survey. Some 31% of projects were exclusively quantitative (postal, telephone and household surveys, plus secondary analysis) and 20% exclusively qualitative (focus group, indepth interview, observation).

Figure 7.4: Methodology of research published by the DSS

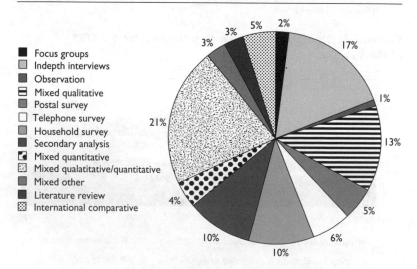

Over time (data not shown) standalone qualitative research has increased in importance (especially indepth interviews), as has secondary data analysis. The former trend may reflect a growing confidence in the value of qualitative research, not merely as a prelude to quantitative research but as a valuable tool with which to investigate issues and systems that lie beyond the scope of survey-based methodology (Walker, 1985a; Lessof and Squires, 1997). Secondary analysis includes the exploitation of computerised administrative records for research purposes. This mode of approach may become increasingly important as policy becomes more proactive and targeted on small sub-groups of the population (Ashworth, 1997).

Creating evidence

The aim in this section is to illustrate the ways in which research evidence has been sought and used by the DSS. A schematic model of the research process is presented in Figure 7.5. Policy questions are generally re-interpreted as research questions and a research design drawn up by inhouse research staff before going out to competitive tender. The design may be revisited by tendering organisations in their tender documents and revised before the research is commissioned and executed. Research contractors are frequently able to report their findings orally to policy customers and the latter will almost invariably receive the research report (normally accompanied by a briefing prepared by inhouse research staff). Sometimes research contractors report their findings directly to ministers (who will have been briefed by policy makers).

Figure 7.5: Research process

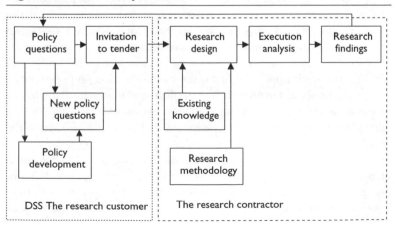

Four research projects in which the author was involved illustrate some of the differing kinds of research evidence and the contribution that they can make to the policy process. While this selection is not necessarily representative, it does offer an informed assessment of some of the uses made of the research findings.

Example 1: Policy development – Housing Benefit

The implementation of the 1982/83 Housing Benefit scheme by local authorities proved to be exceedingly problematic, which led the Thatcher government to commission an independent review of Housing Benefit. This, in turn, informed Green and White Papers on social security reform (Cmnd, 1985a, 1985b).

Research for the Review Team had demonstrated that some of the administrative difficulties were inherent in the structure of the scheme, which had merged earlier schemes within a common framework but largely failed to unify them (Walker, 1985b). This led to great complexity and made effective functioning of the scheme dependent on a degree of interagency liaison that was difficult to sustain. The White Paper addressed many of these issues but left key aspects of the reform to be decided. The Department chose to use research to tap into the expertise of those directly responsible for administering Housing Benefit in local authorities so as to ensure that new procedures would work (Walker et al, 1987).

The research was let by negotiated single tender. Senior Housing Benefit officials from a stratified random sample of 66 local authorities participated in a series of day-long research workshops, run at different times with groups varying in size from two to eight people. Two groups of officials met on two occasions a week apart. Their task was to review the government's detailed proposals and, on the second occasion, to suggest alternatives. Six other groups met once to evaluate the full set of proposals. Two self-completion questionnaires were administered, one before and one after the workshops. The first gathered information on performance indicators, the second mainly elicited a reflective response to all the policy proposals as refined during the course of the workshops. Follow-up telephone interviews were also conducted with a view to enriching the written responses.

One aspect of the consultation concerned the change in the definition of income used to assess a person's entitlement from gross to net. Initially, the government proposed that, rather than attempting to collect information on actual net income, a formula be used to assess a proxy 'notional' net income. Participants rejected the government's proposal as being too complex for rough and ready assessment but not sensitive enough to ensure equity. Over the course of the research, they moved increasingly in favour of assessment of actual net income, the approach that the government finally adopted.

Example 2: Policy analysis – barriers to moving off Income Support

In 1988 Income Support replaced Supplementary Benefit (the scheme studied by Berthoud). By 1994 it was paid in respect of 10 million people and the number of claimants of working age had increased markedly over time. So, too, had the average time that claimants spent on benefit. Policy developments in the USA were encouraging policy makers to think about the possibility of moving away from passive policies of income support to proactive ones that sought to help and encourage people to move off benefit. In this context the DSS issued an Invitation to Tender for largely qualitative research to:

> Examine the circumstances which permit people of working age to move off Income Support (and identifying those factors which inhibit movement) so as to provide a basis for developing strategies for reducing the lengths of spells on benefit.

However, the Department was persuaded in the tendering process that adequate qualitative material was available and that quantitative data was required if proactive policies were to be designed and implemented. To provide such data, a novel sampling strategy was devised to address the distortion inherent in cross-sectional samples of welfare recipients (which serve to over-represent long-term recipients at the expense of short-term ones [Ashworth and Walker, 1998]). Exploiting newly introduced administrative computer systems, a nationally representative probability sample was drawn of all people who had claimed benefit during almost a two-year period (the time since the computer system had been introduced). This sample, combined with employment and benefit histories collected using life-history techniques, enabled the duration of time spent on benefit and the incidence of repeated spells on benefit to be modelled and the socio-economic correlates determined. The research also collected information on the barriers that people reported as inhibiting their movement off benefit and explored these factors in relation to actual flows off benefit and into work or economic inactivity (Shaw, 1996).

The survey evidence, complemented by qualitative research, emphasised the importance of qualifications, work experience and health status as factors trapping people on benefit. There was no evidence that people increasingly became dependent on benefit as a direct consequence of spending long periods as claimants. The research also indicated that features of the benefit system (notably the need to change benefit regimes consequent upon starting work and the associated delays in processing claims) conspired to inhibit people moving off benefit.

Six policy initiatives undertaken by the last Conservative government were officially attributed to this research (DSS, 1996). It additionally helped to sustain the policy shift towards proactive policy that has been moved centre-stage by the 1997 Labour government with the implementation of its New Deal Welfare to Work policies (Bennett and Walker, 1998).

Example 3: Policy evaluation – the Social Fund

Post facto evaluation of national policies of the sort that was unavoidable prior to 1996 is very difficult. One byproduct of this difficulty was the creative use of multi-method designs that exploited ideas of pluralistic evaluation. Pluralistic approaches examine the effectiveness of policy with respect to the various and sometimes divergent objectives of different policy actors (Smith and Cantley, 1985).

One such evaluation concerned the Social Fund introduced in 1988 (Huby and Dix, 1992). The Social Fund is a system of largely discretionary loans and grants to meet the one-off needs of people living on social assistance which are paid from a fixed budget allocated to local offices. It replaced the system for meeting exceptional needs examined by Berthoud (see above).

The evaluation sought to determine the extent to which the Social Fund was targeted on people who were most in need, an objective which was complicated by the discretionary, budget-driven nature of the scheme. Only Social Fund officers using discretion could determine whether a person was eligible, but even their discretion was fettered by the budgetary constraints.

The approach adopted after competitive tender was to define four non-equivalent comparison groups (see Figure 7.6):
1. Successful applicants of the Social Fund
2. Applicants who had been refused an award

3. Income Support recipients who had not applied to the Social Fund (to establish how far need was going unmet)
4. Recipients of Housing Benefit (who are excluded from coverage of the Social Fund, but were included in the study as proxies for low-income families).

Figure 7.6: Evaluating the Social Fund

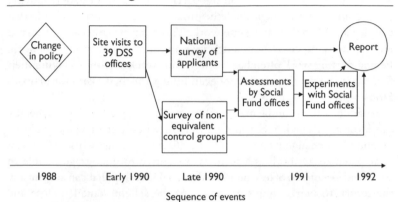

Stratified national samples were drawn from each group, clustered in 39 Benefit Agency Office areas (each office had previously been visited by the research team and officers at all levels were interviewed about the implementation of the scheme [Walker et al, 1992]). In total 1,724 structured home interviews were undertaken to collect information on incomes, perceived needs, 'objective' needs indices and budgeting strategies. Social Fund officers, seconded to the research team, revisited applicants to conduct need assessments with reference to the priorities and budgetary constraints of the appropriate local office in which they were temporarily based. Finally, 'laboratory experiments' were conducted in which Social Fund officers processed applications under different budgetary constraints.

The study showed that it was impossible to predict which applicants would be awarded payments from the Social Fund on the basis of objective or self-assessed measures of need. Officers varied noticeably in their interpretation of the regulations and reached very different decisions on the basis of the same facts, while the 'laboratory work' suggested that budgetary constraints were likely to have reduced the percentage of successful applications by 31%.

The Social Fund did not target help to those in greatest need as was intended. On the other hand, it did successfully cap expenditure on exceptional needs that no previous scheme had done. The scheme continues with only minor modifications.

Example 4: Operational efficiency – extended Housing Benefit

The research reviewed above on the barriers that prevent people moving off Income Support identified the financial uncertainty and risk that people face when they move into work. This often arises because claimants do not know precisely how much income they would receive in work. People starting work often have to wait four weeks before receiving their first wage cheque and sometimes even longer for their claim for in-work Housing Benefit to be processed.

To address these problems a facility was introduced in 1996 whereby the Housing Benefit received by a person while out of work could be extended unchanged for four weeks after taking up work. This was anticipated to act both as a financial incentive to encourage people to work and as a means of lessening the financial hardship that can accompany the return to work. Implementation of the scheme entailed close and timely liaison between Job Centres, Benefits Agency Offices and local authorities (the lack of which, as already noted, had frustrated the 1982/83 reform of Housing Benefit).

The number of people making use of this facility in early 1997 was less than expected and a qualitative project was commissioned via competitive tender to understand the administrative context. The research was necessarily conducted quickly, between mid-February and May 1997. Case studies were conducted in three areas to map the operating systems and patterns of liaison, and to identify the types of staff most knowledgeable about the system. On the basis of this intelligence, 90 staff in nine local authorities were then interviewed by telephone to elicit information of procedures. Finally, after conducting indepth interviews with successful and unsuccessful applicants and eligible non-claimants, group discussions were held with staff drawn from all 12 areas to review the evidence and to consider the policy implications (Stafford et al, 1998).

The study concluded that the scheme was failing to function as a work incentive because jobseekers were not being told about the scheme until they had secured a job. Publicity and promotion of the scheme was limited and liaison systems often broke down because there was no shared ownership of the scheme at local level.

Functions of applied research

The four studies described above serve to illustrate some of the different functions of applied research: policy analysis; policy development; policy evaluation; and the investigation of operational efficiency. They also emphasise the constraints and opportunities that are created by working closely under contract to the DSS. Almost direct access to policy makers, supported by substantial financial resources, is typically counterbalanced by tight research briefs and minimal timescales, often measured in weeks, and sometimes days, rather than years. However, the complexity of policy questions, the constraints of time and the demands of post facto evaluation stimulate creative methodologies that pioneer interdisciplinarity and mixed method approaches. The traditional tensions inherent in the diverse epistemological origins of differing methodologies, that have sometimes crippled intellectual advancement in the academic world, are used in an applied environment to enhance and enrich understanding of the social world with which policy has to interact.

New forms of evidence

While the DSS continues to commission research for a variety of purposes, policy evaluation has become increasingly important under the Labour government. All of the three case studies reported below involved the collection of evidence ahead of the implementation of a new policy and the latter two approach the classic model of evidence-based policy in which evaluation precedes implementation.

Example 5: Before and after designs – evaluation of the Jobseeker's Allowance

This case study concerns the evaluation of the Jobseeker's Allowance (JSA) which was introduced in October 1996 to replace the Unemployment Benefit and Income Support previously available to the unemployed. The new scheme integrated insurance and means-tested provision under a single system and among other changes required jobseekers to sign a Jobseeker's Agreement specifying the actions that they had to take to secure paid work.

The evaluation was initiated under the last Conservative government and was a byproduct of HM Treasury's insistence that all new policy initiatives should be accompanied by an evaluation strategy (McKay et al,

1997, 1999). Even so, while the evaluation was planned before policy implementation, there was never any intention that the evaluation should inform implementation. The early planning did mean that a comprehensive before-and-after design could be employed, although the detailed study design and questionnaire preparation still had to be accomplished within less than two months. The evaluation employed a cohort design with repeated measures and closely followed the approach proposed by the four commissioning departments and agencies in the call for tenders (see Figure 7.7).

A geographically clustered, stratified sample of 2,500 new and 2,500 existing claimants were interviewed twice, six months apart, before the introduction of JSA. A second cohort was drawn for interview in the same way approximately 12 months after implementation. The cohort samples were drawn approximately two years apart in autumn 1995 and 1997. The evaluation also included a number of qualitative studies, some of which focused on the experience of small sub-groups of unemployed claimants whose circumstances could not be addressed in detail in the main survey. Others considered specific aspects of the implementation of JSA.

All before-and-after designs are very susceptible to changes in the external environment and the JSA evaluation was no exception. There can be no guarantee of equivalence between the two cohorts since the sampling took place at different times. Claimant unemployment fell from 2.3 million to 1.6 million between July 1995 and July 1997. So it is possible that the composition of the in-flow into unemployment differed markedly between the different cohorts and that, for similar reasons, the employment opportunities available to jobseekers also changed. Weighting was used to try to disentangle differences in the behaviour of jobseekers that were attributable to these changes in the labour market from those that resulted from the introduction of JSA.

Despite the unavoidable limitations of the design, the full evaluation allowed policy makers to gain insight into the effects of the new system in ways that were not possible in the earlier evaluation of the 1980 Supplementary Benefit reform (Rayner et al, 2000; Smith et al, 2000).

Figure 7.7: Evaluation of Jobseeker's Allowance

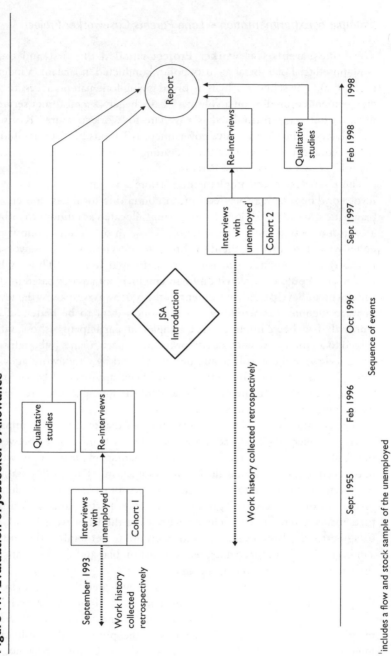

Sequence of events

[1] includes a flow and stock sample of the unemployed

Example 6: Experimentation – Lone Parents Caseworker Project

The Lone Parents Caseworker Project entailed the first and only randomised trial of a social security policy conducted in Britain (Vincent et al, 1996). The scheme, which involved giving lone parents access to an employment counsellor on a voluntary basis, began as a customer service initiative but was reformulated as a Welfare-to-Work measure. Revised and piloted by the Conservative government as 'Parents Plus' it was rapidly re-revised and repackaged by the incoming Labour government under the title 'New Deal for Lone Parents'.

The pilot design was implemented before a research contractor was involved. The scheme operated in four contrasting localities, chosen on pragmatic grounds, with lone parents being allocated at random to either a control or action group (Figure 7.8). Those in the action group were either written to, inviting them to come for interview with a caseworker at the Benefits Agency, or visited in their own homes. Those who participated could be directed on to an employment adviser based in the Employment Service. A key element in the process was to assess the level of wage income that would enable the lone parent to be better off in work. It had been intended that samples of participants (those who agreed to an interview with a caseworker), non-participants (who refused an interview) and controls would be interviewed by a fieldwork agency approximately six months after they had been approached by, or met with, a caseworker. In the event, because of the low take-up, interviews were sought with all participants.

The evaluation suffered many of the problems that tend to afflict impact analyses (Walker, 1997). The administration of the scheme differed between the four areas and changes in the implementation procedures were introduced at various times during the evaluation. The randomisation was carried out manually although this seemed not to destroy equivalence of the action and control groups. However, participants and non-participants differed in their characteristics and the latter were less likely to agree to the later evaluative interview or to remember the initial approach. This introduced a degree of selection bias and further reduced the sample size and power of the analysis.

A cost–benefit analysis was undertaken that evaluated the schemes from the perspectives of the financial well-being of the lone parent and the cost to the administration. Lone parents in the action group were marginally better off than the controls at the point of the evaluative interview. However, the results were largely driven by the experience of a small number of controls in one area who, for reasons which remain unclear, experienced a reduction in their claim on social security benefits that was large enough to offset increases in other incomes among the control group.

It had been intended that the evaluation of Parent Plus would also employ random allocation but the strategy was dropped by Labour ministers when New Deal for Lone Parents was piloted (possibly because of an unwillingness to deny lone mothers access to the putative benefits of the new scheme).

Figure 7.8: Evaluating the Lone Parents Caseworker Project

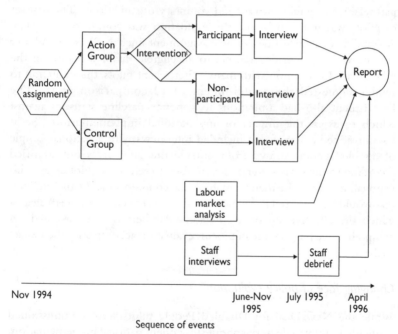

Nov 1994   June-Nov   July 1995   April
            1995   1996

Sequence of events

[1] The random assignment and caseworker interviews took place over the eight months of the pilot. The experiment was undertaken in four localities

Example 7: New Deal for Disabled People – a comparison group design

More typical of the design of the policy evaluations commissioned under the new Labour government is that for the New Deal for Disabled People personal adviser pilots (Walker, 1998). The aim was to determine whether recipients of Incapacity Benefit and certain other disability benefits would respond to an invitation to a work-focused interview with a personal adviser, and whether, with the assistance of personal advisers, more disabled people could secure and retain paid employment.

Two groups of six pilots were established in a range of labour markets, the first group run by the Employment Service and the second by partnerships of public, private and voluntary organisations. The first set of pilots was initiated before the evaluation was commissioned. The design did not allow for randomised assignment since the Personal Adviser Service was to be made available to all eligible disabled people in the pilot areas. In common with many other recent pilots, the invitation to tender suggested the establishment of 12 comparison areas. The Department also had aspirations to generate baseline statistics against which to assess the impact of any national implementation. So it commissioned a design that included interviews with a national sample of disabled people drawn from outside the pilot areas but stratified according to the same criteria as were used to select the pilot areas. This national survey is to be used to establish the counterfactual (ie the situation that would have existed if the New Deal had *not* been introduced) against which the effectiveness of the Personal Advisers is to be assessed. A comprehensive programme of process evaluation accompanies the impact analysis.

Changing face of policy evaluation

While the New Deal for Disabled People pilots were commissioned explicitly to inform decisions about subsequent national implementation, it was always intended that such decisions should be taken halfway through the two-year pilot and before the results of impact analyses were available. In such circumstances the advance of policy cannot fully benefit from sophisticated evaluation, or, at least, not in the short term.

Prospective policy evaluation aims to reduce the risk inherent in policy implementation. To date, the extent to which this has happened has been limited by the fact that policy has been developed ahead of evaluation.

Complex policies with many variants and great scope for varied implementation do not readily lend themselves to impact evaluation. In the US, it is increasingly the norm to design policy and implementation together so that the impact of a policy can be assessed with greater precision (internal validity). In Britain, the use of pilots has been more akin to prototyping than to experimentation, and it remains to be seen whether politicians will ever sacrifice the understandable desire to know more and accept that it may be better to know less but to know it more precisely.

It is also worth noting that the principal goal of impact evaluation in British welfare policy – to test out a policy with a view to large-scale, national implementation – is subtly different from the recent Welfare-to-Work demonstration projects in the US. The latter primarily seek to establish whether a policy works in a particular setting. In the British scenario, issues regarding the generalisability of the pilot results come to the fore. Because experiments are inherently exceptional, due in part to the experimental control that is necessarily exerted, the interpretation of the findings is always likely to be open to debate and external validity of the experiment will be somewhat limited. Since in Britain the use of pilots means that national policy making has to be deferred until at least some results are available, pilots have high visibility and are prone to be overtaken by political events.

Concluding remarks: the place of evidence

Although research-based evidence has played a role in the development of welfare policy since the inception of the modern welfare state, recent policy developments serve to make it more visible. The obligation on departments to develop an evaluation strategy for all new policies, and the Labour government's commitment to piloting ahead of implementation, have already influenced the research programme of the DSS. This is likely to be further affected by the government's commitment to audit the impact of its policies against recently published output criteria ('success measures') (Cm 4445, 1999).

However, several words of caution are in order lest the reader believe that research evidence will ever be the principal determinant of welfare policy. The case studies presented were not drawn at random but in order to illustrate the close symbiosis that is possible between research and policy. Each of the studies, from the 1984 Berthoud evaluation onwards, was commissioned by the DSS (and its predecessor department) explicitly to inform the policy process. However, happenstance still played a large role in determining the impact of each study. Berthoud's evaluation of Supplementary Benefit reported into an unanticipated extensive review of the social security system and was heavily used to justify policy changes (Cmnd 9518, 1985). Likewise, after publication of the White Paper (Cmnd 9691, 1985), the Department relied greatly on the policy development work with local authority Housing Benefit officials. But while the government accepted the local officials' views on the measurement of net income, they rejected many other ideas, including those on local liaison.

The policy analysis of barriers to moving off Income Support was also blessed by fortuitous timing. Reporting coincided with a sea-change in domestic and global policy opinion to reject passive social security policies in favour of active ones; employment came to be seen as a route to self-sufficiency and the antidote to benefit dependency. However, it is more difficult to establish how far the research shaped the six policy measures cited when it was published or whether it was primarily used to justify their introduction.

The Social Fund evaluation had less immediate effect. It is understood that reforms were proposed in the light of the research but found opposition within HM Treasury. Momentum for change was lost with the 1992 General Election and a change of ministerial team. Likewise, reporting on the study of extended Housing Benefit coincided with a change of government and its immediate impact was probably negligible. Nevertheless, it would be unwise to suggest that either project was futile. Policy development is often cyclical and if policy in these areas is revisited, the research findings will undoubtedly be exhumed.

And what are the prospects for new forms of evidence arising from the prospective piloting of policy? Evaluation has become part of the fabric of policy making. On the other hand, the experience to date suggests that the short-time horizons of policy making will outpace those of research. Political considerations, with an upper and lower case 'p', will continue to have precedence over those to do with research design. Ministers are likely to continue to reject random assignment for fear of adverse public reaction even in the rare cases where it is not ruled out by the desire of policy makers to establish system-wide effects. When results are uncomfortable and inconvenient they may well be overlooked in the short term.

So, even research commissioned within the bosom of government that reaches the desks of policy makers is not always influential, supplanted by the powerful political forces of inertia, momentum, expediency, ideology and finance (Greenberg et al, 1999). But, then, modern democracy is not

Plato's Republic. Rather, research evidence is just one influence on the policy process and, while the research community is free to argue that it should receive greater attention, it would be anti-democratic to insist that research evidence should be the prime consideration.

References

Abel-Smith, B. and Townsend, P. (1965) *The poor and the poorest*, London: Bell.

Ashworth, K. (1997) 'Practical applications of longitudinal analysis in social security research: the dynamics of Income Support', *Department of Social Security Research Yearbook, 1996/97*, London: The Stationery Office, pp 24-38.

Ashworth, K. and Walker, R. (1998) *Analysing social security provisions: The case for longitudinal data*, Inhouse report no 38, London: DSS.

Bennett, F. and Walker, R. (1998) *Working with work*, York: YPS for Joseph Rowntree Foundation.

Berthoud, R. (1984) *The reform of supplementary benefit*, London: PSI.

Beveridge, W. (1909) *Unemployment: A problem of industry*, London: Longmans Green.

Booth, C. (1892) *Life and labour of the people of London*, London: Macmillan.

Bruce, M. (1968) *The coming of the welfare state*, London: Batsford.

Bull, D. (1971) 'The rediscovery of family poverty', in D. Bull (ed) *Family poverty*, London: Duckworth, pp 13-18.

Bulmer, M. (ed) (1987) *Social science research and government: Comparative essays on Britain and the United States*, Cambridge: Cambridge University Press.

Carter, N. and Greer, P. (1993) 'Evaluating agencies: Next Steps and performance indicators', *Public Administration*, vol 71, no 4, pp 407-16.

(1999) *Opportunity for all: Tacking poverty and social exclusion, First Annual Report*, Cm 4445, London: The Stationery Office.

(1985a) *Reform of social security: Programme for change*, Cmnd 9518, London: HMSO.

(1985b) *Reform of social security: Programme for action*, Cmnd 9691, London: HMSO.

Deacon, A. and Bradshaw, J. (1983) *Reserved for the poor: The means test in British social policy*, Oxford: Basil Blackwell & Martin Robertson.

DSS (Department of Social Security) (1996) 'New research highlights importance of government's work incentive measures, says Roger Evans', London: DSS Press Release 29 August.

Greenberg, D., Mandell, M. and Walker, R. (1999) 'Learning from random assignment experiments in the US and Britain', Paper presented at the Association of Public Policy Analysis and Management, Washington, DC, 6 November.

Huby, M. and Dix, G. (1992) *Evaluating the Social Fund*, DSS Research Report No 9, London: HMSO.

Lessof, C., and Squires, E. (1997) 'Quality not quantity: using qualitative research for policy analysis and evaluation', *Department of Social Security Research Yearbook, 1996/97*, London: The Stationery Office, pp 39-53.

McKay, S., Walker, R. and Youngs, R. (1997) *Unemployment and jobseeking before Jobseeker's Allowance*, DSS Research Report No 73, London: HMSO.

McKay, S., Smith, A., Youngs, R. and Walker, R. (1999) *Unemployment and jobseeking after the introduction of Jobseeker's Allowance*, DSS Research Report No 87, London: HMSO.

Marshall, T. (1981) *The right to welfare and other essays*, London: Heinemann.

MoP (Ministry of Pensions and National Insurance) (1966) *Financial and other circumstances of retirement pensioners*, London: HMSO.

Rayner, E., Shah, S., White, R., Dawes, L. and Tinsley, K. (2000) 'Evaluating Jobseeker's Allowance: a summary of the research findings', *Research Report 116*, London: Corporate Document Services, DSS.

Rowntree, B.S. (1901) *Poverty: A study of town life*, London: Macmillan.

Rowntree, B.S. (1941) *Poverty and progress*, London: Macmillan.

Shaw, A. (1996) *Moving off Income Support: Barriers and bridges*, DSS Research Report No 79, London: The Stationery Office.

Smith, A., Youngs, A., Ashworth, K., McKay, S., Waler, R. with Elias, P. and McKnight, A. (2000) 'Understanding the impact of the Jobseeker's Allowance', *Research Report 111*, London: Corporate Document Services, DSS.

Smith, G. and Cantley, C. (1985) 'Policy evaluation: the use of varied data in the study of a psychogeriatric service', in R. Walker (ed) *Applied qualitative research*, Aldershot: Gower, pp 156-75.

Stafford, B., Heaver, C., Croden, N., Abel-Smith, A., Macguire, S. and Vincent, J. (1998) *Moving into work: Bridging housing costs*, DSS Research Report No 79, London: The Stationery Office.

Stafford, D. (1998) 'National Insurance and the contributory principle', *In-house Report 39*, London: Corporate Document Services, DSS.

Stewart, J. (1996) 'A dogma of our times – the separation of policy-making and implementation', *Public Money and Management*, July-September, pp 33-40.

Thomas, P. (1987) 'The use of social research: myths and models', in M. Bulmer (ed) *Social science research and government: Comparative essays on Britain and the United States*, Cambridge: Cambridge University Press, pp 51-60.

Townsend, P. (1957) *The family life of old people*, London: Routledge.

Veit-Wilson, J. (1987) 'Paradigms of poverty: a rehabilitation of B.S. Rowntree', *Journal of Social Policy*, vol 15, no 1, pp 69-99.

Veit-Wilson, J. (1992) 'Muddle of mendacity: the Beveridge Committee and the poverty line', *Journal of Social Policy*, vol 21, no 3, pp 269-301.

Vincent, J., Walker, R., Dobson, B., Stafford, B., Barnes, M. and Bottomley, D. (1996) *Lone Parent Caseworker Pilots evaluation*, Final Report, Working Paper 263, Loughborough: Centre for Research in Social Policy.

Walker, R. (ed) (1985a) *Applied qualitative research*, Aldershot: Gower.

Walker, R. (1985b) *Housing Benefit: The experience of implementation*, London: Housing Centre Trust.

Walker, R. (1997) 'Public policy evaluation in a centralised state', *Evaluation*, vol 3, no 5, pp 261-79.

Walker, R. (1998) *Britain's New Deal for disabled people: How will we know if it works?*, Association of Public Policy Analysis and Administration, Annual Conference, New York, 30 October. (Available as Centre for Research in Social Policy Working Paper 2240, Loughborough University.)

Walker, R. (1999) *Ending child poverty: Welfare for the 21st century*, Bristol: The Policy Press.

Walker, R., Dix, G. and Huby, M. (1992) *Working the Social Fund*, London: HMSO.

Walker, R., Hedges, A. and Massey, S. (1987) *Housing Benefit: Discussion about reform*, London: Housing Centre Trust.

Williams, J., Hill, M. and Davies, R. (1999) 'Attitudes to the welfare state and the response to reform', *Research Report 88*, London: Corporate Document Services, DSS.

EIGHT

Housing: linking theory and practice

Joe Doherty

Introduction

There is a long history of an association between housing research and housing policy in Britain. However, recent evaluations of this association show it to be uneven and inconsistent. Maclennan and Moore (1999), for example, conclude that "evidence has had an inconstant impact on UK housing policy and practice" (p 23). They attribute this inconstancy to deficient data "spread thinly on the ground" and to "a persistent unwillingness" on the part of policy makers to "clarify ends and means, so that key policy questions have remained unresolved" (pp 23 and 17). The blame, it appears – if blame is to be attributed – lies with both researchers and policy makers. Deficiencies on the part of researchers are attributed to the adoption of inadequate methodologies and to the relative neglect of policy relevant concepts such as "effectiveness" and "cost-benefit" analysis (p 23). Deficiencies in policy are revealed in the ambiguity and obfuscation that surround the formulation and implementation of housing policy. While successive governments have adopted and proclaimed universalistic objectives such as the provision of 'decent' and 'affordable' homes, these terms have never been clearly defined and the means and methods for their achievement have not been adequately specified (Maclennan and Moore, 1999, p 22).

This chapter starts with an historical overview which suggests that, with some exceptions, the current inconstancy, identified by Maclennan and Moore, has been a common characteristic of the relationship between housing research and British housing policy during the past 150 years. Building on this overview, a more detailed examination of the present day relationship reveals an apparent paradox whereby, at a time of unprecedented output, research evidence – although central to the evaluation of housing practice – seemingly rarely percolates through the machinery of government to impact directly on housing policy formulation and implementation. Two potential and complementary contributions to this paradox are examined:

- the changing nature of housing policy and its increasing complexity as it is implicated in a multitude of social, economic and political problems beyond the mere provision of shelter;
- the 'filtering' role played by political ideology in determining the relationship between evidence and the shaping of policy agendas.

The concluding section of the chapter reflects on the possible opening up of new channels whereby research evidence may have the opportunity to influence policy, and on the changing nature of evidence which has arisen from a re-examination of the research process by feminists and post-structuralists.

Nature of evidence

A history of housing research and housing policy

The association between housing research and housing policy in Britain dates from the 19th century with Edwin Chadwick's work on the links between environmental health and housing. Research and policy expanded thereafter, during the course of the early and mid-20th century, to embrace the sources and adequacy of housing provision and the social conditions of housing, including issues of affordability, tenure and finance. More recently the links between housing and such issues as ethnicity, the quality of life, crime and sustainability have attracted the attention of researchers and policy makers. Today much housing research concentrates on management issues with an emphasis on information gathering and monitoring, a focus which Robertson and McLaughlin (1996) attribute to the recent growth in the research requirements of individual housing organisations and, we can add, central government departments and agencies. Robertson and McLaughlin also note that with the revival of interest in the relationship between housing and health, research and policy have come full circle to embrace again some of the preoccupations of the 19th century.

Paralleling this expansion in the scope of housing research, the past

150 years has seen a vast increase in the number and variety of agencies involved in gathering and presenting evidence and arguing for policy change and innovation. Central and local government and philanthropic individuals and organisations dominated the mid and late 19th century. During the 20th century these were joined first by professional and campaigning groups and then by academics and, particularly in recent years, market research agencies and individual housing organisations.

Edwin Chadwick, the 19th century Poor Law Commissioner (1834-46), is commonly identified as the pioneer of research into housing conditions in Britain. His research initiated a process of improvement, albeit piecemeal, in the housing and environmental condition of Britain's burgeoning industrial cities. Chadwick's investigations were mirrored later in the century by Charles Booth and Seebohm Rowntree (also influential in welfare reform – see Chapter Seven). These studies, together with several philanthropic housing 'experiments' (such as Port Sunlight and Bourneville), furnished significant information on housing conditions and provided clear demonstrations of what could be accomplished by agencies beyond the private sector. However, the most influential research in terms of policy impacts in this period was conducted by local and central government. Municipal Commissions investigated local conditions, while the Royal Commission on Housing (1884-85) looked at the national scene. The accumulated evidence led directly to legislation controlling overcrowding and permitting the selective demolition and rebuilding of slum property by municipal authorities. It also led to the 1890 Housing Act which imposed on these same authorities the responsibility of rehousing those displaced. Though national in scope, the impact of this legislation, while not inconsiderable, was predominantly confined to the larger metropolitan areas such as London and Glasgow, and was on a relatively small scale when compared to the overall dimensions of the problem.

At the turn of the century, pressures from groups such as the Working Men's National Housing Conference (1898) and Scottish Miners' Federation (1909), combined to maintain interest in housing and to stimulate the gathering of evidence on the quality of working-class living conditions. The 1919 Addison Act, along with the 1923 Wheatley Act, gave legislative expression to the conclusion drawn from the accumulated evidence that the private sector could not be relied upon to provide adequate housing for the country's working class. These two Acts are frequently cited as laying the legislative foundations for six decades of council house construction in Britain (Merrett, 1979, pp 31-60).

The interventionist role of the state in housing provision, as in other areas of social policy, steadily increased during the inter-war years. Much of the housing research conducted during this period focused on two areas: the production of technical manuals to assist local authorities in the construction of council houses and on monitoring the impact of rent restrictions introduced after the Glasgow and London rent strikes of 1915 (Robertson and McLaughlin, 1996, p 22). Rapidly accumulating evidence of the limited impact of council housing on inner city slums stimulated further legislation in 1930 and 1933 which switched housing subsidies from the number of houses built to the number of people rehoused. This shift in policy provides an early example of how political expediency (the need to be seen to be doing something about a continuing social problem) and financial exigency (the 1920s subsidies were placing a heavy burden on increasingly pressured government finance) combined to initiate policy change. This change helped to meet short-term ends (the rehousing of inner-city slum dwellers), but in the final analysis it can be judged as undermining the long-term effectiveness of housing policy. In contrast to the council estates of the 1920s, many of which remain as sound dwellings, houses built under the 1930s' subsidy regime led to the creation of stigmatised estates which rapidly revealed construction deficiencies and eventually became slums in their own right. Most have now been demolished and replaced.

A post Second World War national consensus on housing was evident in the adoption by all political parties of a commitment to slum clearance and the making good of war-damaged housing. The central role of the state in this process was also accepted across the political spectrum. In a period in which objectives and methods were uncontested, research was largely confined to technical matters relating to issues of space and design involving predominantly, but not exclusively, architects and engineers. Few academics were involved in housing research during this period and local authorities only infrequently employed professional researchers. As a consequence, Robertson and McLaughlin observe "policy was made solely on the basis of local politics and adhering to centrally generated guidance" (1996, pp 22-3).

Housing policy during the 1950s and 1960s was directed almost exclusively at demolition and rebuild with the provision of replacement housing in situ and of new housing on the peripheries of towns and cities. These redevelopment programmes, together with the construction of New Towns, made considerable inroads across the country into the problems of war-damaged housing and those of slum properties inherited from the 19th century. Yet the persistence of these problems, especially in the larger metropolitan centres, and the emergence of new problems associated with the replacement housing, eventually brought into question the efficacy of the redevelopment policies; a question which was encouraged by the findings of housing research conducted by an emerging and growing body of independent academics. Various studies (Young and Willmott, 1957; Willmott and Young, 1960; Rex and Moore, 1967; Coates and Silburn, 1970) all highlighted the emergence of new problems overlooked by the technical emphasis of research during the postwar drive for new and replacement housing.

While the Conservative Macmillan government of 1957-63 was the first to challenge the postwar consensus by questioning the mass provision of housing by the state, it was under the Labour administration of Harold Wilson (1964-70) that the research on alternative housing policies began to emerge. The independent Joseph Rowntree Trust had been financing housing research since the late 1950s, but it was not until the latter part of the 1960s that urban and housing research began to take off with the opening of three important research establishments: the University of Birmingham's Centre for Urban and Regional Studies (CURS) and two quasi-government 'think-tanks', the CES (Centre for Environmental Studies) and SCPR (Social and Community Planning Research). When the television docu-narrative 'Cathy Come Home' effectively breathed life into the campaigning organisation Shelter in 1968, many of the key players, who were to dominate housing research for the next quarter of a century, were in place: philanthropic organisations, academics, central government-sponsored think-tanks and campaigning groups. The 'team' was completed in the early 1970s with the emergence of local authority housing research units, following the reorganisation of local government in 1974/75, and the reinvigoration of The Housing Corporation (inaugurated in 1964), following the introduction of a subsidy system for financing housing associations in 1974.

With the 1969 Housing Act, policy moved decisively away from two-and-a-half decades of demolition and rebuild towards an emphasis on renovation and conservation. Yet, notwithstanding the accumulation of evidence of mounting problems, it was often other events which moved government to action. For example, while a growing body of research evidence clearly demonstrated the harmful social effects of high-rise housing, it was not until the Ronan Point disaster of 1968, when a gas explosion in a tower block on an East London estate killed several people and destroyed the building, that a halt was finally called to further multi-storey construction.

The creation of the School for Advanced Urban Studies (SAUS), as a joint project of the Department of the Environment and the University of Bristol in 1974, illustrates the continuing growth of the relationship between housing research and housing policy during this period. A liaison which was further cemented with the initiation of a series of government-sponsored urban studies during the early 1970s (for example, CDP, 1976, 1977; Benwell CDP, 1978). It has been argued, with some legitimacy, that for a time during the 1970s, housing research and policy were more closely associated than in any previous or subsequent period (Robertson and McLaughlin, 1996).

The Conservative governments of the 1980s rapidly curtailed many of the more direct links that had been established between research and policy – the CES, for example, was closed – and political ideology and expediency emerged overtly as the engines of housing policy, often to the neglect of substantive research evidence. Such developments were apparent in the manner in which 'Right to Buy' (the right of sitting tenants to purchase their council houses at substantial discounts) was introduced and pursued throughout the 1980s. While this policy clearly bought the government of the day considerable political support, it was enacted and energetically pursued throughout the decade in the face of mounting evidence concerning the detrimental effects of mortgage debt and housing repossessions and the accumulation of problems arising from the neglect of essential repair and maintenance by households whose budgets were over-stretched by the cost of purchase. The English House Condition Survey of 1996 reflected some of these issues in recording the need for £50 billion of expenditure for comprehensive repairs in the owner-occupied sector.

While a disjuncture between housing research and the policy formulation can be identified during the years of Conservative governments, independent research continued to monitor, often critically, the impact of government policies. The academic profile of housing research actually increased during the 1980s: academic professorships in housing were established at several universities and in 1984 the Economic and Social Research Council set up the Centre for Housing Research at Glasgow University. The Joseph Rowntree Trust (benefiting from a buy-out windfall following the takeover of Rowntree chocolate manufacturers by Nestlé) was reinvigorated and renamed the Joseph Rowntree Foundation. Building on the historic role of the Trust, the Foundation developed an explicit remit to influence government housing policy and emerged as a major source of funds for research particularly in housing finance and tenure.

In the 1990s, a number of demands combined to encourage research, particularly in the evaluation and monitoring of policy implementation and practice. These included the research demands of the government-established funders and monitors of the so-called voluntary housing sector (The Housing Corporation, Scottish Homes, and Tai Cymru, in Wales), the statutory requirement for local authorities to draw up housing plans, the introduction of compulsory competitive tendering, and later, 'best value' criteria, and the need for all publicly-funded housing agencies to meet performance targets. Today research and evidence collation on housing are proceeding at an unprecedented rate. In the financial year 1998-99, for example, the DETR spent £5.2 million on housing research. More than 25 new projects were commissioned covering issues such as youth homelessness, difficult-to-let housing, guidance on good practice for housing providers and guidance to local authorities on specifying cost-effective stock condition surveys. As these funded projects indicate, housing research, although strongly policy orientated, has become increasingly reactive and evaluative of practice rather than proactive and innovative of policy.

What evidence for what policy?

The conclusion to the above overview suggests that housing research is flourishing. However, at a time of buoyant output, which is widely distributed in academic, peer-refereed journals and in the research reports of a variety of housing trusts and agencies, research evidence seems to only rarely impact directly on the derivation and formulation of government housing policy. A partial explanation for this paradox is to be found in the nature of the research being conducted (see next sub-section). Driven in part by the requirements currently emanating from government agencies, housing research has moved away from "researching issues to evaluating operations" (Robertson and McLaughlin, 1996, p 27). However, a fuller explanation of the paradox requires an examination of two further issues: the growing complexity of housing policy and the role of ideology in the policy process. These latter two issues are considered below (in the section on 'Using the evidence').

Current state of housing evidence

Driven by the demand for policy and user-orientated research the culture of research contracts has been embraced by universities. Academics now regularly compete with commercial agencies for lucrative contracts that have a predominantly monitoring and evaluative purpose. Examples of such research are to be found in a multitude of reports and findings relating to housing provision at both the local and national scales. While perhaps constituting an example of "poor data" (Maclennan and Moore, 1999, p 23) – in that this type of research is sometimes deficient, even in relation to its own objectives, and does not impact directly on the formulation of policy – it should not be dismissed as insignificant or unimportant. At a national level extensive databases on a variety of housing issues have been accumulating over the past 10 years. Some of these provide only snapshot views (for example, the national House Condition Surveys and the periodic General Household Survey); others attempt to provide a continuous recording of data. The CORE and SCORE (acronyms for COntinuous REcording and Scottish COntinuous REecording) databases are the longest standing examples of continuous recording systems in Britain. They collect information on the dwelling and household characteristics of new tenants of registered social landlords in England (CORE) and housing associations in Scotland (SCORE). Such databases document the 'state of play' and, in monitoring performance, provide valuable evidence of what has been achieved as well as guidance to responsible organisations on what remains to be done. Complementing these national surveys, a plethora of local surveys and assessments of housing provision and housing conditions have been produced over the past decade. Tenant surveys, for instance, are now a regular feature of the activities of housing providers, supplying information on topics as varied as tenants' levels of satisfaction with their present housing and tenant preferences with regard to stock and landlord transfers. Such surveys inform practice and can initiate change. While some of this work is conducted 'inhouse', particularly in larger housing organisations which have their own research staff, the bulk of it is produced by academic researchers and by market research agencies working under commission to central government quangos, local authorities and housing associations.

In concluding their survey of past and present day housing research, Robertson and McLaughlin observe that,

... [i]t has become very much more policy focused, moving downwards from providing research that informs the national policy agenda to providing a similar capacity at a local operational scale. Research, in one sense, could now be viewed as the servant of the housing profession and the wider housing 'policy community'. Rather than helping to set policy agendas, however, in its new operational role research rarely challenges the constraints in which policy operates. There has also been a move away from researching issues to evaluating operations. Such an approach certainly has merit, in better informing those working in housing, but it also has clear limitations. (Robertson and McLaughlin, 1996, p 27)

Clear limitations exist certainly, but such national and local surveys, while having only an indirect influence on policy agendas, have an immediate and direct impact on policy implementation and practice by assisting housing agencies and their funders and regulators in making judgements about the fulfilment of statutory duties and responsibilities. As such they should not be trivialised, for they are central in determining the day-to-day housing experience of tenants with regard to such crucial issues as rent affordability and housing standards. This type of research is likely to continue and to grow in importance. Housing conditions and housing provision are not static; patterns of need, demand and supply alter over time responding to changing social, economic and political contexts. At a basic level, as society becomes more affluent, the demand for inside toilets is satisfied and is replaced by demands for higher insulation standards – the same standards that are of growing concern to environmentalists intent on designing and producing sustainable housing. Demographic transformations such as those reflected in an ageing population, increased household formation and the multiplication of single and childless households, create a need for new and variable house sizes and designs. Shifting regional economic fortunes are reflected in increased demand for housing in one area and decline in another. In such changing circumstances, evidence from periodic surveys and continuous monitoring is an essential prerequisite for effective and efficient delivery of housing provision.

The predilection (if such it is) for housing research to focus on the accumulation of factual and quantitative evidence concerning performance and practice, may reflect the origins of housing research in an empirical, multidisciplinary tradition (Kemeny, 1992, Chapters 1 and 2). Housing studies as an academic discipline has developed in close parallel with a growing professionalism in housing training and has had, in consequence, a decided practical inclination. Even today many housing courses that aspire to recognition by the Chartered Institute of Housing tend to focus on the practice more than the analysis of housing. However, theoretical inclinations have never been entirely absent. Rex and Moore's development in the 1960s of the concept of 'housing classes' provides an early example (Rex and Moore, 1967), as does the work of Clarke and Ginsburg (1976) and Forrest and Lloyd (1978) on the relationship between housing and the state and that of Ball (1983) on housing and the economy. Twenty years on, theoretical and conceptual issues have an increasingly prominent place, with organisations such as the Housing Studies Association and the European Network for Housing Research consciously and deliberately promoting theoretical work. The launch of the journal *Housing Studies* in 1984, its upgrading under a different format in 1994 and its emergence as the premier English language journal for housing research, together with the recent name change of the journal *Scandinavian Housing and Planning Research* to *Housing Theory and Society* are all indicative of the rising status of housing studies as a credible research discipline. This trend has been further enhanced by the relatively recent expansion in comparative research on housing provision in Europe and the USA (see Harloe, 1985; Barlow and Duncan, 1994; Kleinman, 1996; Edgar et al, 1999).

While these developments increase the profile and credibility of housing studies, the paradox remains, that despite a growing and increasingly credible output, housing research continues to be relatively distanced from influencing the development of housing policy agendas. While a number of channels of communication between government and researchers have recently been opened to facilitate the transfer of ideas (such as the Scottish Housing Network established by the Scottish Office in 1997), much of the contact between government policy makers and researchers is ad hoc and at an individual level. Further unravelling of the paradox requires an examination of recent changes in the nature of housing policy, or perhaps more accurately, changing government perceptions of the nature of the housing problem.

Using the evidence

Housing policy

Over the past two decades housing as a policy issue in Britain seems to have slipped down the political agenda. Public investment in housing has been cut year-on-year since the mid-1980s and there was little coverage of housing in the 1992 and 1997 General Elections. The 'national' Green Paper on housing, scheduled for publication in 1999, was postponed to spring 2000, although a Scottish version was published in March 1999. However, to interpret these trends as indicators of a 'terminal decline' of housing policy (Bramley, 1997, p 387) would overstate the case. A more measured interpretation might see them as indicative not so much of a decline in the importance of the issue to government, but of a shift in the way housing policy is perceived by government. In the 1970s housing policy objectives were concisely identified by successive administrations. In both the Conservative government's White Paper of 1971 and in the Labour government's Green Paper of 1977 the emphasis was directed squarely at the provision of 'decent' and 'affordable' housing.

Today, for most of Britain's population (with some notable exceptions), past problems of overall housing shortage and unacceptable accommodation standards have been resolved. Government policy objectives have, as a consequence, moved on and housing has been increasingly absorbed into wider policy considerations. Housing problems are not now seen in exclusively housing terms; they are coupled with issues of sustainability, social exclusion, regeneration, and so on. What might in the past have been seen as a quintessential housing problem – homelessness – is presented in the government's Rough Sleepers Initiative as an issue of life-style, more to do with personal choice and behavioural problems (drug addiction and social dysfunction) than with structural problems in the housing market (shortage of affordable housing). Such interpretations, which focus on the so-called pathological behaviour of individuals and ignore the structural features of the operation of the housing market, have been contested (see, for example, Kemeny, 1992). Similarly, in relation to issues of neighbourhood renewal and estate (formerly known as *housing* estate) regeneration, housing ranks as only one issue alongside employment and community development.

The identification of multifaceted problems in which housing is implicated invariably leads to conflicts and tensions between different government departments and between different vested interests.

Consequently, this obscures, or at least blurs, the housing dimensions of the problem. The current debate concerning the need to cope with the predicted 16-year national increases in the demand for housing demonstrates this point. Overall it is estimated that in order to cope with population increases, new household formation and deterioration of existing stock Britain will require 4.4 million new homes by 2016; it is presently calculated that 900,000 of these will be needed in the South East of England. The debate over this issue is primarily conducted in terms of the environmental impact of such developments, particularly in the already badly congested South East. A second issue of concern is the question of the regional imbalance that will be exacerbated by a further focus of population growth in the south to the detriment of the north. In comparison, questions specifically relating to housing – the accuracy of the estimates with regard to population increases and housing need and the mix required in the provision of market and social housing – receive little attention. It is perhaps indicative of the relative importance that government attributes to housing per se that it has brought in an economist, rather than a housing expert, to review and assess SERPLAN, the regional plan devised by local authorities in the South East to deal with the anticipated expansion.

Yet, in other contexts, housing still has a starring, if controversial role. Accounting for 40% of all personal wealth and one fifth by value of national consumption (Maclennan and Moore, 1999, p 17), housing is an important component of the national economy, as both a barometer of economic health and as a driver of economic change. As such the Treasury, especially since the housing boom of the late 1980s, has a vital and intrinsic interest in housing issues. The decision in November 1999 to lift interest rates (now taken by a panel of government-appointed, independent experts) was motivated by a need to quell rising property prices – led by housing and not other areas of the property market, such as business premises – in the South East of England, a decision bitterly criticised by representatives of the manufacturing industry as being detrimental to their export trade.

The absorption of housing into a wider frame of reference whereby it is seen as a part – and not necessarily the most important part – of wider problems is now a common characteristic of policy development. Housing issues today are no longer seen solely in terms of the provision of shelter; they are now manifest as part of complex problems which require multifaceted solutions. The evidence required to deal with these complex problems must come not just from housing but from a broader range of sources including, among others, social policy, environmental economics and social psychology.

Some explanation of the paradox – whereby increases in housing research output have little or no direct impact on policy making – may then be found in an apparent mismatch between the widening and increasingly complex identification of the nature of housing problems and the type of research being conducted. The challenge to housing researchers, if they are to contribute meaningfully to the derivation and formulation of policy, is to come up with a clear understanding of the manner in which housing is inscribed in these complex problems and the role that it has to play as part of a multifaceted solution. The variety of research topics covered in recent issues of the housing professional and trade journals and in academic publications illustrates the positive manner in which researchers and practitioners are responding to the challenge. The recent special issue of *Housing Studies* (1998) on social exclusion is indicative that researchers have recognised the multifaceted arena in which housing now sits. The growing number of studies which link housing to wider social issues are further testament to this: for example, Gilroy and Woods (1994) on gender, Cowans (1998) on community and Cairncross et al (1996) on tenant empowerment.

Ideology and evidence in the formulation of housing policy

Further decoding of the paradox of the apparent neglect of evidence at a time of accelerated research output, requires a movement from an examination of a possible mismatch between problem definition and research focus, to a consideration of the role of political ideology. Maclennan and Moore identify "strong ideological stances" and "preferences" in the development of housing policy and practices (Maclennan and Moore, 1999, p 17). However, the examples they give – the pre-1975 preoccupation with council housing and the 1980s' obsession with home ownership – while undoubtedly important in directing the details of housing practice, underplay the rather more profound influence of ideology in determining the nature of policy agendas. Maclennan and Moore's account also underestimates the role that housing policy itself has played in promoting ideologically driven programmes; for example, in spearheading privatisation through 'Right to Buy' and assisting in the reduction of direct state involvement in public policy by promoting alternative providers of social housing. The notion that public policy, including housing policy, is evidence driven is itself a reflection of an ideology, the ideology of scientism. Scientism claims that the social and economic world, like the natural world, can be understood by the correct application of science, that it is susceptible to rational and objective examination. It implies that "decisions which might formerly have been considered exercises of power, and hence political, are not in fact political decisions at all, but scientific or rational ones" (Rosenhead and Thunhurst, 1979, p 299). Maclennan and Moore's plea for the adoption by housing researchers of a more scientific methodology such as that associated with "cost-benefit thinking" (1999, p 23) can be cited as an example of the perpetuation of this particular ideological stance.

Crudely put, ideology acts as a purposeful 'filter' through which evidence is passed and selected before it impacts on policy. Evidence which runs counter to current ideological stances tends to be questioned and downplayed; evidence which supports the prevailing ideology is accepted and cited. Scientism accords with a view of the state (and hence of government) as a neutral arbiter, standing above class and other vested interests and working in the 'national' interest of society as a whole. In contrast, an approach that sees the relationship between evidence and policy as ideological, accords with a view of the state as representative of the dominant interests in society, which, in a capitalist society such as Britain, is capital itself. However, the picture is complicated by the fact that the state is not an unity, it is fragmented and divided (as indeed is capital) and in relation to housing policy some of the more important of these divisions are between local and central government, and between successive administrations. The implication of these observations is that while, at a particular historical conjuncture, a dominant ideology may be identifiable, it is rarely hegemonic; dominant ideologies will have rivals and be contested. But the fact that we need to talk in plural rather than singular terms does not invalidate the observation that ideology enters the policy process to mediate the impact of evidence.

Ideological conflict runs deep in the development of housing policy. Since its emergence in the first half of the 19th century, housing policy in Britain has been characterised by two contrasting views of housing as either a commodity or as a social service; that is, as a consumption good, catered for by the market, or as a public good provided by the state. While no administration has committed itself exclusively to one or other of these positions, traditionally the former has been favoured by Conservative governments and the latter by Labour administrations. Conservative administrations, although inclined to a commodity view, have (at least until the advent of the Thatcher governments of the 1980s) accepted elements of a service approach in attempts to ensure the provision of a decent home for all at an affordable cost. Labour administrations, again until recently, have ostensibly favoured a service approach, but have been unwilling to challenge market provision and have ended up with what we might label as a 'social utility' approach. Unlike health and education, housing as a public policy issue has never been fully taken on board; it has only ever been partially decommodified. One of the, perhaps inevitable, results has been an uncertain role for local authority housing. While undoubtedly providing high amenity housing for the first time for many households across the nation, particularly in the immediate postwar years, the historic judgement has been effectively to characterise council property as residual housing.

Ideological conflicts of the past have been replaced today by a growing convergence between political parties. Over the past two decades, both Conservative and Labour governments have shown an increasing commitment to individualism. Advanced vigorously under Thatcherism and manifest most famously in the declaration that 'there is no such thing as society, only individuals and their families', a less strident version of individualism was adopted under John Major in the pursuit of 'active citizenship' and it remains a founding principle of Blair's 'third way' communitarianism. The ideology of individualism, in advancing the notion that people have to take responsibility for themselves and their own actions, has at least two practical consequences which impinge on housing policy. First, it implies opposition to the interference of the state in the affairs of individuals and, second, it creates a framework for the adoption of a 'blame the victim' diagnostic when assigning responsibility for social ills, thereby apparently obviating the need for structural reforms.

In the realm of housing policy, individualism leads to privatisation and the 'rolling back of the state', of which Right to Buy is the clearest demonstration, now reinforced by large-scale stock transfers of housing from public to semi-public (housing associations) and quasi-market (local housing companies) organisations. These developments have the effect of further exacerbating residualisation particularly since no new investment is being made in replacement council housing.

However, the problem of residualisation or – in the language of individualism – 'unbalanced communities' is not exclusive to council properties; it is also a feature of some housing association estates (Power, 1999). Under the conceptual umbrella of social inclusion, government proposals for a solution to the problems of these 'unbalanced' estates illustrates clearly the way in which ideology filters evidence in determining policy.

In the current Labour government's proposals, difficult-to-let, stigmatised, residual housing estates are defined by the overconcentration of poor, predominantly unemployed households. The solution is the creation of 'mixed tenure' and 'mixed income' communities. The mechanism for achieving this is the abandonment of the traditional needs-based allocation system used by social landlords to permit the allocation of housing to a greater range of households, a proportion of which would be economically active and who would make a positive contribution to the community. These ideas have been widely debated (for example Housing Standing Conference, 1998) and frequently enthusiastically endorsed (for example, Cowans, 1999). Such notions are consistent with an individualist ideology that views employed homeowners as the epitome of respectability; individuals who have taken responsibility for themselves and can provide role models of exemplary behaviour for the seemingly 'feckless' residents of 'unbalanced' housing estates. The pre-Budget report (November 1999) from the Chancellor of the Exchequer previewed these policies. A 'sounding board' team was established to work up details of the programme for inclusion in the Green Paper on Housing which was published in early 2000 (*Housing Today*, 1999; DETR, 2000). They were also aired in the Scottish Green Paper on housing (Scottish Office, 1999)

Cautionary comments, from organisations such as Shelter and Demos (*Housing Today*, 1999; Jupp, 1999) on these proposals are, it seems, being disregarded. Similarly, it seems that the wealth of historical evidence on the past success of low-income, single tenure estates (Young and Willmott, 1957) and more recent evidence from Europe and the USA which throws doubt upon and questions the efficacy of such policies (see Schwartz and Tajbakhsh, 1997; Power, 1997) has also been ignored. Anne Power, for example, concludes her authoritative, six-year study of five low-income housing estates across northern Europe – estates on which the ownership, management and letting patterns diverge sharply – with the judgement that "in no case did the ownership structure protect the estates from cataclysmic decline" (Power, 1997, p 271).

Concluding remarks

Evidence that can effectively inform housing policy and practice comes from several sources – national surveys as well as local indepth investigations. This chapter has identified several reasons as to why such evidence may be more effective at informing policy practice than policy formulation. However, the 'open' government policy initiated under the Conservative administration in 1994 in association with the launch of its 'Citizen Charter' and the subsequent development of this concept by the present Labour administration might provide an opportunity for researchers to increase their influence on housing policy formulation.

It is tempting to dismiss the 'open government' stance as political expediency, and time will tell. However, the Labour administration supports more than 300 task forces and advisory panels, has convened numerous discussion forums and devotes considerable expenditure to canvassing the opinions of the public (Cohen, 1999). The recent Scottish Green Paper (Scottish Office, 1999) includes a series of invitations to readers to convey their views and opinions to the Scottish Executive.

The door to influencing policy formulation, as well as practice, may have opened a crack, offering an opportunity to researchers. Whether the door can be prized open further may be as much in the hands of the research community as in the hands of government.

However, there are other challenges to housing research emanating from within the discipline of housing studies as it has become theoretically more sophisticated, embracing and applying some of the concepts developed elsewhere in the social sciences. These raise questions about the worth and relevance of some of the evidence presently being developed. The challenge within housing studies is to the prevailing scientism or, perhaps more accurately, the residual scientism of the research agenda. Inspired by both feminist and post-structuralist approaches, the demand is for 'experiential' evidence that moves beyond the collection of statistical indicators of prevalence and trends to record the voices of the 'other', the 'subaltern' (see; for example, Gilroy and Woods, 1994 and Neale, 1997a). Building on the work of social theorists such as Anthony Giddens and Michel Foucault, research in housing studies has tentatively begun to explore the relevance of notions such as that of 'social construction' and to interrogate power structures as they relate to issues of, for example, homelessness and mixed communities (Somerville, 1998; Neale, 1997b).

Such challenges, for the moment at least, can be seen as complementary to the prevailing focus of policy orientated housing research, as part of an emerging multimethod and multidisciplinary approach which is needed to produce the "complex evidence" required "to support housing policy demands" (Maclennan and Moore, 1999, p 22).

References

Ball, M. (1983) *Housing policy and economic power*, London: Methuen.

Barlow, J. and Duncan, S. (1994) *Success and failure in housing provision*, London: Pergamon.

Benwell CDP (Community Development Project) (1978) *Private housing and the working class*, Newcastle: Benwell CDP.

Bramley, G. (1997) 'Housing policy: a case of terminal decline?', *Policy & Politics*, vol 25, no 4, pp 387-407.

Cairncross, L., Clapham, D. and Goodland, R. (1996) 'The social basis of tenant organisations', *Housing Studies*, vol 8, no 3, pp 179-93.

CDP (Community Development Project) (1976) *Profits against housing: An alternative guide to housing finance*, London: CDP Information and Intelligence Unit.

CDP (1977) *Gilding the ghetto: The state and the poverty experiments*, London: Home Office.

Chadwick, Edwin, Sir, (1842) *Report to Her Majesty's Principal Secretary of State for the Home Department from the Poor Law Commissioners on an Inquiry into the sanitary condition of the labouring population of Great Britain*, London: HMSO.

Clarke, S. and Ginsburg, N. (1976) 'The political economy of housing', *Kapitalistate*, no 4/5, summer, pp 66-99.

Coates, K. and Silburn, R. (1970) *Poverty: The forgotten Englishman*, Harmondsworth: Penguin.

Cohen, N. (1999) 'An explosion of puffery', *New Statesman*, 29 November, pp 14-16.

Cowans, D. (ed) (1998) *Housing participation and exclusion*, Aldershot: Ashgate.

Cowans, D. (1999) 'Backdoor', *Roof*, vol 24, no 2, p 48.

DETR (Department of the Environment, Transport and the Regions) (2000) *Quality and choice: Decent housing for all*, Housing Green Paper, London: DETR.

Edgar, B., Doherty, J. and Mina-Coull, A. (1999) *Services for homeless people: Innovation and change in the European Union*, Bristol: The Policy Press.

Forrest, R. and Lloyd, J. (1978) 'Theories of the capitalist state: the implications for housing policy', *Papers in Urban and Regional Studies*, vol 2, pp 28-45.

Gilroy, R. and Woods, R. (eds) (1994) *Housing women*, London: Routledge.

Great Britain (1971) *Fair deal for housing*, Cmnd 4728, London: HMSO.

Great Britain (1977) *Housing policy: A consultative document*, Cmnd 6851, London: HMSO.

Harloe, M. (1985) *Private rented housing in the United States and Europe*, Beckenham: Croom Helm.

Housing Standing Conference (1998) *Mixed communities*, East Hanley: National Housing Forum.

Housing Studies (1998) 'Special issue: housing and social exclusion', *Housing Studies*, vol 13, no 6.

Housing Today (1999) 'Allocations system overhaul', no 159 (November), p 1.

Jupp, B. (1999) 'Social structures', *Housing Today*, no 157 (October), pp 14-15.

Kemeny, J. (1992) *Housing and social theory*, London: Routledge.

Kleinman, M. (1996) *Housing, welfare and the state in Europe: A comparative analysis of Britain, France and Germany*, London: Routledge.

Maclennan, D. and Moore, A. (1999) 'Evidence, what evidence? The foundations for housing policy', *Public Money and Management*, vol 19, no 1, pp 17-24.

Merrett, S. (1979) *State housing in Britain*, London: Routledge & Kegan Paul.

Neale, J. (1997a) 'Homelessness: contemporary sociological and feminist analysis', in R. Burrows, N. Pleace and D. Quilgars, *Homelessness and social policy*, London: Routledge, pp 35-49.

Neale, J. (1997b) 'Homelessness and theory reconsidered', *Housing Studies*, vol 12, no 1, pp 47-62.

Power, A. (1997) *Estates on the edge: The social consequences of mass housing in Europe*, Houndsmills: Macmillan.

Power, A. (1999) 'A plague on all our houses', *Housing Today*, no 132 (May), pp 12-13.

Rex, J. and Moore, R. (1967) *Race, community and conflict*, Oxford: Oxford University Press.

Robertson, D. and McLaughlin, P. (1996) *Looking into housing: A practical guide to housing research*, Coventry: Chartered Institute of Housing.

Rosenhead, J. and Thunhurst, C. (1979) 'Operational research and cost-benefit analysis: whose science?', in J. Irvine, I. Miles and J. Evans (eds) *Demystifying social statistics*, London: Pluto Press, pp 289-304.

Schwartz, A. and Tajbakhsh, K. (1997) 'Mixed income housing: unanswered questions', *Cityscape*, vol 3, no 2, pp 71-92.

Scottish Housing Advisory Committee (1948) *Planning our new homes*, Edinburgh: HMSO.

Scottish Office (1999) *Investing in modernisation: An agenda for Scotland's housing*, Edinburgh: Scottish Office.

Somerville, P. (1998) 'Explanations for social exclusion: where does housing fit in?', *Housing Studies*, vol 13, no 6, pp 761-80.

Willmott, P. and Young, M. (1960) *Family and class in a London suburb*, London: New English Library.

Young, M. and Willmott, P. (1957) *Family and kinship in East London*, London: Routledge & Kegan Paul.

NINE

Transport:
beyond predict and provide

Francis Terry

Introduction

Framework for transport research

Research in transport covers a wide field, embracing the main branches of engineering, economics, statistics and others of the social sciences. A substantial proportion of the UK national research effort in transport is funded by government either directly or indirectly, although the transport industries themselves also play a significant role. The principal channel for direct support by government used to be the Transport Research Laboratory (TRL), which was formerly part of the Department of Transport (DoT) and was privatised in 1996. The majority of TRL's work continues to be funded on a contract basis by government, but the Department (now the Department of the Environment, Transport and the Regions) makes use of a much wider range of external contractors in fulfilling its research agenda: there is no longer any presumption in favour of TRL. Indirect support from government is primarily channelled through the funding arrangements for universities and research councils.

Despite the substantial volume of transport research in total terms, very little of this has been directed towards collecting and evaluating evidence to inform policy or towards assessing the effectiveness of policy in action. This chapter seeks to probe the question of why this has been so, particularly in the case of research funded directly by government, and what the consequences have been. Within the transport industries themselves, policy-relevant research and development, as might be expected, has been primarily driven by considerations of the market and orientated towards the improvement of safety, speed and technical efficiency – often involving an increasing level of automation. If anything, this is more true in the post-privatisation era than in the days when major transport undertakings such as British Rail and British Airways were nationalised. In the case of research supported through universities and research councils, little of such work is, nor is intended to be, relevant to policy. There is no barrier to relevance in principle, it is simply that the incentives in the university system have been largely directed more towards the advancement of academic disciplines and the pursuit of more fundamental scientific enquiry.

In understanding the role of research-based evidence in relation to transport policy, it is important to remember that ever since the recommendations of Lord Rothschild were accepted (Central Policy Review Staff, 1971) each government-funded research project has been expected to have a clearly identified customer, who commissions a contractor to carry out the work on specified terms. One effect of this reform (and the evidence is impressionistic) seems to have been a reduction in the scope for government-sponsored research and development (R&D) to range very far outside the framework of current policies. If research could not be shown to further the implementation of the agenda set by ministers of the day, it was *ipso facto* a poor candidate for financial support.

This reduction in the flexibility of government-funded researchers, particularly in research establishments such as TRL, to think outside the confines of current policy objectives was in retrospect a serious flaw. However, it was partially offset, probably coincidentally, by the creation of a separate unit – the Central Policy Review Staff (CPRS) – with an explicitly questioning and broad-ranging remit in relation to policy (Blackstone and Plowden, 1988). Much of the work undertaken by CPRS used applied research techniques and employed the skills of academic researchers seconded into it, but its mission was completely different from that of government laboratories or university researchers. It was an early example of attempts to collect, sift and evaluate evidence, including from overseas experience, which would rationally inform policy making at the centre of government.

The agenda of CPRS was fixed partly in accord with what were seen to be the major policy problems of the day, but were also a reflection of the interests of its staff (Blackstone and Plowden, 1988). Industrial policy featured strongly in both the published and unpublished reports of CPRS, reflecting the economic situation of the United Kingdom at the time; but transport was almost completely ignored. This is surprising, given the scale of investment then being pumped into new road construction, and the seemingly inexorable rise in subsidies to the nationalised bus and rail undertakings. Major new projects such as the channel tunnel and the third London airport were under intense debate, while projects in progress (such as the Dartford tunnel and the Humber bridge) were running into major financial difficulties. Yet the CPRS did not examine any of these. After the demise of the CPRS in 1983, governments continued to need a source of alternative policy thinking, but by this time the focus of interest had moved outside Whitehall, with the rise of 'think-tanks', independent of government itself but often aligned with some political interest group.

The agenda of the TRL meanwhile continued to be dominated by the central Departments responsible for environment and transport, at various times operating together or as separate entities. Staff at the Laboratory would annually propose an agenda of projects for funding, which were screened by the civil servants at headquarters acting as research 'customers', sometimes with advice from an external Planning and Transport Research Advisory Committee or similar body. Apart from the availability of funds, a key test of whether TRL's proposals were endorsed was their relevance to current policies and established spending programmes.

While the Rothschild reforms achieved a clearer focus on the perceived needs of research customers, and a tighter control of resources, their effect in the transport field was to constrain the scope of work undertaken. The vast majority of TRL's work throughout the 1970s and 1980s was geared to the operation and use of the road network, paralleling departmental expenditure on road construction and improvement, rather than transport problems in a wider sense. Huge volumes of research were commissioned on the physical aspects of building, operating and maintaining road traffic infrastructure, while the social sciences were applied to studies concerned with driver and pedestrian behaviour usually in an effort to improve road safety. It is possible to regard this work as producing evidence that contributed to the more effective use of public resources (practice), but it did not address the more basic questions of 'what works' in achieving the policy goals of a transport system, the key one being to improve access to destinations for various social and economic purposes.

The framework within which so much research on transport was commissioned had another important implication for its practical application. Since each item of DoT research needed a customer, there was a strong incentive to show that commissioned research had some practical application; otherwise, the research budget was liable to be cut. However, a large majority of the customers for the transport research programme were professional staff – chiefly highway planners and engineers employed in central government – rather than civil servants whose task it was to develop policies in a broader sense. Research was shown to be valuable because the findings were disseminated in the form of detailed guidance to local highway authorities and construction firms about such matters as road alignments, drainage, surfaces, sight-lines, traffic signal phasing and so on.

The dominance of professionals in setting the research agenda, and their strong professional culture, was reflected in the way research findings were disseminated as standards and codes of practice. Through the 1970s and 1980s, this process became highly organised and tightly controlled. The smallest departure from the standard, or a variation in practice, necessitated Departmental approval – usually given only after some bureaucratic delay. The Highways Agency, an executive agency created in 1994 to manage the national roads programme on behalf of the DoT, has continued to utilise many of the outputs of this past research investment. It is only now, at the beginning of the new century, that the elaborate standards and codes applied to highway design, operation and maintenance are being rewritten by the Agency to support a radically new vision of transport policy.

Transport policy debate

The transport research programmes funded by government in the 1970s and 1980s enjoyed the support of Parliament and professional bodies and were largely uncontentious. However, it is regrettable that wider policy issues were so firmly excluded. As the economy grows, demand for travel and transport typically expand; yet the capacity of UK government to fund the necessary improvements in infrastructure and services has always lagged behind. Even when, in 1989, the nation's largest-ever road construction programme was announced, it was becoming clear that such investment could not cater for more than a tiny fraction of the likely increase in road vehicle movements during the next 25 years.

The realisation of this stark fact among local authorities, pressure groups and others outside government exposed a fundamental divergence in the national objectives for transport policy which, eventually, the White Paper, *A New Deal for transport: Better for everyone* (Secretary of State for the Environment, Transport and the Regions, 1998), sought to address. It is possible to argue that a divergence of objectives had existed prior to the 1990s, but was latent, or less explicit. That may perhaps explain why government spending programmes were allowed to support a diversity of ad hoc and sometimes inconsistent measures, catering for different constituencies without facing hard choices between them.

By contrast, in other policy areas, a government's basic objectives quite often remain stable for long periods. In health, for example, there has been at least a broad agreement over many governments about the basic aims of promoting good health, treating illness and providing medical care. In the operation of the criminal justice system most people would subscribe to the aims of deterring crime, as well as punishing and rehabilitating offenders (although the relative balance between these remains a matter for debate). In these services, the focus of debate among professionals and politicians is about the *means* to achieve aims that are largely uncontentious. The contribution of research then is to establish 'what works' from an intellectually coherent reading of the evidence.

The current debate over transport policy can, in simple terms, be reduced to a contrasting pair of arguments: on the one hand, there is concern to reduce the negative impacts of transport and travel on the environment and society, and even to reduce the volume of transport per se; on the other hand, there are demands, especially from business and motoring organisations, to improve transport flows in the interests of economic development and competitiveness. Evidence from research and elsewhere has typically been used to support policy preconceptions on either side of the argument, rather than to resolve it. This is not just a peculiarity of the UK: the same is true in other European Union countries (ICCR, 1997). The reasons are not difficult to find. For most of us, passenger transport (by car, bus, train, bicycle and so on) is a much more integral part of normal daily life than, say, healthcare or the operation of the criminal justice system. All of us have frequent, regular and direct experience of the transport system and have views about it, conditioned by an enormous range of locational, economic, social, environmental and even emotional factors (Steg and Tertoolen, 1999).

The tension between individual preferences and collective impacts is a key characteristic – perhaps the defining dilemma – of transport policy. 'Freedom of movement' – at least within national borders and, increasingly, across them – is generally regarded as a basic human right. By extension, the means by which individuals nowadays exercise the greatest range and flexibility of movement is via the use of motor vehicles; yet the unlimited exercise of freedom of movement by car has detrimental effects which a responsible government, sooner or later, has to address. Research in connection with the preparation of the *Second Dutch National Environmental Policy Plan* (Dutch Ministry of Housing, Physical Planning and the Environment, 1993) is instructive in this context. It showed that while public consciousness of environmental issues (in general) was high, this was not accompanied by any wish to restrain one of the principal causes of pollution and damage to the environment, namely car use.

Ambivalence in official policy making could be seen as no more than a reflection of inconsistencies in attitudes and behaviour at the individual level. Government limitations on car use could easily be represented as infringing the rights of individuals and, in such circumstances, democratic governments would be wise to tread with caution. It is tempting for them to think instead of providing attractive alternatives to cars, particularly for urban and inter-city journeys, in the hope that motorists will make enlightened choices. Yet the experience of cities in continental Europe suggests that this is a 'false trail'. Cheap and efficient public transport has little appeal for the habituated car driver and more often encourages people who do not have access to a car to make journeys that were previously awkward or impossible. We are back to the thorny issue of restricting freedom of movement.

Against this background, a consideration of 'what works' in transport policy is at least partly determined by your philosophical starting point, and the key questions are easier to answer at the tactical level than to do so in terms of total strategy. Nevertheless, the government appears more interested in addressing the strategic question now than for a long time in the past. The creation of a unified Department of the Environment, Transport and the Regions in place of the former Department of Transport may be seen as a reflection in institutional terms of a new-found will to reconcile the fundamental arguments. Since debates over policy are often sharply focused in relation to the growth of road transport, evidence in this area is examined in the remainder of this chapter. However, parallel issues and arguments do arise over the provision of public transport facilities by rail, air and to a more modest degree by bus.

Growth of road traffic

In the decade after 1952, the number of passenger-kilometres travelled by car in the UK doubled; after 1958, cars accounted for more journeys than any other single mode; within another five years, car journeys accounted for more than twice the passenger-kilometres travelled by all other surface transport modes combined (DoT, 1996a). The trend moved inexorably upwards until 1989, when it seemed to falter, before continuing upwards at a reduced rate. The trend in passenger-kilometres has been accompanied by a huge growth in the numbers of vehicles using the road system (now more than 25 million) and the numbers of people holding licences to drive.

The response from government to this pattern of demand has been characterised as 'predict and provide' (Goodwin, 1993). Throughout the 1960s, 1970s and 1980s, spending on new road construction averaged more than £2 billion annually (in today's prices). The determination to respond to soaring demand was restated in the 1989 White Paper *Roads for prosperity* (DoT, 1989a), in which the then government set out proposals for expenditure on road schemes of around £18 billion (1997 prices) for the following 10 years.

These grandiose plans were progressively modified as the recession of the early 1990s took hold, making it essential to cut public spending. However, the government hoped (DoT, 1989b) that the private sector would replace at least part of the cuts through the development of the Private Finance Initiative (PFI) and that motorway tolling would raise new income for road schemes (see DoT, 1993). Use of the PFI in a road construction context was strongly promoted by the then Conservative government, resulting in a few major schemes going ahead. The PFI contractor is remunerated under these schemes by 'shadow tolls', which are paid by central government in proportion to the level of use made of the road, rather than by motorway users themselves. This approach, by failing to transfer significant risk to the private sector, has been shown to represent questionable value for money (Buchan, 1996; National Audit Office, 1998) and it seems unlikely that many more such schemes will now be built. A summary published by the DoT (1996b) showed that, despite the ambitions of Cm 693 (DoT, 1989a), real-terms expenditure on national road construction and improvement in England fell from £5.2 billion in 1990-93 to a projected £3.8 billion for the period 1996-99. Support to local authorities, chiefly for maintenance of the existing system, was set to fall from £2.7 billion in 1990-93 to £2.3 billion in 1996-99.

Signs that the declared policy was becoming unsustainable appeared with the Green Paper (Cm 3234), *Transport – The way forward* (Secretary of State for Transport, 1996) which canvassed a range of diverse and more environmentally-friendly objectives for transport policy. The incoming Labour government announced a major review of trunk road and motorway spending shortly after it came to office in May 1997, leading to an announcement in August 1998 that out of 156 schemes, roughly one third would go ahead with public funding, 13 with private funding and the rest would be either cancelled or referred to other bodies (chiefly regional or local authorities) for decision. The transport White Paper (Secretary of State for the Environment, Transport and the Regions, 1998), published earlier the same month, made it clear that the thrust of transport policy would in future be towards promoting alternatives to car use, with a very much lower level of public spending available for new road schemes.

We turn now to the nature of the evidence that has underpinned the very substantial investment in road building during the previous 30 years, the way it was interpreted and used, and the rise of alternative interpretations lying behind the shift of policy signalled in the White Paper.

Nature of evidence

We have already seen how the transport research programmes commissioned by government were led by the requirements of highway professionals and focused on technical issues. Meanwhile, the evidence used to support major road construction relied heavily on statistics and forecasts of traffic growth. Collection of statistics about car ownership and numbers of qualified drivers is administratively simple (through the licensing system), and few people would seriously doubt that the task was performed other than to the highest professional standards: in that sense, road transport statistics constituted 'hard evidence'. The DoT allocated on average about £30 million annually to research on transport, much of it spent on commissioned work at TRL. Although the findings from such research also constituted evidence, its impact on policy towards road construction (as has been seen) was typically at the technical level of implementation, being focused on better ways of achieving the goal of building roads rather than suggesting alternatives.

Forecasts

The former DoT's practice was periodically to produce National Road Traffic Forecasts (NRTF) for a period of at least 30 years ahead. Although the relationship of these forecasts to public expenditure planning has never been precisely defined, they were used as part of the general case to the Treasury in annual public expenditure negotiations. The forecasts made in 1989 (DoT, 1989c) are especially interesting because they acted as the touchstone of policy for most of the Conservatives' remaining period in office up to 1997. The published forecasts consisted of two variants: a high forecast of 142% increase in traffic between 1988 and 2025 and a low forecast of an 83% increase. The growth projections were closely linked to forecasts of economic growth, such that over the period 1988 to 2000, the increase in traffic was expected to be virtually the same as assumed growth of GDP, although traffic was assumed to grow more slowly thereafter.

Separate forecasts were made for each major class of vehicle, as follows:
- *cars:* it was assumed that the observed relationship between increase in income and increase in car ownership would continue until 90% of the population of driving age (17- to 74-year-olds) own a car; the distance travelled by each car was assumed to increase one fifth as fast as GDP per head, and to be reduced by 1.5% for every 10% increase in the price of fuel in real terms;
- *light good vehicles:* vehicle-kilometres were assumed to increase in direct proportion to GDP;
- *heavy goods vehicles:* again, growth was assumed to be directly related to GDP, although other factors were incorporated, such as an assumption that road's share of freight would continue to increase and that most of the additional freight would be carried by the heaviest vehicles;
- *buses and coaches:* vehicle-kilometres were expected to remain static at 1989 levels;
- *others:* remarkably, no forecasts at all were made for travel on foot, by bicycle, moped or motorcycle.

Aside from the forecasts, detailed statistics are also kept of road accidents, and have been for more than 70 years. These too are relatively simple to collect from police records, although the way in which the data are recorded does not always make it easy to analyse the causes of accidents. Nevertheless, it constitutes an important ancillary source of evidence on which policy has been based over many decades.

Using the evidence

For much of the postwar period, road traffic forecasts were the driving force behind British transport policy and a principal criterion for deciding on the level of public investment in transport infrastructure. Priorities for investment were, to some extent, influenced by accident statistics ('black

spots' being targeted for improvement). However, a number of other, more politically important, reasons guaranteed high public expenditure on road building. These included:
• attracting support from voters by catering for massive potential increases in personal mobility;
• the importance of maintaining, through the 1960s and 1970s, a sizeable indigenous car manufacturing industry (for employment and trade reasons) and a strong construction industry;
• scepticism, or outright prejudice, about the value of sustained high levels of investment in the rail network, as an alternative to road provision.

In the 1989 roads White Paper, the principal reasons for investment acknowledged by the then government (DoT, 1989a, paras 6-8), were to:
• help economic development by reducing transport costs;
• improve the environment by removing through-traffic from unsuitable roads;
• enhance road safety.

Considering the scale of investment promised, it was a surprise to find that the methodology of the forecasts was not more robust. Yet it was not until 1994, when the Royal Commission on Environmental Pollution (RCEP) made a damning criticism of the assumptions behind the forecasts in its *Eighteenth Report* (RCEP, 1994) that official views began to change. For example, it had been assumed by government that real incomes in Britain would continue to rise and that the life-styles of higher income groups would progressively spread more widely across the population. The official assumption that car ownership would ultimately reach 90% of the population implied that the ratio of cars per 1,000 population would increase from 331 in 1988 to between 529 and 608 by the year 2025. According to RCEP, this assumption was based on the 1990 level of car ownership in the United States, with its wealthier and much less dense pattern of settlement – hardly an appropriate yardstick for the UK. Despite such weaknesses, the NRTF were extensively used at local levels to model the impact of proposed improvements to the road network.

In the present context, the important point is that the NRTF were in themselves *treated as evidence*. The point was clearly demonstrated in the case of *Bushell and Brunt v Secretary of State for the Environment* (1980), in which the House of Lords ruled that the NRTF were part of the policy context within which specific road schemes were proposed and therefore were not challengeable at planning inquiries. Although the government stated that its traffic forecasts were not a target, and even that it was not desirable that they should be met, they continued to be used as evidence of the need for specific schemes throughout the 1980s and early 1990s. As a result, planning inquiries were largely restricted to considering the route of a proposed road, and ruled out examination of alternative strategies which might remove the need for the new road. The official justification was that inquiries were intended to deal with objections, not with the formulation of policy, for which Parliament was the proper forum. But, as the RCEP commented,

> This argument would be more convincing if ... Parliament is regularly offered the opportunity of scrutinising the road programme.... In our view, there is a need both for Parliamentary scrutiny of the broad thrust of policies and for opportunities for local people to question the policies as applied to their locality. The failure to allow the latter is symptomatic of a flawed policy. (RCEP, 1994, p 156)

Economic benefits

Ministers have for a long time required a cost-benefit analysis (CBA) to be conducted for major road schemes before giving approval. Guidance by the former DoT (1985) has had the effect of limiting CBA to three main classes of benefits:
- journey time savings, which may accrue to the uses of the new road and to other roads where congestion is likely to be reduced;
- savings in operating costs on the road network as a whole;
- accident costs savings.

These benefits were then compared to the costs, in two ways: in relation to capital costs, such as the acquisition of land and construction costs, and in relation to maintenance costs in the future. Arguments about the appropriate methodology for CBA have long been debated, one of the basic problems being that final conclusions are heavily dependent on the actual numbers ascribed to the value of time saved or accidents reduced. Figures of £10 per hour for working time saved and £5 per hour for leisure time are typically used, with £1m as the average value of a life saved. Validation of such numbers is problematic, depending largely on the perceptions of respondents to social surveys who are asked, directly or indirectly, to place monetary values on hypothetical benefits and amenities, or the loss thereof.

While it is easy to criticise the numerical values built into CBA, the more interesting point perhaps is that the conclusions of CBA calculations were for a long time accepted as an important category of evidence in determining priorities for road investment. Fundamental criticisms of this were eventually made by RCEP (1994) and later by the Standing Advisory Committee on Trunk Road Assessment (SACTRA, 1994), on the grounds that CBA did not address the problem of induced traffic. In other words, there is a strong case for believing that the extension and improvement of the road network leads to an increase in the total amount of road traffic, as distinct from redistributing a pre-set level of traffic on to the enhanced network.

For example, the M25 motorway generated leisure journeys from the South West of London to the North, with traffic flows at weekends much higher than predicted and congestion occurring around Heathrow airport during the morning peak times (7-10am). Many of the additional trips, as compared to the time before the M25 existed, have little economic value, and once congestion occurs it enters the equation as an economic cost in terms of time wasted, rather than as benefit. Despite such findings, which came from local authorities and pressure groups outside government, the DoT's view was for a long time that any effect that the road programme had in generating additional traffic was of minor importance, and that its comparisons of forecast levels with actual levels occurring one year after the completion of schemes supported this interpretation.

Use of the DoT's recommended method for conducting CBA has recently been replaced by a new approach to scheme appraisal based on qualitative judgements alongside quantitative calculations where possible. The approach starts from the transport problem to be solved, rather than launching straight into the costs and benefits of a specific scheme put forward by DoT road planners. It therefore makes no presumption in favour of a road-based solution to the problem and will, apparently, be applied to all types of transport projects. Information about the nature of the problem is collected and tested against five broadly-based criteria:
- contribution to the goals of an integrated transport policy;
- improvement in safety;
- impact on the economy;
- impact on the environment; and

- contribution to accessibility (ie helping people to reach their chosen destinations).

The new-style appraisal then looks at the contribution of different forms of transport in developing alternative solutions, before a final choice of scheme is made.

Apart from the limitations of CBA methodology, evidence of the relationship between road investment and economic growth is also unclear. The assumption was invariably made in postwar transport planning that new roads promote growth; this was a central theme of the 1989 White Paper. Yet the evidence for these arguments was inconclusive to say the least. A study for the Department of the Environment by Parkinson (1981) revealed that the proportion of a firm's costs accounted for by transport is small, typically 5–10%. Of this, 70% is incurred at terminals and is virtually unaffected by transit times or road access. A 10% cut in movement costs would reduce total production costs by around 0.3%. Parkinson concludes "it is implausible that the fall in price which could result from this small reduction in transport costs is likely to lead to a significant increase in demand and output".

More recently, the findings of the inquiry by the Standing Advisory Committee on Trunk Road Assessment (SACTRA, 1999) has shown the relationship between infrastructure provision and economic growth to be complex and uncertain. That relationship is believed to be powerful in underdeveloped economies, but in other areas quite weak. Better road links may have the aim of opening up markets, but this does not mean that investment in roads is necessarily an effective lever for inducing economic growth. Traffic congestion on other parts of the network may cancel out the benefits of a particular scheme (Headicar and Bixby, 1992), while the evidence from work by Dodgson (1973) and others is that new roads may actually suck economic activity out of a region as easily as they stimulate it. As a means of creating jobs, road building has also been shown to be relatively poor value for money. Pound for pound, it creates considerably fewer jobs than spending on other assets such as housing and public transport (Vanke, 1988; German Road League/IG Bau Steine Erden, 1992).

Nevertheless, while a variety of evidence from independent experts has cast doubt on the assumption that a general rise in movements signals greater economic activity at the micro-level, official policy was for a long time reluctant to accept this. In the 1996 Green Paper, the Conservative government at last conceded that many of its assumptions about traffic growth needed to be revised. The scene was set for the reforms promised in Labour's White Paper a year later. Interestingly, the idea that growth in car ownership is a proxy indicator of national prosperity, which appeared in the 1989 White Paper, is repeated in 1998. But the evidence shows that levels of ownership in the UK, relative to the rest of Europe, are not related to other indicators such as GDP per head.

Environmental benefits and accidents

On the question of the environmental case for road building, a serious challenge was raised by RCEP (1994) and by others (Transport 2000, 1994). It was pointed out that bypasses, which tend to bring the most direct environmental benefits to towns and villages, accounted for a relatively small proportion of total public expenditure on roads through the 1970s and 1980s, while trunk roads and motorways (including motorway widening) were pressed through against heavy opposition based on the levels of noise, pollution and loss of rural amenity that would result. In relation to accidents, the all-party Parliamentary Advisory Committee on Transport Safety (PACTS) found that "many large schemes produced very small accident reductions ... we believe that the small benefits that might accrue might be achieved by other methods for a fraction of the costs" (PACTS, 1993).

The evidence from local authorities, which independently of central government began to implement traffic calming and speed reduction measures in the early 1990s, is that such measures often show substantial gains in noise abatement, air quality and pedestrian safety for very much smaller outlays than large-scale new construction.

Concluding remarks

It appears that the principles for commissioning government R&D, and the institutional framework for research which prevailed in the UK from 1970 onwards, acted as a significant discouragement to wider policy thinking and, in particular, evidence-based approaches in transport. However, the divergence of views on strategic policy objectives (notably in relation to road construction), which became increasingly apparent in the 1990s, called for a more extensive range of evidence to be admitted in the policy process. The preoccupation with research geared simply to fulfilling established and unquestioned policy objectives began to fall away. In 1993, research at the Transport Studies Unit at Oxford University

(Goodwin et al, 1993), demonstrated that even if the 1989 White Paper proposals were fulfilled, the problems of congestion would not be solved, or that if the official projections of traffic growth were realised, there would be no possibility of increasing road space on a commensurate scale. The policy implication of Goodwin's work – dubbed 'the new realism' – was that since the supply of road space is not going to be matched by demand, demand must be matched to supply.

Up to that point, road construction had been identified with the belief that constraints on movement are undesirable, almost on principle. As a result, greater *mobility* tended to be confused with better *access* to destinations. Accordingly, policy making emphasised the evidence of traffic growth as a justification for large allocations of public investment. As time passed, new road schemes had to be driven through in the face of growing local opposition, on the assumption that government was thereby conferring generalised benefits on large numbers of road users and the national economy. Eventually, after witnessing police and bailiffs clearing protesters from the path of a new section of the M11 motorway in 1994, Brian Mawhinney, as Transport Secretary, recognised the need for a broader national debate on transport issues.

The limited evidence used to support large-scale road construction contrasts with the precise records of road accidents and the extensive research into their causes. Although road safety may be improved by new construction projects (by removing accident 'black spots'), a range of other initiatives can be undertaken. On a number of these, the government has been slow to act because of anticipated negative public reaction and the lower priority (compared to new construction) given to the necessary expenditure. For example, the benefits of wearing seat belts were conclusively demonstrated during tests in the early 1960s, but ministers did not feel that they could introduce a seat-belt law until more than 50% of the population were wearing them voluntarily, as a result of intensive public information campaigns (DoT, 1997). Again, while the introduction of experimental 20 mph zones, starting in 1990, showed dramatic reductions (typically 60%) in the number of pedestrians killed or seriously injured, it was at least five years before the DoT would consider giving any priority to spending on 20 mph zones more generally.

In retrospect, it seems remarkable that the growth trends in vehicle miles and car ownership were elevated to a position where they received a dominant position over all other evidence, and indeed evidence about the effects of the policy itself. The contrast between evidence from official sources and that from independent professional and academic sources is also striking. For a long period, evidence from within, or commissioned by, the DoT was the only evidence admissible in policy making. It was not until the 1990s, when organisations outside government – ranging from the RCEP to local pressure groups – successfully challenged the traditional direction of transport policy, that alternative evidence was given much weight.

While the barriers to a more evidential approach to transport policy seem to be coming down, the reasons can only be surmised at this stage. Changes in the political climate during the mid-1990s allowed evidence produced by bodies external to government to enter the decision process not only in transport but also in other public policy arenas such as housing and welfare. The volume and quality of research outside government seems to have increased, as the government's own research budgets have shrunk in response to public expenditure constraints, and as universities have been encouraged to undertake more 'applied' research relevant to policy making. Another factor may be that during the 1990s local authorities – despite the wide-ranging reductions in their powers – began to conduct practical experiments to find alternatives to road building.

It can be argued that the initiative in forward thinking about transport issues was partially lost by central government in favour of local authorities. The widespread pedestrianisation of historic centres such as York and Chester is one example, but innovative partnerships with bus companies to improve the appeal of public transport, and experiments with community transport, are others. The results of these experiments have been disseminated by networks of urban planners and by voluntary groups preoccupied with highway matters, acting as alternative channels to the manuals of official guidance. The dissemination of evidence about 'what works' in transport policy has arguably become more pluralistic in the 1990s compared to the 1970s and 1980s.

The conclusion from this brief review is that 'what works' in transport policy can be understood at more than one level of analysis. At the strategic level (and assuming that the policy objectives are established through appropriate political and consultative processes), deciding 'what works' will need a receptiveness to alternative perspectives and approaches that has not always been the hallmark of official thinking. If the goal is clear, there may be more than one way of reaching it, and this is especially important in the context of tight constraints on public expenditure. More research could be done on how political processes assimilate and use evidence, especially when it does not conform to popular views and beliefs.

At the tactical level of individual measures − whether constructing new roads or introducing limitations on the use of cars − it is clear that government sometimes feels strong enough to pursue its course in the face of substantial local opposition, while at other times it is reluctant to force the pace. There does not seem to be much obvious correlation between these responses and what research or experimental evidence say about such issues; nor incidentally, with the size of a government's Parliamentary majority. Public acceptability is often a more important criterion than whether the evidence supports a particular course of action. Nevertheless, the diversity of sources, from which evidence about 'what works' now comes, seems a positive feature of the present scene, and the contribution from locally-driven initiatives can have a strong practical value. After a long period in which the use of evidence in transport policy has been restricted and confused, the mid-1990s have seen a greater openness and clarity. However, there is much more to be done before the full value of an evidence-based approach is recognised.

References

Blackstone, T. and Plowden, W. (1988) *Inside the think tank*, London: William Heinemann.

Buchan, K. (1996) *For whom the shadow tolls − The effects of design, build, finance and operate (DBFO) on the A36 Salisbury Bypass*, London: MTRU/Transport 2000.

Central Policy Review Staff (1971) *A framework for government research and development* ('Rothschild Report'), London: HMSO.

Dodgson, J.S. (1973) 'Motorway investment, industrial transport costs, and sub-regional growth: a case study of the M62', *Regional Studies*, vol 8, pp 145-58.

DoT (Department of Transport) (1985) *COBA 9 Evaluation Manual and Highway Economics Note 2* (Update), London: DoT.

DoT (1989a) *Roads for prosperity*, Cm 693, London: DoT.

DoT (1989b) *New roads by new means*, Cm 698, London: HMSO.

DoT (1989c) *National Road Traffic Forecasts (Great Britain)*, London: HMSO.

DoT (1993) *Paying for better motorways*, Cm 2200, London: HMSO.

DoT (1996a) *Transport statistics Great Britain 1996*, London: HMSO.

DoT (1996b) *Transport report 1996*, London: HMSO.

DoT (1997) *Road casualties Great Britain 1997*, London: DoT.

(Dutch) Ministry of Housing, Physical Planning and the Environment (NEPP) (1993) *Second Dutch National Environmental Policy Plan*, The Hague: NEPP.

German Road League/IG Bau Steine Erden (1992) quoted in *Going Green Report*, London: Environmental Transport Association.

Goodwin, P. (1993) *Key issues in demand management* (Paper to Surrey County Council's Workshop on Demand Management), Oxford: University of Oxford, 25 April.

Headicar, P. and Bixby, B. (1992) *Concrete and tyres – Local development effects of major roads: A case study of the M40*, London: CPRE.

ICCR (Interdisciplinary Centre for Comparative Research in the Social Sciences) (1997) *Comparative report on national transport policies* (Report of EU-TENASSESS project), Vienna.

National Audit Office (1998) *The Private Finance Initiative: The first four design, build and operate roads contracts* (HC 476), London: The Stationery Office.

PACTS (Parliamentary Advisory Committee on Transport Safety) (1993) *Working Paper on road investment and accident reduction*, London: HMSO.

Parkinson, M. (1981) *The effect of road investment in economic development in the UK*, London: Government Economic Service Working Paper No 430.

RCEP (Royal Commission on Environmental Pollution) (1994) *Eighteenth Report – Transport and the environment*, Cm 2674, London: HMSO.

SACTRA (Standing Advisory Committee on Trunk Road Assessment) (1994) *Trunk roads and the generation of traffic*, London: HMSO.

SACTRA (1999) *Transport and the economy*, London: The Stationery Office.

Secretary of State for Transport (1996) *Transport – The way forward*, Cm 3234, London: HMSO.

Secretary of State for the Environment, Transport and the Regions (1998) *A New Deal for transport: Better for everyone*, Cm 3950, London: The Stationery Office.

Steg, L. and Tertoolen, G. (1999) 'Sustainable transport policy: the contribution from behavioural scientists', *Public Money & Management*, vol 19, no 1, pp 63-9.

Transport 2000 (1994) *Transport 21: An alternative transport budget*, London: Transport 2000.

Vanke, J. (1988) 'Roads to prosperity', *The Planner*, December, pp 426-31.

TEN

Urban policy: addressing wicked problems

Tony Harrison

Introduction: urban policy and the problem of evidence

Urban policy – or policy designed to arrest the economic and social decline of either parts of cities, whole settlements, or even (more recently) cities in general (Urban Task Force, 1999) – has been a feature of UK policy for more than 30 years. Its origins are generally traced back to the Educational Priority Area programmes of the late 1960s and to the launch of the Urban Programme by Harold Wilson in 1968 following Enoch Powell's 'rivers of blood' speech (Edwards and Batley, 1978; Laurence and Hall, 1981). It is variously described as 'inner-city policy', 'urban policy' and more recently as 'urban regeneration' (terms which will be used interchangeably in this chapter). It is characterised by a number of features that make the idea of an 'evidence-based' urban policy problematic, in the strict sense of linking predictable outcomes with discrete interventions, so as to say with confidence 'what works'.

The first characteristic is that urban policy has a very strong political dimension. Events that have prompted central government to address the 'problem' of our cities have often assumed a high media profile (Cottle, 1993). The consequent involvement of leading politicians in urban policy is, according to Mossberger and Stoker (1997), difficult to explain in rational terms. This could be because urban policy has commonly been grounded in strong political philosophies for which supporting evidence may have been either absent or extremely difficult to produce. These features have led to urban policy being described by one commentator as "political in the meanest sense of the word, point scoring and sweeping damaging issues under the carpet rather than seriously confronting and resolving them" (Cheshire, 1987, p 22). The extensive critical literature on urban policy includes a strong strand of such cynicism about the extent to which it is anything other than a policy area in which the political imperatives of visibility dominate (Robinson and Shaw, 1994; Oatley, 1998).

The second characteristic is that because urban policy involves complex interventions their impact or effectiveness is difficult to isolate and measure. In contrast to many other areas of policy and practice they are designed to be effective at a community (defined in geographical terms), not individual level. Although individuals experience the ultimate benefits (such as jobs created), the objective of urban policy is improvement across a defined geographical area. This raises two problems. First the displacement effect, or the impact of any improvement on other areas (whether jobs created in a targeted area, for example, are simply relocated from other areas). Second whether in-and-out migration (on a daily or permanent basis) means that the beneficiaries are not those originally living and working in the area – and indeed whether this actually matters. Although in principle displacement in one form or another can be measured in evaluation there remains controversy over whether gains in some areas are worth paying for in terms of losses elsewhere. Urban policy interventions are not like those in education or clinical practice where there is wide consensus around the objectives, for example of improved reading skills or more rapid recovery. They involve trade-offs – and judgements about whether these trade-offs are worthwhile are inevitably political.

The cross-sectoral nature of interventions in urban policy also makes the measurement of their effectiveness difficult. In the current jargon, urban policy is holistic (DETR, 1997a) and involves 'joined-up' working. It involves, for example, aspects of housing, local economy, community safety and crime prevention, land-use planning, transport, education and training, in mixes that reflect local conditions and involve public, private and voluntary agencies working in partnership. Other contributions in this volume deal with different policy sectors that form part of urban policy (housing, transport and so on); consequently this chapter concentrates on integrative, multisector and holistic urban policy.

The third characteristic of urban policy that presents problems for evidence-based policy is that of the nature of the policy and practitioner community to which evidence may be addressed. Since urban policy is multiagency, involves central and local government, and the private and voluntary sector, and places considerable emphasis on public participation and community capacity building, it brings together policy makers, practitioners and stakeholders from a range of backgrounds. If there is a policy community in this area it is not necessarily bound together by common views about the nature of the problem, or of what constitutes evidence.

One of the main objectives in urban policy in the UK at present is to ensure that partnerships (the current delivery mechanisms for urban policy) work effectively. To this 'process' objective can be added others, such as encouraging public participation, or community capacity building. Urban policy currently, then, is not *only* concerned with evidence of the extent to which different interventions improve urban *outcomes*, but also with evidence of what works in developing more inclusive and participatory processes of policy making and implementation that may ultimately improve urban conditions. The objectives are often long term – particularly if any improvements are to be judged by the extent to which they are sustained. This may mean, paradoxically, that a desire for short-term measurable benefits of the type that a push towards evidence-based policy may involve, could be counter-productive for an urban policy with long-term goals.

In the light of these complex features it is not surprising that a literature review of urban policy (Mossberger and Stoker, 1997, p 380) reveals it as being variously described as "disjointed ... ad hoc ... uncoordinated ... incoherent ... marginal ... lacking impact ... symbolic ... presentational or public relations oriented ... fragmented ... (and) ...reactive". In spite of this there are sufficient common threads to the chequered history of urban policy that allow it to be characterised for the purposes of identifying any evidential base in the following terms:

- It is area based, focusing on localities demonstrating high levels of social stress, multiple deprivation, physical decay, and, in the current terminology, social exclusion. These areas are identified by central government to receive targeted funding. This raises questions about evidence of need.
- It aims to "work across traditional programmes and subject boundaries to achieve holistic impact" (DETR, 1997a, p 3, para 4.6). It is, therefore, multisector based and concentrates on partnerships as a means of delivery.
- It involves a process of competitive bidding for funding (particularly from the Single Regeneration Budget [SRB]), with a formal appraisal of proposals and the subsequent monitoring and evaluation of funded

schemes. This raises questions about the use of evidence in the different stages of the policy process.

• It concerns processes of policy making and implementation that challenge traditional ways of service delivery. Consequently, evidence on how to make these ways of operating work (for example, how to overcome blockages to multiagency working and engage communities) is currently an objective of urban research. This particular aspect of policy implementation is not unique to urban policy and is not discussed in depth here.

The scope of urban policy as it is referred to in this chapter closely follows that implied by the DETR discussion document on regeneration (DETR 1997a, p 3, paras 2.1, 2.2):

> Government's regeneration policies and programmes are part of the drive to tackle the combination of local needs and priorities associated with poverty and deprivation.... The task of regeneration is most urgent (and difficult) where all or most of these problems come together – areas of multiple deprivation.... The goal is to break the vicious circle of deprivation and provide the foundation for sustainable regeneration and wealth creation.... Regeneration policy ... cuts across departmental boundaries.

This chapter does not examine evidence-based policy in those vertically defined sectors, financed through main programmes, which, by virtue of expenditure may make substantial contribution to helping solve problems *in cities* (for example, employment policies such as those in the New Deal). It concentrates instead on policy directed at the multifaceted problems *of cities*, in particular those concentrated in specific neighbourhoods where problems of housing, health, employment and crime, for example, seem to reinforce each other and demand a multiagency approach.

Each of the above issues will be discussed in turn, and illustrated from urban policy research. But first the nature of the evidence produced from some 30 years of urban policy and associated research is summarised.

Nature of evidence

The nature of urban research from which an evidence base for policy could be produced is briefly summarised with examples from key stages of the development of urban policy. All come from work designed to inform policy, and which has in the main been carried out or sponsored by government departments.

The 1970s and 1980s

The Home Office directed the early stages of urban policy. This reflected its origin as a response to problems of multiple deprivation in areas of large immigrant populations (Hall, 1981). An example is the Community Development Projects (CDPs) – 12 experimental initiatives involving local action teams, backed by a research facility, that worked closely with the local population to assess needs, improve service delivery and enhance self-sufficiency. The research output included a radical series of reports documenting conditions in these areas and attributing these in particular to structural economic causes, reinforced by government action (for example, CDP, 1977; CDP/PEC, 1979). Although these may contribute little to the current 'what works' debate they illustrate a basic problem of urban policy; the causes of urban decline often lie in global and national processes of restructuring and so may, in the short run, be beyond the capacity of local policy to address.

The Department of the Environment took over formal responsibility for the urban programme in 1975, but prior to this had initiated what was to become a large number of studies, good practice guides, monitoring exercises and evaluations of urban policy. For example, the Making Towns Better studies (for example, DoE, 1973) came close to being early versions of 'what works' guides and were designed to help local authorities to develop a 'total approach' to the urban environment. More substantial in both analysis and scope were Inner Area studies of 1977. These were carried out in three areas suffering the classic symptoms of urban decline: Liverpool, Birmingham and Lambeth (DoE, 1977) and were again designed to take a total approach to both understanding and prescription. Although different in flavour, these studies developed their theme from the CDP work of understanding the economic roots of urban decline. However, they laid greater stress on reversing this and improving the living conditions of inner area residents through more vigorous government policy, and through better coordination of policy and service delivery between central and local government, and between different service departments.

The 1980s saw the development of a stronger economic development focus in urban policy. This included the 'experiments' with Enterprise Zones (EZs) and Urban Development Corporations (UDCs) (see Box

10.1), which were subject to extensive monitoring and evaluation. This contributed both to providing an evidence base about the effectiveness of area-based urban policy and to the development of evaluation methodologies. This work is discussed below. Another development in the 1980s was the publication by the Department of the Environment of a series of good practice guides in urban regeneration. These were case study based (each containing up to 20) and dealt not with urban policy in general, but with the implementation of specific projects (particularly involving property and the physical environment). Examples were: reusing redundant buildings, greening city sites, improving urban areas and creating development trusts. They included general guidance of a 'how to do it' (and, by implication, 'what works') type. This included advice on key stages in the development process, drawn from case study evidence, on topics such as getting started, critical choices, the management of projects, and finance. These come closer to a 'what works' guide for practitioners than anything else produced up to that time but they do not satisfy rigorous criteria for being evidence-based urban policy in the sense of providing transferable evidence about the effect of specific interventions.

Box 10.1: Some urban development initiatives

Enterprise Zones (EZ) – area-based designations in which a deregulated regime involving the lifting of selected fiscal and administrative requirements was used to try to encourage industrial and commercial investment as part of the process of economic regeneration.

Urban Development Corporations (UDCs) – areas of economic decline designated by government under the 1980 Local Government, Planning and Land Act, in which a specially appointed corporation was given comprehensive powers (including planning and land assembly and finance) to revitalise the area.

City Challenge (CC) – a 'challenge fund' set up by central government to which local partnerships could bid for funding on the basis of strategies that would tackle severe local problems on a significant scale; now superseded by the Single Regeneration Budget (SRB).

Estate Action (EA) – a multifaceted programme under which the problem of run-down estates was addressed by a mix of physical, social and economic measures; also now replaced by SRB.

Single Regeneration Budget (SRB) – a programme of funding from the Department of the Environment, Transport and the Regions for urban regeneration based on a combination of need and competitive bidding.

The 1990s and recent developments

The 1990s have seen the development and dissemination of a more substantial and systematically organised evidence base for urban policy. This is briefly illustrated, before some of the research output is examined. Sources of data (for example, demographic data from the Census, labour market, housing, transport and crime statistics) are not examined, although it should be noted that the development of electronic databases (for example, the National Online Manpower Information Service [NOMIS]) has greatly facilitated access to data for urban policy.

Three sources of evidence illustrate the current state of development of infrastructure for evidence-based urban policy. First, the DETR website (http://www.regeneration.detr.gov.uk/rs/index.htm) provides summaries of all research commissioned by the department. Separate home pages for housing, local government, local transport, planning and regeneration give access to summaries of recent research. Those for regeneration, which are most relevant to this chapter, are reviewed below. Second, the Joseph Rowntree Foundation website (www.jrf.org.uk/knowledge/default.htm) provides clear, user-friendly summaries of research findings and work in progress. The search facility is organised into more than 100 categories (including urban, housing, community involvement, governance and local government, as well as numerous more detailed breakdowns). This is easy to access and use and the summaries provide clear reviews of findings, although they are generally less transparent on research methods. A third source worth mentioning is the net site developed by the Planning Exchange for the DETR and the Urban Regeneration Group of the Department for Social Development in Northern Ireland (www.regen.net). Although not a source for evidence-based policy in the strict sense, regen.net does provide ready access to a range of information, including reports on policy, good practice and specific initiatives.

These sources greatly facilitate access to up-to-date information, including research findings and examples of current practice and new initiatives. However, they are not currently designed as a source for evidence-based urban policy in the strict sense. While useful as a source for narratives and descriptive reviews of practice and findings they do not yet provide an adequate basis for systematic reviews involving the synthesis of research data and the production of reliable summary data on 'what works'.

The nature of most of the recent research and the extent to which it provides a foundation for evidence-based urban policy is illustrated from the regeneration research summaries on the DETR website. By 1999, 24 research summaries were available. A simple categorisation of these is not possible since they reflect the multisector and integrative nature of urban policy, and the pluralistic nature of urban research. But of these:

- *14 are monitoring or evaluation studies of urban policy.* Some analyse the impact of national policy initiatives – for example, urban policy in general through the 1980s (Robson et al, 1994), Enterprise Zones (PA Cambridge Economic Consultants, 1995a, 1995b) or English Partnerships (PA Consulting Group, 1999). Some evaluate the impact of policy in particular places – for example, the Urban Development Corporations in Leeds, Bristol and Manchester (Robson, 1998), or the London Docklands (DETR, 1998a). Others examine the effect of interventions in housing either in the form of wide-ranging 'Estate Action' policy (DoE, 1996a) or of the impact of design improvements on a range of social and environmental factors (PIEDA, 1995). All adopt a mix of quantitative and qualitative methodologies. Attempts at isolating the impact of interventions on outcomes range from multivariate statistical analysis to the use of control areas (districts or estates not subject to the intervention) in a quasi-experimental design methodology. Case study methodologies are common, and although the basis of selection of cases is normally explicit it is not always clear that they are representative of a wider population or of the conditions found in other places and therefore allow for generalisation. All demonstrate that triangulation (the use of different methodologies) is an essential feature of urban policy evaluations and that the impact of context on outcomes cannot be ignored. Some attempt to draw out lessons for good practice – but they do not go so far as to claim to be evidence-based policy.
- *Six are primarily concerned with establishing the facts of urban change.* One of these is methodological (DETR, 1998b) and develops an index of deprivation to be used in identifying need; two use either this indicator or its predecessor to identify the extent of deprivation on estates and in different districts (DETR, 1996b, 1998c). Two examine patterns of resource allocation in relation to need; one (DETR 1998d) analysing the distribution of SRB funds and the other (Bramley et al, 1998) of public funds more generally. The latter makes methodological developments in that it develops ways of analysing public spending flows to small areas. One study (Atkins et al, 1996) uses 1991 Census data to analyse urban trends – particularly with respect to urban rural divisions and conditions in inner-city areas.

- *Three are essentially about processes of urban policy.* One (Alcock, 1998) examines the interaction between two policy vehicles designed to tackle social and economic disadvantage (SRB and local authority anti-poverty strategies), a second reviews the structure and processes used in English Partnership work (DETR, 1998e) and the third looks at the factors influencing the success of regional and sub-regional partnerships (Fordham, 1998).
- One is unique in that it is *mainly concerned with the implications for London of developments in the finance and business sectors* in three other 'world cities' (DETR, 1996c).

Evidence of need and its relationship to spending

Any rational urban or area-based policy must be based on the ability to identify geographical areas demonstrating high levels of deprivation and need. Blackman (1998) makes this the central theme of a discussion of evidence-based local government, where he uses local authority social care services to examine formula-based funding and targeting of spending. Evidence of need, of the extent to which spending follows need, and of the impact of policy on reducing deprivation must be central to evidence-based urban policy. Three key problems of geographical measures or indicators of need are:

- selecting and using data that is regarded as valid in the sense that it measures need, as defined by the objectives of policy, and is reliable in reflecting current social and economic conditions (there are obvious problems in using Census data towards the end of the decennial cycle);
- the availability of data at the appropriate geographical scale;
- combining different datasets so as to produce a single index – this involves both value judgements (which data to use and whether differential weighting is required), and technical issues of data transformation (for example the use of z scores or chi squared so as to make different datasets comparable).

This approach to demonstrating evidence of need is illustrated by the method used by the DETR to construct an indicator of local conditions (now an Index of Deprivation). Originally produced in 1981, and updated in 1991 and 1998, the current index is produced at three spatial scales, local authority district, ward and enumeration district (ED) (DETR, 1998b). This provides "a more sensitive description of the complex geography of deprivation" and thus allows for the identification of pockets of deprivation in what are otherwise less deprived areas (Robson et al, 1995, p 195). The district level index (the most comprehensive and up-to-date data) uses 12 indicators. The ward level uses six (two of which are part of the district level set) and the ED level uses five. The 12 district level indicators represent a range of socioeconomic 'domains' of deprivation (health, shelter, security, physical environment, education, income and unemployment), and are devised as direct measures of deprivation. Consequently, they do not include groups at risk of deprivation (such as single-parent families). Where data requires standardisation, chi squared rather than z scores are used (to reduce the weight on potentially unreliable small numbers), and differential weightings are in general avoided. Exceptions are made for data already in index form (Standardised Mortality Rates for under-75s, and a crime proxy that uses home insurance weightings). In summing indicators to produce an overall index only positive values (greater than the average for England) are used.

Evidence of need is essentially descriptive and can be used to inform decisions about urban policy. However, this data can also be used to analyse the extent to which urban policy funding and public spending in general are *allocated* according to need – in other words whether the complex mechanisms by which public funding is allocated 'work' in reaching the most needy areas. Robson et al (1994), in a major evaluation of urban policy in the 1980s, examined the fit between the designation of 57 Urban Priority Areas (UPAs) (which were not based solely on the index of local conditions) and funding from both Action for Cities (AfC) (the specific urban policy funding), and main programmes (such as Revenue Support Grant [RSG] and Housing Investment Programmes [HIPs]). They found a general lack of fit between designation and funding, for urban and general funding, both in the 1980s in general and between 1988 and 1990 when the 57 areas were officially designated as target areas. Similar outcomes were found for the more substantial main programme funding. On one level this work could demonstrate the significance of political processes in allocating funding – but in terms of long-term policy development it could be interpreted as part of a process of accumulating evidence through which urban policy becomes more evidence based.

More recent work looks specifically at the link between the index of local conditions and the distribution of the first three rounds of SRB Challenge Fund resources (Tyler et al, 1998). This study found that although 20% of SRB funding went to partnerships in less deprived districts, 80% went to the 99 most deprived districts (42% of the population). There thus appears to have been some rationality (based on the measurement of need) behind the distribution of urban funding, bearing in mind that such distribution is also a result of a bidding process. It is a matter of speculation as to whether the outcome seen reflects research evidence being used to inform policy decisions.

However, as the Robson et al (1995) study demonstrates, targeted urban funding represents a small fraction of total public expenditure (2% in the case of AfC funding). More recent research (Bramley et al, 1998) develops a methodology for measuring about 70% of total public spending flows (excluding, for example, defence and foreign affairs) to local and small areas (down to ward levels). This study contains numerous caveats and notes of caution, but presents findings from case study cities that demonstrate the possibility of measuring public spending at ward level. It shows some relationship (but wide variation) between deprivation at ward level and spending (spending for the most deprived wards in case study cities being about 45% above that for least deprived wards). Such evidence on the incidence of spending could inform public policy programmes so that they are targeted on areas of deprivation and social exclusion. It demonstrates the possibility of urban policy at the national level, where decisions are made about the distribution of funds, becoming less political in Cheshire's (1987) 'mean' sense and more rational in the sense of it being based on evidence of where need is located.

Using the evidence

The monitoring and evaluation of urban policy initiatives, such as Enterprise Zones, Urban Development Corporations, City Challenge, and now the Single Regeneration Budget Challenge Fund, has produced a wealth of data of potential use at a number of stages of the policy process (see Box 10.1).

As a result of the competitive nature of urban funding the bidding stage involves an appraisal process in which forecasts of the costs and benefits of what is being proposed are required; these obviously require evidence. Details depend on the nature of the projects being proposed. Apart from costings they are likely to include quantifiable outputs such as number of jobs created, new businesses started up, housing association dwellings to be completed and voluntary organisations supported (DETR, 1998f).

This process requires a statement of baseline conditions in the targeted area from which improvements attributable to the funded programme can be measured. There is now considerable evidence available in published studies carried out for the DoE and DETR on baseline conditions in areas targeted by particular urban policy measures. For example, a report on the performance and good practice of eight UDCs (Howick and Lawrence, 1998) sets out initial conditions in these areas, documenting the vacancy and dereliction left behind by large-scale industrial closures in the 1970s and 1980s, and then analysing the land reclaimed, property and infrastructure developed and jobs created from this baseline. Similar evidence is available for other studies of UDCs (Robson, 1998).

The terms on which funding is made available requires monitoring of conditions (including perceptions of stakeholders as well as measurable outputs) through the life of the programmes. This, like other material collected as part of the appraisal and monitoring process, includes qualitative as well as quantitative data. For example, an interim evaluation of the SRB Challenge Fund as a whole, based on 20 case studies (Brennan et al, 1998), included household surveys which produced evidence on dissatisfaction with dwellings, perceptions of crime problems associated with drugs, and of serious traffic problems. Targeted areas were compared with comparable national statistics.

Evaluation of schemes requires an analysis of outcomes in which outputs (jobs created in the area, houses constructed and so on) are analysed for their actual final impact. This involves identifying the impact on different groups, displacement effects, and additionality that is genuinely attributable to the programme as opposed to other factors.

Although much of the data coming from the appraisal and evaluation requirements of urban funding is designed to ensure value for money and rigorous project management it also provides an evidential basis for analytical studies of what works in urban policy. The evidence coming from the use of this and other evidence in evaluations is considered in the next section.

Evidence of what works from the monitoring and evaluation of urban policy

Full-scale evaluation, providing evidence on the relationship between interventions and outcomes, which is transferable, would arguably provide the gold standard for 'what works' in urban policy. For reasons already identified this is difficult, if not impossible, to achieve. However, in spite of the problems, considerable effort has been directed at evaluation. This can be divided into:

- evaluation of urban policy in general;
- evaluation of the overall effect of specific initiatives (for example, Enterprise Zones, Urban Development Corporations, or Estate Action) and the instruments used within those;
- evaluation of interventions in particular places (for example, the work in the London Docklands Development Corporation);
- thematic studies (for example, of the impact of estate improvement, or environmental improvement on urban regeneration).

Examples of a selection of studies relevant to these themes are briefly reviewed, methodologies are discussed and conclusions drawn about the extent to which this work provides evidence about urban interventions that could be replicated.

The evaluation by Robson et al (1994) of the overall impact of urban policy (Action for Cities) through the 1980s is an attempt to answer the big question of whether the targeting of special funds on specific areas by central government 'worked' in improving conditions in those areas. Strength of policy was measured using AFC spending levels, and attempts were made to discover statistical associations between this and selected socioeconomic output measures. Three rates (unemployment, job change and small firm creation) were used as indicators of local economic conditions, and two rates (house price change and migration of 25- to 34-year-olds) were used as measures of residential attractiveness. Conditions in three types of areas reflecting different levels of intervention were analysed to see whether any convergence of circumstances was attributable to urban policy. Given the conceptual and technical problems of this analysis, results obviously have to be interpreted with care. Many of the relationships between inputs and outcomes showed no statistical significance, but a few significant relationships were identified: urban programme spending between 1986 and 1990 was positively associated with some improvements in unemployment, and spending appeared to be linked with residential attractiveness as measured by house prices and migration of the 25- to 34-year-old group. However, these findings have to be set against others, which showed a widening gap between the urban areas and others, and complex patterns of change within conurbations that showed increased 'within district' polarisation. This study demonstrates very clearly the problems of this 'macro-level' evaluation of urban policy. The mix of interventions in AFC was such that it is impossible to tell whether results reflected geographically targeted urban policy in general (and therefore whether such targeting 'works') or (more likely) the very particular policies of that period. Other conclusions from the Robson study about processes of urban policy implementation using qualitative data are discussed in the next section.

A number of studies evaluate the impact of specific urban policy programmes. For example, work on Enterprise Zones (EZs) (PA Cambridge Economic Consultants, 1995a, 1995b) used a combination of annual monitoring data (such as employment, firms established, impact on property markets), company surveys (revealing perceptions of the importance of different EZ benefits) and indepth studies of property markets and environmental improvements. As part of this triangulation methodology attempts were made to isolate the impact of different instruments (for example, property tax relief, capital allowances and the relaxation of planning controls) using qualitative survey data of perceptions. Potentially this gives some 'what works' data – for example property tax relief was reported as being the main attraction. Analytical work included attempts to measure the extent to which property tax relief was capitalised in higher rents, and therefore benefited owners rather than occupiers, and also deadweight and displacement effects. Consequently, although this work evaluated the specific combination of instruments used in EZs (and provided data specific to that experiment), it provides a base of evidence that could inform policy judgements about the effects of geographical targeting of incentives on small areas.

Similar work has evaluated the effect of Urban Development Corporations (Howick and Lawrence, 1998; Robson, 1998). Gross measures of outputs of UDCs include jobs created within the areas, roads and infrastructure constructed, land reclaimed, commercial floorspace and housing units completed and private sector investment levered in. Results include evidence on the extent to which most of the new activity in UDCs is simply a displacement effect and would otherwise be occurring elsewhere (either in the same town or region or elsewhere in the UK). This fundamental problem of evaluation of area-based programmes is analysed in one UDC study (Robson, 1998) through property vacancy chains (that is, an exploration of displacement effects caused by relocation). Conclusions are that only where chains of property vacated as a result of relocations end in long-term vacancy or demolition can the impact of a UDC be said to be purely the result of displacement. In another study, evaluating the effect of the London Docklands, it is estimated that additionality (gains from the policy intervention itself) is high and displacement is low *within* the Docklands area, but additionality fell to about 26% of the jobs created if a wider area including the Cities of London and Westminster were included (DETR, 1998a). In other words, concentrated, targeted action worked in creating jobs within that area – but was less impressive if other neighbouring areas were brought into the frame.

The emphasis of these programmes was economic. Housing has also been central to urban policy, and linked not only to improving physical conditions in properties and on estates, but also to bringing empty properties back into use, reducing crime, improving health and resident satisfaction through participative estate management, and attracting private investment and improving opportunities for training. A number of studies adopting quasi-experimental methodologies have provided evidence on the extent to which housing based strategies 'work' as elements of urban policy. An evaluation of six early Estate Action schemes (DoE, 1996a) adopted a longitudinal approach (with data gathering before the programme to establish baseline conditions, immediately after completion and one year later), in which comparator estates were used in an attempt to measure genuine additionality. Data collection involved physical, environmental and social surveys, and interviews. Results indicated that although regeneration and physical improvements were evident in most cases, perceptions of success were greater in local authorities than among residents. With exceptions, reductions in crime were few and the difficulties of using housing investment as a basis for social and economic benefits were demonstrated. The main lessons concerned the need for a multifaceted strategic approach to estate regeneration.

Halpern (1995) reports a more sharply focused study of the impact of physical improvements under the Estates Action programme on the mental health of residents. This study, carried out in an unpopular New Town estate characterised by fear of crime, distrust, and a view that it was a bad place to raise children, attempted to link the mental health of residents to three stages of estate improvement intervention. Assessments of residents' mental health (using the Hospital Anxiety and Depression Scale to measure anxiety and depression, and the Rosenberg Self Esteem Scale) took place at all stages. A longitudinal element was included in which the same individuals were compared at different times. Statistical methods were employed to act as a control for different factors that could account for any changes. Halpern concludes that:

... there were clearly substantial improvements in mental health coinciding with residents consultation with the Council and with physical improvements to the estate ... the study provides evidence that, at least in some important instances, mental health can be improved through an environmental intervention.... The methodology ... demonstrates that the intervention worked.... Clearly the environment is just one of many factors that can affect mental health, but nonetheless it is a factor, and it can be a very important one among those living on society's problem estates. (1995, pp 199-200)

Other work on housing and estates demonstrates some of the basic problems of interpreting evidence on the effectiveness of spatially targeted urban policy. Pinto (1993, p 54), for example, shows that "targeting and concentrating funds for specific schemes in predefined localities does seem to work" at one level. But Power and Tunstall (1995, p 73), in a study of changing social and housing conditions over 15 years on 20 council estates spread throughout the country, found that although wider social changes led to increased polarisation, and government initiatives led to short-term physical improvements, intensive localised management (for which there was "no substitute ... and for which no exit strategy can or should be devised") was as important in arresting decline as the physical improvement process.

The impact of housing design on a range of physical and social conditions has been the subject of one of the only attempts at a controlled experiment in urban policy. Coleman, in well-publicised work (1990), attributed a range of social and economic problems to poor estate design. On the basis of this a series of full-scale trials was designed to test whether a range of monetary and non-monetary benefits could be brought about from the design measures advocated in Coleman's work (DoE, 1997b). Benefits examined in this study included: reduced maintenance costs, improved estate management, lower tenant turnover, reductions in vacancy rates and rent loss, reductions in crime, and improvements in children's behaviour and in residents' mental and physical health. The evaluation of this DICE (Design Improvement Controlled Experiment) initiative involved comparison of pre- and post-scheme conditions on DICE and control estates. Results indicate not only less benefit from design improvements than those predicted, but also the extreme difficulty of experimental trials as a means of obtaining evidence of 'what works'. Although some benefits were attributed to DICE improvements, in general they were no more successful than Estate Action schemes, and demonstrated that local context and other specific factors strongly influenced or modified the effects of the design interventions. Not only do initial conditions vary from place to place in such a way that the impact of interventions will vary, so do the details of the intervention and the processes through which it is implemented. Consequently, the range of factors involved is such that it is impossible to use control to isolate the effect of a specific intervention. In the light of methodological problems of this sort it is instructive to look briefly at a different sort of evidence in urban policy – that which concerns 'good practice' in the processes of policy development and implementation.

Process-based evidence

Of the 24 DETR projects listed above, three are primarily about processes of urban regeneration policy and most of the others include sections on the policy process. One (Alcock, 1998) examines the interactions between two parallel policy vehicles, SRB projects and local authority anti-poverty strategies, both of which are designed to tackle social and economic disadvantage. This is case study based, and draws lessons about coordination. Another (DETR, 1998e) looks at the procedures used by English Partnerships to support area-based regeneration strategies, including what this body requires in the appraisal process. The third (Fordham, 1998), again using a case study methodology, looks at the formation and operation of regional and sub-regional partnerships and the ways in which they contribute to regeneration objectives.

Most other urban research studies include substantial contributions to understanding processes of urban regeneration. The Robson et al (1994) study discussed above includes an examination of the way in which particular circumstances in different places affect the viability of creating partnerships, and of the problems of coordination between central and local government. This work was based on interviews with experts involved in urban policy. A study of the impact of three UDCs, again making extensive use of interviews (Robson, 1998) includes an assessment of the importance of good networking between regeneration agencies and other local stakeholders. Its conclusions included recommendations about the need for agencies not to adopt narrow property-led strategies but to include the social dimension. This has implications for the geographical boundaries of regeneration agencies, which, he argues, should incorporate resident communities.

An increasingly important objective in spatially targeted urban policy is that of ensuring that improvements in the area are sustained beyond the time period of the initiative. The 'what works' question here is that of how to develop capacities within an area so that any improvements brought about by intervention are sustained by internal social and economic processes. Processes of capacity building, from tenant participation and management to community-based schemes for crime reduction have been the subject of numerous studies and experiments, many of which are concerned with sectoral policy (housing, crime reduction and so on) rather than urban policy as defined here. However, the question of what works in sustaining any area-based improvements brought about by urban policy is an important one, and one to which the policy research in general on capacity building and sustainability is highly relevant.

Conclusions: is an evidence-based urban policy possible?

It is clear from the nature of urban policy that the concept of evidence-based policy here must take on a rather different meaning from that associated with, for example, medical or education practice. If evidence-based policy means 'what works' in the simple sense of what interventions are necessary to bring about certain predictable outcomes then urban policy seems to have some distance to travel. The complexity of urban problems and the significance of context (the impact of the conditions in which intervention takes place on the outcomes achieved) casts doubt on the relevance of a mechanistic approach to urban policy in which diagnosis leads to prescriptions that are universally applicable.

However, the problems in achieving evidence-based urban policy do not just relate to the nature of that policy. They also reflect the limited availability of methodologies and analytical tools that are up to the task of providing reliable and valid evidence. The research reviewed here shows that existing approaches are pluralistic, relying on methodologies that range from trials (rarely), quasi-experiments and statistical analysis, to attitude surveys and interviews with experts. The data produced is both qualitative and quantitative, and is commonly based on case studies in which the uniqueness of local conditions is recognised. Even where trials and quasi-experiments have been carried out, the results point to the importance of evidence based on 'softer' methodologies that acknowledge the importance of context, local conditions and process. The nature of urban research suggests it would be wrong to expect the same sort of evidence base as that available, for example, from randomised controlled trials in the medical field. Systematic reviews and meta-analyses would undoubtedly take forward the concept of evidence-based urban policy, but are difficult to carry out given the validity of different research paradigms in this area. They would also require greater transparency about methods than is sometimes available on the current websites used to disseminate findings in urban research.

So a fully developed evidence-based urban policy would be different from, for example, evidence-based health policy. The policy judgements that stem from it would still be open to question. However, that does not invalidate the notion of evidence-based urban policy – if anything it reinforces it. Only with evidence can urban policy move away from being in Cheshire's terms 'political in the meanest sense'. If the claims of many commentators that urban policy simply serves a political function (in the sense of providing visible reassurance that something is being done about some of society's most intractable problems) are correct, then some cynicism about the search for an evidence-based urban policy would be justified. But if urban policy 'will not go away', if it continues to make significant claims on financial and other resources, and it develops new, holistic and integrative ways of addressing 'wicked' problems that vertical, sector-based approaches have clearly failed to achieve, then evidence must be an essential part of this. The fact that this evidence is not based on a simple mechanistic view of the relationship between interventions and outcomes should not be justification to reject the very notion of evidence-based urban policy.

References

Alcock, P. (1998) *Inclusive regeneration: The impact on regeneration of local authorities' corporate strategies for tackling regeneration*, London: DETR.

Atkins, D., Champion, T., Coombes, M., Dorling, D. and Woodward, R. (1996) *Urban trends in England: Evidence from the 1991 Census*, London: HMSO.

Blackman, T. (1998) 'Towards evidence-based local government: theory and practice', *Local Government Studies*, vol 24, no 2, pp 56-70

Bramley, G., Evans, M. and Atkins, J. (1998) *Where does public spending go? A pilot study to analyse the flows of public expenditure into local areas*, London: DETR.

Brennan, A., Rhodes, J. and Tyler, P. (1998) *Evaluation of the Single Regeneration Challenge Fund: A partnership for regeneration – An interim evaluation*, London: DETR.

CDP (Community Development Project) (1977) *Gilding the ghetto*, London: The Home Office.

CDP/PEC (1979) *The state and the local economy*, London: PDC.

Cheshire, P. (1987) 'Urban policy: art not science?', in B. Robson (ed) *Managing the city*, London: Croom Helm, pp 22-39.

Coleman, A. (1990) *Utopia on trial: Vision and reality in planned housing*, London: Hilary Shipman.

Cottle, S. (1993) *TV news, urban conflict and the inner city*, Leicester: Leicester University Press.

DETR (Department of the Environment, Transport and the Regions) Regeneration research website: http://www.regeneration.detr.gov.uk/rs/index.htm

DETR (1996b) *Mapping local authority estates using the Index of Local Conditions*, DETR Regeneration Research Summary No 06 (now Housing Research Summary No 65), DETR website.

DETR (1996c) *Four world cities*, Urban Research Summary No 7, DETR website.

DETR (1997a) *Regeneration – The way forward, DETR Regeneration website*.

DETR (1997b) *An evaluation of DICE schemes*, DETR Regeneration Research Summary No 11, DETR Regeneration website.

DETR (Corporate Author) (1998a) *Regenerating London's Docklands*, London: DETR.

DETR (1998b) *1998 Index of Deprivation*, DETR Regeneration Research Summary No 15, DETR website.

DETR (1998c) *The 1998 Index of Local Deprivation: Patterns of deprivation and 1991-6 change*, DETR Regeneration Research Summary No 21, DETR website.

DETR (1998d) *The distribution of SRB Challenge Fund Resources in relation to local area needs in England*, DETR Regeneration Research Summary No 13, DETR website.

DETR (1998e) *Interim evaluation of English Partnerships: Review of structure, strategy and practices*, DETR Regeneration Research Summary No 22, DETR website.

DETR (1998f) *SRB Challenge Fund Guidance Manual*, London: DETR.

DoE (Department of the Environment) (1973) *Making Towns Better: The Sunderland Study*, London: HMSO.

DoE (1977) *Inner Area studies: Summaries of consultants' final reports*, London: HMSO.

DoE (Corporate Author) (1996a) *An evaluation of six early Estate Action schemes*, London: HMSO.

Edwards, M. and Batley, R. (1978) *The politics of positive discrimination: An evaluation of the Urban Programme*, London: Tavistock.

Fordham, G. (1998) *Building partnerships in the English Regions*, London: DETR.

Hall, P. (1981) *The inner city in context*, London: Heinemann.

Halpern, D. (1995) *Mental health and the built environment*, London: Taylor and Francis.

Howick, C. and Lawrence, D.: Roger Tym and Partners (1998) *Urban Development Corporations: Performance and good practice*, London: DETR.

Laurence, S. and Hall, P. (1981) 'British policy responses', in P. Hall (ed) *The inner city in context*, London: SSRC/Heinemann, pp 88-111.

Mossberger, K. and Stoker, G. (1997) 'Inner city policy in Britain; why it will not go away', *Urban Affairs Review*, vol 32, no 3, pp 378-401.

Oatley, N. (1998) 'Urban policy and regeneration in Britain. The way forward', Unpublished discussion paper, Faculty of the Built Environment, University of the West of England.

PA Cambridge Economic Consultants (1995a) *Final evaluation of Enterprise Zones*, London: HMSO.

PA Cambridge Economic Consultants (1995b) *Second interim evaluation of Enterprise Zones*, London: HMSO.

PA Consulting Group (1999) *Interim evaluation of English Partnerships, Final Report*, London: DETR.

PIEDA (1995) *The impact of environmental improvement on urban regeneration*, London: HMSO.

Pinto, R. (1993) 'An analysis of the impact of Estate Action schemes', *Local Government Studies*, vol 19, no 1, pp 37-55.

Power, A. and Tunstall, R. (1995) *Swimming against the tide: Polarisation or progress on 20 unpopular council estates*, York: Joseph Rowntree Foundation.

Robinson, F. and Shaw, K. (1994) 'Urban policy under the Conservatives: in search of the big idea', *Local Economy*, vol 9, no 3, pp 224-35.

Robson, B. (1998) *The impact of Urban Development Corporations in Leeds, Bristol and Central Manchester*, London: DETR.

Robson, B., Bradford, M. and Tye, R. (1995) 'The development of the 1991 local deprivation index', in G. Room (ed) *Beyond the threshold: The measurement and analysis of social exclusion*, Bristol: The Policy Press, pp 191-211.

Robson, B., Bradford, M., Deas, I., Hall, E., Harrison, E., Parkinson, M., Evans, R., Garside, P., Harding, A. and Robinson, F. (1994) *Assessing the impact of urban policy*, DoE Inner Cities Research Programme, London: HMSO.

Tyler, P., Rhodes, J. and Brennan, A. (1998) *Discussion Paper 91, The distribution of SRB Challenge Fund Expenditure in relation to local area needs in England*, Cambridge: Department of Land Economy, University of Cambridge

Urban Task Force (Chair Lord Rogers of Riverside) (1999) *Final Report. Towards an urban renaissance*, London: DETR, distributed by E & FN Spon.

ELEVEN

A strategic approach to research and development

Huw Davies, Gloria Laycock[1], Sandra Nutley,
Judy Sebba and Trevor Sheldon

Introduction

Previous chapters have examined the nature of the research evidence which has been generated in different sectors. Much of the knowledge base has been contributed by researchers pursuing their own disciplinary and intellectual interests. This has been productive, leading to important contributions to our understanding of the world and improved effectiveness of interventions. However, this investigator-led approach has often left important gaps in knowledge, particularly in areas that are relevant to policy and policy makers but which may not be of such interest or gain kudos in more academic circles. More recently, policy makers in various service areas have sought to ensure that the balance of research carried out more adequately reflects their needs. They have done this in the UK by further developing inhouse research capacity (for example, at the Home Office) or by establishing the mechanisms for commissioning relevant research from external research groups, principally university-based.

Some £350m is estimated to have been spent on policy-related research by UK central government in 1998/99 (Cabinet Office, 1999). A government review of the use of such research does not make edifying reading:

> Recent work by the Council for Science and Technology found that no department was really organised to make the best possible use of science and technology either in delivering its immediate objectives or

in formulating its strategy for the long term. Our evidence suggests that the same is true of social and economic research. (Cabinet Office, 1999, para 7.6)

This chapter examines and compares how different service areas have sought to develop well-directed research capacity to generate information on the effectiveness of interventions and how such information is integrated into the policy process and communicated to practitioners. Three key policy areas are considered: the National Health Service, the Home Office and the Department for Education and Employment.

The National Health Service *by Trevor Sheldon*

Background

There has been international interest in the way that the UK National Health Service (NHS) developed a strategy for acquiring and disseminating the research evidence needed for policy and clinical decision making. Other countries have invested heavily in medical research and the evaluation of healthcare, but the NHS was probably the first to develop a research and development (R&D) strategy that lay at the core of the service and central to the management of that service (Black, 1997)

Over the years increasing concern was expressed about both the quality of UK health-related research and its increasingly biomedical emphasis, which did not reflect the research needs of the service. Researchers were keen to obtain funds to carry out research in areas that interested them and they were not overly bothered about ensuring that their results had an impact. Even if they were concerned with dissemination of their results, the traditional route of publication in academic journals rarely led to change. The result was that research that was relevant to practice and policy too often lay under-utilised. The lack of producer push was matched by little in the way of consumer pull – "no one ... really believed that health services research could help them solve their problems. They thought that all problems, ... were solved administratively" (Cochrane, 1989, p 245).

A review of the state of medical research, with special reference to the needs of the NHS, by the House of Lords Select Committee on Science and Technology (1988) found UK medical research to be in a low state of morale, with inadequate funding, and poor career prospects. Above all the NHS was run with little awareness of the needs of research or what research could contribute. This last deficit is what led to the main recommendation of the report – the creation of a national health research authority within the NHS with greater funding, which would support an "applied science base which matches the service needs of the NHS" (House of Lords, 1988, para 4.8). Clinical research would from then on be funded by reference to service needs rather than the interests of the investigator.

The House of Lords report led to both the appointment of a Director of R&D in the NHS (Professor [now Sir] Michael Peckham, who became a full member of the NHS Management Executive), and the launching of a national strategy *Research for health* in 1991 (DoH, 1991, 1993). The national strategy had a target for increasing the spending on research by the NHS from 0.9% to 1.5% of the total NHS budget. The resulting increase in research spending led to the NHS R&D programme becoming the biggest single public funder of research in the health area in England (see Table 11.1), although it is still small compared to industrial funding (mostly from pharmaceutical companies). While the R&D programme has been significant in shaping the agenda for NHS-funded research, much of the research evidence on what works in healthcare is commercially funded, and those funders have their own agenda.

Table 11.1: Health R&D funding in England

Department of Health R&D (1999/2000)	£467m
Charities (1998/9)	£417m*
Medical Research Council (1997/8)	£296m*
Higher Education Funding Council for England (HEFC) (1997/98)	£137m†

Notes: * UK figure; † Includes research funding to medical schools.

Sources: DoH; MRC Annual Report; Association of Medical Research Charities

The key features of the NHS R&D programme launched in 1991 are summarised in Box 11.1. The following discussion looks firstly at the way in which it established priorities for NHS-funded research, and secondly at how it sought to ensure research synthesis and dissemination.

Box 11.1: Key features of the NHS R&D programme

- Focused on meeting needs of the service and of policy makers

- Based in the heart of the national and regional management structure of the NHS

- Most research commissioned based on assessment of service/policy needs

- Emphasis on systematic reviews of research before new primary research is commissioned

- Regional structure to better involve and respond to the service

- Involvement of managers as well as clinicians and academics

- Emphasis on dissemination and not just production of knowledge

---

The R&D strategy

Establishing priorities

An advisory Central Research and Development Committee was established with representation from NHS managers, industry and academic researchers. The strategy which they put forward favoured a 'problem-led' approach in which priority areas were established for fixed time periods and research topics were prioritised within those areas. A lead regional health authority then took responsibility for overseeing the commissioning of the research. This was in contrast to the previous predominantly investigator-led or science-driven approach. Problem areas for which time-limited programmes were established included: mental health and learning disability; cardiovascular disease and stroke; cancer; asthma; oral health. Programmes were also established in areas more related to management and organisation such as the interface between primary and secondary care, and also ones focusing on specific client groups such as maternal and child health, and physical and complex disabilities.

Subsequently, centrally commissioned research was restructured within the NHS R&D programme. The nine time-limited, specific problem-based programmes were subsumed by three more generic continuing programmes: Health Technology Assessment; Service Development and Organisation; New and Emerging Applications of Technologies. Alongside these core programmes, a methodology panel prioritises research into, and gives support for, methodological research crucial to rolling out the substantive programmes of research.

The Health Technology Assessment (HTA) programme illustrates the potential importance of the R&D programme to the NHS (Stein and Milne, 1998). Since its inception in 1993, more than 7,600 potential research topics have been submitted for consideration by advisory panels. The main Standing Group has prioritised nearly 400 topics and 233 have so far been commissioned at a cost of nearly £40 million (NHS Executive, 1999). These range from evaluations of screening programmes (such as for prostate cancer), diagnostic technologies, pharmaceuticals, technologies used in acute care or primary or community care. The assessment may consist of a systematic review of existing research and possibly some extra modelling or primary research such as a new trial. Technologies are prioritised for evaluation because there is uncertainty in the NHS about their value in terms of patient outcomes in relation to their cost.

In addition to these central activities, a key aspect of the strategy was the development of R&D programmes in the regions headed up by regional R&D directors. As well as helping to manage the national programmes, regions were also expected to fund research to meet local priorities, invest in local research capacity and provide responsive funding for local researchers.

In tandem with these stipulations, major changes were made to the way that R&D was supported financially within the NHS. The Culyer Report (1994) recommended a clear separation in the NHS between money for R&D activity per se, money to support the excess service costs of hosting R&D activity (for example, extra tests, medications or clinic visits), and other regular NHS activity. These recommendations were implemented across the UK fostering a greater clarity about how R&D money was spent and providing clearer incentives for well articulated R&D activity.

Research synthesis and dissemination

One of the key features of the NHS R&D programme was a concern with the use of research outputs (Smith, 1993). One of the time-limited, problem-specific R&D programmes was for commissioning research into implementing the results of research.

The central Information Systems Strategy (ISS) includes a project register (the National Research Register) in order to keep a record of publicly-funded research projects across the country. Another part of the ISS is the UK Cochrane Centre. This supports the conduct and maintenance of meta-analyses of (mainly) randomised controlled trials in the UK, as part of an international Cochrane Collaboration. A sibling organisation – the NHS Centre for Reviews and Dissemination (CRD) – also carries out and commissions systematic reviews. However, these are carried out in direct response to policy and practice needs in the NHS. The CRD also has a national responsibility to transfer this R&D information to NHS databases and to publish six times each year the *Effective Health Care* bulletin (Sheldon and Melville, 1996).

Over the first few years of the R&D programme there was an increase in easy-to-access, high-quality synthesised information in electronic form (such as the Cochrane Library) or in paper form (such as the *Effective Health Care* and *Effectiveness Matters* bulletins from the NHS CRD). However, these did not always reach the relevant target audience and relied heavily on self-motivated use. While there were individual and often heroic efforts to get research into practice (such as Getting Research Into Practice and Purchasing [GriPP] in Oxford, Promoting Action on Clinical Effectiveness [PACE] promoted by the King's Fund and Framework for Appropriate Care Throughout Sheffield [FACTS] in Sheffield), these were not part of an integrated aproach across the NHS. This was because there was a clear division of national responsibility within the NHS Executive between the R&D Directorate and those in the Health Services Directorate responsible for the activities of the service including 'evidence-based' healthcare. As a result of the failure of coordination across these directorates, and the lack of a national dissemination/implementation framework, the increasing output of health service research relevant to the NHS was not matched by a corresponding implementation effort. Instances of successful dissemination/ implementation, such as the national policy not to establish a national screening programme for prostate cancer in the light of research commissioned by the HTA programme, have been more due to individual efforts and luck rather than by design.

Recent initiatives and future challenges

The NHS R&D strategy was bold and original. However, it has been criticised even by its supporters (Baker, 1998; Black, 1997). There are two main areas of concern:
• the injection of funds for new projects has not been accompanied by a corresponding and balanced investment in the capacity of the country

to carry out research, particularly in the areas of primary care, nursing, midwifery and other non-medical areas;
• perhaps the weakest element of the R&D programme has been dealing with dissemination and implementation of the research evidence.

The latter situation has changed recently with the government's quality initiative (DoH, 1998). This establishes a framework and a number of supporting institutions to develop and monitor the implementation of evidence-based standards (see Chapter Three). The National Institute for Clinical Excellence (NICE) will develop guidelines that, along with the National Service Frameworks, will set quality standards for the service. Clinical governance sets a duty on healthcare organisations and practitioners to assure the quality of their practice (including use of research evidence) and the Commission for Health Improvement will monitor the implementation of national standards. This regulatory structure provides a mechanism for the implementation of research results via quality standards. The challenge will be to ensure that these standards are based on the knowledge base and are not simply captured by professional groups and bureaucrats.

The Home Office (police research) by Gloria Laycock[1]

Background

The Home Office has a long history of centrally-funded social science research (Lodge, 1974; Croft, 1981, 1983). Since 1948 the Home Secretary, by virtue of Acts of Parliament, has had statutory authority to carry out and commission research. In 1957 the Home Office set up its own unit for funding and carrying out research in the crime and criminology fields, partly to fill a gap in provision by the other major social science research funders, but also to provide a central resource for ministers and senior officials seeking an empirical base in the formation of policy.

The current remit of the Home Office Research Development and Statistics Directorate (RDS) is to provide information that helps ministers and policy makers take evidence-based decisions. It also seeks to help the police, probation service, the courts, immigration officials and firefighters do their jobs as effectively as possible. It does this by maintaining the various statistical services published by the Home Office and by carrying out research (either directly or through commissioning others).

In establishing its research programme, RDS has operated a traditional

UK government research agency customer/contractor relationship with policy units. This involves an annual cycle for establishing research priorities. Such a cycle might typically start in the summer with an invitation to research customers (those in policy units) to identify their forthcoming research needs over the next 12 months. The contractor (the inhouse research team) develops these bids during the autumn with the aim of publishing an agreed research programme the following spring, for funding during that financial year.

In this section it is not the R&D strategy of the Home Office RDS per se that is described, but rather a separate group (the Police Research Group [PRG]) established in 1992 within the Police Department of the Home Office. The reason for focusing on the PRG is because of the way it set out to establish a different approach to R&D than the traditional model described above. This approach has subsequently been adopted as a template for developing the Crime Reduction Programme.

The PRG was given the remit of carrying out research that addressed the needs of ministers, officials and the police themselves. Its aim was to increase the influence of research on police policy and practice. In the way in which it operated, the PRG set out to address directly the criticisms of research, justified or not, as seen by some civil servants. With some notable exceptions research was characterised as always too late, too esoteric, more or less irrelevant to the current panic, and expensive. The police held a similar view. There was a history of academic police research, which was essentially critical in nature and often hostile in content. The police were used to being the subjects of research rather than being involved in the process by which research questions are defined and research commissioned. The way in which these various criticisms were addressed within the PRG is described below.

R&D strategy for police research

The following guiding principles of the R&D strategy of the PRG are discussed below:
- relevance to policy
- timeliness
- strategic programmes, not projects
- intelligibility
- engaging practitioners.

Relevance to policy

The location of the PRG physically and organisationally within a major policy directorate contributed to ensuring the relevance of PRG work to the policy agenda. The head of the PRG worked directly to the head of the Police Department. It was this same person who was organisationally responsible for the determination of police policy in England and Wales and who similarly managed all the major policy unit heads. The proximity of the research staff to the 'policy process' was also useful in bringing home to the researchers involved the speed with which senior policy advisers work and the rate at which the agenda changes.

Timeliness

The fact that research was usually seen to be untimely is hardly surprising given the traditional annual bidding system. There was frequently as much as a 12-month delay in starting a project, never mind producing a useful set of conclusions. This annual cycle was not the approach taken in PRG. Instead, an 'open door' policy applied to the identification of research topics, with policy colleagues encouraged to approach research staff at any time with a research problem. Such approaches did not, by any means, consume the totality of the research budget available and resources were identified which allowed a more programmatic approach as outlined below.

Strategic programmes, not projects

Inviting bids for research on an annual cycle at a low level within an organisation tends to lead to expenditure on ad hoc projects, which bear little relationship to one another and do not constitute a strategic programme. There is a synergy from programmed work, which is missing when projects are disconnected and not set in a broader strategic framework. In an ideal world individual projects should build on each other, adding to the body of knowledge and extending it.

In 1992, the newly-established PRG was in the fortunate position of having a substantial budget for external research of one million pounds and no commitment to any specific programme of work. This allowed the Group to offer a strategic framework, within which the research agenda, at the more detailed project level, could be negotiated with relevant stakeholders – in this case the police and the policy units. A five-year programme of work on police operations against crime was initiated (see PRG, 1996). By 1998 the PRG operated four strategic programmes covering crime control, management and organisational issues, traffic and vehicle crime, and serious and organised crime. These programmes accounted for approximately 90% of the PRG research expenditure with the remainder spent on ad hoc, generally urgent requests from ministers or policy units. In order to maintain a strategic focus to these programmes they were negotiated at a relatively high level within the Home Office and at senior officer level within the police service.

Intelligibility

Many research reports are not an easy read for policy advisers or practitioners. In response to this a new series of research reports was established by the PRG, which were produced as quickly as possible after the conclusion of the work. They were to be concise, written in plain English and small enough to be easily carried in a briefcase. They were accompanied by an A4 sheet, which summarised the research and listed points for action either by the police or other agencies. The emphasis in the reports was on clarity and conciseness combined with a clear statement of what the policy or practical implications of the work might be.

Engaging practitioners

For research to be immediately relevant to the problems of the day requires those commissioning research to be prescient in a way that few are. Getting ahead of the game requires a different approach to the research task. One possibility is for researchers to work more closely with the practitioners to develop initiatives based on previous work or established underlying principles. The approach taken to the development of knowledge in the work of the PRG was more akin to a theory-driven research and development programme than an evaluation programme (see Chapter Twelve on theory-driven evaluations). In most cases it involved identifying a crime problem and then testing a hypothesised solution to that problem. The researchers often worked closely with the practitioners in developing initiatives that were not vulnerable to failure because of implementation (as opposed to theory) problems. Such partnerships between researchers and practitioners tested articulated implementation tactics that were context sensitive (Pawson and Tilley, 1997). As such, equal attention was paid to the implementation process as to the research and development programme itself (Laycock and Tilley, 1995). This way of working has recently been described by Kennedy (1999) as representing 'new collaborations' between researcher and practitioner partners.

Practitioner interest in research evidence has been stimulated by the move towards outcome measures in local and national operations (such as percentage reductions in car crime). A focus on outcomes begs the question of how to deliver them, and this sets up an incentive to look to the research community seeking to know 'what works'. The Home Office has published its targets in its Business Plan (Home Office, 1999a). In policing there is increasing pressure to demonstrate reductions in crime and to set targets through the police performance regime or the Crime and Disorder Act (1998) partnerships.

Simply producing hard evidence of what works, where and why, is not, of itself, sufficient to change practice. One of the insights from the PRG operation was the realisation of just how much extra effort was required to get the research results and their implications, out to practitioners on the ground. This constituted an independent exercise, which was separately conceived and funded. In 1994 the PRG strengthened an already existing information desk, which provided a computerised research information service, with a senior administrator and a seconded police officer whose task it was to 'sell' what were judged to be important research papers to the police. They saw their work as essentially one of marketing the results and they used traditional marketing strategies and practices in doing so. A useful tactic was to periodically pull research themes together into a single publication with an emphasis on what should be *done*. This was particularly relevant when there was simultaneous pressure, through the performance-monitoring regime, to encourage initiatives in the reviewed area.

However, the answer to the 'what works' question is often rather more complicated than practitioners (and policy makers) might wish. What seems to work universally is strategic thinking and a systematic, data-driven approach to defining the problem, determining a possible solution on the basis of some principles of human behaviour, proper implementation, and monitoring or evaluation thereafter. This is a process, not an off-the-shelf solution, and encouraging its use has exposed a skills shortage in the practitioner community (Tilley et al, 1999).

Recent initiatives and future challenges

There is an ongoing commitment from the Home Office to fund research and development. There has been a major injection of research funds into the Home Office (£25m over three years) as part of the Crime Reduction Programme (Home Office, 1999b). For the criminological research community this is proving a major challenge. Trained researchers are not sufficient in number to deliver the required volume of work.

The PRG approach to R&D is seen as an exemplar and its remit was expanded in 1998 to include the coordination of the crime reduction programme (Home Office, 1999b). It changed its title to the Policing and Reducing Crime Unit in recognition of this expansion. The Crime Reduction Programme presents an exciting opportunity to demonstrate the potential relevance of an evidence-based programme to policy and practice. However, it may be a relatively short window of opportunity and much is riding on the ability of researchers to deliver relevant and intelligible advice in the short to medium term.

The Department for Education and Employment (schools research) *by Judy Sebba*

Background

There has been an ongoing debate in education about the quality of research and about its relevance and capacity to influence policy and practice (Furlong, 1998; Gray, 1998; Hargreaves, 1994, 1996, 1998; Mortimore and Mortimore, 1999; Rudduck and McIntyre, 1998). This section has more modest aims: to consider how research needs are identified and prioritised in education and to outline some of the ways in which the Department for Education and Employment (DfEE) is developing its research strategy to make this process more effective. The focus is on schools research rather than on further education, higher education or employment, but many of the strategies described are being developed and used across the whole Department.

The debate about quality of education research was fuelled by David Hargreaves (1996) when in an annual Teacher Training Agency (TTA) lecture he compared the quality of education research unfavourably with that of medicine. In 1998, the DfEE commissioned a review of research in schools (Hillage et al, 1998) which concluded that the relationship between research, policy and practice needed to be improved. One of its conclusions suggested that the research agenda was too supplier-driven and that this was exacerbated by the process of research funding. Pressure on researchers to produce empirical findings in published journals of international repute reflected different priorities to those which 'users' in the system need to inform policy and practice. There was little evidence of teachers, local education authority staff or policy makers influencing research priorities.

R&D strategy for schools

Whose priorities?

If one main purpose of research is to inform policy and practice there are implications for who is responsible for identifying the priorities. The client group in education might include teachers, governors, education administrators, parents and even pupils. It also includes other disciplines working in education such as psychologists, therapists and social workers who all require evidence of effectiveness in selecting methods for their work. These people may all be viewed as *users* of research but the part they have played in determining research priorities has traditionally been relatively minor and, in the case of pupils, virtually non-existent.

In identifying research priorities for its own programme the DfEE has been developing a more consultative approach with input from users. Previously, policy teams identified research priorities in their areas and then prioritised these. The programme that emerged was fragmented, lacking in strategy and took no account of users' views. In 1998 for the first time, outside organisations such as universities, research institutes, local education authorities, teacher unions and others were consulted. This produced a huge number of suggestions in a range of areas, some of which were incorporated into the programme. In 1999, a similar exercise was undertaken but this time comments were invited on a Research Prospectus, which listed 10 broad priority themes identified by ministers. The prospectus also outlined the Department's research strategy and invited comments on this. This produced helpful feedback that enabled the Department to develop a programme which reflected better users' and researchers' priorities, as well as those of policy makers.

Involving teachers in the research process, in particular in identifying priorities, contributes to making it practical in its focus and relevant to improving teaching and learning. The Teacher Training Agency (TTA), with some support from the DfEE, set up a panel of teachers (in 1999) with substantial research experience to assist government agencies and others to identify appropriate priorities, provide a user perspective on research applications, take part in research project steering groups and provide feedback on how research is influencing practice. For the 2001 Universities Research Assessment Exercise one quarter of the education panel will for the first time be users of research.

Another mechanism for involving a wider range of stakeholders in the R&D process is the National Educational Research Forum (NERF) (whose members include funders, policy makers and practitioners – chaired by a non-educationist, Professor Sir Michael Peckham, former head of the NHS R&D strategy). This forum provides a steer in the development of an overall framework for research.

Identifying areas of priority

Priority areas may be identified via a number of routes: theoretical or strategic demands, user demands, gaps identified through previous reviews, replicating and extending existing studies, and the need for international comparative data. How each of these has influenced the thinking of the DfEE is outlined below.

Some research needs are prioritised because theoretical understanding needs to be advanced or a longer-term strategy needs to be considered. In many cases, this may contribute to longer-term policy and practice outcomes but in the short term it will remain predominantly in the world inhabited by other researchers. The timing of decisions about sharing these ideas with others outside research who may benefit is an issue. Going public too soon, many researchers argue, may result in messages that are misleading since further work may change their interpretations; too late and so many decisions will have been made that the impact of the research is minimised. The DfEE's recent decision to invest in more longitudinal studies will involve establishing ongoing links with researchers which will facilitate evidence informing policy irrespective of timing.

High quality research reviews have been published in education. These include areas of direct relevance to the classroom such as pupil grouping, class size, and the impact of gender differences and ethnicity on attainment. Mapping those that have been completed will provide a picture of gaps, areas that need to be updated and areas where the context has changed. Reviews of 'effective practice' through visits, case studies and reports (the 'grey' literature) will also assist in identifying research priorities. While generalisations from these may be inappropriate, they may reveal areas of unresearched territory that need to be addressed. Similarly, the data from school inspections are a further source of information to be considered, provided the differences in the status of the data are made clear.

In education, there are relatively few randomly controlled trials, large quantitative studies or evaluations of experimental interventions. While all these should be encouraged, the existing evidence base would be strengthened through replications and extensions of some existing studies and systematic reviews. The perception may be partly that replications are less well received than new, original work. However, many areas would benefit from further reworking and this will be the task of the newly established evidence centre (see below).

The development of a nation's education system can benefit from international comparisons for two reasons:
- international benchmarks enable a country to identify its strengths and weaknesses and thus help to prioritise resources;
- countries with different patterns of education attainment can learn from one another by interrogating the differences.

Hence, there is a continuing need to try to develop further comparable data and to undertake studies that involve the collection of these data across countries.

Centre for evidence-informed policy and practice

In 1999 the Social Science Research Unit, at the University of London, was commissioned by the DfEE to set up a centre to develop a collaboration in education similar to the Cochrane Collaboration in healthcare intervention. The centre has two main functions, to:
- set up a database of published and ongoing research that is accessible at a variety of levels;
- register research review groups who undertake research syntheses in an area and are committed to updating these.

The centre is expected to work closely with the Evidence-based Policy and Practice Coordinating Centre being set up by Economic and Social Research Council and to collaborate with the nascent international Campbell Collaboration (a body modelled on the Cochrane Collaboration, but one that focuses on social, criminological and educational interventions). These latter developments are seen as broader but complementary to the setting up of a centre specifically to focus on education.

Challenges for the future

In order to become effective, the newly established evidence centre and associated review groups will need the cooperation and support of most education researchers. Researchers will need to share information and collaborate, which they may have reservations about doing in the context of competition for research funding. Some researchers are understandably suspicious that these developments are based on the government's desire for greater control or power over education research. However, the role of the government in this initiative is to lead and establish national coherence in the approach, not to assume control of the research agenda or the overall research programme.

The ultimate success criterion for the evidence unit might be to find pupils accessing the best evidence on classroom practice in order to challenge their teachers; teachers can challenge themselves and others, and parents can challenge schools all on the basis of 'best evidence'. The same information that gives rise to challenge should provide greater confidence, but not complacency, that decision making at every level can be done in the knowledge of the best possible evidence. Government departments face the considerable challenge of creating a culture of expectation that policy makers will ask for, consider and use research findings in their work. This needs to happen both in formulating policy and in evaluating policy implementation.

In many areas the research evidence is unavailable either because it does not exist or occasionally because it has not been published or only appears in a unknown source. As Davies (1999) has noted we need to improve both the high quality research evidence available and the use made of it. The cost-effectiveness of educational interventions is an example of an area in which until very recently there was no research evidence at all. Those working in the area are grappling with the need to adapt a methodology developed in economics to fit education. The DfEE has commissioned a dedicated research centre in the economics of education (based at the London School of Economics) in response to this perceived need.

There are considerable challenges ahead for the DfEE in developing and implementing its R&D strategy, but important steps in the right direction have already been made.

Concluding remarks by Sandra Nutley and Huw Davies

The above overview of R&D in the NHS, and parts of the Home Office and the DfEE reveals a number of common themes. All areas have suffered in the past from a lack of connection between research on the one hand and policy and practice on the other. The reasons for this are echoed across the three areas:

- a history where the research agenda has been predominantly investigator-led, and a recognition that investigators may be more concerned with gaining academic kudos than connecting with policy and practice needs;
- a difference between research and policy/practice modes of working, particularly in the timescales they work to, their methods, and their reporting styles;
- the lack of demand for research findings from policy makers and practitioners due to a cultural disbelief in the usefulness of research in the *real-politik* of everyday life.

However, there is one core difference between healthcare and the other two areas: that is the large incentive to outside interests to develop and test new interventions (such as drugs) for health services. This has led to massive investment by the private sector on both basic and applied research into what works, albeit activity strongly influenced by market prospects. This situation is not paralleled in education and criminal justice.

The lack of connection between research and policy/practice has been increasingly commented on in all three policy areas during the last decade. This has culminated in concerted efforts to turn this situation around. Again there are many similarities in the R&D strategies that have emerged to achieve this. All three areas have developed mechanisms for improving the way in which government research funding is prioritised. This has entailed a shift from reactive to proactive funding. In prioritising research needs the emphasis has been not only on filling gaps but also on extending and building on existing research to develop a cumulative evidence base. The R&D strategies have thus emphasised the importance of secondary research – systematic reviews and meta-analyses – as well as trying to direct primary research.

In order that research connects more with the needs of policy makers and practitioners, R&D strategies have sought to engage users throughout the research process – from priority setting through to implementation. All three sector areas are developing closer partnerships between researchers and a wide variety of research users. In some cases these partnerships extend to include service users as well as policy makers, managers and service delivery professionals. Partnerships (such as the NERF) are intended to ensure that research topics are relevant to users and provide more robust research designs, which produce evidence that is not 'vulnerable to implementation failure' (Pawson and Tilley, 1997).

There is widespread recognition of the need for research findings to be disseminated in different forms and at different stages to address the needs of a variety of stakeholders. There is also a common acknowledgement of the need to move beyond simple dissemination if R&D strategies are to be effective. However, this has not proved easy. The implementation process itself has been the subject of new research programmes, and implementation is beginning to be built into research and evaluation projects. Yet the experience to date is that the 'development' aspects of R&D require more focused attention and concerted action than they have received hitherto. Finally, all three service areas have only latterly begun to address the question of not just what works but whether it is worth it. To date the investigation of cost–effectiveness remains an underdeveloped aspect of R&D strategies, although the late 1990s witnessed an increasing concern to address this lacuna.

In pursuing their R&D strategies all three areas have faced similar dilemmas. At a most basic level, there is a lack of research capacity in the UK to support the strategic aspirations for evidence-based services. There are also concerns about the possible diminished objectivity and impartiality of research in the new environment of user-led research. In building capacity and safeguarding objectivity all three areas have sought to achieve the delicate balance that needs to be struck between developing internal capacity and outsourcing research via competitive tendering for project-based contracts.

The lack of analytical capacity not only affects the supply of research, it has also been identified as a problem among those who are the policy customers for research (Cabinet Office, 2000). The lack of good quality analysts in government has led to calls for policy makers to be given a grounding in economics, statistics and relevant scientific disciplines in order that they are able to act as 'intelligent customers' for complex policy evidence (Cabinet Office, 1999). The Centre for Management and Policy Studies in the Cabinet Office is expected to contribute to a programme of cultural change within the policy-making process, so that rigorous evidence is both demanded and used. Training of ministers and officials is one tactic for achieving this. There are also plans to establish a 'knowledge pool' of experiences of policy making in order to disseminate best practice and assist in knowledge management. "Government should know what it knows", and this will be assisted by the "better management and organisation of knowledge within government" (Cabinet Office, 2000, para 1.10).

The Cabinet Office (1999) has stated that all government departments should be taking a strategic and forward-looking approach to their use of research and that a mechanism for achieving this is the development of a single, overarching research strategy, related to the priorities and objectives set out in the departments' Public Service Agreements.

Overall, the experiences reported in this chapter suggest that R&D strategies need to make headway on three main fronts:

• ensure the development of an appropriate research evidence base;
• establish mechanisms to push the evidence out to policy makers and practitioners;
• encourage a situation where there is a pull for evidence among policy makers and practitioners.

In doing so, those responsible for R&D strategies are likely to face a number of common problems. These include the lack of research capacity to achieve the first goal; the lack of credible interventions to achieve the third goal, and the general volatility of the situation due to the politicisation of both research and researchers. The agenda for the future is further complicated by the fact that drawing up area (or departmental) research strategies alone is not enough: they also need to be 'joined-up' to ensure that cross-cutting research questions are addressed.

Note

[1] Gloria Laycock's contribution to this chapter was written during her fellowship in the USA. This fellowship was supported by grant No 1999-IJ-CX-0050 awarded by the National Institute of Justice, Office of Justice Programs, US Department of Justice. The points of view in this document are those of the author and do not necessarily represent the official position or policies of the US Department of Justice.

References

Baker, M. (1998) 'Taking the strategy forward', in M. Baker and S. Kirk (eds) *Research and development for the NHS: Evidence, evaluation and effectiveness* (2nd edn), Oxford: Radcliffe Medical Press, Chapter 2, pp 9-24.

Black, N. (1997) 'A national strategy for research and development: lessons from England', *Annual Review of Public Health*, no 18, pp 485-505.

Cabinet Office – Performance and Innovation Unit (2000) *Adding it up: Improving analysis and modelling in central government*, London: Cabinet Office.

Cabinet Office – Strategic Policy Making Team (1999) *Professional policy making for the twenty first century*, London: Cabinet Office.

Cochrane, A.L. (1989) *One man's medicine: An autobiography of Professor Archie Cochrane*, London: British Medical Journal.

Croft, J. (1981) *Managing criminological research*, Home Office Research Study No 69, London: HMSO.

Croft, J. (1983) 'Criminological research in Great Britain', in M. Tonry and N. Morris (eds) *Crime and justice: An annual review of research, Volume 5*, Chicago, IL: University of Chicago Press, pp 265-80.

Culyer, A. (1994) *Supporting research and development in the NHS*, A report to the Minister for Health by a Research and Development task force chaired by Professor Anthony Culyer, London: HMSO.

Davies, P. (1999) 'What is evidence-based education?' *British Journal of Educational Studies*, no 47, pp 108-21.

DoH (Department of Health) (1991) *Research for health: A research and development strategy for the NHS*, London: HMSO.

DoH (1993) *Research for health*, London: DoH.

DoH (1998) *A first class service: Quality in the new NHS*, London: DoH.

Furlong, J. (1998) 'Educational research: meeting the challenge', An inaugural lecture, University of Bristol, 30 April.

Gray, J. (1998) 'The contribution of educational research to the cause of school improvement', Professorial Lecture, Institute of Education, University of London, 29 April.

Hargreaves, D. (1994) *The mosaic of learning: Schools and teachers for the next century*, London: DEMOS.

Hargreaves, D. (1996) 'Teaching as a research-based profession: possibilities and prospects', The Teacher Training Agency Annual Lecture.

Hargreaves, D. (1998) *Creating professionalism: The role of teachers in the knowledge society*, London: DEMOS.

Hillage, J., Pearson, R., Anderson, A. and Tamkin, P. (1998) *Excellence in research on schools*, London: DfEE.

Home Office (1999a) *Business plan: 1999-2000*, London: Home Office.

Home Office (1999b) *Reducing crime and tackling its causes – A briefing note on the Crime Reduction Programme*, London: Home Office.

House of Lords Select Committee on Science and Technology (1988) *Priorities in medical research*, London: HMSO.

Kennedy, D. (1999) 'Research for problem solving and the new collaborations', in *Viewing crime and justice from a collaborative perspective: Plenary papers of the 1998 Conference on Criminal Justice Research and Evaluation*, Washington, DC: US Department of Justice.

Laycock, G.K. and Tilley, N. (1995) 'Implementing crime prevention programs', in M. Tonry and D. Farrington (eds) *Building a safer society, crime and justice: A review of research*, vol 19, Chicago, IL: University of Chicago Press.

Lodge, T.S. (1974) 'The founding of the Home Office Research Unit', in R. Hood (ed) *Crime, criminology and public policy: Essays in honour of Sir Leon Radzinowicz*, London: Heinemann.

Mortimore, P. and Mortimore, J. (1999) 'Does educational research influence policy or practice?', in I. Abbott (ed) *The future of education research*, London: Falmer.

NHS Executive (1999) *The annual report of the NHS Health Technology Assessment Programme 1999*, London: DoH.

Pawson, R. and Tilley, N (1997) *Realistic evaluation*, London: Sage Publications.

PRG (Police Research Group) (1996) *PRG in focus*, London: Home Office, PRG.

Rudduck, J. and McIntyre, D. (eds) (1998) *Challenges for educational research*, London: Paul Chapman.

Sheldon, T.A. and Melville, A. (1996) 'Providing intelligence for rational decision-making in the NHS: the NHS Centre for Reviews and Dissemination', *Journal of Clinical Effectiveness*, vol 1, pp 51-4.

Smith, R. (1993) 'Filling the lacuna between research and practice: an interview with Michael Peckham', *BMJ*, vol 307, pp 1403-7.

Stein, K. and Milne, R. (1998) 'Taking the strategy forward', in M. Baker and S. Kirk (eds) *Research and development for the NHS: Evidence, evaluation and effectiveness* (2nd edn), Oxford: Radcliffe Medical Press, Chapter 7, pp 67-85.

Tilley, N., Pease, K., Hough, M. and Brown, R. (1999) *Burglary prevention: Early lessons from the Crime Reduction Programme*, Crime Reduction Research Paper 1, London: Home Office.

TWELVE

Debates on the role of experimentation

Huw Davies, Sandra Nutley and Nick Tilley

Introduction

As the preceding chapters show, different service areas adopt very different approaches towards identifying what works. On the one hand, the health sector has in general adopted a research culture in which it is accepted that the services provided should in principle be exposed to rigorous scientific evaluation (see Chapter Three). Central to this culture is the notion of experimentation, usually taken to mean randomised controlled trials. In practice many medical practices have not been properly evaluated in this sense, or the studies that have been undertaken fall some way short of providing incontrovertible guidance. Much activity remains untested through randomised trials (Smith, 1991). Strategic policies, such as the introduction of 'fundholding' in general practice (and its subsequent abandonment), have not hitherto received the same form of evaluative attention as individual medical procedures (Ham et al, 1995; Davies and Nutley, 1999). Yet the principle is enshrined: interventions should be tested before widespread use, and experimentation (in the form of randomised controlled trials) lies at the apex of a hierarchy of evidence (see Chapter Three, Box 3.3).

In contrast, research on effectiveness takes a different form, and is often less visible, in other parts of the public sector. In areas such as education, social services and criminal justice, there has been considerable research activity over several decades. However, coverage is patchy, there is less consensus regarding appropriate methodology, and there is little agreement as to how to use research evidence to inform policy and practice (see Chapters Four to Six). Although experiments (including randomisation) have at times been conducted in education and criminal justice, and some too in social care, their use is highly contested for a range of ontological, epistemological, methodological, ethical and practical reasons. The arguments in these areas go beyond disputes over rational/technical matters, and the debates about the role of experiments (and randomisation in particular) expose deep philosophical divides. In other parts of the public sector the use of experimentation in the form of randomised controlled studies is largely absent in guiding policy or practice, for example, in housing, transport, welfare or urban policy (see Chapters Seven to Ten). It remains moot whether the absence of randomisation from evaluations in these policy areas arises because of intrinsic limitations of the method, practical reasons, or lack of fit with the dominant service cultures.

Some might argue that this apparent neglect of experimentation suggests missed opportunities. On the face of it, there are numerous issues in, say, education, which could be examined using such methods. For example, identifying the most effective approach to teaching reading; or assessing the impact of calculators on the child's mathematical development; or evaluating the introduction of a new homework policy. Such questions may be amenable to experimental study (although seeking randomisation may be problematic) but concerted research effort seems to have been lacking. In contrast, there are many other public policy questions which appear less amenable to the use of randomised controlled trials, such as whether legalising soft drugs decreases or increases the use of hard drugs; or whether the Right to Buy scheme leading to extensive council house sales was an effective strategy. There is a vast 'middle ground' where experimentation may be feasible in principle, but where the cost of implementing such methodologies renders them practically infeasible. Here, whatever the value of randomised controlled trials, alternative methodologies and analytic techniques may yield more useful evidence from a policy perspective.

This chapter begins to explore these themes. In particular, it aims to investigate the methodological schism on randomisation that exists between different parts of the public sector and runs deep within some individual service areas. The opening section reviews some of the methodological difficulties of assessing what works. In particular, it focuses on the possibility of bias and hence erroneous attributions of effectiveness. Next we elucidate the design of experimental evaluations which emphasise randomisation, and highlight some of the key concerns over their application. Finally, we explore some of the more radical critiques of experimentation, focusing particularly on the epistemological challenges made by theory-led, non-randomised approaches to evaluation. Subsequent chapters take these arguments further by addressing first the role of non-experimental quantitative methods in evaluation (Chapter Thirteen) and then the contributions made by qualitative approaches (Chapter Fourteen).

Before proceeding a number of clarifications are in order. First, this is a highly selective review of evaluation methodology. A survey of evaluators in the US showed tremendous diversity in the approaches to evaluation (experimental, quasi-experimental and observational) and in the purposes of those evaluations (Shadish and Epstein, 1987). We do not aim to explore such diversity in depth. Instead, we explicate the competing claims of just two broad methodological thrusts (randomised experimental designs and theory-led evaluations). Second, this review is studiedly neither prescriptive nor judgmental. The divisions that exist run deep and reflect serious ontological and epistemological misgivings. It is again not our objective to attempt to resolve such misgivings. Our aim instead is to map out some of the terrain of these disputes and explain how evaluators currently face some of the challenges. In the process we hope to illuminate some of the assumptions, implications and consequences of choosing one evaluative approach rather than another, as well as distinguishing the contextual factors that might influence such a choice.

Assessing what works: addressing the issue of bias

Many different purposes to evaluation studies have been described, including providing guidance on implementation, elucidation of mediating variables, and an assessment of wider institutional effects (Shadish and Epstein, 1987). Nonetheless an overriding goal of much evaluation research lies in distinguishing any specific effects of the intervention from other factors. Evaluators are interested in discerning any effects of the intervention over-and-above what could have been expected if the intervention had not been applied. Typically, such estimates of effects are provided in *aggregate*, in the form of a mean effect size (for example, changes in relative risks, odds ratios or event rates [Davies, 1998]). In order to provide evidence to influence both the policy and the practice agendas, good evaluations need to tease out and isolate the specific effects of interventions. They need also to say something valid about how such effects might be replicated elsewhere: for policy purposes, conclusions confined to specific populations at specific times and places are of little or no value. Worthwhile evaluations should be able to demonstrate both *internal* and *external* validity. It is only the first of these issues that randomisation can address.

Evaluating different methods

Experimentation in the natural and social sciences

In the dominant view of science, scientists conduct experiments where as many variables as possible are controlled in order to isolate any relationships between the relatively few variables that are the subject of study. Only by exerting such experimental control can the observer be confident that any relationships observed are meaningful and are not due to extraneous factors. This postivistic view of the world underlies much of what has become known as the 'natural sciences' model of research. When the elements of study are inanimate items readily reduced to their essential components, then this approach has much to commend it. However, transplanting this research model to the social world (where the elements of study are complex, conscious, sentient actors) proves problematic. In particular, assessing the impact of interventions or programmes on people embedded in social systems poses some distinct challenges.

Individualistic and programmatic interventions

'What works?' evidence is concerned with evaluating the impact of interventions. Sometimes such interventions are aimed at *individuals*: the archetype here being the care of the sick using diagnostic and therapeutic interventions aimed at improving health outcomes. This *individualistic* model − an intervention applied to an individual in pursuit of some outcome for that individual − fits many of the services delivered not only in healthcare, but also in social care, education, welfare and criminal justice services.

By no means all public sector interventions are delivered direct to individuals. Many interventions are *programmatic* in nature, in that packages of measures are applied to whole groups or communities in the hope of influencing both individual and collective outcomes. In both cases (individualistic or programmatic interventions) these services are delivered in a wider context which is likely to influence the impact of the intervention (Figure 12.1).

Figure 12.1: Interventions in context

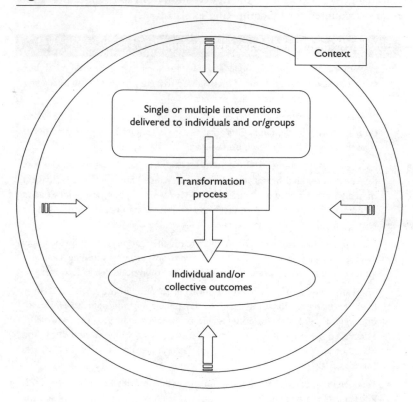

Identifying true intervention effects

The need for rigorous evaluation springs from a number of observations that demonstrate the potential to be misled (Box 12.1). There are two main ways in which we can be deceived: we may see apparent benefits of interventions that are not in fact attributable to that intervention; or we may miss important benefits as they become obscured by other random or non-random factors. The effects of interventions are rarely unidimensional, and we may fail to discern a complete picture of the intervention's impact, good or bad. Useful evaluations should reveal not just potential benefits but also, for example, the side-effects of drugs or the dysfunctional consequences of organisational interventions (Smith, 1995). In essence, the difficulty in evaluation lies in disentangling *all* the real change(s) attributable to the intervention from apparent change more readily accounted for by competing explanations.

Box 12.1: Need for methodological rigour

- *Ineffective interventions abound.* Many interventions have promised much but failed to deliver. Recognition of such has led to a certain scepticism bordering on nihilism among some policy makers.

- *The limitations of theory.* Theoretically well-supported interventions often do not flourish in the field. Empirical testing is required to buttress a belief that theoretical benefits will be realised.

- *Spontaneous improvements.* Interventions aimed at ameliorating deficiencies may be confounded by naturally occurring change. For example, evaluation of programmes aimed at reducing recidivism among young offenders needs to take account of natural reductions as most young people spontaneously emerge from brief criminal careers.

- *Contemporaneous change.* The world moves on. Larger secular trends may swamp the effects from specific interventions either by hiding real and important benefits or falsely suggesting gains when none are in fact present.

- *The Hawthorne Effect.* Any attention at all to people in a social system is likely to bring about some change. Distinguishing the specific effects of interventions from those non-specific remains a challenge. (*The Hawthorne Effect* is so named as it was first discovered during a study carried out in the Hawthorne Western Electric Company Plant in Illinois in the 1920s [Gill and Johnson, 1997]).

- *Variation.* Variability of effect between and within individuals and communities adds another layer of uncertainty. This may confuse in two ways: by obscuring real and important gains or by falsely suggesting effects that are in fact spurious.

- *The importance of small effects.* Dramatic impacts are unfortunately rare. The best hope for many service interventions lies in accumulating small beneficial effects through well-targeted programmes. Also important is discovering any unwanted dysfunctional or deleterious responses. Finding small effects (good and bad) among the background noise requires meticulous attention to bias.

Using controls

One way in which the sources of various effects might be differentiated is through the use of comparison or control groups. The logic here is straightforward: comparing outcomes (individual and collective) in similar circumstances for two groups – one subjected to the intervention, and one not – should help clarify intervention-specific benefits. This observation, helpful as it is, introduces new difficulties: how should experimental, comparison or control groups be selected, and what sort of comparison is appropriate?

Two broad strategies present themselves. On the one hand, comparison groups can be *selected* in such a way as to try and ensure equivalence, and thus the fairness of any comparison. This might entail matching groups on many attributes except the intervention under study, or using historical data to provide some benchmarks. Such *observational* approaches may take advantage of naturally occurring variation (so-called 'natural experiments') but do not involve the deliberate allocation of individuals or groups by the evaluator. The second broad strategy assumes some degree of experimental control, and involves the evaluator selecting which *individuals* are to receive the intervention under test, and which are to receive some comparison intervention. However, when the level of control is incomplete (for example, with a staggered roll-out of an intervention) such approaches to evaluations are known as *quasi-experiments* (Campbell and Stanley, 1966). Only when the investigators have complete control over group allocation (enabling random allocation to new intervention or comparator) is the evaluation said to be a *true experiment*.

Observational and quasi–experimental approaches

Observational and quasi-experimental approaches may take many forms but at the core is the presumption that the evaluator cannot exert full control over group allocations. Even when some control is available it is limited in extent or timing. Instead, the evaluator tries to select suitable comparison groups, and attempts to make up for lack of experimental control by using statistical adjustments (see Chapter Thirteen). Comparison groups used may include the study cohort before intervention (before-and-after designs), past cohorts who have received different interventions previously (historical controls), or current cohorts receiving different interventions, for whatever reasons, at the same time as the study group (concurrent non-randomised controls). The key issue that arises is one of equivalence: how to ensure that any comparison compares like-with-like, so that only the application of the intervention differs between the two groups.

Asserting such equivalence in observational approaches is problematic (Ellenberg, 1994). We have no guarantees that individuals receiving the new intervention are directly comparable with those receiving different interventions either now or in the past. There is every reason to suppose that those identified and selected for the new intervention may well differ in real and important ways (Sheldon, 1994). For example, those selected to receive a new surgical intervention over traditional conservative approaches may well be those most fit and able to survive surgery. Thus any comparisons will tend to bias judgements in favour of the new approach. Conversely, individuals selected to try out a new delinquency reduction programme may be those with the most intractable problems, thus biasing any judgements against the new approach. The key point is that bias may work in either direction (either for or against a novel intervention), but we have no reliable prior way of knowing which is most likely.

Substantial empirical work has been carried out that seeks to test the potential for bias in observational and quasi-experimental studies. Most of this work has been carried out in healthcare where the findings are mixed. Some studies do seem to show that observational approaches to evaluations are likely to suggest larger effect sizes than are actually so (Gilbert et al, 1977; Colditz et al, 1989; Miller et al, 1989). However, such comparisons are not straightforward and more recent work suggests that it is less the basic design which influences findings and more the extent of flaws or biases within those designs (Ottenbacher, 1992; Kunz and Oxman, 1998; Reeves et al, 1998). It is certainly true, however, that many medical advances predicated on small observational studies have subsequently been shown to be ineffective or even harmful (Pocock, 1983; Elliott, 1991); sadly even some large quasi-experimental studies have suffered the same fate (Sherman, 1992), as have meta-analyses of whole collections of randomised studies (Egger et al, 1997).

Randomisation

Randomisation involves allocating at random individuals (or groups) either to the intervention under test or to the 'control' intervention (often 'usual practice'). This strategy brings with it a number of crucial advantages. First, allowing *chance* to choose group allocation (to new intervention or old) reduces the possibility of bias creeping in through differential allocation. The strategy obviates the need for deliberate allocation and thus any biases attendant to such an approach. Second, in the long run, such random allocation will tend to lead to balanced groups. Crucially, balance is likely not just for all those factors that are known to influence outcomes (which could be matched for under a non-randomisation strategy), but also for all those *unknown* prognostic factors (of which no matching strategy could possibly take account). Although such balance is not guaranteed, it becomes more likely the larger the groups randomised. Finally, randomisation provides the statistical basis on which inferences can be made as to whether observed differences in outcomes lie within likely limits due to chance. Crucially, this final judgement relates only to the study population (*internal* validity) and extrapolation to other groups (*external* validity) requires some circumspection.

Randomisation developed quite separately within the fields of education, psychology and agriculture, before being widely applied in medicine, healthcare, education and experimental sociology (Oakley, 1998). The US in particular experienced a 'Golden Age' of experimental evaluation in many aspects of social interventions from the mid-1960s to the early 1980s (Rossi and Wright, 1984). Robert Boruch's bibliographies of 'randomised field experiments' in the late 1970s listed around 250 studies on criminal justice, legal policy, social welfare, education, mass communication and mental health (Boruch, 1974, 1978; Oakley, 1998).

Additional methodological rigour

Randomisation deals with one specific and important bias – *selection* bias – that leads to invalid comparisons. This advantage in isolation is insufficient to eliminate other potential sources of bias. Thus randomisation is often combined with a range of other methodological features aimed at distinguishing real effects from spurious findings (Box 12.2). The basic design in randomised studies is as shown in Figure 12.2. In essence, these features aim to ensure that all activities after randomisation preserve balance and do not admit any differential treatment (other than the intervention under test) that may tip the balance in favour of one group or the other. Any differences in outcomes between the two groups should then rightly be attributable to the interventions.

Figure 12.2: Basic design of randomised evaluations

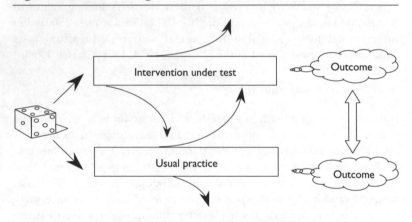

Note: Arrows show individuals leaving their initial group of allocation, either to transfer to the alternate group or to leave the study. Nonetheless, an unbiased analysis requires that these individuals be analysed according to their initial group allocation.

Empirical work, again largely from the medical field, shows that these methodological safeguards are not just academic niceties. Studies not attending to them may provide misleading results (Kunz and Oxman, 1998; Moher et al, 1998). For example, studies without blinding, or with blinding that is not maintained, can lead to an overestimation of beneficial outcomes in the group receiving new treatments (Noseworthy et al, 1994); and studies with poorly concealed randomisation tend to show larger treatment effects probably due to differential allocation of individuals between groups, that is, selection bias arising because clinicians subvert the randomisation schedule (Chalmers et al, 1983; Schulz et al, 1995).

Use of randomisation

Randomisation in programmatic interventions

Randomisation has largely been applied to *individualistic* interventions (the treatment model), where it has had a long history of methodological development and refinement. This is not to say that randomisation has not been applied in *programmatic* interventions. Randomisation has been used here too, most especially in assessing social interventions, where groups or communities are randomly allocated to one programme or another. The rationale behind such interventions is the same although the practical, methodological and analytical constraints and difficulties are rather larger (Campbell and Grimshaw, 1998; Bloom et al, 1999; Wood and Freemantle, 1999). In particular, because individuals in groups tend not to be independent, the effective power of a study is determined not just by the number of individuals but also by the group size, number of groups allocated and the amount of within-group correlation (Ukoumunne et al, 1998).

Factors making randomisation problematic

Circumstances of the context, intervention, or targeted group can conspire to make randomised comparative studies difficult or impossible to design or sustain. It is not just ethical concerns that can preclude randomisation. Many other obstacles may subvert randomisation as the most appropriate means of evaluation (see Box 12.3). In healthcare, where randomised experiments have been most fully exploited, recognition of these problems has led to considerable methodological refinement. Two broad strategies to deal with some of the difficulties can be discerned. First, there has been a trend towards simpler protocols for uniform interventions that are easier to maintain in large multi-centre studies. This approach has led to a number of 'mega-trials', which have been able to detect quite small effects of medical interventions (Woods, 1995) but are not without their critics (Charlton, 1995). The second approach takes the opposite tack. Rather than recruiting large numbers to simple uniform interventions, it seeks instead greater experimental control through careful selection of study participants, puts in place elaborate arrangements to control bias, and uses more complex designs (such as Latin-squares allocation, and crossover designs) to deal with some of the problems outlined in Box 12.3.

Box 12.3: Methodological challenges in randomised evaluation studies

- *Ethical concerns.* Randomly allocating individuals to different interventions raises serious ethical and sometimes legal issues to do with informed consent.

- *Learning curves.* Many interventions may take time to be perfected. The question then arises as to when evaluations of these should be undertaken. Too soon and even those with potential are likely to be rejected; too late and ethical considerations may preclude randomisation.

- *Variable delivery.* The delivery of many interventions may rely on the skill of the deliverer. Ensuring consistent and replicable delivery may be difficult leading to concerns about what, exactly, is being evaluated.

- *Interactions.* There may be interactions between the intervention deliverer and the intervention recipient, which affect the likelihood of achieving beneficial outcomes.

- *Individual preferences.* Individuals may have strong prior preferences that make their random allocation to groups problematic or even unethical.

- *Customised interventions.* Some interventions may need considerable customising to individuals to achieve best effect. Concerns again rise as to what is being evaluated.

- *Lack of group concealment.* Knowledge of group allocation may lead to changes in behaviour or attitudes, which undermine the unbiased nature of any evaluation.

- *Contamination.* Understanding by participants of the nature of the evaluation may lead to convergence between the groups diminishing any effect sizes.

- *Lack of blinding.* Blinding is difficult or impossible for many interventions, with the attendant risk of bias being introduced by study subjects' behaviour, compensatory activities by external agents, or differential outcome assessment.

- *Poor compliance.* Individuals allocated to one intervention or another may fail to comply with stipulations thus undermining the assessment.

Application of randomisation

Randomisation has had its furthest reach in healthcare where its use has become *de rigueur* for the evaluation of healthcare interventions (see Chapter Three). However, even here there is recognition of certain limitations in application. Black, for example, lists reasons why experimentation may be unnecessary, inappropriate, impossible or inadequate (1996): *unnecessary* because the intervention effects are so dramatic as to be incontrovertible; *inappropriate* because of the need to detect very small effects, or rare or far distant outcomes; *impossible* because of practical and ethical restrictions; or *inadequate* because of low generalisability to groups not included in the studies. To add to this list, randomisation might prove too expensive and/or impractical. When such circumstances pertain, observational and quasi-experimental methods may offer more appropriate, practical, cheaper and ethical evaluations. Nonetheless, in medicine at least, and in healthcare more generally, randomisation has emerged as the 'gold standard' against which other forms of evaluation are assessed for methodological 'purity' in their attempts to eradicate bias.

Critiques of randomisation in evaluation

Randomised intervention studies, with other appropriate methodological safeguards, can provide unbiased estimates of aggregate effects in the studied population. Herein lies both their major strength and the root of the criticisms levelled against them. If intervention effects are homogenous (in that, each individual to whom the intervention is applied gains more-or-less an equivalent amount) or if, at the very least, there are no damaging effects of the intervention, then such aggregation may be highly appropriate. However, when intervention effects are heterogeneous, and especially when there are both winners and losers, then such aggregation may obscure more than it reveals (Longford, 1999). When the intervention effects are not homogenous, some disaggregation for different groups is desirable and may indeed be possible (although statistical power considerations may preclude even this). However, such disaggregation presupposes that we know in advance the defining variables of those groups to be disaggregated – and, more usually, we do not.

Appropriateness of aggregation

When interventions have diverse effects on individuals, randomisation aggregates these into a 'mean effect size'. If individual effects are randomly distributed with low variance then this information about an 'average' impact may be helpful in assessing what works. However, if the individual effects are highly idiosyncratic, depending on not just the individual, but also particular aspects of the intervention, or the interaction of the intervention and the individual perhaps mediated through contextual variables, then the desirability of assessing 'average' impacts becomes much less clear. In particular, when some individuals gain from the intervention and others lose then aggregating these diverse effects may be misleading. At the very least, it contains the utilitarian assumption that benefits for some may legitimately be traded for losses to others.

Real world randomised evaluation studies usually do examine aggregate effects, and tend to emphasise intention-to-treat analyses (when groups are compared according to initial group allocation rather than what interventions they actually received). These trials regard any variability as 'noise' to be dealt with statistically in order to reveal any underlying net effect. Such trials are *pragmatic* rather than *explanatory* (Schwarz and Lellouch, 1967; Russell and Wilson, 1992). That is they do not seek to explain any causal mechanisms between interventions and outcomes. Rather, such evaluations answer the pragmatic question of what *allocation strategy* (allocating individuals to intervention A or intervention B) will produce the overall best aggregate outcomes *regardless of whether individuals actually receive or complete the interventions allocated to them*. The intervention–individual interaction is regarded as a 'black box' whose internal mechanisms may remain unelucidated.

External validity and the impact of context

A second major thrust of the critique of randomised evaluations centres on their generalisability to other individuals in other contexts (Britton et al, 1999). Individuals included in randomised evaluations are almost always highly selected (the use of stringent inclusion criteria being used to select groups for whom the intervention is most likely to show beneficial effects). Further selection is imposed by the need to obtain informed consent from participants. The context within which such studies are mounted is always distinctive, at least in so much as it includes intensive attention, data gathering and the need for consent to be randomised. Other factors too may be distinctive, for example, randomised evaluations are more likely to be run in expert centres rather than run-of-the-mill service settings. It is highly unlikely that those included in many randomised evaluations are *representative* of the populations from which they were drawn, and certainly the contexts within which interventions are applied are likely to be significantly non-standard. If intervention effects are relatively homogenous and stable across diverse groups (as, for example, might be expected of an analgesic drug) then this may not be of much import. However, when intervention effects are idiosyncratic, synergistic and contingent (such as might occur in schemes designed to confront offenders with the impact of their behaviour), then there are obvious concerns about whether the (aggregate) findings discovered in any particular randomised evaluation will still hold when translated to different individuals in different contexts.

These critical questions coalesce around one crucial issue: whether we have sufficient understanding of the linkages between a desired set of outcomes, and the interactions between the context(s), intervention(s) and target group(s) that may lead to such outcomes. Without such understanding, the aggregation that is implicit in randomised studies risks mixing not only apples and oranges but also fish heads and the odd sock too. This lack of understanding about mechanisms of action means that the results generated from randomised studies cannot readily be extrapolated beyond the study population because those included in the study were highly selected, and examined in a highly specific and atypical context. The importance of context–intervention–group interactions and contingencies precludes generalisability. It is from this basis that an alternative approach to the evaluation of social interventions has grown up – an approach that is largely hostile to randomisation alone as the key to unbiased assessments.

Theory-driven evaluations

Pragmatic evaluations using randomised controls elevate empirical knowledge over theoretical understanding. They seek as much control as possible over both the contexts within which experiments take place and, most especially, those mediating factors that intervene between intervention and outcome. In contrast, these issues are precisely those that 'theory-led' or 'realistic' evaluations (Chen, 1990; Pawson and Tilley, 1997) seek to bring to the fore. Within this critique, experimentalists' efforts to 'cancel out difference' and isolate change from the wider context of that change have been described as "absurd ... an effort to write out what is essential to a program – social conditions favourable to it" (Pawson and Tilley, 1994).

The criticism of randomisation as an approach to evaluation centres around the assertion that experimentation has "pursued too single-mindedly the question of *whether* a program works at the expense of knowing *why* it works" (Pawson and Tilley, 1997, p xv, emphasis added). The primary aim in theory-driven evaluation is to 'unpack the box' of the transformation process shown in Figure 12.1, using *within-programme* experimentation. In doing so it brings centre-stage theories of individual and group change. Some of the key concepts underlying such approaches are outlined in Box 12.4.

Box 12.4: The new rules of realistic evaluation

• Evaluators need to attend to how and why social programmes have the potential to cause change.

• Evaluators need to penetrate beneath the surface of observable inputs and outputs of a programme.

• Evaluators need to focus on how the causal mechanisms that generate social and behavioural problems are removed or countered through the alternative causal mechanisms introduced in a social programme.

• Evaluators need to understand the contexts within which problem mechanisms are activated and in which programme mechanisms can be successfully fired.

• Evaluators need to understand what are the outcomes of an initiative and how they are produced.

• To develop transferable and cumulative lessons from research, evaluators need to orient their thinking to context-mechanism-outcome pattern configurations.

• In order to construct and test context-mechanism-outcome pattern explanations, evaluators need to engage in a teacher–learner relationship with programme policy makers, practitioners and participants.

• Evaluators need to acknowledge that programmes are implemented in a changing and permeable social world, and that programme effectiveness may thus be subverted or enhanced through the unanticipated intrusion of new contexts and new causal powers.

Source: Abstracted from Pawson and Tilley (1997)

An example: CCTV as a crime reduction strategy in car parks

An example – extracted from Pawson and Tilley's book *Realistic evaluation* (1997) – helps explicate the approach and sets it in stark contrast to simple randomisation. Consider the problem of whether or not closed-circuit television (CCTV) deters criminal activity in car parks. A classic (randomised) experimental approach to this problem would involve randomly allocating car parks so that half had CCTV installed and half did not. The study would then compare subsequent crime rates between the two groups to estimate the aggregate impact of CCTV on crime levels. This approach side-steps many of the issues of bias in the assessment of interventions. For example, it overcomes the confounding factors that might be expected in before-and-after studies, matched designs or even quasi-experiments. However, even if positive impacts were demonstrated by this approach, it would leave unanswered the question of why benefits were obtained and how these might be maximised elsewhere. It would also be unable to address the important policy question of whether or not crimes were simply displaced elsewhere.

A theory-driven approach takes a different tack. The mechanisms by which interventions such as CCTV impact on crime are many and varied. Box 12.5 lists eight more-or-less plausible mechanisms ranging from simply catching and apprehending current offenders, through deterring would-be offenders, to encouraging more security-conscious behaviour on the part of car park users. These 'mechanisms for change' may operate simultaneously and independently, and which (if any) apply in any given car park will vary widely. Pawson and Tilley argue that which (again, if any) of these mechanisms are actually triggered will also depend on the larger context. Some possible contexts, such as the nature of local offenders (for example, many occasional offenders or a few repeat offenders), or the availability of alternative easier crime targets, are described in Box 12.6. The likelihood of these contexts impacting on individual car parks will also be variable.

Box 12.5: Mechanisms by which CCTV can reduce crime in car parks

- *Caught in the act:* CCTV can make the apprehension of offenders more likely

- *Deterrence:* CCTV may deter would-be criminals who fear being caught

- *Increased informal surveillance:* CCTV may increase car park usage by non-criminals leading to a greater level of informal surveillance

- *Effective deployment:* CCTV may make the deployment of existing security personnel more efficient, enabling them to respond more effectively to crime

- *Signal of intent:* The presence of CCTV may signal a willingness to take crime seriously indicating that car parks are no longer 'soft targets'

- *Reduced time for crime:* The duration of time available for committing crime may be reduced making certain crimes less feasible

- *Encouraging defensive behaviour:* The presence of CCTV may remind some car park customers to be more careful and vigilant

- *Appeal to the cautious:* The presence of CCTV may serve to attract to the car park 'cautious users' who present little opportunity for crime

Note: These mechanisms need not be either independent or uniform in action.

Source: Abstracted from Pawson and Tilley (1997)

The lesson from such an analysis is that CCTV will be more or less effective depending on the dominant mechanism–context interactions that pertain in a given car park. Understanding of these causal pathways then allows unpacking of the intervention to see which aspects are most effective – fostering not just an appreciation of whether the intervention works as a whole, but also which bits work and how these might be adapted and refined. The job of the evaluator is to use this understanding to frame a data and research strategy that is quite different from making blind comparisons, but aims instead at testing some of the assumptions and hypotheses embedded in Boxes 12.5 and 12.6. Such a strategy will use a multiplicity of methods both quantitative and qualitative. It may even involve randomised experiments to evaluate specific mechanism–context interactions. The theory-driven approach seeks explanations as to why interventions work which also allows an assessment of whether they do.

> **Box 12.6: Contexts within which car park crime should be considered**
>
> - *Criminal clustering:* Are crimes committed by a few very active criminals or by many opportunistic thieves?
>
> - *Style of usage:* Are there periods when the car park is full of tempting targets but generally devoid of people, or is usage (and hence presence of people) relatively constant?
>
> - *Coverage of CCTV:* Does the CCTV cover all areas of the car park or are there blind spots?
>
> - *Crime displacement:* Are there other tempting crime targets nearby or is the car park isolated in this respect?
>
> - *Other security resources:* Is the CCTV backed up by local security personnel? Are police readily available to assist?
>
> - *Other surveillance:* Does the CCTV reinforce existing surveillance strategies? Is the CCTV particular to the car park or a regular and accustomed feature of the locality?

Source: Abstracted from Pawson and Tilley (1997)

Divergence between social and natural sciences evaluation

This theory-driven approach to evaluations recognises that the 'natural science' model has serious shortcomings when dealing with interventions aimed at people in social contexts. Several powerful reasons exist as to why naturalistic evaluations of programmatic interventions differ significantly from the natural sciences ideal of experimentation:

- The context of experimentation in the natural sciences is usually controlled, isolated and closed. In contrast, the contexts within which social programmes are delivered are complex, fragile, dynamic and often unpredictable. Rather than seeking control over this, realistic evaluation seeks to capitalise on the 'natural experimentation' offered by unexpected perturbation.

- Natural science experimentation focuses on single interventions operating through well-understood mechanisms. Programmatic evaluations tend to be multiple, with diverse impacts effected through multiple pathways and poorly-understood mechanisms.

- In the natural sciences there is a large body of taken-for-granted background theory about what matters and what is inconsequential. It is on this (largely) stable platform that empiricism rests. The social sciences have no such luxury. Here understanding, such as it exists, tends to be rougher, more uncertain and contingent.

At their root, critiques of controlled experimentation contain recognition that social programmes involve both deliverers and recipients who are human agents, with their own idiosyncratic knowledge, reasoning and reflectiveness. For complex social interventions, a key concern is whether or not we can ever reach the point where the understanding of the context-mechanism-outcome interaction is so complete that large-scale randomised experimentation becomes sensible.

Concluding remarks

Interventions in social and public policy areas range from simple, direct, well-delineated and well-understood prescriptions (for example, many medical technologies) to complex, multilayered, multifaceted broad strategies underpinned by only limited understanding of causal mechanisms (for example, crime reduction or urban regeneration programmes). Nonetheless, each requires evidence to assess its effects. In healthcare, the hegemony of the randomised controlled trial (with all its methodological bells and whistles) has built up during the past 50 years. In education, criminal justice, social care and elsewhere (notwithstanding the presentation of some powerful arguments – see Chapters Four, Five and Six) the perceived role of randomisation has ebbed and flowed, never becoming as established in the rest of the world as it has in the US.

Much of the debate about the potential of randomisation to contribute to evidence on effectiveness has been hampered by a lack of clarity over the nature of the interventions being studied, the contexts within which these interventions are delivered, and the type of evidence required. To take the last of these first: there is a world of difference between *pragmatic* and *explanatory* studies. The first seeks to answer the question, 'Has intervention strategy A provided, in aggregate, better outcomes than intervention strategy B in the sampled population?'. Explanatory studies, in contrast, ask the more testing question of whether and what aspects of interventions are *causally responsible for a prescribed set of outcomes*. In healthcare, much of the emphasis of intervention assessment has been (and remains) on the very pragmatic question of whether or not the intervention offers overall benefits in aggregate. However, in criminal justice and social care there is a much greater concern to 'unpack the box' of the intervention, to seek understanding of *why* it works. This stems from a recognition that interventions do not work for all persons under all circumstances, and that not all parts of an intervention necessarily contribute to its effectiveness. There is a desire to tease out the effectual elements from the ineffectual in a highly contextualised manner, in other words *an emphasis on explanatory studies*. In pursuing these goals, theories of human behaviour and qualitative methods play prominent roles, counter-balancing the empiricism of pure experimentation.

Theory-driven evaluations emphasise the importance of unravelling the causal mechanisms that make interventions effective in context – what Pawson and Tilley refer to as the context-mechanism-outcome configurations (1997). Only when these have been clearly elucidated does it begin to make sense to look for aggregate effects – for then such aggregations can be set up so that heterogeneity of effect is minimised. Such understanding also emphasises the important role of the context in supporting beneficial change (rather than trying to squeeze it out of the equation which can happen in randomised experiments). Thus contextualised understanding of effectiveness provides a more secure basis for extrapolating research findings to other sites and settings – increasing confidence in external reliability.

Robust evidence of *what works* is needed to inform policy and practice, evidence that is robust both in terms of its *internal persuasiveness* as well as its *external applicability*. What is also needed is robust evidence of *how things work* to allow progress in intervention design and tailoring to specific contexts. Both randomised and theory-driven approaches have much to offer, and a judicious mix of the two may provide rich evidence on which to devise interventions, inform policy and shape professional practice. The appropriate balance between these methodological approaches depends on the complexity of the interventions and the context of delivery, as well as on the sophistication, clarity and substantiation of theories about possible causal mechanisms. Interventions in stable settings where human agency plays a small part are well suited to randomised evaluations. Interventions where human agency is central and the settings are unstable may need more imaginative theory-driven evaluation strategies.

References

Black, N. (1996) 'Why we need observational studies to evaluate the effectiveness of health care', *BMJ*, no 312, pp 1215-8.

Bloom, H.S., Bos, J.M. and Lee, S.W. (1999) 'Using cluster random assignment to measure program impacts: statistical implications for the evaluation of education programs', *Evaluation Review*, vol 23, no 4, pp 445-69.

Boruch, R.F. (1974) 'Bibliography: illustrative randomized field experiments for program planning and evaluation', *Evaluation*, vol 2, pp 83-7.

Boruch, R.F. (1978) 'Randomized field experiments for program planning, development and evaluation', *Evaluation Quarterly*, vol 2, no 4, pp 655-95.

Britton, A., McKee, M., Black, N., McPherson, K., Sanderson, C. and Bain, C. (1999) 'Threats to applicability of randomised trials: exclusions and selective participation', *Journal of Health Services Research and Policy*, vol 4, no 2, pp 112-21.

Campbell, D.T. and Stanley, J.C. (1966) *Experimental and quasi-experimental designs for research*, Boston, MA: Houghton Mifflin.

Campbell, M.K. and Grimshaw, J.M. (1998) 'Cluster randomised trials: time for improvement. The implications of adopting a cluster design are still largely being ignored', editorial, *BMJ (Clinical Research Edition)*, vol 317, no 7167, pp 1171-2.

Chalmers, T.C., Celano, P., Sacks, H.S. and Smith Jr, H. (1983) 'Bias in treatment assignment in controlled clinical trials', *New England Journal of Medicine*, vol 309, no 22, pp 1358-61.

Charlton, B.G. (1995) 'Mega-trials: methodological issues and clinical implications', *Journal of the Royal College of Physicians of London*, vol 29, pp 96-100.

Chen, H.-T. (1990) *Theory-driven evaluations*, Newbury Park, CA: Sage Publications.

Colditz, G.A., Miller, J.N. and Mosteller, F. (1989) 'How study design affects outcomes in comparisons of therapy, I: Medical', *Statistics in Medicine*, vol 8, no 4, pp 441-54.

Davies, H.T.O. (1998) 'Interpreting measures of treatment effect', *Hospital Medicine*, vol 59, pp 499-501.

Davies, H.T.O. and Nutley, S.M. (1999) 'The rise and rise of evidence in health care', *Public Money and Management*, vol 19, pp 9-16.

Egger, M., Davey Smith, G., Schneider, M. and Minder, C. (1997) 'Bias in meta-analysis detected by a simple, graphical test' (see comments), *BMJ (Clinical Research Edition)*, vol 315, no 7109, pp 629-34.

Ellenberg, J.H. (1994) 'Selection bias in observational and experimental studies', *Statistics in Medicine*, vol 13, nos 5-7, pp 557-67.

Elliott, S.J. (1991) 'Neonatal extracorporeal membrane oxygenation: how not to assess novel technologies', *Lancet*, vol 337, no 8739, pp 476-8.

Gilbert, J.P., McPeek, B. and Mosteller, F. (1977) 'Statistics and ethics in surgery and anesthesia', *Science*, no 198, pp 684-9.

Gill, J. and Johnson, P. (1997) *Research methods for managers* (2nd edn), London: Paul Chapman.

Ham, C., Hunter, D.J. and Robinson, R. (1995) 'Evidence based policymaking', *BMJ*, vol 310, pp 71-2.

Kunz, R. and Oxman, A.D. (1998) 'The unpredictability paradox: review of empirical comparisons of randomised and non-randomised clinical trials', *BMJ (Clinical Research Edition)*, vol 315, no 7167, pp 1185-90.

Longford, N.T. (1999) 'Selection bias and treatment heterogeneity in clinical trials', *Statistics in Medicine*, vol 18, no 12, pp 1467-74.

Miller, J.N., Colditz, G.A. and Mosteller, F. (1989) 'How study design affects outcomes in comparisons of therapy, II: Surgical', *Statistics in Medicine*, vol 8, no 4, pp 455-66.

Moher, D., Pham, B., Jones, A., Cook, D.J., Jadad, A.R., Moher, M., Tugwell, P. and Klassen, T.P. (1998) 'Does quality of reports of randomised trials affect estimates of intervention efficacy reported in meta-analyses?', *Lancet*, vol 352, no 9128, pp 609-13.

Noseworthy, J.H., Ebers, G.C., Vandervoort, M.K., Farquhar, R.E., Yetisir, E. and Roberts, R. (1994) 'The impact of blinding on the results of a randomized, placebo-controlled multiple sclerosis clinical trial', *Neurology*, vol 44, no 1, pp 16-20.

Oakley, A. (1998) 'Experimentation and social interventions: a forgotten but important history', *BMJ*, vol 317, no 7167, pp 1239-42.

Ottenbacher, K. (1992) 'Impact of random assignment on study outcome: an empirical examination', *Controlled Clinical Trials*, vol 13, no 1, pp 50-61.

Pawson, R. and Tilley, N. (1994) 'What works in evaluation research?', *British Journal of Criminology*, vol 34, no 3, pp 291-306.

Pawson, R. and Tilley, N. (1997) *Realistic evaluation*, London: Sage Publications.

Pocock, S.J. (1983) *Clinical trials: A practical approach*, Chichester: John Wiley & Sons.

Reeves, B.C., Maclehose, R.R., Harvey, I.M., Sheldon, T.A., Russell, I.T. and Black, A.M.S. (1998) 'Comparisons of effect sizes derived from randomised and non-randomised studies', N. Black, J. Brazier, R. Fitzpatrick and B. Reeves (eds) *Health services research methods: A guide to best practice*, London: BMJ Publishing, pp 73-85.

Rossi, P.H. and Wright, J.D. (1984) 'Evaluation research: an assessment', *Annual Review of Sociology*, vol 10, pp 331-52.

Russell, I.T. and Wilson, B.J. (1992) 'Audit: the third clinical science?', *Quality in Health Care*, vol 1, pp 51-5.

Schulz, K.F., Chalmers, I., Hayes, R.J. and Altman, D.G. (1995) 'Empirical evidence of bias: dimensions of methodological quality associated with estimates of treatment effects in controlled trials', *JAMA*, vol 273, pp 408-12.

Schwarz, D. and Lellouch, J. (1967) 'Explanatory and pragmatic attitudes in clinical trials', *Journal of Chronic Disease*, vol 20, pp 637-48.

Shadish, W.R. and Epstein, R. (1987) 'Patterns of program evaluation practice among members of The Evaluation Research Society and Evaluation Network', *Evaluation Review*, vol 11, no 5, pp 555-90.

Sheldon, T.A. (1994) 'Please bypass the PORT – observational studies of effectiveness run a poor second to randomised controlled trials', *BMJ*, vol 309, pp 142-3.

Sherman, L. (1992) *Policing domestic violence*, New York, NY: Free Press.

Smith, P. (1995) 'On the unintended consequences of publishing performance data in the public sector', *International Journal of Public Administration*, vol 18, pp 277-310.

Smith, R. (1991) 'Where is the wisdom...?', Editorial, *BMJ*, vol 303, pp 798-9.

Ukoumunne, O.C., Gulliford, M.C., Chinn, S., Sterne, J.A.C., Burney, P.G.J. and Donner, A. (1998) 'Evaluation of health care interventions at area and organisation level', in N. Black, J. Brazier, R. Fitzpatrick and B. Reeves (eds) *Health services research methods: A guide to best practice*, London: BMJ Publishing, pp 117-28.

Wood, J. and Freemantle, N. (1999) 'Choosing an appropriate unit of analysis in trials of interventions that attempt to influence practice', *Journal of Health Services Research and Policy*, vol 4, no 1, pp 44-8.

Woods, K.L. (1995) 'Mega-trials and management of acute myocardial infarction' (see comments), *Lancet*, vol 346, no 8975, pp 611-14.

THIRTEEN

Non-experimental quantitative methods

John Hutton and Peter Smith

Introduction

As Chapter Three noted, the use of the randomised controlled trial (RCT) has become widespread, and in many senses obligatory, in many areas of healthcare. However, there are legitimate grounds for concern about uncritical adoption of RCT methods, even in healthcare. As the chapters in this book indicate, the extent to which the principles of controlled experimentation have penetrated other areas of public sector activity has been much more limited. Even in education services, which share many of the characteristics of healthcare, the RCT methodology has not been embraced with enthusiasm (see Chapter Four), in other services – such as welfare (Chapter Seven) – its use clearly poses substantial problems.

There are numerous reasons why RCT methods might not be adopted in a particular setting. For example:
- it might be difficult to recruit participants willing to enter a trial;
- professionals might be reluctant or unable to administer a trial;
- a trial might for a number of reasons be considered unethical;
- the costs of undertaking a prospective trial might be considered unacceptably high;
- the length of time before results emerge from a prospective trial might be considered unacceptably long;
- it might be considered impractical to design a scientifically acceptable RCT for the intervention in question;
- the intervention under investigation may have population as well as individual effects, bringing into question the relevance of the traditional RCT;

- any trial would have to be undertaken in an artificial setting, which might compromise the general relevance of the results;
- outcomes and side-effects of an intervention may be difficult to capture in any meaningful way;
- the impact of the intervention may be widely heterogeneous making the assessment of aggregate effects inappropriate (see Chapter Twelve).

Underlying several of these concerns is the fact that participants in a behavioural trial (either professionals or subjects) are conscious of their own role in the experiment, and are therefore capable of subverting the outcome. More generally, there is often a concern that the very act of studying a social phenomenon changes its behaviour, frustrating the intended purpose of the examination (the so-called 'Hawthorne effect'). For these and other reasons (see Chapter Twelve), there appears to have been a marked reluctance on the part of UK researchers to pursue experimental methods in public services, especially when compared to their US counterparts, who have developed a distinctive 'evaluation' tradition.

If an RCT is precluded, the question arises: can scientific methods nevertheless be used to evaluate an intervention? In some, rather rare, circumstances the answer is no. For example, lack of any meaningful outcome data may effectively mean that the decision as to whether an intervention should be implemented is essentially an act of faith. Certain aspects of the defence and public protection services might be included in this category.

However, in most circumstances the opportunity will exist for undertaking some non-experimental evaluation of the proposed intervention. These evaluations are frequently referred to as observational studies. This chapter examines the scope for such non-experimental evaluation, describes the methodological problems that arise, assesses some of the techniques now available to undertake such evaluation, and offers some conclusions on non-experimental methods. The next section explores the notion of an observational study and its associated problems; this is followed by a section that discusses approaches to analysing observational data; the chapter concludes with a discussion of the role of observational studies in yielding evidence.

Observational study

The concept of an observational study covers a vast spectrum, from a casual glance at a two-dimensional graph to a complex simultaneous equation econometric estimation. This should not suggest that simple methods are necessarily unsatisfactory, or that complex methods are always appropriate. Nevertheless, the huge range of methodologies employed indicates that there are often substantial research problems to be addressed before an observational study can be said to have offered evidence that is at all useful for policy purposes.

This warning is not always heeded. Inadequate observational studies appear only too regularly, and are seized on when convenient, either by policy makers or by their opponents. To take just three (slightly disguised) examples:

- A multivariate study of local education authorities examines the association between examination results and a number of supply and demand variables in a single year. It fails to find any significant association between outcome and either average class size or average expenditure levels. To a casual observer, the inference might be that these policy variables 'do not matter'.

- A study of police forces finds that there was a *positive* relationship between levels of expenditure and levels of crime rate! Does this mean that police activity causes crime?!

- A study of general practitioners finds that there is a significant reduction in prescribing expenditure in the first year of becoming a fundholder. Does this mean that fundholding will help contain increases in prescribing expenditure?

The associations detected by these studies cannot be gainsaid. However, the policy inferences that flow from the analysis are far more questionable. In particular, there are profound shortcomings in both the data available and the modelling procedures used which raises the question of whether these studies are leading policy makers down a sensible route. For example: educational outcomes are the results of years of endeavour, so use of a single year's data appears highly questionable; the positive relationship between crime and police expenditure might reflect the political tendency to increase resources where recorded crime levels are high; the apparent virtues of fundholding might reflect the fact that only general practitioners who knew they had scope for savings in prescribing expenditure chose to become fundholders. Doubtless the reader can supply numerous alternative explanations.

Criticisms such as these can be excessively fastidious, and seeking to answer all of them would probably rule out almost all study of observational data. Yet the use of observational methods can open up enormous possibilities for analysis, in the form of large-scale datasets, which – although not collected for the specific purpose of the study – might offer large samples of timely and low-cost information. Nonetheless, our examples do illustrate the difficulties that can arise when you start to explore observational data. The purpose of this chapter is to highlight problems in examining observational data, and to outline the methods that have been developed to address some of these problems.

In an observational study, it is usually possible to observe subjects (individuals or populations) that have been exposed to different interventions or different levels of the same intervention. For example, it may be straightforward to identify the average size of class in which graduating schoolchildren have been taught (although the choice of measure of class size experienced is clearly open to debate). Furthermore, we must assume that some measure of outcome is available – in our example this might be employment status five years after graduation. In such circumstances there should be no problem in measuring the association between intervention and some indicator of outcome.

However, the essence of the problem confronted by the observational analyst is the need to identify the variation in outcome that is *attributable* to the intervention of interest. In a RCT it is assumed that all possible systematic causes of variation other than the type of intervention have been removed. Any variations between experimental and control group must – it is assumed – be due either to random noise or to the effects of the intervention under scrutiny. So if a statistical association between intervention and outcome can be established, there are strong grounds for inferring that the outcome is *caused* by the intervention.

In the observational study, no such assumption can be made. The burden of the analysis centres on the need to ensure that all possible confounding causes of variation in outcome have been captured. In our example, pupils will not have been randomly assigned to classes of different sizes. For example, it may have been the case that pupils with behavioural difficulties were placed in small classes in order to give teachers the opportunity to effect remedial interventions. Alternatively, it may have been the case that schools with more challenging pupil behaviour had teacher recruitment difficulties, which has then led to larger class size. If such pupil characteristics had an impact on outcome (future employment status), then careful statistical modelling is required to accommodate their confounding influence.

The 'treatment' may not be a simple construct. In an RCT it is usually possible to ensure that all elements of treatment other than the intervention of interest are kept constant. This might entail use of a double blind trial (in which neither the subject nor the professional undertaking the trial are aware of whether the subject is an experiment or control), and the construction of elaborate placebos. In an observational study it will frequently be the case that – along with the policy intervention of interest – many other aspects of the service provided might vary. In our school example, it may be the case that more accomplished teachers were assigned to larger classes, and that some of the variation in outcome associated with class size is due to teacher effects rather than class size effects.

Observational study methodology

In medicine, the traditional method for examining observational data is the *case control study*. Often referred to as a retrospective study, this seeks to examine the histories of patients with a designated disorder (the 'cases') and compare their exposure to a putative causal factor with a set of otherwise similar individuals who did not suffer from the disorder (the 'controls').

There is no reason in principle why the case control study should not be applicable to many public sector interventions. In our education study, we might seek to identify a set of past pupils who were suffering unemployment five years after graduation. This would be compared with a set of employed controls who were matched in as many respects as possible (except class size) with the unemployed cases. Once the control population is in place, it becomes possible to test statistically whether there is a significant difference in exposure to the intervention (class size) between the two groups. A fundamental difficulty that arises with this methodology is that the required sample size is very large, even controlling for just a modest number of characteristics. For example, if just five age categories, two sex categories and six employment categories are used, this implies a need for an adequate sample in $5 \times 2 \times 6 - 60$ cells, implying the need for an extraordinarily extensive and well-designed sample.

Although sometimes accepted as necessary in epidemiology, the observational study is considered especially vulnerable to distortion, and is afforded a cursory half page in the 5,000 page *Encyclopedia of biostatistics*

(Gail, 1998). Numerous potential sources of bias arise, often centering on the danger of certain types of cases being systematically over- or under-represented (Lilienfeld and Stolley, 1994). Even if selection of controls has been satisfactory, the retrospective study can only indicate association between exposure and outcome, and cannot prove causality. This issue has been particularly problematic in retrospective studies of smoking in healthcare, which demonstrate a clear association between smoking and many adverse health outcomes. Such studies can be criticised on the grounds that the association may not be causal, and that predisposition towards smoking could be merely an indicator of some more fundamental and unidentified tendency towards poor health.

It is also possible to design *prospective* observational studies, in which an attempt is made to construct two populations that are identical in all respects other than exposure to the intervention. This suffers from similar problems to the retrospective study, with the added potential complication of adjusting for increasing levels of missing data as the study progresses (a problem which it shares, of course, with prospective experimental studies).

Econometrics and the role of multiple linear regression

Beyond the field of medicine, problems such as small samples, selection bias and missing cases are endemic to the data sources on which observational studies are based. It is for these reasons that, towards the end of the 19th century, the new science of econometrics evolved out of the disciplines of economics and statistics (Morgan, 1990). The discipline of econometrics represents the apotheosis of the statistical analysis of observational data. Although, as Kennedy (1999) and many other commentators note, there is no formal definition of econometrics, it is generally accepted to involve the statistical analysis of observational data in line with an economic theory in circumstances where there is no scope for controlled experimentation. Among the earliest econometric techniques were those devised to examine trade phenomena, for example in the form of business cycles and agricultural markets. However, the interests of the discipline soon extended to the analysis of firms, households and individuals. There is no reason why econometric techniques cannot be applied to many social systems not usually thought of as the domain of economists. The distinctive feature of the statistical approach of the econometrician is that the datasets to be analysed are affected by the behavioural responses of human agents.

The core model of the econometrician is the classical multiple linear regression (MLR) model, now familiar to scientists in numerous disciplines (see Box 13.1). The purpose of the MLR is to model variation in a phenomenon of interest (the dependent variable) as a function of a number of independent explanatory variables. From our perspective, the usefulness of such modelling is that it enables you in principle to model separately multiple influences on an outcome of interest, and in particular to isolate the influence of a particular policy intervention on outcome. In contrast to the case control approach, MLR methods can be a very efficient approach towards controlling for variations in subject characteristics, and can offer useful results with limited samples. The use (and abuse) of MLR techniques has become legion.

Box 13.1: Multiple linear regression

Suppose Y_i is the i-th observation of the dependent variable, and $X_{1i}, X_{2i}, ..., X_{ki}$ are the associated measures of the k explanatory variables. Then multiple linear regression models the dependent variable as follows:

$$Y_i = \alpha_0 + \alpha_1 X_{1i} + \alpha_2 X_{2i} + ... + \alpha_k X_{ki} + u_i$$

where u_i is the unexplained random element. The α_is are unknown fixed coefficients, the values of which are inferred from the set of observations available to the analyst. The usual method of estimating the α_is is ordinary least squares, which minimises the sum of the squared u_is. The more observations available, the more reliable are the estimates of the α_is.

The validity of the classical ordinary least squares MLR model rests on numerous limiting assumptions which are often not satisfied in practice. In short, many applications of the classical MLR model are in some sense inappropriate. The distinctive contribution of econometricians has been to detect departures from the classical assumptions, and to develop techniques for specifying and estimating models in situations where the classical model does not apply.

To this end, numerous econometric techniques have been reported, many developed to accommodate peculiar modelling requirements of specific situations. A comprehensive treatment can be found in any advanced textbook, such as Greene (2000). Here we merely report some examples that illustrate important issues likely to arise in any examination of observational data with relevance to 'what works' in the public sector.

- *Misspecification*. In many disciplines, researchers report MLR results without much regard for whether the associated model appears to be well specified. In contrast, econometricians have devoted a great deal of effort to developing an extensive armoury of tests to examine consistency with the classical model (Godfrey, 1988). For example, it may be the case that the relationship being modelled is non-linear, in contrast to the linear form assumed in classical MLR. It is to be hoped that use of such consistency tests becomes accepted practice among all users of MLR. Once a correctly specified class of models has been identified, use of specification tests can also play an important part in the difficult art of selecting the most appropriate model from a range of competing alternatives.

- *Multicollinearity.* A common problem in analysis of observational data is that many of the potential explanatory variables do not in general vary independently. Instead, they are to a greater or lesser extent collinear. This means that selection of models and interpretation of results is often a complex issue. For example, height and weight are highly correlated, but both might have separate effects on (say) blood pressure. Omitting one variable might appear to 'improve' the model, but might be highly misleading in inferring cause and effect. While offering no definitive guidance on what is often a matter for judgement, econometricians have played an important part in highlighting the need to take full account of collinearity in interpreting results. Omission of variables collinear with included variables is an important and common form of model misspecification.
- *Missing data and outliers.* The presence of anomalous data, in the form of either missing or outlying observations, is intrinsic to observational datasets. For example, a single outlier can substantially change the estimated coefficients. A range of techniques have been developed to examine and accommodate the complications that such issues give rise to.
- *Time series.* A lot of observational data is in the form of time series, and some of the earliest developments in econometrics sought to develop statistical methods consistent with economic theories of dynamic systems. Here a particular interest might be in modelling the lag between stimulus and response, and in distinguishing between short-run and long-run influences.
- *Panel data.* A lot of observational data is in the form of panels (a series of repeated observations from the same sources). For example, extensive data on UK local governments is routinely collected on an annual basis. This situation offers the potential for developing far more secure statistical models of behaviour, but in general invalidates the use of classical MLR. It has therefore given rise to a rich set of panel techniques

(Baltagi, 1996). These help the analyst to examine the stability of a model over time, and, by isolating secular effects, to offer secure estimates of explanatory variables over the time period for which data are held.

- *Limited dependent variables.* In many observational studies the dependent variable fails to conform to the continuity requirements of the classical MLR model. It may be reported in categorical rather than continuous form (for example, participation or non-participation); it may be censored, in the sense that it can be observed only within certain ranges (for example, a survey of occupancy rates of NHS beds is bounded above by 100%); or it may be truncated, in the sense that observations lying outside a particular range are not captured (for example, small nursing homes may not have to register and therefore may not be captured in a survey). A range of techniques has been developed to specify and estimate models under such circumstances, which in many respects are the econometrician's response to the problem of selection bias (Maddala, 1983; Greene, 2000).

- *Endogeneity.* The classical MLR model assumes that the explanatory variables vary independently, or (in the econometrician's terminology) are 'exogenous'. In practice, in many observational studies some of the explanatory variables used are effectively determined in part by the level of the dependent variable – in other words some of the explanatory variables, as well as the dependent variable, are 'endogenous'. To take an example mentioned earlier, the level of expenditure on police services may in part be influenced by past levels of criminal activity – that is, there is *feedback* from responses to stimulus. Another example might be that the very roads built on the basis of traffic forecasts inevitably invalidate those same forecasts (see Chapter Nine). Such feedback gives rise to a model comprised of a system of simultaneous equations, rather than a single equation. The development of methods (such as the use of instrumental variables) to accommodate systems of equations is perhaps the crowning achievement of econometrics.

- *Measurement error.* In general, all of the variables used in observational studies are measured with a degree of error, which is sometimes very large. Such measurement error is endemic to all statistical methods, and econometricians have developed a range of techniques to model measurement error, and address the inconsistency and bias to which it may give rise.

The essence of the traditional econometric methodology is to assume a particular data generating process (or theory), and then to develop an estimation procedure that enables the analyst satisfactorily to model a specific situation for which such a process is thought to apply. Misspecification tests are in many circumstances available to test ex post facto whether the data appears to be consistent with the chosen model.

The econometric approach is not without its critics. For example, when the results of an econometric study are used to derive policy conclusions, a now famous pitfall must be avoided: any change in policy may quite radically change the behaviour of the individuals or households studied, thus changing the effect of the policy change. This is the 'Lucas critique' (see Lucas, 1976), initially applied to macroeconomic policy, but applicable to any situation where behaviour depends on people's understanding about current policy rules.

It is not difficult to think of more general public sector applications of the Lucas critique. For example, suppose that a study of general practitioners' (GPs') referral under a budget-holding experiment is used to inform policy makers about whether or not to implement a universal fundholding scheme. If those GPs in the experiment did not believe that the experiment would be sustained, then the responses observed may be very different to those that occur once the scheme becomes universal policy. In short, expectations about the nature and longevity of the policy may have been changed, and responses may become very different to those observed in the experiment. This problem of policy design is not confined to the use of observational data. However, it is more difficult to control with evaluations that use observational data.

In this chapter the perspective has largely been one of testing or estimating the effects of alternative policies. In this context, the role of econometrics or statistics can appear rather negative: rejecting theories that conflict with evidence, or that even just have weak evidential support. In practice, the role of statistical analysis may be much more constructive, by revealing relationships and thus suggesting causal connections: smoking and lung cancer were connected by a statistical correlation between observational data before any causal link was established. The danger here is 'data-mining', or 'fishing expeditions'. The analyst may discover a (typically partial) correlation, think up some reason why it should exist, and then test-and-verify the new 'hypothesis' using the same data. The whole apparatus of hypothesis testing set out in any statistical text is thereby jettisoned. To inject some intellectual coherence into this activity has long been a major preoccupation of all observational analysts. Important contributions have come from the Bayesian camp, and Leamer's

(1978) *Specification searches* clarified the issues, pointing the way to at least partial solutions (see Box 13.2).

Box 13.2: Leamer's six types of specification search	
Type of specification search	**Designed to ...**
Hypothesis testing	Choose a 'true model'; test a theory
Interpretive	Interpret multidimensional evidence; discover what is hidden in the data
Simplification	Construct a 'fruitful model'; make the model comprehensible
Proxy	Find an alternative measure positively correlated with the ideal but one that is an unobserved measure to compensate for poorly measured phenomena
Data selection	Select a data set; transform the data; weed out anomalous observations
Post-data model construction	Improve an existing model; create testable hypotheses

Source: Darnell and Evans (1990)

However, in practice it is often the case that a large number of plausible competing models cannot be rejected by econometric modelling (Epstein, 1987). The econometrician feels unable to offer definitive guidance. This outcome may be for a number of reasons which can be summarised under two headings: the systems being modelled may be more complex than assumed, and the data being used is not adequate for the intended purpose. System complexity is endemic to human endeavour, and there exist few solutions other than to develop better theory, or to seek to model a simpler sub-problem. Inadequate data may reflect small samples, unmanageable selection bias, or poor measurement instruments. Here the prescription is for the analyst to seek to become involved when data collection mechanisms are being designed. In practice, the disappointing results emanating from many econometric studies probably reflect an element of both system complexity and data inadequacy.

Notwithstanding such reservations, the discipline of econometrics is a major intellectual achievement. As Epstein (1987) points out it is "unique among the sciences for aspiring to great precision without controlled experiments or large samples". It offers analysts in fields well beyond the traditional concerns of economists a sound methodological framework for analysing observational data.

Discussion

This chapter has indicated that the methodology associated with the analysis of observational data is fraught with difficulty. However, it would clearly be absurd to reject the use of such data as an important source of evidence on which to base policy and practice recommendations. The importance of observational methods is likely to increase rapidly, as the revolution in IT capabilities releases a wealth of hitherto unavailable data. It becomes important therefore to ensure that the observational methods that are used are appropriate to the data sources under scrutiny, and that the analytic strategies applied are subjected to sustained critique.

The key skills in analysing observational data are firstly, to make the model sensitive to the situation under investigation, while acknowledging any shortcomings in the data. Second, any subsequent use of analytic techniques must then be consistent with the specification of the model. Thus evidence-based policy requires evidence to be not only prepared carefully, but also presented and interpreted fairly. By their nature, observational studies rarely offer unequivocal findings, and are always open to criticism. The analyst therefore needs to develop a variety of skills (and a thick skin).

The statistician has introduced the notion of two types of error – Type 1 and Type 2. In the context of this book, these might be reinterpreted as Type 1: wrongly implementing a policy that does not work; Type 2: failing to implement a policy that would work. The job of the observational analyst is to give an honest opinion of the probability of each type of policy error emerging from their analysis. It is then for the policy maker to judge how 'costly' each type of error might be, and to come to a decision accordingly.

It is possible to envisage a range of approaches towards communicating the results of observational analysis to policy makers. At one extreme is the stark conclusion that A works better than B (with probability P). An example of a more subtle approach to the treatment of uncertainty is the type of 'fan chart' published by the Bank of England in its quarterly 'Inflation Report', which shows statistical confidence bands for its 'constant policy' forecasts as they evolve over time. In the extreme, econometric results might be embedded in a complex microsimulation model, capable of simulating the distribution of population responses across a wide range of policy interventions (for example, modelling the responses of individual pupils to a new method of teaching reading).

These approaches may imply very different commitments of analytic resources. However, in general the application of observational methods to existing datasets will be a relatively low-cost approach towards evaluating policy and practice. Such methods are not always applicable and – even where they are – may not generate useable results. But, given the explosion of data availability, there is in practice an increasingly wide range of circumstances in which they are likely to generate some useful evidence.

In short, observational methods constitute a valuable weapon in the armoury of evaluation work. They offer an efficient, fast and cheap alternative to controlled experimentation, and can generate useful results even in apparently unpromising circumstances. However, observational methods are vulnerable to numerous misapplications and misinterpretations, so great care is needed in interpreting results, and improved training is almost certainly needed, both among analysts and among their policy customers. Rather than its traditional role of hypothesis testing, the analysis of observational data can often be used as part of a continuing process of suggesting hypotheses and indicating promising avenues for further exploration. It is in this more constructive role that observational methods are likely to yield their most useful results.

References

Baltagi, B.I. (1996) *Econometric analysis of panel data*, Chichester: John Wiley.

Darnell, A.C. and Evans, J.L. (1990) *The limits of econometrics*, Aldershot: Edward Elgar.

Epstein, R.J. (1987) *A history of econometrics*, Amsterdam: North-Holland.

Gail, M.H. (1998) 'Observational study', in P. Armitage and T. Colton (eds) *Encyclopedia of biostatistics*, Chichester: John Wiley.

Godfrey, L. (1988) *Misspecification tests in econometrics*, Cambridge: Cambridge University Press.

Greene, W.H. (2000) *Econometric analysis* (4th edn), Englewood Cliffs, NJ: Prentice Hall.

Kennedy, P. (1999) *A guide to econometrics* (4th edn), Oxford: Blackwell.

Leamer. E.E. (1978) *Specification searches: Ad hoc inference with non-experimental data*, Chichester: John Wiley.

Lilienfeld, D.E. and Stolley, P.D. (1994) *Foundations of epidemiology* (3rd edn), Oxford: Oxford University Press.

Lucas Jr, R.E. (1976) 'Econometric policy evaluation: a critique', in K. Brunner and A.H. Meltzer (eds) *The Phillips Curve and labor markets*, Carnegie-Rochester Conference Series on Public Policy, vol 1, Amsterdam: North Holland.

Maddala, G.S. (1983) *Limited dependent and qualitative variables in econometrics*, Cambridge: Cambridge University Press.

Morgan, M. (1990) *The history of econometric ideas*, Cambridge: Cambridge University Press.

FOURTEEN

Contributions from qualitative research

Philip Davies

Introduction

The relationship between qualitative and quantitative research has challenged social scientists and public policy researchers for most of the past two centuries. The survey research tradition of Charles Booth and Joseph Rowntree has been developed and refined greatly since the early 19th century, part of which has involved integrating qualitative data on people's perceptions, experiences, values and priorities with respect to a range of public policy issues. At the same time, the interpretive tradition of sociologists such as Max Weber has introduced the notion of *idiographic* and particularistic inquiry alongside that of generalisable, law-like findings of the nomothetic tradition. Social science and public policy research also has a distinguished history of using, and developing, experimental methods of investigation (Oakley, 1998) which, despite pursuing a clearly positivist approach, necessarily involve qualitative research, if only in terms of developing and using outcome measures that are contextually valid and relevant.

Qualitative and quantitative data, then, have a long history of contributing to social science and public policy research. Both types of research and evidence are essential in terms of defining:
- the questions for which evidence is sought;
- what counts as evidence;
- the appropriate methodological procedures for finding and critically appraising the best available evidence.

The calls from evidence-based practitioners, especially in medicine (see

Chapter Three), for more and better evaluative studies using controlled experimental designs, and the insistence by many that randomised controlled trials (RCTs) constitute the 'gold standard' of evidence-based practice, may have served to undermine the value and contribution of qualitative research and evidence. Similarly, the notion of a 'hierarchy of evidence', with RCTs and meta-analyses of RCTs at the top, and the opinions of respected authorities, expert committees and descriptive studies at the bottom (see Box 3.3, Chapter Three), may also serve to suggest that qualitative research is inferior to quantitative data and findings.

This chapter seeks to redress any such demeaning of qualitative research and evidence by:

- describing what constitutes qualitative research;
- reviewing what constitutes evidence;
- exploring how qualitative research has informed public policy and practice in healthcare, education and other substantive areas of inquiry.

It will be argued that the polarisation between quantitative and qualitative research is artificial, and that both types of research and data are usually required in order to provide the highest quality of evidence in public policy.

What is qualitative research?

Qualitative research is a collection of methodological approaches to studying the social world, in which activities are studied in naturalistic settings rather than under experimental conditions, and where the subjective experiences of ordinary people are of greater interest than the objective categories and measurements of researchers. In this research tradition, the 'facticity' or incontrovertible nature of social facts is frequently called into question by the variable practices, meanings, interpretations and values of ordinary people. Qualitative research pays considerable attention to the variety of ways in which people from different social and cultural backgrounds, and in different situations, make sense of the world in which they live, give meaning to it, establish relationships within that world and, thereby, *construct* social reality (Berger and Luckman, 1967). Qualitative research is more concerned with *idiographic* explanations of particular events, activities and social groups (that is, rich descriptions) rather than *nomothetic* (or law-like) explanations involving invariant or generalisable laws relating variables to each other in a quantitative manner.

This account of qualitative research reveals the rather different language and vocabulary that is used, compared to the language and vocabulary of quantitative research based on the positivistic tradition of social inquiry. The latter tends to follow Durkheim's (1895, p 1) dictum to "treat social facts as things", and to count, hypothesise, test, measure, theorise and conclude about these 'things' as if they had little or no relationship to the people they affect. The much-used example of suicide provides a useful illustration of the contrast between the qualitative-interpretative approach to social research and evidence, and the quantitative-positivistic tradition. Durkheim's classic study of suicide (1897) took official statistics on deaths by suicide as social facts (in that they were readily available in official records), and analysed the variability in rates of suicide in terms of other social facts such as the religion, geography, and degree of social integration of the people who had apparently died by suicide. Durkheim's analysis was that suicide tends to occur in greater numbers among people who are less integrated (or indeed over-integrated) into society than those who are well integrated. Statistical analysis and manipulation showed this, inter alia, to be a function of the religious background of people. People in highly integrated religions, such as Jewish people, have lower incidences of suicide than people in less integrated religions (such as Protestants). Durkheim's study of suicide provided sociology with a prototype of inquiry and evidence which has become so commonplace that many regard it as the industry standard of the discipline.

The qualitative-interpretative tradition of social research, however, challenges the very basis of Durkheim's analysis by calling into question the validity of official suicide statistics as social facts (Douglas, 1967; Atkinson, 1978). What counts as a suicide and, therefore, what gets into official statistics, is dependent on the judgement, categorisation and classification of coroners and other officials who compile official statistics. This may be influenced by the perceived status or social position of the deceased person, or their relatives, the interpretation of any notes or personal effects that may (or may not) have been left by the deceased, and the policies and procedures of different coroners' offices and other parts of officialdom. Moreover, the apparent 'facticity' of a deceased person, such as their religion, may vary greatly in importance depending on their devoutness, the orthodoxy of their beliefs, the frequency of practising their religion, and the meanings they gave to their religious status or identity. As a result, qualitative research on suicide has tended to explore the processes, procedures and practices whereby official statistics are generated, and the chain of interpretations, meanings and ascription that are invoked in both generating official statistics and using them analytically.

The qualitative approach to inquiry and evidence is not confined to social research, nor is it mutually exclusive of quantitative and positivistic inquiry. It is, for instance, at the very heart of good practice in epidemiology and medical statistics. It is readily acknowledged in these two areas of inquiry that comparative analysis of death rates may be an artefact of the classification procedures of doctors and coroners or, in the case of morbidity data, of variations in how people define and interpret health and illness. Good epidemiology and medical statistics take these important qualitative factors into consideration when using measures of outcome or process, and integrate them into the interpretations that are made of epidemiological and statistical findings.

Qualitative research uses a variety of methods, including interviews, observations of naturally occurring activities, detailed descriptions and ethnography, conversation and discourse analysis, analysis of texts and semiotic representations, and personal accounts, biographies and oral histories (Silverman, 1993; Denzin and Lincoln, 1994, 1998; Wolcott, 1994; Creswell, 1998). Creswell (1998) has suggested that there are five traditions of qualitative research: biographical life history, phenomenology, grounded theory, ethnography, and case studies. Denzin and Lincoln (1994) also stress the diversity of methods used by qualitative researchers and suggest that qualitative research "privileges no single methodology over any other" (p 3). Rather, qualitative researchers:

> ... use semiotics, narrative, content, discourse, archival, and phonemic analysis, even statistics. They also draw upon and utilize the approaches, methods, and techniques of ethnomethodology, phenomenology, hermeneutics, feminism, rhizomatics, deconstructionism, ethnographies, interviews, psychoanalysis, cultural studies, survey research, and participant observation, among others. (Denzin and Lincoln, 1994, p 3)

Such diversity of research methods, many of which may be unfamiliar to public policy makers and practitioners, may raise questions about the appropriateness and applicability of qualitative research for public policy and practice. There is a long, and at times heated, debate within sociology and other social sciences about whether social science should have anything at all to do with policy or practice concerns. Although sociology grew out of the Enlightenment, and the belief that the scientific study of society might pave the way for the social and political world to be understood and engineered in ways that might emulate the control and manipulation of the physical world by the natural sciences, such views have been fiercely contested. Bloor (1997) reviewed these issues most succinctly, and has concluded that addressing social problems and public policy is a legitimate objective of social research, and that "qualitative research has a two-fold advantage in these processes of influence" (p 236). First, says Bloor, the degree of close personal contact which qualitative researchers have with research subjects means that "those research subjects will have interest in implementing the researcher's suggestions on changes in practice" (Bloor, 1997, p 236). Second, the rich descriptions of everyday practice provided by qualitative research "enable practitioner audiences imaginatively to juxtapose their own everyday practices with the research description". This may affect policy and practice by questioning the assumptions upon which both of these activities are based, by questioning the ways in which policy or practice issues are framed, by providing insight into the views, activities and priorities of the people who are affected by policy and practice, and by ensuring that the evidence that is used to develop policy and practice is *ecologically* valid (that it works in the contexts of people's everyday lives and environments). This, in turn, raises an equally important question: what is evidence?

What is evidence?

Evaluative evidence

Much of the work to date in evidence-based practice has been evaluative. That is, it seeks to establish valid, reliable and relevant evidence of the most effective and efficient interventions in medicine, healthcare, education and other areas of public policy and practice. Evaluative research asks questions such as 'Does intervention x have a better outcome than intervention y in terms of achieving outcome z?'. More specifically, evaluative research seeks evidence of the *relative* costs and effects of using intervention x as opposed to intervention y. Consequently, evaluative research asks questions such as 'Is intervention x more, or less, *cost* effective than intervention y at achieving outcome z?' Evaluative questions such as these require either the strictures of controlled trials, where everything other than the interventions under investigation is held constant (see Chapter Twelve), or methods involving sophisticated statistical control (see Chapter Thirteen). Such research typically determines the relative effectiveness and efficiency of interventions x and y by measuring the difference between the outcomes of these two interventions and establishing whether this difference is statistically significant.

Qualitative contributions to defining policy questions

It is sometimes assumed that there is little, or no, role for qualitative research in RCTs, quasi-experiments or other types of evaluative methods. This is incorrect. Qualitative issues are almost always involved in determining the evaluative question(s) to be addressed. One of the central tenets of evidence-based healthcare, and of evidence-based policy and practice in other substantive areas, is that getting the question right is crucial to gathering the appropriate data and establishing best evidence. The process of asking the right question(s) involves careful thought, critical appraisal, and qualitative consideration of who the appropriate subjects are, what interventions (or manoeuvres) are to be investigated, what contextual and ethical issues are involved in introducing these interventions (and withholding their introduction to the control group), and what outcomes are to be measured. These questions arise when contemplating using *existing* evidence as well as when planning new research to establish or replicate evidence. Evaluative studies are always undertaken in a particular sociodemographic, cultural and political–economic context. They are also affected by temporal factors. Consequently, when using existing evidence the evidence-based practitioner must ask whether the particular conditions under which a controlled trial, systematic review or meta-analysis were undertaken are sociologically, culturally and contextually relevant to the client groups, subjects, or environments for which this evidence is to be invoked. Similarly, when planning a controlled trial, systematic review or meta-analysis these same contextual factors must be taken into consideration in order to ensure prospectively that appropriate, ecologically valid data is gathered. Qualitative research assists with all of these considerations.

A contribution to external validity

An example of the need to consider such qualitative issues comes from the use of a high quality RCT of treatment for alcohol problems (Orford and Edwards, 1977). This study randomly allocated *selected* problem-drinkers in south London into an experimental group, which provided a single counselling session based on giving advice plus providing certain back-up support, and a control group, which received what was considered 'normal' psychiatric treatment for alcohol problems in the mid–1970s. There were no statistically significant differences between the quantitative outcomes of the experimental and control groups at 12 and 18 months, but some of the (non-significant) differences in outcomes favoured those in the experimental group. The trial was undertaken to a high standard and met the ACP (American Council of Physicians) Journal Club criteria of a good RCT.

In terms of using the findings of this trial as best evidence for treating problem-drinkers elsewhere, it is imperative to ask questions – and establish best evidence – about the subjects included in the trial, the skills and competencies of the counsellors involved in the single session of advice-giving, the nature of the communication and advice-giving between the counsellors and clients, and the replicability of this communication in different contexts and with different subjects. It is also necessary to ensure that the support services that were provided during the follow-up period of the trial can be reproduced in the context being considered, and that the sociocultural context of alcohol use and misuse in the experimental locale compares with that in the localities where this evidence is to be used. Also, what counted as 'normal' or 'regular' psychiatric treatment for alcohol problems in the mid–1970s may be very different from what is provided at the beginning of the 21st century, thereby establishing a temporal specificity to the Orford and Edwards' study. Similarly, if a trial is being planned to establish further evidence of the effectiveness of minimal intervention with alcohol problems elsewhere, or to replicate the Orford and Edwards study, it is equally important to ask (and answer) these same qualitative questions.

Assessing fairness in comparisons

Qualitative data are also important in establishing whether experimental and control groups are matched at the outset of a trial. It cannot be assumed that the random allocation of subjects to experimental and control groups will necessarily result in matched samples on appropriate variables at the outset. There may be qualitative, and quantitative, differences between the experimental and control groups on variables that will affect the validity of the trial. For instance, it may be that despite matching on *drinking* behaviour, there will be important qualitative differences in the sociodemographic, sociological, cultural and psychological backgrounds of subjects in the experimental and the control groups, all of which have been shown to be highly *clinically* significant in terms of affecting positive and negative outcomes of treatment for problem drinkers. While randomisation will on average allocate such factors evenly to experimental and control groups, it is important to test that this has been achieved at the outset of a trial, and to know which of these qualitative factors are likely to be significant for clinical and real-life outcomes. Similar considerations are necessary when undertaking, or using, a systematic review or a meta-analysis (Preiss, 1988; Hedges, 1992; Hunter and Schmidt, 1995).

Determining appropriate outcomes

Another important role of qualitative research in evaluative studies is in determining appropriate and valid outcome measures. One of the major challenges of establishing best evidence is doing so in terms of outcomes that are meaningful and relevant to the people who are affected by the interventions concerned. The relationship between objective and subjective measures of outcome is imprecise, in that people who may be considered to have had a positive outcome on an objective measure may actually consider themselves to have had a negative experience, and vice versa. Also, objective outcome measures may measure variables that have no (or quite different) significance or relevance to the people whose health status, education achievement, or consequence of criminal behaviour is being assessed. Activities of daily living (ADL) indices, for instance, usually measure patients' or respondents' ability to walk unaided for 50 metres. This may have little relevance or significance to patients or respondents who do not need to walk 50 metres unaided, or to those who need to walk further than 50 metres unaided in order to catch a bus, visit a supermarket, or pay their bills. Similarly, students' achievements on standard attainment tests (such as GCSEs, A levels or higher degrees) may have little relevance to employers or the real-life demands of the employment or problem-solving worlds. In other words, the contingent and contextualised nature of measured outcomes needs to be appreciated and accommodated (Davies, 1996).

Establishing outcome measures that have subjective and objective meaning, as well as having the propensity for meaningful quantitative measurement and analysis, can be greatly assisted by good qualitative research. One example of this was the way in which the Nottingham Health Profile (NHP) was developed (Hunt and McEwen, 1980). It was done so in a way that would:

- provide assessment of a person's need for care which was not based on purely medical criteria;
- enable the subsequent evaluation of care provided;
- provide an indicator of population health status.

The creators of the NHP began to construct the profile by undertaking 768 qualitative interviews with patients experiencing a variety of acute and chronic ailments. From these indepth interviews, which revealed respondents' own concepts and categories of health and illness, a total of 2,200 statements were extracted which "describe the typical effects of ill health" (Hunt and McEwen, 1980, p 234). These effects encompassed social, psychological, behavioural and physical functioning. From this large number of statements 138 were selected, and after further testing and piloting, these were further reduced to 82 statements. A closer look was then taken at these 82 statements in order to develop a questionnaire that would be suitable for inclusion in a population survey. As a result of these qualitative interviews and methods of data analysis, the NHP (Part I) was generated consisting of 38 statements representing six dimensions of health *that are meaningful to ordinary people*: physical mobility, pain, sleep, energy, emotional reactions and social isolation.

Assessing context specificity

Another way in which qualitative research can enhance the measurement of outcome in evaluative studies is by identifying the context specificity of both objective and subjective measures. There is a considerable literature (Christmas et al, 1974; Andrews and Stewart, 1979; Newcombe and Ratcliff, 1979; Davies and Mehan, 1988) which reports on the variability of patients' abilities and health status according to the contexts in which the assessments are carried out. Patients' independence in activities of daily living, cognitive functioning, and communicative ability have all been shown to be different when assessed in hospital than when measured in their own homes. This not only calls for extreme caution when using and interpreting so-called 'objective' measures of health (or education, or criminal) status, but also highlights the need to supplement, or substitute, such measurements with more detailed observational and ethnographic data from different real-life contexts in which people live and attempt to function.

Observational and ethnographic evidence

Evaluative research is only one type of research, providing one type of evidence. Other research does not seek to compare, contrast, or evaluate the differential effectiveness and/or efficiency of interventions, but attempts instead to provide qualitative descriptions of health, illnesses and their management, education processes and activities, criminal behaviour and responses, and their consequences. These descriptions are usually based on careful observations and recordings of ordinary, everyday activities that take place in naturally occurring contexts, using the range of qualitative methods outlined above. The term 'observational' in qualitative social science research refers to studies based on detailed observations and recordings of naturally occurring everyday activities. This is somewhat different from how the term is used in quantitative approaches such as epidemiological inquiry, where it refers to non-experimental methods such as surveys, cohorts and case–control studies (see Chapter Thirteen).

An early example of the contribution of such qualitative research to policy issues was Erving Goffman's (1961) detailed observations and qualitative analysis of mental illness institutions. This, along with other types of data and evidence, accelerated the movement towards deinstitutionalisation of the care of people with mental illnesses and the closure of mental asylums and other types of total institution. Other examples are the work of Labov and Fanshel (1978), Byrne and Long (1984), Cicourel (1985), Heath (1986) and many others, whose detailed observations and qualitative analyses of doctor–patient discourse and interaction has greatly influenced the training of doctors in communication and interactional skills (Pendleton and Schofield, 1988).

Qualitative examination of processes

Evidence from such qualitative research can take a number of forms. One of these is evidence concerning the *processes* by which the daily activities of education, healthcare, criminal justice and other areas of public policy and practice are undertaken, and the consequences that these have for various stakeholders, such as learners/patients/criminals as recipients of services, teachers/healthcare professionals/criminal justice personnel as service deliverers, and school governors/healthcare executives/criminal justice authorities as service managers. In education, for instance, a number of qualitative studies (Cicourel and Kitsuse, 1963; Hargreaves, 1976; Cicourel and Mehan, 1985; Mehan et al, 1986; Mehan, 1992) have demonstrated the ways in which teachers and other educational personnel typify students, and use various categories, procedures and practices, to open up and close down opportunities for advancement in education. These studies have shown, for instance, that inequalities in education attainment are less a feature of students' genetic or racial background (Herrnstein and Murray, 1994) or gender per se, and more a consequence of the everyday activities and processes of school life and school organisation.

An early qualitative study of a mid-West high school in the United States (Cicourel and Kitsuse, 1963), for instance, used ethnographic methods of observation and interviews with school personnel and students to examine how students from different socioeconomic backgrounds proceeded through high school. Cicourel and Kitsuse noted that whereas students from low-income families with low grades and low test scores tended to proceed into lower ability tracks (streams), students from middle- and higher-income families with similar grades and test scores tended to proceed into higher ability tracks. Students from low-income families, with *adequate* grades and test scores, did *not* generally proceed into higher ability tracks but remained in classes and courses that would prohibit them from preparation for college entrance. Thus students' scholastic abilities were less important in determining their educational careers than teachers' and counsellors' differential treatment of students from different parental and home backgrounds.

Cicourel and Kitsuse also found that black students were significantly less likely to apply for college than white students, and that those white students with modest grades and test scores were nonetheless tracked for college preparation. The authors found that school counsellors played a significant role in these differential pathways of students by consistently advising black students not to prepare for, or apply to, college even when they had good grades and test scores. However, white students were far more often advised by school counsellors to prepare for college entrance despite their modest or low grades and test scores. Counsellors' labelling and sorting practices were key factors in black students not applying to college, and provided an alternative explanation for low college attainment among blacks and lower-income students than their genetic inheritance or social deprivation.

In a review of a number of qualitative studies of education inequality and stratification, Cicourel and Mehan (1985) found that these 'sorting practices' were common in many American high schools. They found that the allocation of students to different ability groupings was based on teachers' perceptions of students, as well as on grades and test scores, and that students from different linguistic environments, and with different backgrounds of 'cultural capital' (Bourdieu and Passeron, 1977; Bourdieu, 1986), had differential access to educational curricula, instructional methods and interactional opportunities. Cicourel and Mehan's findings suggest that there is an inverse teaching law, similar to the inverse care law in healthcare (Tudor-Hart, 1971), whereby students who need the most intensive teaching receive it less, and those whose abilities and social backgrounds are such that they may need less teaching and instruction in schools receive more input.

John Ogbu (1983) also used qualitative methods in his research and has provided yet further evidence that minority status per se does not determine educational achievement. Ogbu argues that there are different kinds of minorities experiencing different types of school success and failure, and for different reasons. He suggests that education achievement is related to the degree of autonomy and voluntarism in the minority status of different social and ethnic groups. Autonomous minorities, such as the Amish, Jews and Mormons, have tended not to be subordinated by dominant groups, despite persecution and prejudice, and have maintained a distinctive identity. These groups have successfully maintained a separate existence and a cultural frame of reference that encourages success. They can be characterised as having avoided persistent school failure. Other groups, such as Blacks, Indians, Mexican-Americans, and Puerto Ricans have had less control over their immigration to the US, sometimes arriving as slaves, and have been subordinated by dominant groups within America. Ogbu argues that the caste-like status of such groups is usually permanent and is acquired at (or attributed to) birth. These groups are usually regarded as inferior and of the lower ranks of society with little or no political power. This type of group, says Ogbu, experiences disproportionate school failure.

Qualitative studies such as these show the limitations of quantitative studies of education achievement that report only on aggregated variables, without considering the sociological and cultural variability that exists within them. They also challenge those explanations of statistical patterns of education achievement that attribute causality to genetic, hereditary and racial characteristics (Jensen, 1969; Herrnstein and Murray, 1994).

Combining qualitative and quantitative insights

Qualitative findings are not mutually exclusive of quantitative data. They can complement quantitative data and begin to explain social survey findings, such as those of Modood (1993) in the UK and Kao and Tienda (1995) in the US, both of which have shown improved educational performance and participation of students from ethnic minorities. Kao and Tienda's suggestion that the parental immigrant status of students may be pivotal in determining the superior educational performance of new immigrants to the US, compared to that of white, third generation, native-born Americans, is given greater empirical and evidential weight by qualitative findings of researchers such as Matute-Bianchi (1986), Gibson and Bhachu (1988) and Ogbu (1983). These studies not only confirm, but more importantly *explain why,* some students from some ethnic minorities are doing better in British and American schools than others.

The empirical findings of the AVID (Advancement Via Individual Determination) project (Mehan et al, 1996), provides further evidence of the combined strength of quantitative and qualitative research in explaining improvements in the educational achievement of able, but hitherto underachieving, students. The project was partly inspired by the qualitative findings of the studies reviewed above, which identified the sorting, labelling and stratifying practices of teachers and other school personnel in the tracking, underparticipation and under-achievement of ethnic minority and low-income students in American schools. The AVID project was designed to reverse these sorting and stratifying practices by 'seeking to "motivate and prepare underachieving students from underrepresented linguistic and ethnic minority groups or low-income students of any ethnicity to perform well in high school and to seek a college education" (Mehan et al, 1996, p 14). It did this by 'untracking' schools and placing hitherto bussed students into regular college preparation classes. Curriculum and teaching methods were based on some of the social constructivist principles of Bruner (1961a, 1961b, 1966), Cole et al (1978), Tharp and Gallimore (1989) in that they provided structured learning opportunities in writing, inquiry and collaboration, as well as social 'scaffolding' to support students until they were ready to learn on their own. AVID also provided professional development opportunities and support to school principals, teachers, school counsellors and other school personnel so that they would be familiar with effective teaching strategies and the principles of teaching and learning that underlay the AVID project.

These were innovative processes inspired and developed by qualitative research from sociology, psychology, and educational theory and practice.

Qualitative research – a different type of evidence

Observational and ethnographic studies, then, provide invaluable qualitative evidence about policy and practice by going beyond, behind and below the surface level of experimental and statistical evidence, and identifying variations *within* apparently independent variables as well as providing explanations for why these variations occur. They also provide valuable evidence about the role of institutional and organisational processes in generating a *sense* of social structure and the appearance of ordered activity in public policy and practice, both of which may be subject to challenge and reinterpretation. There is a need for such evidence to be summarised and synthesised with the same degree of rigour as evidence that is based on RCTs and other experimental and observational methods. This will involve the development of an agreed set of criteria for establishing the quality of qualitative observational and ethnographic studies, and will be one of the tasks of the proposed Campbell Collaboration on the effects of social and educational interventions (Davies et al, 1999; see also Chapters Four and Six of this book). There are already a number of attempts to provide such criteria for establishing the quality of qualitative research (see, for example, Beck, 1993; Boulton and Fitzpatrick, 1997; Creswell, 1998; Forchuk and Roberts, 1993; Greenhalgh and Taylor, 1997; Kuckelmann-Cobb and Nelson-Hagemaster, 1987; Medical Sociology Group, 1996; Seers, 1999).

Conversation and discourse analysis

Another form of qualitative approach that helps to inform service delivery is conversation and discourse analysis, which studies naturally occurring talk and conversation in institutional and non-institutional settings. Following the pioneering work of Sacks (1972, 1992), Schegloff (1972, 1982, 1984), and Sacks et al, (1974), which showed that there are systematic structures and rules of turn-taking and sequencing in naturally occurring talk, conversation analysts have built a body of empirical evidence of how these structures and rules operate in different organisational and institutional settings (Atkinson and Drew, 1979; Davies, 1979; Mehan, 1979; Cicourel, 1981, 1985, 1987; Fisher and Todd, 1983; Heath, 1984, 1986; Sharrock and Anderson, 1987).

Turn-taking, and the structure of sequences in conversation, are central concerns of conversation analysis. Sacks et al (1974) have proposed that there are at least three rules of everyday conversation:
• one speaker speaks at a time;
• turn-taking occurs smoothly with no, or minimal, overlap of speakers;
• there are speaker selection rules whereby current speakers can exit and new speakers can enter the conversation.

Failure to observe these 'turn-taking rules' in everyday conversation is noticeable and usually requires some sort of repair, such as "I'm sorry, I thought you had finished". In other words, turn-taking is one of the basic rules of social interaction and social order.

Studies of turn-taking and naturally occuring talk in institutional settings have noted variations to the two-part sequences, such as Questions and Answers, Greetings and Responses, that Sacks (1967) and Schegloff (1968) identified as the most basic structures of everyday talk and social interaction. Mehan (1979), for instance, found that classroom interaction is structured in terms of three-part sequences made up of: *Initiation, response,* and *evaluation.* For example:

Teacher: "Now, who knows what this one says? [Holds up new card] This is the long word. Who knows what it says?" [Initiation]

Student: "Cafeteria" [Reply]

Teacher: "Cafeteria, Audrey. Good for you." [Evaluation] (Taken from Mehan, 1979)

Here, the basic two-part question (initiation) and answer (reply) sequence is supplemented by a third part (evaluation) which allows the teacher to not only accept or reject the student's reply, but to appraise it, correct it if necessary, challenge the student, ask another student (or the whole class) for an answer and, thereby, to control the lesson and the classroom. There are other rules of classroom interaction that supplement these verbal exchanges, such as students raising their hands and waiting to be recognised (selected) by the teacher before replying (Mehan, 1979). Failure to follow the rules of 'bidding for the floor' will constitute a breach of social order in the classroom. Again, the three-part sequence, and accompanying rules of bidding for the floor, are structures that students must learn and 'orient to' if they are to participate appropriately in lessons and avoid being labelled as troublemakers or badly behaved.

Todd (1983) has noted the use of three-part sequences in doctor–patient interactions whereby the first part (question) is usually taken by the doctor, the second part (answer) by the patient, and the third part (evaluation, or 'reactive') is taken by the doctor. Todd argues that the third part in doctor–patient interactions, which she calls 'reactives', "provide the doctor with the means to change topic, swerve the talk back into the doctor's turn and maintain control of the conversation, thereby manifesting medical institutional power" (Todd, 1983, p 166). Heritage (1997) has suggested that this is a more general feature of asymmetry in institutional discourse and interaction. He suggests that:

> In many forms of institutional discourse, by contrast [with ordinary conversation], there is a direct relationship between institutional roles and tasks, on the one hand, and discursive rights and obligations, on the other. For example, institutional representatives commonly ask questions and require of lay participants that they answer them. In this way, they may secure the initiative in determining (i) when a topic is satisfactorily concluded, (ii) what the next topic will be and, (iii) through the design of their questions, how that new topic will be shaped (Drew and Heritage, 1992; Mishler, 1984). Thus institutional representatives can often direct the interaction in ways that are not found in ordinary conversation. (Heritage, 1997, p 176)

There is an abundance of evidence that doctor–patient interaction is asymmetrical, in that doctors overwhelmingly ask questions and patients do not. West (1983) found that only 9% of questions between patients and family practitioners were initiated by patients. West also confirms Frankel's (1984) claim that patient-initiated questions are 'dispreferred' in medical exchanges. Such findings may have important implications for the patient acceptability of therapies, patient adherence to treatment or advice, and subsequent patient satisfaction. Thus qualitative findings from such research can help inform the delivery and improvement of evidence-based practice.

Conversation and discourse analysis, as with observational and ethnographic analysis, goes beyond the summary information that is provided by quantitative data, and provides deeper and more specific, contextualised explanations for why, and how, policy and practice may be effective or ineffective. Ethnographic and conversation analytic data can provide evidence of the *sorts* of reasons why, and how, communication and interaction can be successful, and how it can go wrong. Also, it can help clarify, if not determine, what *counts* as successful (and unsuccessful) communication, interaction, process and outcome from, for example, the viewpoint of patients, doctors and third-party observers. Such insight is very important to evidence-based practice and evidence-based outcomes in many professional settings, and needs to be made accessible to the policy and practice community.

Using qualitative approaches to inform ethical issues

Another way in which qualitative data contributes to evidence-based policy and practice is by providing principles and procedures for determining whether or not it is right or justifiable to pursue a particular policy or practice initiative. In all areas of public policy and practice, ethical issues arise as to whether the people who will be affected by some aspect of policy or practice have been adequately informed about its nature and consequences, about the values on which the policy or practice are based, about the priorities that have been established and the choices that have to be made in order to pursue this approach. It is ethically important that the values, priorities, and choices of the people affected by policy and practice are elicited adequately and taken into consideration by policy makers and people who put policies into practice. In vitro fertilisation of human ova, for instance, is able to increase the happiness and fulfilment of thousands of infertile couples, and is based on reasonable evidence of treatment effectiveness. This still leaves open the issue of whether or not it is ethically right for human life to be conceived in this way, and whether the scarce healthcare resources that are needed to do so should be used in this way when there are many other equally compelling demands on those resources.

Some of the principles and procedures for making ethically informed decisions about the allocation of scarce resources in healthcare include QALYs (Quality Adjusted Life Years), Needs Analysis, the Fair Innings Theory, and the Lottery Theory (Fulford, 1990; Hope, 1995; Rawls, 1972). Such decisions require both qualitative and quantitative evidence of the needs, values and priorities of the population. Methods such as social surveys, panels surveys, indepth interviews, and observations of how people act when faced with choices and moral decisions, are all necessary to ensure that ethical decisions are made on empirical and evidential grounds as well as on the basis of sound philosophical judgement. Citizens' juries (Lenaghan, 1997) and town meetings, such as those used in the Oregon initiative (Ham, 1992), are other ways to gather qualitative data that will inform ethical decision making in public policy and practice.

The ethics of public policy and practice make further calls for qualitative data and evidence, and require that a corpus of best evidence based on case studies and the accumulation of ethical judgements and considerations is readily accessible to the policy and practice community.

Concluding remarks

This chapter has attempted to clarify what is meant by qualitative research and how it may contribute to evidence-based policy and practice. Qualitative research is a broad church of methodological approaches, only a very few of which have been considered in any detail in this knowingly *unsystematic* review. This chapter has examined observational and ethnographic evidence, conversation and discourse analysis, and the ethical considerations of public policy and practice. It concludes that they, like the many other qualitative approaches that can inform policy and practice, go beyond, behind and below the surface level of experimental and statistical evidence. These methods identify variations *within* apparently independent variables as well as providing explanations for why these variations occur. As such, qualitative methods provide additional perspectives on what *counts* as evidence in policy and practice, and how experimental and quantitative evidence can be more thoroughly and meaningfully appraised for its validity and relevance in the everyday world.

Qualitative research, like its quantitative counterpart, has limitations. Some of these limitations are derived from the attention it gives to the context specificity of observations, descriptions, accounts, meanings and underlying structures of activity and interaction that are its hallmark. Those who have tried to go beyond this context specificity and "venture towards achieving more general conclusions from the ethnographic specifics of the separate cases" (Wax, 1979, p 1) have found that this usually violates the "meaning in context" and the "ethnographic uniqueness" that is so central to qualitative inquiry (Noblit and Hare, 1988, p 21). Consequently, it is important that agreed criteria of the quality of qualitative research be determined, and that studies that meet these criteria should be made accessible to the public policy and practice community.

From a more positivistic perspective qualitative research is often seen as being limited by its inability to provide statistical accumulation of findings, its inability to allow prediction or to specify any degree of confidence about qualitative findings, and by its inability to allow for the statistical control of bias. The apparent lack of any systematic way for qualitative research to test for, and control, the heterogeneity/homogeneity of different studies, also concerns those who are more disposed to quantitative approaches to research and evidence. However, these concerns and limitations are somewhat cross-paradigmatic and seem to miss the point of what qualitative studies are trying to achieve. It is rather like trying to decide between the virtues of a saw and a hammer; they do quite different things and serve quite different purposes.

However, the different approaches of qualitative and quantitative research also offer considerable potential for their combined use in evidence-based policy and practice. Mention has been made in this chapter of the use of qualitative research in determining: the nature of the questions to be addressed by quantitative and evaluative research; who the appropriate subjects are; what interventions (or manoeuvres) are to be investigated; what contextual and ethical issues are involved in introducing these interventions (and withholding their introduction to the control group); and what outcomes are to be measured. Qualitative research also enhances quantitative studies by helping to determine the social, cultural, temporal and ecological conditions under which the findings of evaluative and experimental studies are likely to be generalisable and non-generalisable. Qualitative research is usually essential if evidence-based policy and practice is to go beyond the evidence and make sense of its implications for everyday people, situations and circumstances. By the same token, quantitative research can often take the findings of qualitative studies and consider (if not test) their broader applicability and relevance in different contexts. Evidence-based policy and practice requires both types of research and needs to foster an intellectual environment in which the complementary nature of qualitative and quantitative research can flourish.

References

Andrews, K. and Stewart, J. (1979) 'Stroke recovery: he can but does he?', *Rheumatology and Rehabilitation*, vol 18, pp 43 8.

Atkinson, J.M. (1978) *Discovering suicide*, London: Macmillan.

Atkinson, J.M. and Drew, P. (1979) *Order in court: The organisation of verbal interaction in judicial settings*, London: Macmillan.

Beck, C.T. (1993) 'Qualitative research: the evaluation of its credibility, fittingness, and auditability', *Western Journal of Nursing Research*, vol 15, no 2, pp 263-6.

Berger, P.L. and Luckman, T. (1967) *The social construction of reality*, New York, NY: Free Press.

Bloor, M. (1997) 'Addressing social problems through qualitative research', in D. Silverman (ed) *Qualitative research: Theory, method and practice*, London: Sage Publications, pp 221-38.

Boulton, M. and Fitzpatrick, R. (1997) 'Evaluating qualitative research', *Evidence-Based Health Policy and Management*, vol 1, no 4, pp 83-5.

Bourdieu, P. (1986) 'The forms of capital', in J.G. Richardson (ed) *Handbook of theory and research for the sociology of education*, New York, NY: Greenwood Press, pp 241-58.

Bourdieu, P. and Passeron, C. (1977) *Reproduction in education, society and culture*, London: Sage Publications.

Bruner, J. (1961a) 'The act of discovery', *Harvard Educational Review*, vol 31, pp 21-32.

Bruner, J. (1961b) *The process of education*, Cambridge, MA: Harvard University Press.

Bruner, J. (1966) *Toward a theory of instruction*, Cambridge, MA: Harvard University Press.

Byrne P.S. and Long, B.E.L. (1984) *Doctors talking to patients: A study of the verbal behaviour of doctors in the consultation*, Exeter: Royal College of General Practitioners.

Christmas, E.M., Humphrey, M.E., Richardson, A.E. and Smith, E.M. (1974) 'The response of brain-damaged patients to a rehabilitation regime', *Rheumatology and Rehabilitation*, vol 13, pp 92-7.

Cicourel, A.V. (1981) 'Language and Medicine', in C.A. Ferguson and S.B. Heath (eds) *Language in the USA*, New York, NY: Cambridge University Press, pp 407-29.

Cicourel, A.V. (1985) 'Doctor–patient discourse', in T.A. van Dijk (ed) *Handbook of discourse analysis, Volume 4*, London: Academic Press, pp 193-205.

Cicourel, A.V. (1987) 'Cognitive and organisational aspects of medical diagnostic reasoning', *Discourse Processes*, vol 10, pp 347-67.

Cicourel, A.V. and Kitsuse, J.I. (1963) *The educational decision makers*, Indianapolis, IN: Bobbs-Merril.

Cicourel, A.V. and Mehan, H. (1985) 'Universal development, stratifying practices, and status attainment', *Research in Social Stratification and Mobility*, vol 4, pp 3-27.

Cole, M., John-Steiner, V., Scribner S. and Souberman, E. (eds and translators) (1978) *Mind in society: The development of higher psychological processes*, L.S.Vygotsky, Cambridge, MA: Harvard University Press.

Creswell, J.W. (1998) *Qualitative inquiry and research design: Choosing among five traditions*, Thousand Oaks, CA: Sage Publications.

Davies, P.T. (1979) 'Motivation, responsibility and sickness in the psychiatric treatment for alcohol problems', *British Journal of Psychiatry*, vol 134, pp 449-58.

Davies, P.T. (1996) 'Sociological approaches to health outcomes', in H.M. Macbeth (ed) *Health outcomes: Biological, social and economics perspectives*, Oxford: Oxford University Press, pp 94-139.

Davies, P.T and Mehan, H. (1988) 'Professional and family understanding of impaired communication', *British Journal of Disorders of Communication*, vol 23, pp 141-51.

Davies, P.T., Petrosino, A.J. and Chalmers, I.G. (1999) 'The effects of social and educational interventions', Report of a meeting held at the School of Public Policy, University College London, 15-16 July (available from P.T. Davies, Department for Continuing Education, University of Oxford).

Denzin, N.K. and Lincoln, Y.S. (eds) (1994) *Handbook of qualitative research*, Thousand Oaks, CA: Sage Publications.

Denzin, N.K. and Lincoln, Y.S. (eds) (1998) *Collecting and interpreting qualitative materials*, Thousand Oaks, CA: Sage Publications.

Douglas, J.D. (1967) *The social meanings of suicide*, Princeton, NJ: Princeton University Press.

Drew, J. and Heritage, J. (1992) 'Analyzing talk at work: an introduction', in P. Drew and J. Heritage (eds) *Talk at work: Interaction in institutional settings*, Cambridge: Cambridge University Press.

Durkheim, E. (1895; English-language version 1964) *The rules of sociological method*, New York, NY: Free Press.

Durkheim, E. (1897; English-language version 1970) *Suicide*, London, Routledge and Kegan Paul.

Fisher, S. and Todd, A.D. (1983) *The social organisation of doctor–patient communication*, Washington, DC: Centre for Applied Linguistics.

Forchuk, C. and Roberts, J. (1993) 'How to critique qualitative research articles', *Canadian Journal of Nursing Research*, vol 25, no 4, pp 47-56.

Frankel, R.M. (1984) 'Talking in interviews: a dispreference for patient-initiated questions in physician-patient encounters', in G. Psathas and R. Frankel (eds) *Interactional Competence*, New York, NY: Irvington Press, pp 231-62.

Fulford, K.W.M. (1990) *Moral theory and medical practice*, Cambridge: Cambridge University Press.

Gibson, M.A. and Bhachu, P.K. (1988) 'Ethnicity and school performance: a comparative study of South Asian pupils in Britain and America', *Ethnic and Racial Studies*, vol 11, pp 239-62.

Goffman, E. (1961) *Asylums: Essays on the social situation of mental patients and other inmates*, Harmondsworth: Penguin.

Greenhalgh, T. and Taylor, R. (1997) 'How to read a paper: papers that go beyond numbers (qualitative research)', *BMJ*, vol 315, pp 740-3.

Ham, C. (1992) *Health policy in Britain: The politics and organisation of the National Health Service*, London: Macmillan.

Hargreaves, D. (1976) *Deviance in the classroom*, London: Routledge and Kegan Paul.

Heath, C.C. (1984) 'Participation in the medical consultation: the co-ordination of verbal and non-verbal behaviour', *Journal of the Sociology of Health and Illness*, vol 5, no 2, pp 36-74.

Heath, C.C. (1986) *Body movement and speech in medical interaction*, Cambridge: Cambridge University Press.

Hedges, L.V. (1992) 'Meta-analysis', *Journal of Educational Statistics*, vol 17, no 4, pp 279-96.

Heritage, J. (1997) 'Conversation analysis and institutional talk', in D. Silverman (ed) *Qualitative research: Theory, method and practice*, London: Sage Publications, pp 161-82.

Herrnstein, R.J. and Murray, C. (1994) *The Bell Curve*, New York, NY: Free Press.

Hope, T. (1995) 'Quality Adjusted Life Years', Notes for a course on Rationing of Health Care, Oxford Practice Skills Project, Oxford: Institute of Health Sciences.

Hunt, S.M. and McEwen, J. (1980) 'The development of a subjective health indicator', *Sociology of Health and Illness*, vol 2, no 3, pp 231-46.

Hunter, J.E. and Schmidt, F.L. (1995) 'The impact of data-analysis methods on cumulative research knowledge: statistical significance testing, confidence intervals and meta-analysis', *Evaluation and the Health Professions*, vol 18, no 4, pp 408-27.

Jensen, A. (1969) 'How much can we boost IQ and scholastic achievement?', *Harvard Educational Review*, vol 39, no 1, pp 1-123.

Kao, G. and Tienda, M. (1995) 'Optimism and achievement: the educational performance of immigrant youth', *Social Science Quarterly*, vol 76, no 1, pp 1-19.

Kuckelmann-Cobb, A. and Nelson-Hagemaster, J. (1987) 'Ten criteria for evaluating qualitative research proposals', *Journal of Nursing Education*, vol 26, no 4, pp 138-43.

Labov, W. and Fanshel, D. (1978) *Therapeutic discourse: Psychotherapy as conversation*, New York, NY: Academic Press.

Lenaghan, J. (1997) *Citizens' juries*, London: Institute of Public Policy Research.

Matute-Bianchi, M.E. (1986) 'Ethnic identities and patterns of school success and failure among Mexican-Descent and Japanese descent students in a California High School: an ethnographic analysis', *American Journal of Education*, November, pp 233-55.

Medical Sociology Group (1996) 'Criteria for the evaluation of qualitative research papers', *Medical Sociology News*, vol 22, no 1, pp 68-71.

Mehan, H. (1979) *Learning lessons: The social organisation of classroom instruction*, Cambridge, MA: Harvard University Press.

Mehan, H. (1992) 'Understanding inequality in schools: the contribution of interpretative studies', *Sociology of Education*, vol 65, no 1, pp 1-20.

Mehan, H., Hertwick, A. and Lee Meihls, J. (1986) *Handicapping the handicapped: Decision making in students' educational careers*, Palo Alto, CA: Stanford University Press.

Mehan, H., Villaneuva, I., Hubbard, L., and Lintz, A. (1996) *Constructing school success*, Cambridge: Cambridge University Press.

Mishler, E. (1984) *The discourse of medicine: Dialectics in medical interviews*, Norwood, NJ: Ablex.

Modood, T. (1993) 'The number of ethnic minority students in British education: some grounds for optimism', *Oxford Review of Education*, vol 19, no 2, pp 167-82.

Newcombe, F and Ratcliff, G. (1979) 'Long term psychological consequences of cerebral lesions', in M. Gazzangia (ed) *Handbook of behavioural neurology, Volume 2*, New York, NY: Plenum Press, Chapter 16, pp 495-540.

Noblit, G.W. and Hare, R.D. (1988) *Meta-ethnography: Synthesizing qualitative studies*, Newbury Park: Sage Publications.

Oakley, A. (1998) 'Experimentation and social interventions: a forgotten but important history', *BMJ*, vol 317, no 7167, pp 1239-42.

Ogbu, J.U. (1983) 'Minority status and schooling in plural societies', *Comparative Education Review*, vol 27, no 2, pp 168-90.

Orford, J. and Edwards, G. (1977) *Alcoholism*, Maudsley Monograph No 26, Oxford: Oxford University Press.

Pendleton, J. and Schofield, T. (1988) *The consultation process*, Oxford: Oxford University Press.

Preiss, R.W. (1988) *Meta-analysis: A bibliography of conceptual issues and statistical methods*, Annandale, VA: Speech Communication Association.

Rawls, J. (1972) *A theory of Justice*, Oxford: Oxford University Press.

Sacks, H. (1967) *Unpublished Transcribed Lectures*, 1964-1972, University of California, Irvine, Edited by Gail Jefferson as *Lectures on Conversation*, Oxford: Blackwell, 1992.

Sacks, H. (1972) 'An initial investigation of the usability of conversational data for doing sociology', in D. Sudnow (ed) *Studies in social interaction*, New York, NY: Free Press, pp 31-74.

Sacks, H. (1992) *Lectures in conversation, Volumes I and II* (edited by G. Jefferson), Oxford: Blackwell.

Sacks, H., Schegloff, E.A. and Jefferson, G. (1974) 'A simplest systematics for the organisation of turn-taking for conversation', *Language*, vol 50, pp 696-735.

Schegloff, E.A. (1968) 'Sequencing in conversational openings', *American Anthropologist*, no 70, pp 1075-95.

Schegloff, E.A. (1972) 'Notes on a conversational practice: formulating place', in D. Sudnow (ed) *Studies in social interaction*, New York, NY: Free Press, pp 75-119.

Schegloff, E.A. (1982) 'Discourse as an interactional achievement: some uses of "uh huh" and other things that come between sentences', in D. Tannen (ed) *Analyzing discourse*, Washington, DC: Georgetown University Press, pp 71-93.

Schegloff, E.A. (1984) 'On some questions and ambiguities in conversation' in J.M. Atkinson and J. Heritage (eds) *Structures of social action*, Cambridge: Cambridge University Press, pp 28-52.

Seers, K. (1999) 'Qualitative research', in M.G. Dawes, P.T. Davies, A. Gray, J. Mant, K. Seers and R. Snowball (eds) *Evidence-based practice: A primer for health care professionals*, Edinburgh: Churchill-Livingstone, pp 111-26.

Sharrock, W. and Anderson, J. (1987) 'Work flow in a paediatric clinic', in G. Button and J.R.E. Lee (eds) *Talk and social organisation*, Clevedon: Multilingual Matters Ltd, pp 244-60.

Silverman, D. (1993) *Interpreting qualitative data: Methods for analysing talk, text and interaction*, London: Sage Publications.

Tharp R. and Gallimore, R. (1988) *Rousing minds to life: Teaching, learning and schooling in social context*, Cambridge, MA: Harvard University Press.

Todd, A. (1983) 'A diagnosis of doctor–patient discourse in the prescription of contraception', in S. Fisher and A. Todd (eds) *The social organisation of doctor–patient communication*, Washington, DC: Centre for Applied Linguistics, pp 159-87.

Tudor-Hart, J. (1971) 'The inverse care law', *Lancet*, pp 405-12.

Wax, M. (1979) *Desegregated schools: An intimate portrait based on five ethnographic studies*, Washington, DC: National Council of Education.

West, C. (1983) '"Ask me no questions...": analysis of queries and replies in physician–patient dialogues', in S. Fisher and A. Todd (eds) *The social organisation of doctor–patient communication*, Washington, DC: Centre for Applied Linguistics, pp 75-106.

Wolcott, H.F. (1994) *Transforming qualitative data: Description, analysis, interpretation*, Thousand Oaks, CA: Sage Publications.

FIFTEEN

Making a reality of evidence-based practice

Sandra Nutley and Huw Davies

Despite progress in some public policy domains, as reported in the first half of this book, making a reality of evidence-based policy and practice remains a major challenge. Chapter Two has considered the issue of the relationship between evidence and policy making (particularly at the central government level); this chapter is concerned primarily with the relationship between evidence and front-line practice.

The literature on research utilisation (for example, Weiss, 1998) tells us that much research appears to have little or no impact on practice. Many reasons have been cited as to why this is the case. Much of the focus has been on the gaps between researchers and policy makers/practitioners. Policy makers and practitioners are said to live in a different world to that occupied by researchers – they have different sets of interests and concerns in relation to any research project and hence find it difficult to communicate with one another (Caplan et al, 1975; Higgins, 1978 ; Husen, 1984). Social science knowledge is necessarily imprecise, inconclusive, complex and contingent, whereas policy makers and practitioners, it is argued, can only use knowledge if it is precise, gives clear guidance, and is formulated in sufficiently simple terms to be directly applied (Merton, 1957; Lindblom and Cohen, 1979). There are also practical differences in the ways in which research and policy/practice are organised; for example, they operate to different timescales and have contrasting dynamics – research is slow while policy situations change quickly. There are also differences in relative status – in the context of central government policy making researchers are likely to be relatively low-status in relation to those whom they wish to influence.

Part of the disillusionment of policy makers and practitioners relates to the hope that research will result in building a cumulative knowledge base. One of the key aspirations of social scientists and policy makers is that as research multiplies, knowledge will converge and produce cumulative findings. However, in reality the opposite often happens (Cohen and Weiss, 1977). More recently there has been progress towards developing a cumulative evidence base in some public service areas (particularly in healthcare). However, even in healthcare, as reported in Chapter Three, despite recent effort in systematically reviewing and disseminating the results of research, much practice appears to be unaffected by these efforts.

The aim of this chapter is to consider what might be done to improve the impact of research evidence on practice across a range of policy domains. It considers in more detail the development aspects of the research and development (R&D) strategies introduced in Chapter Eleven. The chapter begins by considering the strategies currently used for changing individual and organisational practices, and the effectiveness of these strategies. Given the limited success of such initiatives, the chapter proceeds by providing two alternative conceptual frameworks (Modes 1 and 2) that outline the four main components of evidence-based practice (EBP) and how they might be linked together. These four components are identified as knowledge generation, validation, dissemination and adoption; because the emphasis of this chapter is on the implementation of research evidence, the focus will largely be on the last two of these. It is less concerned with how knowledge is generated and validated (the concerns of Chapters Twelve to Fourteen), although it is acknowledged that both of these activities are likely to influence the process of dissemination and adoption.

The third section of the chapter argues that the literature on innovation diffusion is helpful in providing additional frameworks for informing the process by which the uptake of research evidence might be improved. Diffusion theories attempt to explain how innovations are communicated to and adopted by members of a social system. Innovations are ideas, objects or practices that are perceived as new. In the context of achieving EBP it is argued that diffusion relates not only to which interventions work with which client groups but also to the ideology of EBP, and to the organisational arrangements that enable this ideology to be translated into practice.

The fourth section considers two approaches (macro and micro) to achieving the changes envisaged by an EBP ideology. A macro approach is aimed at changing whole systems and as a result is predominantly top-down in nature. A micro approach tackles the issue of bringing about change in a more bottom-up manner, starting with the practice of particular individuals and/or targeted organisations. The two approaches are not mutually exclusive and can be used in combination.

The fifth section discusses the micro concern of changing individual practice. In doing so it considers how practitioners acquire, update and deploy knowledge. The concept of EBP is hotly debated, with several writers preferring the term 'evidence-influenced practice' to emphasise that practice needs to be context sensitive and hence cannot be driven by evidence in a deterministic way. The way in which evidence is blended with other forms of knowledge is one of the keys to understanding change in individual and organisational practice.

The final section of the chapter shifts the emphasis away from individuals and focuses on the organisations within which they work. Much of the existing literature on the implementation of research findings focuses on either the macro concerns of policy change and top-down diffusion or on the micro concerns of changing individual practice. Both are important, but potentially overlook the need to redesign organisational practices. Individual practitioners neither work in isolation nor are they always able to make autonomous decisions. They work in organisations that have embedded routines, established cultures, limited and largely committed resources, and a variety of stakeholders. This section considers how systems theory and the concept of the learning organisation can illuminate the organisational issues that need to be addressed for EBP to take hold.

Existing interventions for changing individual and organisational practice

The various public service areas covered in this book provide many examples of interventions aimed at changing individual and organisational practice so that it is more evidence focused. For example, the:

- dissemination of research evidence via continuing professional development activities (as in some forms of inservice teacher education);
- issuing of evidence-based guidelines as exemplified by clinical guidelines in medicine;
- establishment of audit and feedback mechanisms which may (as is the case in probation services) be linked with accreditation regimes; the audit process may be voluntary and peer-led (as with clinical audit) or may be statutory and led by nationally appointed auditors (as is the case with HM Inspectors of Probation and Social Services);

- identification and promotion of good or best practice – an approach which lies at the heart of the Beacon schools initiative;
- dissemination of research results using marketing techniques, coupled with the creation of demand for these results through the establishment of outcome measures and targets – an approach adopted by the Home Office for police research (for example, see Box 15.3 at the end of this chapter).

There is a small, but growing body of literature that considers the effectiveness of particular 'developmental' interventions for changing the practice of individuals. Some of these interventions are also aimed at changing the practice of groups of individuals and even whole organisations. Most research has been carried out within specific policy domains, rather than across domains. By far the most accessible research is that relating to interventions with healthcare professionals. Much of this research has been identified and catalogued by the Effective Practice and Organisation of Care (EPOC) review group within the Cochrane Collaboration. This group has conducted a number of systematic reviews of the effectiveness of particular forms of intervention (such as educational outreach visits). This section first briefly summarises the findings to emerge from EPOC and then compares these with the findings relating to the effectiveness of interventions aimed at achieving change in education (particularly in schools).

EPOC undertakes reviews of education, behavioural, financial, organisational and regulatory interventions designed to improve the practice of healthcare professionals. Their taxonomy of interventions is set out in Box 15.1. EPOC has drawn a number of tentative conclusions (based on systematic reviews) about the effectiveness of these interventions in achieving the desired behaviour change (Bero et al, 1998) and these were updated in a recent review (*Effective Health Care Bulletin*, 1999). To date they have found that the passive dissemination of educational information (such as educational materials and didactic lectures) is generally ineffective. Many other interventions are found to be of variable effectiveness. These include: audit and feedback; the use of local opinion leaders; local consensus-generating procedures; patient–mediated interventions (for example, where an intervention seeks to change practitioner behaviour by giving information to patients). In a more positive vein, certain interventions *are* found to be consistently effective. These include: interactive education meetings; education outreach visits; reminders. A key finding is that multifaceted interventions (those that combine two or more of audit and feedback, reminders, local consensus processes and marketing) seem to be more effective than single interventions.

Box 15.1: Interventions aimed at achieving practice change

Professional interventions

- Distribution of educational materials
- Educational meetings
- Local consensus processes
- Educational outreach visits
- Local opinion leaders
- Patient-mediated interventions
- Audit and feedback
- Reminders
- Marketing
- Mass media

Financial interventions

- Provider interventions
- Patient interventions

Organisation interventions

- Revision of professional roles
- Multidisciplinary teams
- Formal integration of services
- Skill mix changes
- Continuity of care
- Interventions to boost morale
- Communication and case discussion

Patient-oriented interventions

- Consumer participation in governance of healthcare organisation
- Mail order pharmacies
- Mechanisms for dealing with patient suggestions and complaints

Structural interventions

- Changes to setting/site of service delivery
- Changes to physical structure
- Changes in medical records system
- Changes in scope and nature of benefits of services
- Presence and organisation of quality monitoring
- Ownership of hospitals and other facilities
- Staff organisation

Regulatory interventions

- Changes in medical liability
- Management of patient complaints
- Peer review
- Licensure

Source: EPOC (1998)

There are concerns in education, as in healthcare, about the effectiveness of single interventions. For example, Fullan with Stiegelbauer (1991) concludes that much inservice education is ineffective. Several reasons for this ineffectiveness are cited and include:
- frequent use of one-shot workshops;
- follow-up support for ideas and practices introduced during inservice programmes occurs in only a small minority of cases;
- inservice programmes rarely address the individual needs and concerns of participants;
- the majority of programmes involve teachers from many different schools and/or school districts, but there is no recognition of the differential impact of the positive and negative factors within the systems to which they must return.

The literature on achieving education change emphasises the importance of considering context and of choosing change interventions that suit that context. The focus is less on individual practitioners and more on the organisations within which they work. For example, one important strand of the education change literature has taken as its core concern the achievement of school improvement. This is defined as "an approach to educational change that has the twin purposes of enhancing student achievement and strengthening the school's capacity for managing change" (Hopkins et al, 1994, p 68). The assumptions underlying this approach are outlined in Box 15.2. The long-term goal is to create learning organisations at the school level referred to as the 'self-renewing school' (Hopkins et al, 1994).

The importance of multifaceted interventions is a finding echoed in the literature on achieving education change (Fullan with Stiegelbauer, 1991; Hopkins et al, 1994; Stoll and Fink, 1996). The school improvement literature argues for the balancing of push and pull change tactics – that is, external and internal pressures for change should be counterbalanced by external and internal sources of sustained support (Miles, 1986; Fullan with Stiegelbauer, 1991; Hargreaves and Hopkins, 1991; Hopkins et al, 1994). The interventions to achieve change may begin by targeting individuals, but if change is to endure it needs to move beyond the individual and become embedded within a school's structures, systems and resources (Miles, 1986).

Box 15.2: Assumptions underpinning the school improvement approach to educational change

The school as the centre of change This is the focus for change – reforms need to be sensitive to the situation of individual schools

A systematic approach to change Change is envisaged as a planned and managed process that takes time (several years)

The 'internal conditions' of schools as a key focus for change This includes the schools' procedures, role allocation and resource use as well as its teaching-learning activities

Accomplishing education goals more effectively Education goals and desired outcomes are defined more broadly than academic achievement

A multilevel perspective The school is embedded in an education system and hence change strategies need to pay attention to the broader system while focusing on the school as the centre of attention

Integrative implementation strategies Strategies need to integrate top-down and bottom-up interventions to achieve change

The drive towards institutionalisation The need to move beyond implementation to ensure that new ways of working become part of the natural behaviours of teachers in a school

Source: Adapted from Hopkins et al (1994, p 69)

Central government-led initiatives in education have focused on ways of achieving system-wide change. For example, the identification and labelling of some schools as Beacon schools. On the basis of inspections, the Office for Standards in Education identify such schools. They are then given money to act as Beacon schools so as to spread the good practice to others. The problem is that it remains unclear just how this dissemination and subsequent adoption of good practice is meant to occur (Hargreaves, 1998). It requires more than simply providing information about Beacon schools – "transfer is the conversion of information about one person's practice into another's know-how" (Hargreaves, 1998, p 46). It remains to be seen whether the Beacon schools initiative can achieve this:

> Beacon schools may be more effective schools than average, but there is no reason for believing that they have particular skills or experience in disseminating their professional practices.... Government policy, that

effective practice should be disseminated from a minority of effective schools to the rest in a short time scale, depends on the creation of professional knowledge on effective dissemination. (Hargreaves, 1998, p 48)

Taken as a whole, the existing empirical evidence on the effectiveness of particular interventions for achieving practice change is somewhat equivocal. Multifaceted interventions seem to work best. However, given that it is likely that nothing works all of the time and that everything works some of the time (Pawson and Tilley, 1997) there is a need to explore not only what seems to work but also why it might be expected to work and in what circumstances. The remainder of this chapter explores the conceptual and theoretical foundations on which these change interventions are based.

Conceptualising evidence-based practice

The term evidence-based practice assumes that it is practical and desirable to base practice on knowledge of what works. This begs the questions of how this knowledge is generated, validated, disseminated and adopted, and, importantly, who is involved in each of these activities. A traditional model of this process is represented in Figure 15.1. Here there are four stages in a linear process that starts with knowledge creation and ends with adoption. The final stage provides the raw data for the process to begin again. It is envisaged that the process involves two main communities: experts (mainly researchers based in universities) and users (practitioners based in the field). There is limited interaction between these two communities; the experts are the main actors at the start of the process and they deliver the fruits of their labours to the users towards the end of the process. The concept of knowledge embodied in this model is what Gibbons et al (1994) refer to as Mode 1: university-centred knowledge creation.

The traditional model has been challenged both as a descriptive model and as a normative model (for example, Hargreaves, 1998). The challenge has been mounted on two fronts: first the presumed linearity of the traditional model and second the distinct and separate domains occupied by university researchers and practitioners. An alternative conceptualisation of the process is represented by Figure 15.2. This alternative model eschews notions of a linear set of stages, with sharp boundaries between knowledge production and utilisation. Instead the assumption is of a continuous interaction between knowledge creation, validation, dissemination and adoption. None of these activities belongs to the separate domain of experts as opposed to users. Instead both experts and users are partners in the generation and utilisation of knowledge. The concept of knowledge embodied in this model is what Gibbons et al (1994) refer to as Mode 2: knowledge creation though applied partnerships.

Figure 15.1 Mode 1 – a traditional model of evidence-based practice

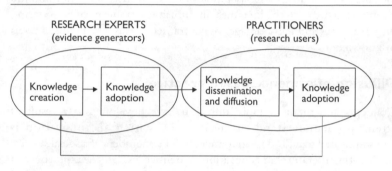

Figure 15.2: Mode 2 – an alternative model of evidence-based practice

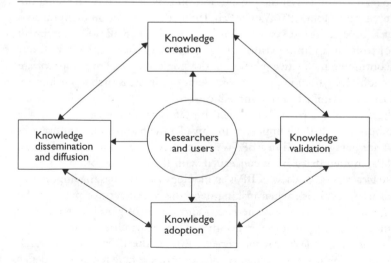

The above models have implications for how we think about issues of dissemination and diffusion. In the traditional model, knowledge is centralised and hence flows from the expert centre(s) to the periphery (local practitioners). In the alternative model, knowledge is held locally as well as in so-called centres of expertise and flows in many directions via local and national networks. Hargreaves (1998) characterises these knowledge flows from the perspective of the practitioner and argues that the traditional model conceives of dissemination as 'outside in', whereas the alternative model sees it as 'inside out'. With these ideas in mind the chapter now turns to the literature on diffusion as a means of considering the advantages and disadvantages of centralised versus decentralised flows of knowledge.

Diffusion of evidence-based practice

Concepts and theories about diffusion have developed as a result of attempts to understand the process by which an innovation is communicated to and adopted (or rejected) by members of a social system. Within this literature an innovation is defined as "an idea, practice, or object perceived as new by an individual or other unit of adoption" (Rogers, 1995, p 35). Diffusion theories have their origins in the explanation of the adoption of technological innovations by farmers (Rogers, 1958). Given the pro-innovation bias of much of the literature (Downs and Mohr, 1976; Van de Ven, 1986), the assumption often made is that a good diffusion system is one that results in swift and widespread adoption of an innovation. The literature has less to say about discontinuing ineffective practice, or slowing the uptake of inappropriate technologies – both important considerations in areas such as healthcare, social care, criminal justice and education.

In drawing the parallels between the diffusion of innovations and the promotion of EBP it is important to consider the nature of the innovations that are being diffused in EBP. We have elsewhere (Nutley and Davies, 1999a) argued that EBP is concerned with the diffusion of:
- *an ideology* – at one level EBP is an ideology that stresses the importance of using evidence when making decisions about service practice; the objective is to win over the hearts and minds of practitioners so that they adopt a frame of reference that values research evidence;
- *technical innovations* – at the core of EBP is the diffusion of research evidence on the effectiveness of interventions; where research evidence recommends changes to the content or mode of service delivery this

will often be perceived as a new intervention by practitioners (thus, an innovation) but evidence may also relate to the need to cease an existing practice without necessarily promoting a new practice;

- *organisational innovations* – research evidence relates not only to the effectiveness of treatment interventions (technical innovations), it also addresses the effectiveness of particular ways of organising service delivery (organisational or administrative innovations); in the context of EBP an important question is whether there are particular forms of organisation and management (including: structures, systems, skills base and style) that enable or inhibit EBP.

Much of the current emphasis in EBP initiatives focuses on the diffusion of what we have labelled as technical innovations. This reflects a concern to ensure that evidence relating to what works is disseminated to all practitioners and adopted by them. While this is important, initiatives also need to convince people about the idea of EBP (to diffuse the ideology) and to ensure that organisational arrangements are consistent with the adoption of an evidence-based approach (to diffuse appropriate organisational innovations).

What about the process by which an innovation is communicated to potential adopters and a decision made on its adoption? The classical diffusion model is a relatively centralised one. It proposes that decisions about which innovations to diffuse, to whom and by what means should be made centrally. In a highly centralised system there is: centralised (often government) control of decisions about which innovations should be diffused; a top-down diffusion of the innovations, from experts to users; a low degree of local adaptation of the innovations when adopted by users. This has obvious parallels with Mode 1 (university-centred) knowledge creation.

Schon (1967, 1971) challenged the adequacy of this centre-periphery model. He argued that, in practice, there is often no clear centre and that the diffusion process is frequently more decentralised and iterative in nature (innovations evolve as they are diffused). It is now recognised that the process of diffusion can range on a continuum from highly centralised to highly decentralised (Rogers, 1995). In a highly decentralised diffusion system there is: wide sharing of power and control among members of the diffusion system; peer diffusion of innovations through horizontal networks; a high degree of local adaptation as innovations diffuse among adopters. In turn, this mirrors Mode 2 (applied partnerships) knowledge creation.

If the process of diffusion can range from highly centralised to highly decentralised what are the conditions under which one is to be preferred over the other? Rogers (1995) considers the advantages and disadvantages of centralised and decentralised systems of diffusion. His findings are summarised in Table 15.1. His tentative conclusion is that decentralised systems are most appropriate when innovations do not involve a high level of technical expertise and when users are relatively heterogeneous. He adds that the potential for users to run their own diffusion system is greatest when the users are highly educated and technically competent practitioners (he cites the example of cardiovascular surgeons). However, he argues that such a conclusion is speculative because "our understanding of decentralised diffusion systems is still limited owing to the general lack of investigations of such user-dominated diffusion" (Rogers, 1995, p 365).

The extent to which a diffusion process is centralised or decentralised is not the only factor that effects the likelihood that a particular innovation will be adopted. Other factors found by researchers to affect the extent of adoption include: adopter characteristics, the social network to which adopters belong, innovation attributes, environmental characteristics, and the characteristics of those who are promoting an innovation. A brief summary of research findings relating to these five areas is provided in Table 15.2. One important conclusion for EBP that can be drawn from these findings is that no matter how strong the evidence is that one form of intervention (eg a novel approach to teaching mathematics, a new drug or an innovative offender programme) is to be preferred over another, this is unlikely to result in adoption unless other favourable conditions prevail.

As noted earlier, widespread adoption of an innovation is not necessarily a good thing; an innovation may not be suited to a wide range of circumstances or may be relatively unsupported by evidence. There is much to be learned from exploring why and how interventions inappropriate to a particular context are nevertheless adopted. Many researchers have documented examples of innovations (such as ineffective therapies or surgical interventions) being adopted in the absence of good evidence of their effectiveness (see, for example, Stocking, 1985; Westphal et al, 1997). This suggests that it is naive to assume that adopters make rational and technically efficient choices about whether to adopt or not. Research on the adoption of organisational innovations suggests that the decision-making process is influenced more by peer group pressures and other institutional factors. For example, studies by Abrahamson and colleagues (Abrahamson, 1991, 1996; Abrahamson and Rosenkopf, 1993;

Abrahamson and Fombrum, 1994) have broadened the understanding of how administrative innovations are diffused or are rejected within organisational groups. They argue that choices about whether to adopt or not often relate to the institutional pressures associated with certain fads or fashions.

Table 15.1: Comparing centralised and decentralised diffusion systems

	Advantages	*Disadvantages*
Centralised	• Central quality control of which innovations to diffuse	• User resistance to central control
	• Can diffuse innovations for which there is as yet no felt need	• May result in low adaptation to local circumstances
Decentralised	• High degree of user control	• Possible for ineffective innovations to be diffused because of lack of quality control
	• Closer fit between innovations and user needs and problems	
	• Users like such a system	• Not suitable for diffusing innovations for which there is not a felt need
		• Local users, who control the system of diffusion, may lack knowledge about other users' problems and about the available innovations that could solve them

Source: Based on Rogers (1995)

It may be that decision making by early adoptors is more in line with the model of technical rationality. It is only later in the life cycle of adoption that decisions are influenced more by non-technical factors. Drawing on the work of DiMaggio and Powell (1983), O'Neill et al (1998) argue that adoption of an innovation may at first relate to the prospect of improved performance, but that as the innovation gains acceptance others adopt in order to seek legitimacy (a finding supported by Westphal et al, 1997). A high proportion of organisations adopt a change "because stakeholders define the change as accepted practice" (O'Neill et al, 1998, p 99). This pattern of behaviour is heightened during times of high uncertainty, when organisations are more likely to imitate other organisations, especially those deemed to be norm-setters (DiMaggio and Powell, 1983).

Table 15.2: Factors affecting the likelihood that a particular innovation will be adopted

Factors	Examples of research findings
Adopter characteristics	• Adopters can be categorised according to their tendencies to adopt – innovators, early adopters, early majority, late majority and laggards (Rogers, 1983)
	• Organisations with a long history of success are unlikely to adopt new approaches (Sitkin, 1992; Levinthal and March, 1993; O'Neill et al, 1998)
The social network to which adopters belong	• Choices about whether to adopt or not can relate to the existence of fads and fashions among members of a social network (Abrahamson, 1991, 1996)
Innovation attributes	• Rogers (1995) argues that there are five attributes of an innovation that influence its rate of adoption: relative advantage, compatibility, complexity, trialability and observability
	• Kimberly (1982) identified three key characteristics: adaptability, evidence of improved performance, extent of change required to adopt an innovation
	• Characteristics identified by Stocking (1985) include appeal to local power holders and little requirement for visible resources
Environmental characteristics	• Low environmental uncertainty increases the tendency of organisations to remain stable or to avoid change (O'Neill et al, 1998)
	• Need for legitimacy may encourage immitation in the adoption of innovations (DiMaggio and Powell, 1983)
The characteristics of those promoting the innovation	• The level of contact the change agent has with potential adopters is positively related to the decision to adopt (Rogers et al, 1970)
	• Change agent credibility in the client's eyes is positively related to the decision to adopt (Coleman et al, 1966)

What lessons can the literature on diffusion provide for those seeking to achieve EBP? A decentralised approach to diffusing EBP is likely to encounter less user resistance than a centralised approach. It is also likely to result in a greater level of re-invention and adaptation of the recommendations of research. This may be appropriate (and as a result facilitate adaptation to local circumstances), but it may also facilitate the diffusion of ineffective interventions. User reactions to evidence-based innovations are likely to be shaped by the nature of these innovations. Evidence of improved effectiveness is not the only factor; the compatability, complexity, trialability and observability of an innovation also affect user reaction. Institutional pressures will also shape the rate of adoption, particularly during times of uncertainty. Diffusion strategies need to recognise that adoption decisions are frequently made in order to seek legitimacy. The extent of government exhortation on service delivery organisations to adopt a particular practice is just one aspect of institutional pressure. An equally important factor is the behaviour of those organisations deemed to be the norm-setters. Institutional pressures can help to explain the diffusion of ineffective practice as well as offer suggestions about how best to diffuse effective practice. In the case of the latter, diffusion strategies that target norm-setting organisations may be an effective means of ensuring that evidence impacts on practice.

Bringing about change to achieve EBP

In the previous section it was argued that to achieve EBP there is a need to diffuse an ideology that stresses the worth of basing practice on validated knowledge of what works. This ideology needs to be supported by enabling systems and structures. The achievement of ideological and systemic change might adopt a macro or a micro approach. A macro approach to bringing about change is likely to emphasise systems thinking, which is a methodology for seeing in wholes and for recognising the patterns and interrelatedness of the parts which go to make up these wholes. The key questions to be addressed in such an approach are:
- What would an evidence-based system look like?
- What implications would this have for the functioning of the constituent parts and how would they need to change from their present mode of operation?
- Which parts of the system should be changed first and how will this impact on other parts of the system?

- How best can functionality in any new system design be ensured?

Having addressed these questions a macro approach is likely to recommend top-down system redesign, which is to be achieved as a result of deliberate change interventions. Change is managed by adhering broadly to a planned strategy for achieving a predetermined goal.

In contrast, a micro approach to change focuses on the parts rather than the wholes. The argument is that grand plans have limited worth and that an emphasis on wholes is in danger of ignoring the importance of human agency. It is the actions of individuals that determine the extent to which practice is evidence based. Thus a micro approach focuses on changing the attitudes and behaviour of individuals, the assumption being that overall system change will emerge as a result of growing numbers of individuals and groups changing their own ways of working.

This is rather a stark and stylised contrast between macro and micro approaches to change. Existing initiatives to achieve EBP often combine elements of both (Nutley and Davies, 1999b). Initiatives that stress education and continuing professional development are at the micro end of the spectrum. Those that focus on issuing guidelines for practice backed up by audit and inspection regimes are more macro in nature. The next section explores in more detail the micro issue of changing individual practice.

Changing individual practice

Following on from the traditional model of knowledge production and utilisation (see Figure 15.1), there is a simple (many would argue too simple) model of the relationship between evidence and individual practice (shown in Figure 15.3). This latter model posits a direct, predominantly linear and uninterrupted relationship between evidence and practice. In such a model, evidence of what works is consciously and readily adopted by practitioners once they know about it. Their practice, in turn, provides the data on which researchers draw in determining what works. If such a model were an adequate representation of reality, then implementing EBP would largely entail improving dissemination. This would ensure that practitioners were informed about the latest evidence.

Figure 15.3: Simple model of relationship between evidence and practice

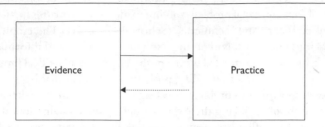

One of the problems with such a model is that it overestimates the generalisability of research evidence and thus underestimates the extent to which practitioners need to interpret the findings of research to assess their applicability to the situation in hand. Schon (1987) refers to the need for 'reflective transfer', which he describes as thinking about the conditions under which the original study was done and analogising the results to other places when conditions are 'similar enough'. Conditions are unlikely ever to be the same – practice has been characterised as consisting of a series of unique events (for example, in healthcare Erikson, 1958, describes each patient as a 'universe of one').

Because of the shortcomings of the simple model of the relationship between evidence and individual practice it has been modified in current debates about EBP. A revised model (exemplified by the evidence-based medicine model) allows for the importance of individual craft knowledge and experience (see Figure 15.4). Sackett et al (1996, p 71) refer to evidence-based medicine as:

> ... integrating individual clinical expertise with the best available external clinical evidence from systematic research.... By individual clinical expertise we mean the proficiency and judgement that individual clinicians acquire through clinical experience and clinical practice.

In the context of education, Davies (1999) describes the interaction between evidence and expertise as a two-way process that involves broadening the basis of individuals' experience and judgement by locating it within the available evidence, and generating research studies that explore and test the experience of professionals and other constituents of learning communities.

While the EBM model allows for the influence of other information and pressures via the exercise of individual expertise, both models (Figures

15.3 and 15.4) have a tendency to reflect what Schon refers to as technical rationality. This is said to be the dominant view about practice and consists of "instrumental problem solving made rigorous by the application of scientific theory and technique" (Schon, 1991, p 21). The emphasis is on conscious problem solving using explicit knowledge and information. The practitioner is confronted with a problem (such as a medical problem, a learning problem or an offending problem). The ends that he/she wish to achieve in solving this problem are clear and his/her task is to determine the best means of achieving these ends. Such a conceptualisation of EBP naturally leads to efforts to change practice by improving practitioners' problem-solving skills.

However, Schon (1991) argues that a model based on instrumental problem solving does not provide an adequate descriptive or normative representation of practice. He comments that practice is more like a "swampy lowland where solutions are confusing 'messes' incapable of technical solutions" (p 45). Practitioners survive and succeed in the confusion of the swamplands by drawing on their tacit knowledge of what works there:

> He [sic] makes innumerable judgements of quality for which he cannot state adequate criteria, and he displays skills for which he cannot state the rules and procedures. Even when he makes conscious use of research-based theories and techniques, he is dependent on tacit recognitions, judgements and skillful performances. (Schon, p 50)

Figure 15.4 : Evidence-based medicine model

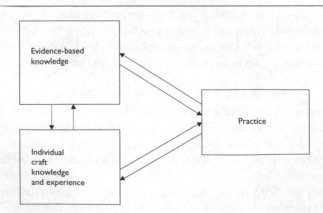

The references in the above quote to the importance of a tacit rather than explicit understanding of problems and their possible solutions relates to a substantial literature in psychology about the nature of memory and how this produces different types of knowledge. Since Polanyi wrote about the tacit dimension in 1967 there has been increasing interest in exploring this partially unconscious dimension of knowledge. It is common now to distinguish between 'declarative' and 'procedural' memory/knowledge. Declarative memory provides the storage of facts, propositions and events. Procedural memory appears to be the form that stores the components of individual skills actions (Squire, 1987; Singley and Anderson, 1989). Declarative knowledge is thus explicit knowledge, knowledge that you can state. In contrast, procedural knowledge is tacit knowledge; you know how to do something (such as ride a bike) but cannot readily articulate this knowledge and hence instruct someone else to do the same. This tacit knowledge is said to be inherent in being a professional; Hargreaves (1999) refers to it as craft expertise.

The reason why it is important to focus on tacit knowledge is because of its deeply embedded nature. Individuals are not self-conscious and emotionally neutral learners and problem solvers. Instead practice is a dynamic, embedded process that gives rise to partially unconscious skilled performances. This has important implications for an approach to changing individual practice that focuses on enhancing individuals' problem-solving skills. Practitioners are said to develop routines based on their procedural knowledge (Cohen, 1996). Hence for EBP problem-solving activity to become engrained in the routines of practitioners, individual development activities (such as continuing professional development) need to develop tacit procedural knowledge and not just expand explicit declarative knowledge. Procedural knowledge is acquired by practical problem solving, a process which is likely to be different from the instrumental problem solving of the EBM model. For example, Schon refers to practical problem solving as 'reflection in action'. This process he describes thus:

> When someone reflects-in-action, he [sic] becomes a researcher in the practice context. He is not dependent on the categories of established theory and technique, but constructs a new theory of the unique case. His inquiry is not limited to a deliberation about means which depends on a prior agreement about ends. He does not keep means and ends separate, but defines them interactively as he frames a problematic situation. He does not separate thinking from doing, ratiocinating his

way to a decision which he must later convert to action. Because his experimenting is a kind of action, implementation is built into his inquiry. (1991, pp 68-9)

However, Schon has been criticised for setting up a false dichotomy in making this distinction between technical rationality and reflective inquiry (Shulman, 1988).

Another aspect of procedural knowledge may also have important implications for continuing professional development activities. Cohen (1996) comments that procedural memory in individuals appears to be specific to the mode of communication in which it was initiated. The result is that a skill learned in one mode (such as via verbal communication) may not be triggered if information is presented in another mode (such as written communication). He argues that this has implications for understanding the tensions between theory and practice.

The model of EBM outlined in Figure 15.4 is an improvement over the simple model of the relationship between evidence and individual practice shown in Figure 15.3. The former gives central importance to the influence of craft knowledge. The preceding discussion has demonstrated that the concept of craft knowledge is complex, as is the process by which this tacit knowledge combines with the explicit knowledge embodied in research evidence. The main limitations of the EBM model arise from the fact that it is concerned with the micro issues of developing evidence-based individual practitioners. It is this that leads it to focus on types of knowledge, how people learn, and how they apply that knowledge in practice. While the category of individual craft knowledge and experience in the EBM model may provide the conduit for a multiplicity of other factors to influence practice, there is a danger that the model underplays the importance of these factors. The next section discusses these broader influences, focusing in particular on organisational influences.

Changing organisational practice

A broad representation of the manifold influences on practice is provided in Figure 15.5. This signals the importance of the organisational context within which practitioners work. Weiss (1998) argues that to think about the use of research evidence without considering the organisational context is to miss a good part of the story. At the very least she argues there is a need to remove impediments to new ways of working and more often to

supply supportive structures to incorporate and sustain new appr
and activities.

Figure 15.5: Broad influences on practice

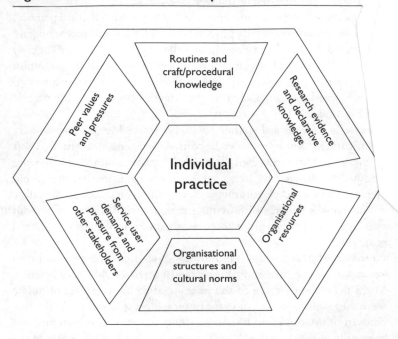

Two of the categories of influences shown in Figure 15.5 have already been discussed – 'research evidence and declarative knowledge' and 'routines and craft/procedural knowledge'. However, before moving on to outline the remaining four categories a few more comments are in order about the concept of routines. Routines develop not only as a result of individual activity but also in interactions between individuals. Cohen and Bacdayan (1996) argue that it is via this interactive process that organisational routines emerge. They also argue that these routines account for much of what happens, good and bad, in organisations. It follows that attempts to make practice more evidence-based will need to consider and probably change these organisational routines. However, this is likely to be difficult because of the three basic characteristics of organisational routines outlined by Cohen and Bacdayan: they are multi-actor and hence difficult to observe and grasp; they emerge through gradual multi-actor learning and exhibit tangled histories; the underlying knowledge of the parts of routines held by individual actors is often partial and inarticulate.

Moving anti-clockwise around Figure 15.5 the remaining four categories are characterised as follows:

- *Peer values and pressures* are an important influence on individual practice. Theoretical modelling of the process by which these influences operate is provided by social learning theory (Bandura, 1971). This suggests that individuals learn from others by a process of imitation. Recognition of the role of peer values has been reflected in certain initiatives to achieve practice change such as the identification and targeting of opinion leaders.
- *Service user demands and pressure from other stakeholders* are increasingly significant as public services become more consumerist in their orientation. This is reflected in the way initiatives aimed at achieving practitioner change may target service users in order that they bring pressure to bear on practitioners. For example, research studies have considered the benefits of providing patients with information about post-operative pain in order to change pain control practices (Gould et al, 1992).
- *Organisation structures and the cultural norms* that prevail within an organisation can enable or disable particular forms of individual practice. Much is frequently made of the bureaucratic characteristics of public service organisations and the way in which these constrain individual innovation (Metcalfe and Richards, 1990). Organisational culture can be equally enabling or disabling (Davies et al, 2000). One strand of the organisational cultures literature refers to the way in which managers need to model the behaviour expected of other staff. For example, in the private sector, Hampden-Turner (1990) found that the encounter between service delivery staff and service users is most often a reflection of the experience that those service delivery staff have of their own managers. As a result of this, Lewis (1999) considers the need for 'pro-social modelling' by managers and argues that the behaviour of managers should mirror that which is expected of practitioners. So, if the goal is evidence-based practice, this needs to be reflected in the culture of the organisation and reflected in the practice of evidence-based management.
- *Organisational resources available* to public service organisations (people, property/equipment and operational budgets) are limited and relatively fixed. This has the effect of reinforcing the status quo. Where practice change requires significant changes to the property and equipment

portfolio of the organisation, this may be difficult to achieve in the short term. The extent to which budgets are devolved to practitioners may affect their ability to respond quickly to evidence-based innovations.

There are at least these six broad categories of influence on individual practice. The question remains of how best to configure an organisation in the light of these influences in order to encourage evidence-based practice. What impediments need to be removed and what supporting systems and processes need to be put in place? It is possible to begin answering these questions by considering what an evidence-based practice organisation might look like. One way of thinking about such an organisation is to conceive of it as an information processing or cybernetic system.

Cybernetic systems and learning organisations

Cybernetics is a technique for designing self-regulating systems. Monitoring, feedback and adjustment lie at the heart of a cybernetic system. The core insight from early work on cybernetics was that a system's ability to engage in self-regulating behaviour depends on building information flows that enable negative feedback. It is the negative feedback loops within a system that allow it to detect when it veers away from a desired course and this in turn triggers corrective behaviours to bring it back on course. Argyris and Schon (1978, 1996) refer to this basic level of detection and correction of error as single-loop learning.

If evidence-based practice organisations are thought of as information processing systems, then the design of appropriate information flows is a central task. Morgan (1997, p 86) argues that there are four key principles to incorporate into such a design. Systems must be able to:
• sense, monitor, and scan significant aspects of their environment;
• relate this information to the operating norms that guide system behaviour;
• detect significant deviations from these norms;
• initiate corrective action when discrepancies are detected.

An example of the way in which this might be incorporated into the routines of an evidence-based healthcare organisation will help to illustrate these points. A hospital examines its care of obstetric patients. Through clinical audit, it finds various gaps between actual practice and established standards (derived from evidence-based guidelines). Meetings are held to discuss the guidelines, changes are made to working procedures, and reporting and feedback on practice are enhanced. These changes increase the proportion of patients receiving appropriate and timely care that is in compliance with the guidelines.

The self-regulating behaviour resulting from this system design is determined by the operating norms or standards that guide it. This is fine so long as the action defined by these guidelines remains appropriate. When this ceases to be the case the system becomes dysfunctional. This has led modern cyberneticians to consider the design of more complex learning systems. For example, Argyris and Schon argue that beyond basic error correction, a more sophisticated learning is possible: that which changes fundamental assumptions about the organisation. Examples are learning that leads to a redefining of the organisation's goals, norms, policies, procedures or even structures. This Argyris and Schon termed 'double-loop learning' as it calls into question the very nature of the course plotted and the feedback loops used to maintain that course.

Referring back to the example of obstetric care, it might be that in examining this care, some patients are interviewed at length. From this it emerges that the issues that are bothering women have more to do with continuity of care, convenience of access, quality of information and the interpersonal aspects of the patient–professional interaction. In the light of this, obstetric care is dramatically reconfigured to a system of midwife-led teams in order to prioritise these issues. The standards as laid down in the evidence-based guidelines are not abandoned, but are woven into a new pattern of interactions and values. This is an example of double-loop learning.

There is clearly a danger that if organisational systems are designed to ensure better single-loop learning, this in turn may limit their capacity for double-loop learning. In the context of evidence-based practice, if organisational systems are designed around the principle of monitoring and adjusting performance against evidence-based guidelines they may get stuck in a cycle of single-loop learning. This raises questions about how new knowledge is generated. What are the mechanisms for the development of new 'treatments' that may work better than existing interventions? The generation of new knowledge relies on local invention and experimentation (Hargreaves, 1998), but this may be stifled by centralised models of the knowledge generation and adherence to centrally produced guidelines.

It is desirable that systems built around single-loop learning incorporate the scope for questioning and changing existing guidelines. Argyris and Schon found that many organisations have difficulties in moving beyond single-loop learning regimes. One reason is the existence of what they describe as inhibitory loops. These include a self-reinforcing cycle in which errors in action provoke individuals to behaviours that reinforce these errors. Morgan (1997) argues that managers wishing to encourage double-loop learning need to avoid detailed objectives and targets in order to enable staff to break out of such inhibitory loops. Instead managers are encouraged simply to place overall limits or broad constraints on action, so as to create the space in which new learning can occur. In the context of EBP this raises the crucial question of whether any centralised control system should only be concerned with avoiding ineffective practice, as opposed to requiring practice to be in line with current evidence on what works. At present the emphasis is on the latter rather than the former. The novel approach of creating space for learning would certainly run against the grain in healthcare. Notwithstanding the fact that much of current healthcare has little solid evidence to support such an approach, an explicit move towards merely avoiding therapies known to be ineffectual would certainly encounter ethical objections.

The growth of problem-based learning in the training of practitioners and the rise of approaches such as evidence-based medicine are both trends that seek to equip individuals with skills rather than a reservoir of facts. As such they may contribute to a culture of both single- and double-loop learning. But improving individual capabilities is only part of the story. There is also the need to address the configuration of the influences on individual practice outlined in Figure 15.5 above. There is much advice on this to be found in the literature on learning organisations (for example, Senge, 1990; Argyris and Schon, 1996; Pedlar and Aspinwall, 1998; Davies and Nutley, 2000). For example, Senge argues that there are five disciplines to master in order to become a learning organisation:

- *open systems thinking* – this encapsulates the idea of teaching people to integrate activities, to see how what they do and what others do are interconnected; this integration needs to stretch beyond the boundaries of the organisation itself to encompass suppliers, customers, and the wider community;
- *improving individual capabilities* – the individuals within the organisation must constantly be improving their own personal proficiencies;
- *updating mental models* – these deeply-held assumptions influence how people make sense of the world; changing and updating these mental models is important if new ways of doing things are to be conceived;

- *a cohering vision* – this relates to providing clear strategic direction and articulating a coherent set of values in order to guide individual actions;
- *team learning* – individual virtuosity is insufficient, individuals must work and learn as part of a team.

It is tempting to provide specific recommendations about the ways in which structures, cultures, business systems and resources should be configured and deployed to encourage ongoing evidence-based practice and organisational learning. However, such recommendations would be speculative given that they would be based, at best, on a nascent evidence base. It is also unlikely that there will be one best configuration. The concept of the learning organisation is not a well-defined package of practices; nor does it provide a blueprint for organisational design – "the learning organisation has to be realised from within" (Pedlar and Aspinwall, 1998, p 55). Nonetheless, exploring organisations from this viewpoint does allow some insight into some of the facilitating and debilitating factors that affect the uptake of EBP. Operationalising these in specific settings will require careful customisation and subsequent empirical testing before the implementation of EBP will itself be evidence-based.

Concluding remarks

That evidence of what works frequently has a disappointing impact on policy and practice is a consistent finding across the public sector. This review of some of the issues germane to research implementation suggests that this should be of no surprise. Traditional conceptions of the role of evidence have placed unreasonable and unhelpful boundaries between the creation and the use of research. The very term 'R&D' itself encapsulates the split between 'research' (expert-led, esoteric and frequently external) and 'development' (practitioner-based, workaday, internal). 'R&D strategies' (Chapter Eleven) tend to emphasise dissemination as a core activity, suggesting that it is merely lack of knowledge/information at the right time in the right place that inhibits evidence-based policy and practice. As the discussion in this chapter highlights, such a simplification both misrepresents the process and hampers the search for more effective implementation models.

There is much to be gained from viewing evidence-influenced practice as a partnership activity between all the key stakeholders, with no clear discontinuities between evidence creation, validation, dissemination or use. Diverse literatures such as those on personal learning and professional decision making, the diffusion of innovation, the dynamics of organisational change, and learning organisations can all contribute insight into these partnerships. What emerges is a clear understanding that provoking the uptake, whenever appropriate, of even single pieces of evidence is no simple matter, much less the shifting of whole organisational cultures so that they are more 'evidence orientated'. What is needed is an approach that combines:

- insights from systems thinking (in terms of setting the contexts within which evidence is to be used);
- understanding of individual decision making and behaviour change (which acknowledges the importance of craft routines and tacit knowledge held by professionals);
- awareness that the nature of the innovation being promulgated will influence its diffusion (and in particular, the 'fit' between the innovation, the context and the those who are potential adopters);
- ownership of evidence through partnerships in the evidence generation process.

One example of the implementation of EBP that combined many of the above lessons is the repeat victimisation story (Box 15.3).

These requirements represent a tall order for those involved in implementing an evidence-based approach to public services. They shift the emphasis away from simply seeing the problem as one of fostering information flows. They also pose considerable challenges for organisational implementation and the development of a refined research agenda to inform that process.

Box 15.3: Getting evidence into practice – the repeat victimisation story

The story begins in England in 1983 when the Home Office decided to give crime prevention a higher profile and established a new policy unit – the Crime Prevention Unit (CPU). Unusually for that time, a small team of research staff was located within the unit – a group that eventually evolved into the Police Research Group (PRG) in 1992. It quickly became clear that there was very little information available to the police on what works in crime prevention. In order to fill this lacuna a series of research projects were commissioned.

An early research project, which focused on the Kirkholt Estate, Rochdale, proved to be particularly influential. The remit given to the researchers was to 'find an area with a high burglary rate, make it go down, and tell us how you did it'. An interagency project team was brought together of academics, police, probation staff and others. Their analysis showed that there was a great deal of 'repeat victimisation' on the estate. If a house had been burgled there was a significantly higher risk of it being burgled again than if it had not been burgled in the first place. This led them to focus on victims as a way of reducing crime. By a variety of means they protected victims and reduced repeat victimisation to zero in seven months. The burglary rate fell on the whole estate by 75% during the following three years.

A series of further research projects were commissioned to test out the repeat victimisation findings in other settings and for crimes other than burglary. These projects confirmed the importance of repeat victimisation in burglary and also showed how it featured in certain types of violent offending and bullying. The conclusions were pulled together in a review report entitled *Once bitten, twice bitten: Repeat victimisation and its implications for crime prevention* (Farrell and Pease, 1993).

The challenge then became to make the findings of this research impact more generally on crime prevention policy and practice. Contrary to the normal pattern of handing such a task over to a policy unit, it was agreed that ongoing responsibility for the programme of work should remain in the PRG.

In rolling out the research findings a great deal of effort was put into engaging practitioners (particularly police forces) in the repeat victimisation story. There were a series of six 'road shows' on repeat victimisation across the country. This was followed by the establishment of a task force comprising a task force head and a seconded police officer. The head of this task force was neither a career civil servant nor a researcher; she was a specialist in organisational development and had some marketing expertise.

The task force used a variety of means to reach practitioners:

- a repeat victimisation liaison officer was designated in each police force, whose task it was to ensure that the research was properly disseminated – in effect a local champion;

- a series of liaison officer meetings was arranged to share good practice and iron out any emerging practical difficulties in implementing strategies to tackle repeat victimisation;

- a publication designed specifically for practitioners at middle manager level was produced (*Preventing repeat victimisation: The police officers' guide*);

- a computerised database of good practice was established within the PRG for use by UK police forces.

However, probably the most significant action in forcing repeat victimisation on to the police agenda was its adoption as one of the Home Secretary's police performance indicators for the prevention of crime. Given the sensitivity of introducing such an indicator, an incremental approach was adopted. This aimed to take the police from the point many of them were at in 1995 of not being able to measure repeat victimisation, to being able to tackle it and deliver real results. The increments were:

- 1995-96 – demonstrate capability of identifying repeat victims

- 1996-97 – develop a strategy to reduce repeat victimisation for any locally relevant offence

- 1997-98 – implement the strategy

- 1998-99 – set targets for reduction in repeat victimisation.

By 1998 all forces claimed to be able to identify repeat victims to some degree; all but one force was able to identify repeat victims of domestic burglary, and all forces had developed a strategy to tackle such crimes.

The repeat victimisation task force was formally disbanded in 1998, although the staff involved continued the work of ensuring implementation of research results on a broader scale.

Source: Abstracted from Laycock (2001)

References

Abrahamson, E. (1991) 'Managerial fads and fashions: the diffusion and rejection of innovations', *Academy of Management Review*, vol 16, pp 586-612.

Abrahamson, E. (1996) 'Management fashion', *Academy of Management Review*, vol 21, pp 254-85.

Abrahamson, E. and Fombrum, C.J. (1994) 'Macroculture: determinants and consequences', *Academy of Management Review*, vol 19, pp 728-55.

Abrahamson, E. and Rosenkopf, L. (1993) 'Institutional and competitive bandwagons: using mathematical modelling as a tool to explore innovation diffusion', *Academy of Management Review*, vol 18, pp 487-517.

Argyris, C. and Schon, D.A. (1978) *Organizational learning*, London: Addison-Wesley.

Argyris, C. and Schon, D.A. (1996) *Organizational learning II*, Reading, MA: Addison-Wesley.

Bandura, A. (1971) *Social learning theory*, New York, NY: General Learning Press.

Bero, L.A., Grilli, R., Grimshaw, J.M., Harvey, E., Oxman, A.D. and Thomson, M.A. (1998) 'Closing the gap between research and practice: an overview of systematic reviews of interventions to promote the implementation of research findings', *BMJ*, vol 317, pp 465-8.

Caplan, N., Morrison, A. and Stambaugh, R. (1975) *The use of social science knowledge in policy decisions at national level*, Ann Arbor, MI: University of Michigan.

Cohen, D.K. and Weiss, C.H. (1977) 'Social science and social policy: schools and race', in C.H. Weiss (ed) *Using social research in public policy making*, Lexington, MA: Lexington/DC Health, pp 67-83.

Cohen, M.D. (1996) 'Individual learning and organisational routine', in M.D. Cohen and L.S. Sproull (eds) *Organisational learning*, London: Sage Publications, pp 188-94.

Cohen, M.D. and Bacdayan, P. (1996) 'Organisational routines are stored as procedural memory: evidence from a laboratory study', in M.D. Cohen and L.S. Sproull (eds) *Organisational learning*, London: Sage Publications, pp 403-29.

Coleman, J.S., Katz, E. and Menzel, H. (1966) *Medical innovation: A diffusion study*, New York, NY: Bobbs-Merill.

Davies, H.T.O. and Nutley, S.M. (2000) 'Developing learning organisations in the new NHS', *BMJ*, vol 320, pp 998-1001.

Davies, H.T.O., Nutley, S.M. and Mannion, R. (2000) 'Organisational culture and quality of health care', *Quality in Health Care*, vol 9, pp 111-19.

Davies, P. (1999) 'What is evidence-based education?', *British Journal of Educational Studies*, vol 47, no 2, pp 108-21.

DiMaggio, P. and Powell, W. (1983) 'The iron cage revisited: institutional isomorphism and collective rationality in organisation fields', *American Sociological Review*, vol 48, pp 147-60.

Downs, G.W. and Mohr, L.B. (1976) 'Conceptual issues in the study of innovations', *Administrative Science Quarterly*, vol 21, pp 700-14.

Effective Health Care Bulletin (1999) vol 5, no 1, London: Royal Society of Medicine Press.

EPOC (Effective Practice of Organisation and Care) (1998) *Organisation of Care Review Group: The data collection checklist* (http://www.abdn.ac.uk/public_health/hsru/epoc/index.htm).

Erikson, E. (1958) 'The nature of clinical evidence', in D. Learner (ed) *Evidence and inference*, Glencoe, IL: The Free Press of Glencoe.

Farrell, G. and Pease, K. (1993) *Once bitten, twice bitten: Repeat victimisation and its implications for crime prevention*, Crime Prevention Unit Paper 46, London: Home Office.

Fullan, M.G. with Stiegelbauer, S. (1991) *The new meaning of educational change*, London: Cassell Educational Ltd.

Gibbons, M., Limoges, C., Nowotny, H., Schwätzman, S., Scott, P. and Trow, M. (1994) *The production of knowledge*, London: Sage Publications.

Gould, T.H., Crosby, D.L., Harmer, M., Lloyd, S.M., Lunn, J.N. and Rees, G. (1992) 'Policy for controlling pain after surgery: effect of sequential changes in management', *BMJ*, vol 305, pp 1187-93.

Hampden-Turner, C. (1990) *Corporate cultures: From vicious to virtuous circles*, London: Hutchinson.

Hargreaves, D. (1998) *Creative professionalism: The role of teachers in the knowledge society*, London: DEMOS.

Hargreaves, D. (1999) 'Can and should evidence inform policy and practice in education?', Evidence-based practices and policies seminar, London, The Royal Society, 22 June.

Hargreaves, D.H. and Hopkins, D. (1991) *The empowered school*, London: Cassell.

Higgins, J. (1978) *The poverty business: Britain and America*, Oxford: Blackwell/Martin Robertson.

Hopkins, D., Ainscow, M. and West, M. (1994) *School improvement in an era of change*, London: Cassell plc.

Husen, T. (1984) 'Issues and their background', in T. Husen and M. Kogan (eds) *Educational research and policy: How do they relate?*, Oxford: Pergamon.

Kimberly, J.R. (1982) 'Managerial innovation and health policy: theoretical perspectives and research implications', *Journal of Health Politics, Policy and Law*, vol 6, pp 637-52.

Laycock, G. (2001: forthcoming) 'Hypothesis based research: the repeat victimisation story', *Criminal Policy Journal*, forthcoming.

Levinthal, D.A. and March, J.G. (1993) 'The myopia of learning', *Strategic Management Journal*, vol 14, pp 95-112.

Lewis, P. (1999) 'Evidence-based management: the challenge of effective practice', *Vista*, vol 5, no 1, pp 23-36.

Lindblom, C. and Cohen, D. (1979) *Usable knowledge: Social science and social problem solving*, New Haven, CN: Yale University Press.

Merton, R.K. (1957) 'The role of the intellectual in public bureaucracy', in R.K. Merton (ed) *Social theory and social structure*, New York, NY: Free Press.

Metcalfe, L. and Richards, S. (1990) *Improving public management*, London: Sage Publications.

Miles, M. (1986) *Research findings on the stages of school improvement*, Mimeo, New York, NY: Center for Policy Research.

Morgan, G. (1997) *Images of organisation*, London: Sage Publications.

Nutley, S.M. and Davies, H.T.O. (1999a) *Achieving evidence-based practice in UK public service: From dissemination to diffusion*, Working Paper, University of St Andrews.

Nutley, S.M. and Davies, H.T.O. (1999b) 'Introducing evidence-based practice: the contrasting experiences of healthcare and probation service organisations in the UK', *Public Policy and Administration*, vol 14, no 4, pp 39-57.

O'Neill, H.M., Pouder, R.W. and Buchholtz, A.K. (1998) 'Patterns in the diffusion of strategies across organisations; insights from the innovation diffusion literature', *Academy of Management Review*, vol 23, pp 98-114.

Pawson, R. and Tilley, N. (1997) *Realistic evaluation*, London: Sage Publications.

Pedlar, M. and Aspinwall, K. (1998) *A concise guide to the learning organisation*, London: Lemos & Crane.

Polyani, M. (1967) *The tacit dimension*, New York, NY: Doubleday.

Rogers, E.M. (1958) 'Categorising adopters of agricultural practices', *Rural Sociology*, vol 23, pp 345-54.

Rogers, E.M. (1983) *Diffusion of innovations* (3rd edn), New York, NY: Free Press.

Rogers, E.M. (1995) *Diffusion of innovations* (4th edn), New York, NY: Free Press.

Rogers, E.M., Ascroft, J.R. and Roling, N.G. (1970) *Diffusion of innovations in Brazil, Nigeria, and India*, East Lansing, MI Department of Communication, Diffusion of Innovations Research Report 24, Michigan State University.

Sackett, D.L., Rosenberg, W., Gray, J.M., Haynes, R.B. and Richardson, W.S. (1996) 'Evidence based medicine: what it is and what it isn't', *BMJ*, vol 312, pp 71-2.

Schon, D.A. (1967) *Technology and change: The new Heraclitus*, New York, NY: Delacorte Press.

Schon, D.A. (1971) *Beyond the stable state*, London: Norton & Company.

Schon, D.A. (1987) *Educating the reflective practitioner: Toward a new design for teaching and learning in the professions*, San Francisco, CA: Jossey-Bass.

Schon, D.A. (1991) *The reflective practitioner*, Aldershot: Ashgate Publishing.

Senge, P.M. (1990) *The fifth discipline: The art and practice of the learning organization*, New York, NY: Doubleday Currency

Shulman, L.S. (1988) 'The dangers of dichotomous thinking in education', in P.P. Grimmett and G.L. Erickson (eds) *Reflection in teacher education*, New York, NY: Teachers College Press.

Singley, M.K. and Anderson, J.R. (1989) *The transfer of cognitive skill*, Cambridge, MA: Harvard University Press.

Sitkin, S.B. (1992) 'Learning through failure', in B.M. Staw and L.L. Cummings (eds) *Research in organisational behaviour*, Greenwich, CT: JAI Press, pp 231-66.

Squire, L.R. (1987) *Memory and brain*, New York, NY: Oxford University Press.

Stocking, B. (1985) *Initiative and inertia: Case studies in the NHS*, London: Nuffield Provincial Hospitals Trust.

Stoll, L. and Fink, D. (1996) *Changing our schools*, Buckingham: Open University Press.

Van de Ven, A.H. (1986) 'Central problems in the management of innovation', *Management Science*, vol 32, pp 590-607.

Weiss, C.H. (1998) 'Have we learned anything new about the use of evaluation?', *American Journal of Evaluation*, vol 19, no 1, pp 21-33.

Westphal, J.D., Gulati, R. and Shortell, S.M. (1997) 'Customization or conformity? An institutional and network perspective on the content and consequences of TQM adoption', *Administrative Science Quarterly*, vol 42, pp 366-94.

SIXTEEN

Learning from the past, prospects for the future

Huw Davies, Sandra Nutley and Peter Smith

Introduction

In the preceding chapters, our contributing authors have revealed a surprisingly long and rich history of the use of evidence in forming public sector policy and practice in the UK. However, they also point to major shortcomings in the extent of evidence available, the nature of that evidence, and the ways in which the evidence is disseminated and used by policy makers and practitioners. Our invidious task now is to draw some of these themes together.

It is clear that vast differences exist between service areas in the breadth and quality of available evidence, and in the ways in which this evidence is utilised (see Chapters Three to Ten and Box 16.1). Considerable diversity also arises *within* sector areas, and so summaries such as those in Box 16.1 are necessarily broad-brush. These differences may arise for a number of reasons: the nature of the service; the costs of providing evidence; the capacity and culture of the research community; the attitudes and prejudices of practitioners; the attitudes and prejudices of citizens and policy makers; or historical accident. Exploring the diversity between sector areas is interesting not just in helping to explain sector-specific developments but, more importantly, because it promotes the diffusion of learning between sectors.

Learning from diversity requires us to celebrate difference and not always to search for what is common. It is not a question of levelling down to the lowest common denominator: one size does not fit all. On the contrary, diversity is explored to extend understanding of the possible, stimulate creative thinking about new strategies, inject life into tired old debates, and foster a more nuanced and contextualised view of the challenges and possible solutions. To anticipate just two examples, the 'paradigm wars' between quantitative and qualitative approaches to evidence generation seen in some sectors (such as education and social care) may reach some sort of rapprochement from an understanding of how they offer diverse and complementary perspectives on policy problems. This may be easier for the protagonists to see by looking outside of their own sector – for example, by examining the debates over experimentation in criminal justice. Similarly, insight into the difficulties of implementation in one area may foster creative thinking about new strategies in another. If nothing else, an understanding of contingency – recognising that interventions work some of the time, for some of the people in certain contexts only – should militate against overly optimistic recommendations about straight transfers between sectors.

This final chapter focuses on cross-sector learning by using the experiences described thus far to explore key issues relating to evidence-based policy and practice:

- the appropriateness of developing evidence-based approaches;
- the nature of credible research evidence;
- securing the research capacity to meet policy makers' and practitioners' need for evidence;
- ensuring that the evidence is used.

Are evidence-based approaches appropriate?

Most of the arguments set out in this book are predicated on the assumption that the pursuit of evidence-based policy and practice is a desirable aim, in the sense that it will lead to the delivery of services closer to society's preferences than would otherwise have been the case. It is something of an irony that there is little evidence on which to base such an assertion – it remains an act of faith. However, we firmly believe that repudiation of the evidence-based approach will in general be to the detriment of the public sector and the citizens it seeks to serve.

There are many legitimate reasons to question the practicality or desirability of an evidence-based approach in certain circumstances. For example:

- the assembly of evidence may be too costly in relation to the likely benefits such evidence may yield;

- there may be only one viable way to proceed, or there may be a universal consensus as to what needs to be done;
- there may be political imperatives that override any objective evidence;
- the research capacity needed to provide useful evidence may not be available;
- the problem to be investigated may defy meaningful research scrutiny, perhaps because objectives are not clear, outcomes are impossible to measure, or technology is changing too rapidly;
- there may be insuperable practical constraints to assembling useful evidence, such as fundamental ethical considerations.

The circumstances in which considerations such as these arise are likely to be relatively rare and such factors are often likely to be offered more as excuses rather than reasons for not collating evidence. There is considerable scope for increasing the proportion of the public sector for which usable evidence (broadly defined) is available, and for greatly improving the quality of that evidence.

Although progress is variable, the preceding chapters have noted a general trend towards increased awareness of the value of evidence in influencing policy and practice. This shift towards a greater use of evidence might on the face of it appear to signal a move towards some concept of 'rationality' in the form and delivery of public services. However, it is important to bear in mind that there may be other possible interpretations of the phenomenon. At various points in this book, commentators have offered alternative perspectives, for example, where evidence is assembled in order to serve the interests of particular groups, or when evidence is commissioned in order to confuse or delay the policy-making process. For all the progress made in bringing evidence to the fore, the term 'evidence-based' may of itself be rather misleading. In many cases evidence-informed or even evidence-aware policy and practice is the best that can be hoped for.

Nature of credible research evidence

It can be useful to distinguish between the type of evidence needed for policy and the type needed for practice. At the level of policy, evidence is needed to:
- justify the provision (or abandonment) of entire services;
- contribute to an argument for expanding (or contracting) a service;
- justify reorganisation of a service;

- determine the best allocation of resources within a service;
- identify the best ways of delivering a service;
- assess the technical efficiency of service managers and practitioners (in effect, to determine whether policy is being implemented effectively).

In contrast, practitioners need evidence to identify which activities they should undertake, and how they should go about carrying out the chosen activities. Further evidence is then needed to evaluate whether the favoured policies and procedures have been effective in practice.

Earlier chapters have demonstrated progress on all these fronts, although the 'what works' debate has often focused on the practitioner concerns of which intervention to use in a given context. The nature of credible evidence varies according to the purpose for which it is used. Methodologically, it is often more difficult to produce credible evidence to address policy as opposed to inform practice questions.

However, the variability in what constitutes evidence revealed in earlier chapters is not entirely due to whether there is a policy or a practice focus. The most striking feature to emerge from the sector-specific accounts is the sheer diversity of approaches. In some areas (most notably clinical practice in healthcare) the need for evidence and the nature of convincing evidence is a given: evidence is essential, and legitimacy is conferred by rigorous experimentation carried out by objective researchers without conflicts of interest. In other areas (most strikingly, social care), the very nature of evidence is hotly disputed and there is strong resistance to assigning privileged status to one research method over another. Evidence emerges more informally from practitioners' and clients' experience as much as from systematic study carried out by external research organisations.

In assembling evidence, sectors such as transport and healthcare have in general pursued very rigid methodological norms, with little room for alternative perspectives. This has led to high impact (certainly on practice) but may have resulted in important elements of evaluation being ignored or mishandled. For example, only recently have environmental considerations been built into road evaluations, and even now clinical outcomes (mortality and major morbidity) garner more attention in evaluations of therapies than the patient perspective (eg quality of life, patient satisfaction). In contrast, services such as social care and education have a research culture that repudiates the scientific norm of experimentation and emphasises ethnographic observation based around thick descriptions.

The preceding chapters indicate that here is a clear need for quantitative methods to examine whether a putative treatment effect exists. However, there is equally a pressing need for qualitative approaches to inform the sorts of questions to address, the forms of the models to be tested, and the formulation of important elements of quantitative analysis, such as outcome measures. It is ironic to note that our commentators from the more experimentally dominated research cultures tend to call for more qualitative content, while those from the opposite end of the spectrum seek more scientific experimentation. This implies that there may be a need for researchers to be more reflective about the nature of the evidence they are providing, and to be more open-minded about the virtues of a mixture of methodologies. There should in principle be a symbiotic relationship between the two research cultures, rather than – as is too often the case – an unproductive clash.

A number of common observations on methodology can be drawn from the preceding chapters. Firstly, there is a tendency (particularly in quantitative studies) to ignore the potentially important side-effects of an intervention. For example, a limited evaluation of the daily 'literacy hour' in schools may point to considerable improvements in literacy, but ignores possible detrimental impacts on other aspects of learning. Secondly, meta-analysis often brings to light important effects that were not evident in single studies, suggesting that in many circumstances study design or sample sizes may have been inadequate. Thirdly, a recurring theme throughout the book is the notion that what matters is what works *in what context*, yet many studies merely seek an aggregate view on what is best, without exploring the role of context. The rise of mega-trials in healthcare – very large-scale, international randomised controlled trials, which compare two or more simple treatment protocols – and the use of meta-analysis rely on such aggregation to uncover precise estimates of relatively small treatment effects but unavoidably sacrifice contextual variables along the way.

Contention in deciding what works is not confined to choice of research design. The sector areas also differ in their use of theory to unravel questions of effectiveness. In healthcare, much of the emphasis of intervention assessment is on the pragmatic question of whether or not the intervention offers benefits in aggregate across patient groups. However, in criminal justice and social care there is a much greater concern to 'unpack the box' of the intervention, to seek understanding as to *why* it works. A recognition that an intervention will not work for all persons under all circumstances, or that not all parts of an intervention necessarily contribute to its effectiveness, leads to a desire to tease out the effectual elements from the ineffectual in a highly contextualised manner. In this, theories of human behaviour and qualitative methods play a prominent role, counterbalancing the empiricism of pure experimentation. One of the dangers of such an approach is that the emphasis may lie more on the theories underlying interventions than on the pragmatic testing of their effects.

Methodological divergence may arise in part from differences in objectives. In some areas the objectives are relatively clear. For example, in healthcare, clinical practice is aimed at increasing longevity and decreasing morbidity (adding years to life and life to years). With such clarity, assessing 'what works' is greatly simplified. However, policy objectives in healthcare are much less clear and here evidence may be less to the fore. For example, the evidence in support of health service reorganisation is usually less robust than the evidence used to determine first-line treatments. Major policy decisions (such as the implementation and subsequent abandonment of GP fundholding) are frequently more ideological rather than evidence-based.

In many policy areas, objectives may be multiple and competing, and the relative balance between them may change over time. This complicates and politicises the evaluation of what works. For example, an intervention aimed at young offenders may be very successful at punishing but may also be an abject failure at reforming future offending behaviour. In urban policy, identifying, weighing and balancing the full range of impacts that are attributable to initiatives is even more problematic. Under these circumstances, reconciling multiple competing objectives is essentially a political task (although research evidence, especially from qualitative work, clearly has great potential to inform).

Despite the fact that methodological divergence rather than convergence is likely to continue, there is still enormous scope for improving the quality of the evidence provided. In many sectors, evidence comprises quite casual and uncontrolled observation, which in effect is little more than expert opinion bolstered by anecdote. Even in sectors that have embraced a more scientific culture, the accepted methodology is often very narrowly based, and may miss important elements of an evaluation (for example, the failure of transport evaluations fully to consider the long-run effects of road-building programmes). Many public sector interventions involve the interaction of a number of agencies, and these are often difficult to capture within a conventional evaluation methodology.

Securing research capacity and direction

The amount of funding for research activity varies enormously across public service areas. Compared to the other service sectors, healthcare (or at least certain aspects of it) attracts substantial research funds. It is a matter for conjecture as to whether this is because the health system is uniquely enlightened, or because the evidence produced for healthcare is uniquely valuable, or uniquely expensive to generate, or whether it is because there exists a uniquely powerful research lobby (in the form of a formidable element of the medical profession). However, by comparison, the research investment in services such as social care, education and criminal justice – which on the face of it appear to offer similar problems of evaluation – is very modest.

A common concern to emerge from earlier chapters is the frequent absence of independent but well-directed research. In many areas (such as in healthcare, education and social care) there is a history of investigator-led research, much of which has *not* connected with policy or practice needs. At the other extreme (such as in transport and welfare policy) there is a history of user- (in other words government-) led research, which has at times merely reinforced the *status quo* rather than questioned existing policy objectives. Achieving a productive balance between these two approaches, to obtain adequate amounts of independent and relevant research, is not easy.

Until relatively recently, the system has not nurtured a vigorous research community – it seems simply to presume that research capacity can in some way be conjured up when called for. Notwithstanding some recent initiatives to increase research training and resources in, for example, healthcare and education, a key barrier to evidence-based policy and practice in the UK is the lack of appropriate research capabilities and capacity. One of the fundamental difficulties afflicting increasing numbers of researchers is that the research activity on which their livelihood depends can often be funded only if a specific policy 'customer' can be found. In many cases this involves a passive response on the part of researchers, perhaps awaiting invitations to tender for particular projects. Such a research culture is clearly dysfunctional, particularly where there are so few policy customers. Researchers may become dependent on a single customer, and may be mindful to avoid coming up with uncomfortable findings. There is little opportunity for the producers of evidence to cast doubt on whether the right question is being asked or to challenge terms of reference. Important but politically difficult research areas may be neglected, for example, the relative neglect of environmental concerns when planning transport policy.

On the other hand, the culture of curiosity-driven research, as (albeit to a decreasing extent) nurtured by the universities also has its limitations. University peer review appears to attach limited worth to policy relevance, and instead places a premium on methodological novelty. Multidisciplinary enquiry is not encouraged by the current system of incentives, while the emphasis on 'international research reputation' has led researchers away from possibly transient policy and parochial issues towards subjects that are readily transferable across time and across national borders. All of these developments have to some extent conspired against the development of a healthy independent policy and practice research community.

Getting evidence used

The relative weight accorded to different inputs into the policy process varies between policy areas. Ideology, expediency and public preferences compete with scientific evidence for the attention of ministers and, indeed, managers. Development of an evidence-based approach in some public policy areas (such as education or criminal justice) may be constrained because stakeholders (such as parents, victims and politicians) have their own intuitive and strongly held views about what constitutes an effective intervention. Such views may conflict with rigorously obtained research evidence but nonetheless they will influence both policy and practice. Areas where the nature of the interventions makes user-knowledge less secure (for example, medicine) tend to be less influenced by these extraneous factors. But even here, client perspectives are assuming a greater prominence fuelled by a growing public expertise, ready access to technical information (for example *via* the Internet) and increasingly assertive public attitudes.

The starting points of different professional traditions undoubtedly colour the methods and enthusiasm with which professionals engage with evidence (for example, medicine is rooted in the biological sciences, whereas social work begins with a more sociological perspective). In healthcare, the production, collation, dissemination and interpretation of research evidence for healthcare professionals is a vast industry. Other policy areas are much more tentative in approach – hampered by lack of consensus, lack of expertise and great practical difficulties. Even in healthcare, for all the richness of the research base, it remains unclear how best to bring about changes in professional behaviour that are congruent with the evidence.

Ironically, the amount of evidence available in healthcare seems to be part of the problem, and the sheer volume of practice guidance in circulation frequently overwhelms healthcare professionals. What is clear is that there remains in all of the areas examined great potential for research evidence to be vastly more influential than hitherto.

Several authors have noted an apparent paradox: that, as the volume of research evidence has increased, so its impact on policy has diminished. However, identifying an impact is notoriously difficult. It raises the question of what is meant by 'impact'. Those researchers supported by government research funds are challenged interminably to provide evidence that their research has had an impact on policy. Yet, when questioned about the role played by a particular piece of research in influencing policy, the policy maker will usually find it difficult to isolate the impact of a single piece of evidence, especially when the 'enlightenment' effects of research are also considered (Chapter Two). The extent to which research evidence has improved eventual outcomes in terms of service delivery is likely to be highly contingent and often unknowable.

Nevertheless, it remains a recurring disappointment that evidence so often fails to have much impact on policy making or professional practice. While Chapters Two and Fifteen explored in detail some of the processes involved, it is worth considering those circumstances that *are* favourable to research having an impact. Greater attention is paid to research findings when:

- policy makers and practitioners understand and believe in the benefits of using evidence, and are clear of its relative merits *vis-à-vis* expert opinion;
- users of research are partners in the process of evidence generation;
- research is timely and addresses an issue that is relevant with a methodology that is relatively uncontested;
- results support existing political ideologies, are convenient and uncontentious;
- results are reported with low degrees of uncertainty, are robust in implementation, and can be implemented without incurring high costs if the decision needs to be reversed;
- researchers (and key users) seek implementation with skilful advocacy and great stamina.

The penultimate point in the above list, the role of uncertainty in influencing policy and practice decisions, is an important consideration that is often ignored by researchers. It is very rare that research can offer incontrovertible evidence that policy A is preferable to policy B. Rather, the research can (at best) indicate that policy A is preferable to policy B subject to some element of uncertainty. This leads to the possibility of two types of policy error – implementing a new policy when its alternative was in fact preferable; or failing to implement a new policy when it is in fact superior. In deciding which policy to pursue, policy makers are likely to have in mind the relative political and social costs of these types of error, a consideration which the ubiquitous and casual use of some simple decision rule (such as a 95% level of statistical significance) signally fails to address. Tied up with this issue is the extent to which implementation of a new policy or practice is reversible if it is subsequently shown to be inappropriate. Evidence from the diffusion literature reviewed in Chapter Fifteen tells us that the ability to try innovations out a little at a time is an important contributor to the likelihood of their uptake and this fits with concerns about the relative political and social costs of policy errors.

The frequency with which political imperatives appear to dominate evidence is a consistent theme throughout the book. In some senses for researchers to complain about this is both naïve and misses the point that policy is ultimately a political instrument. Rather, researchers should seek to recognise why political considerations dominate and seek out ways to accommodate the political environment within which they operate. Researchers should become more knowing about how best to ensure that their work might affect the policy process. We must, however, once again return to the issue of incentives: under current structures (such as the Research Assessment Exercise and internal promotion procedures), curiosity-driven academic researchers have little or no incentive to put any effort into ensuring that any community other than their academic peers notices the fruits of their labours.

Equally, policy makers and practitioners complain that research is, among other things, slow, impenetrable, irrelevant, expensive and inconvenient or uncomfortable. However, to some extent this reflects failures in the commissioning process and failures to understand the nature of research rather than failures of research. There is a clear need for a more informed dialogue between the users and producers of research evidence.

Concluding remarks

The rhetoric of evidence-based approaches reflects an appropriate and pragmatic response to demands for more effective public services. Notwithstanding critiques from a postmodern perspective, there is a growing confidence that eclectic but nonetheless rigorous methodologies can contribute robust knowledge of great practical use. Much activity atests to this view – from within government itself (both in the Cabinet Office and in key departments), by government agencies such as the Research Councils, and by non-governmental organisations such as Barnardo's and the Joseph Rowntree Foundation.

Those concerned with increasing the influence of research evidence in public policy and practice are faced with a formidable task. The provision of good quality evidence is only part of the battle – and it would be folly to assume that the key to evidence-based public policy and practice rests solely in the widespread adoption of the scientific rigour of the randomised controlled trial. There is a desperate need to identify fundamental conflicts about the nature of evidence and, if not to resolve them, then at least to map out areas of agreement and develop sustainable accommodation of any residual diversity. In this respect, methodological ideology needs to be tempered with pragmatism.

Assuming (as we do) the desirability of both improving the evidence base and increasing its influence on policy and practice in the public services, a number of important goals emerge which would foster an enhanced role for evidence. These are to:

- achieve agreement as to what constitutes legitimate evidence on service effectiveness (within specific policy areas); this may be more than simply a methodological question: it may also cover such questions as the source of the research findings, and their political and public acceptability;
- recognise the policy and practice questions that are best answered using experimentation, and achieve an equal acceptance that many policy questions are unsuited to such an approach (by dint of ethics, expense, practicability or complexity); criteria to distinguish between the two would be helpful;
- establish and continue development of a valid, reliable and relevant evidence base on what works – this would recognise the importance of systematic reviews and meta-analysis as a means of drawing together the results and implications of existing evaluation studies;

- develop a more strategic approach to the commissioning of research on what works to help ensure coverage of key policy questions using appropriate methodologies;
- develop sufficient research capacity in each of the public policy areas, academically rooted but also in tune with practice realities;
- develop effective mechanisms for ensuring that the available evidence influences policy and practice;
- consider simultaneously the costs as well as the effectiveness of policy and practice interventions (given the inevitability of tight constraints placed on public expenditure in all policy areas); this is an area largely left unexplored by this book, yet there is an urgent need to move from questions of 'what works' to address issues of 'what works and whether it is worthwhile given the costs'.

Because of the different rates of progress of different public sector areas in meeting these requirements, there is much to be learned from a cross-sector analysis, to which we offer this book as a contribution. If evidence is to play a more central role in the future there are many challenges ahead, but help is also at hand in the form of understanding and learning from the experience of others.

Box 16.1: Contrasting approaches to evidence-based policy and practice

	Healthcare (especially NHS clinical services)	School education
Methodological preferences and debates	Gold standard of randomised controlled trial with additional methodological safeguards. Growing interest in qualitative methods to give complementary view.	Much research is considered less than robust. Paradigm wars. Eclectic methods competing rather than complementing. Large datasets are analysed but there is relatively little true experimentation.
Nature of the evidence base	Extensive and accessible via national initiatives such as the Cochrane Collaboration, and local clinical effectiveness strategies.	Fragmented research community. No accessible database of research evidence (but fresh initiatives underway). Few systematic reviews.
Dissemination strategies	Largely a push of information out from the centre (clinical guidelines); some local education initiatives to increase practitioner pull.	Newly established Centre for Evidence-informed Policy and Practice in Education will have a dissemination role.
Main initiatives for ensuring that evidence impacts on practice	Guidelines movement (prescriptions for practice). Evidence-based medicine (developing clinicians' problem-solving skills and abilities to use evidence in their clinical decisions). National Quality Framework using National Institute for Clinical Excellence and the Commission for Health Improvement becoming quite prescriptive.	DfEE is currently making major investment in developing accessible evidence-base. Some academic-led seminars for practitioners on evidence-based education. Teacher-led work with the Teacher Training Agency. Central prescription of school practice – but not always rooted explicitly in evidence of what works.
Direction of diffusion of EBP	The top down R&D strategy emphasises dissemination rather than implementation. There is a bottom-up move from evidence-based practitioners who have opted into the diffusion process. Diffusion through professionally-led, horizontal networks.	At present horizontal, but limited diffusion of research-based innovations.
Role of central government	Becoming more hands-on, interventionist and prescriptive. Large funder of R&D, and using economic leverage to encourage service change	Some policy decisions more recently informed by research. Emphasises 'driving up standards'.

Box 16.1: Continued

	Criminal justice	Social care
Methodological preferences and debates	General acceptance of experimental methods in determining what works. Preference for theory- rather than method-driven approach to evaluation.	Preferences for qualitative methodologies. Quantification and experimentation often viewed with suspicion and even hostility.
Nature of the evidence base	Large, but still limited, research base. No online, up-to-date database of research in UK, but Home Office research reports are available online.	No accessible database. Concept of evidence is still hotly contested.
Dissemination strategies	Some push of information from the centre (Home Office). Professional associations, formal training courses and networks remain important.	Dissemination is reliant on academic and practitioner journals, conferences and networks.
Main initiatives for ensuring that evidence impacts on practice	Guidelines on effective practice issued by HM Inspectorates of the police, prison and probation services. Newly established central panel for accrediting prison and probation offender programmes. Partnership working between researchers and police in police research. Use of marketing methods to push out the results of police research.	Rhetoric of DoH expresses commitment to evidence-based social care, but no key initiatives. Professional body (CCETSW) initiative to develop 'research mindedness'. Local initiatives include Centre for Evidence-Based Social Services in Exeter University. Interest in evidence-based social care by bodies such as Barnardo's.
Direction of diffusion of EBP	Initially peer diffusion through horizontal networks. More recently top-down in the police, prison and probation services. Home Office led at national level and management and senior officer led in local areas.	Horizontal diffusion of ideas and practices.
Role of central government	HM Inspectorates of police, prison and probation services identify and disseminate best practice guidance. Inspection process assesses the implementation of that best practice. Performance regime used to push research results.	Monitoring the implementation of legislative and procedural changes. Encourages defensive practice among social workers.

Box 16.1: Continued

	Welfare policy (focus on social security benefits)	Housing
Methodological preferences and debates	Eclectic use of methods to provide complementary insights. Some longitudinal study but almost no experimentation (because of legal impediments due to the statutory duty for equitable benefits).	Predominant use of qualitative and quantitative survey methods. Use of econometrics for forecasting housing needs. The emergence of more multi-method and multidisciplinary approaches.
Nature of the evidence base	Evidence created in response to perceived policy problem. Little apparent collation into a stable evidence resource.	Extensive databases on the state of housing stock used for monitoring purposes. Weaker evidence base in other areas of housing policy. Housing research increasingly related to wider policy considerations (such as social exclusion).
Dissemination strategies	Close linkage between researchers and research customers (policy makers) ensures some connect.	Dissemination reliant on academic and practitioner journals, conferences and networks, as well as professional organisations (such as the National Housing Federation) and charitable research organisations (such as the Joseph Rowntree Foundation).
Main initiatives for ensuring that evidence impacts on practice	Research aimed more at policy – practice is rule-based rather than discretionary.	No clear initiatives to bridge the gap between evidence and policy/practice.
Direction of diffusion of EBP	N/A	Horizontal peer diffusion through professional and academic/research networks.
Role of central government	Defining the policy problem and policy options. Calling for research tenders.	Indirect. Occasional funding of targeted investigations and research initiatives.

Box 16.1: Continued

	Transport (focus on roads policy)	Urban policy
Methodological preferences and debates	Multidisciplinary area. Policy-related research is often rooted in economic modelling and statistical forecasting methods.	Major problems over attribution of effects to interventions and identifying externalities. Diverse methods employed, mostly pluralistic case studies. Little or no true experimentation.
Nature of the evidence base	Tends to focus on technical and operational issues relating to the design of the transport infrastructure. Up until the late 1990s, largely reliant on internal government sources only, chiefly the Transport Research Laboratory.	Strong emphasis on evidence collected in appraisal and evaluation of government-funded schemes.
Dissemination strategies	Initially centrally driven via the DoT. Now more pluralist, for example, using professional networks.	Varied. Links between researchers and policy makers now being supplemented by websites developed by funders (such as the DETR and Joseph Rowntree).
Main initiatives for ensuring that evidence impacts on practice	Research results on operational issues passed to highway planners and engineers in the form of guidance notes. The implementation of research-based standards and codes of practice are monitored and controlled.	Increased emphasis on guidelines (for example, on the Single Regeneration Budget), research summary notes, and new training strategies for DETR Challenge funding.
Direction of diffusion of EBP	Largely top-down diffusion of centrally determined practices. Some horizontal diffusion of local innovations (such as city pedestrianisation).	Some top-down diffusion (such as the use of criteria for funding). Development of informal networks across partnerships and through practice/academic links.
Role of central government	Very much hands-on and interventionist.	Supplier and gatekeeper to urban development funds, therefore making greater demands on bidders for these to make the case and incorporate evaluations.

Index

NOTE: Page numbers followed by *tab* indicate information is to be found in a table. Full titles are given for all organisations and entities: followed by abbreviated form in brackets; to identify an acronym or abbreviation please consult the list on page x.